ARETINO, SCOURGE OF PRINCES

By Thomas Caldecot Chubb

Prose

THE LIFE OF GIOVANNI BOCCACCIO
ARETINO, SCOURGE OF PRINCES

Poetry

THE WHITE GOD, AND OTHER POEMS
CLIFF PACE, AND OTHER POEMS
SHIPS AND LOVERS
KYRDOON

ARETINO

SCOURGE
OF PRINCES

Thomas Caldecot Chubb

REYNAL & HITCHCOCK

MCMXL · NEW YORK

PRINTED IN THE UNITED STATES OF AMERICA
BY THE CORNWALL PRESS, CORNWALL, N. Y.

ARETINO IN 1524

"I tell you I glory in the title which he, to vilify me, has given me; and may it teach the nobility to procreate sons which a cobbler has begotten in Arezzo."—*Aretino.*

To John Milton Berdan

Contents

Illustrations

"Divine Aretino, worthie Ariosto, excellent Tasso, sweet Petrarch . . . four famous heroic poets as valorously brave as delicately fine."

GABRIEL HARVEY: *Marginalia*

"E meglio di fare e di pentirsi che pentirsi e non fare."

(It is better to do and repent, than to repent and not to do.)

ARETINO: Letter to *Beatrice Pia*

Introduction

IN FOLLOWING my life of Boccaccio with a life of Aretino, I have turned from an essentially good man — in whatever sense you use the word — to another for whom good was the very last adjective you could possibly employ. Or rather I have turned from the consideration of a human personality who was actuated and even handicapped by all sorts of moral principles to one who was profoundly unmoral. Aretino recognized but a single law, the law of his own advancement. That, incidentally, was not so much a law as a necessity. Also I have turned from what was clearly the fresh dawn of an astounding era to its hot afternoon and its sullen sunset. But perhaps that is simply another way of saying the same thing.

Much turgid water had flowed under various handsome bridges on the Tiber and the Arno — and on the Seine and the Thames and the Rhine and the Ebro — since the thirty-year-old future "author of the *Decameron*" rode back to Florence from Naples and from his youth on a raw, gusty Spring morning. There this son of the bankrupt banker saw his twin disillusionments, disappointment in an impossible love, and the collapse of worldly security, make him burgeon into a grace and an urbanity that enabled him to produce what is probably the most brilliant creative prose ever written in the western world.

I shall do no more than hint at what is obvious. The spirit of man had grown adventurous. In the physical world, red-headed Christopher Columbus was already sailing westward to discover the east, little realizing that he was to stumble on a new west that would soon equal, at least in energy, the old west and the east together. Copernicus, with his puny inadequate glass, was already peering into the cobwebbed crannies of space and preparing to place man's little dizzying globe in its correct place in the universe. Vesalius would soon earn the hate of the Inquisition by dissecting human cadavers, and then modern medicine would start its climb upward from the potions and witch-doctor stuff which had usurped its name during the Dark Ages. Leonardo, whom we think of as a painter, was making his trips of exploration into the realm of mechanics, and coming back with revolutionary discoveries. The only trouble was he did not know what to do with them. And scholar after scholar grew near-sighted as he pored over manuscripts in Greek, Latin, Hebrew and Arabic. The subject of the manuscripts made little difference just so they were written by the ancients: Medicine, Mathematics, Philosophy, Botany, Literature, Geography, Ethics or Aesthetics or Art. There was a gold standard in those days, and its yellowbacks were anything that could be called knowledge. Thus the world of time was opened up simultaneously with the world of space in that era that was rightly called the *rebirth* or the Renaissance. We are so used to change, which is the present normal order of things, that it is hard for us to realize just how greatly men were stirred by this. We must remember that the world had been stagnant or very nearly stagnant for thirteen hundred years.

The political aspect calls also for consideration. When Boccaccio was alive, though men's minds may have started on their soaring flight or their purposeless journey to the modern, the institutions under which they lived were those of the Middle Ages. The unit was the town. The town was independent. There was a Pope; there was an Emperor; there was a King of France; there was a King of England; there were several Kings of Spain. But these rulers were fairly shadowy. You acknowledged them with sounding phrases; you doffed your cap and bowed the knee to them when they rode through your streets and piazzas; you paid taxes or tribute when you could not get out of it. Otherwise, you were left alone. Left alone, you managed your own affairs.

During the 117 years that elapsed between the death, ridden with scabs, of the father of modern fiction in his home at

Certaldo, and the birth — just across the notched Apennines —
of Pietro Aretino, all this had changed. Almost simultaneously, there had been, in the world politic, a series of large
mergers based on nationalism. They happened too closely
together for coincidence. They were the product of the spirit
of the times.

Lean Henry Tudor led the way. When, after hunchback
Richard's death at Boswell Field, he picked up the fallen
crown from a thorn bush and became Henry VII, he not only
ended more than a century of demoralizing civil war, but he
made England one nation. She never has been other than one
nation since. France followed next. One by one, Louis XI,
who was properly known as King Spider, lured the great lords
of France into his web, and so doing the wizened monarch
made a single entity of a Gaul that up till then had been divided into far more than the three parts of Caesar's classic
apothegm. Then came Spain, Ferdinand of Aragon who hid
not a little ability beneath his affable exterior married strong-
purposed Isabella of Castile and the resolute couple soon proceeded to drive the Mohammedan Moor out of the small part
of the land he still held. As a result, all of the Iberian peninsula except Portugal knew one government. Germany was
still a medley of free cities; small kingdoms, dukedoms and
margraviates; independent bishoprics and electorates; but
Austria — her Archdukes having made the office of Holy Roman Emperor, in fact, if not in theory, hereditary in their
Hapsburg family — was of great importance. Soon this importance would be even greater. The Emperor Maximilian, shifty
and irresolute though he was, found somehow — and on two
occasions — enough decision to take as his wife Mary, daughter
and heiress of the dead Duke of Burgundy, and later to marry
their son, Philip, to "mad Joan" the daughter of the Spanish
rulers. A grandson, Charles, born of this second union, came
into the world when Aretino was eight years old. He was destined to inherit the most extensive regions ruled over by a
single man since the days of the Roman Caesars. Last of all,

in the southeast, new forces of earthquake were arising, and Christendom was menaced seriously by the infidel for the first time since Charles Martel. The Turk, under his great Sultans, Bajezet, Selim and Suleiman, had pushed forward in the plains of Hungary, and soon turbaned armies would approach Vienna. Those overgrown troublemakers, the Great Powers, were coming into existence. They were to have the raw strength of giants and the manners and the quarrelsomeness of small boys and psychopathic ones. The possibility of a super-merger that would engulf them and render them beneficent is still something that only visionaries can see.

Italy alone clung to the old disorganization. Five states — Venice, Milan, Florence, the domains of the Pope, and Naples — did indeed dominate the peninsula; and such of the once independent cities, petty lordships, and small republics as still managed to survive nominally, were actually pretty well under the control of one of these. In fact, it is probable that her having resolved herself into five so equal divisions — one of which, incidentally, was ruled by a foreigner and another by a priest — was the very thing that prevented further union. Each one of these states visualized more than one time a united nation, but always under its own hegemony. The idea of an entirely new state that would be simply Italian, was at least three hundred years too far into the future to be anything but a fantastic dream.

And in the meantime a higher intelligence, and a happy interlude in which she was at least free from foreign wars, gave her the opportunity to become the richest geographical unit in the world. Arts flourished and the wheels of industry turned. Venice, with her commerce, drew in the wealth of the Orient, and Florence, with her bankers, snared her blood-percentage out of Europe. The Pope had his cut. He got it both from the alms which were given to what was still widely regarded as a universal religion and from the tribute exacted as lord temporal. Nor did the golden benevolence evade even the most insignificant of places. There were potent kingdoms not having either the solid or the liquid resources of the smallest Italian principality.

What followed was inevitable.

When the King's mistress, decked in pearls and emeralds, is left in the roadside for the barbarians by the fleeing King, she is both robbed and raped. So it was with Italy. Louis XI's spindle-legged son, Charles VIII, who was not even a complete physiological man, and who was scarcely a complete mental one, merely happened to be the first person to see the chance. The sound of his caissons was enough, and he marched through the country from Mt. Cenis to the Bay of Naples with so little resistance that he was said to have conquered it with chalk marks. (The French indicated the houses where they planned to billet troops by marking them with chalk.) The French were followed by the Spaniards, the Spaniards by the Austrians. Presently the victors began to quarrel over the spoils and in due order a battle royal was raging. With some intermissions, it lasted for four decades—those between 1494 and 1530—and the once prosperous "garden of the Empire" was both the cockpit and the prize. When it was over, it was a question whether there was enough left to make even a medal for the winner's chest. The wealth had been drained deeply, if not utterly used up. The morals had been debauched. Creativeness had disappeared, and productivity— whether physical, artistic or intellectual—was ended. The great race of Michelangelo, and Lorenzo the Magnificent, and Dante had become a motley crew of toadies and valets, expert at bowing and obsequiousness. There are, of course, exceptions, for one of the most vital people that history has ever seen does not disintegrate utterly even in its darkest days. But not until Garibaldi—whose shining deeds are not yet a hundred years old—was there anything like a national return.

It was in the midst of all this confusion that the Italian spirit, whose good qualities are inextricably mingled with its bad, found it opportune to hasten on destruction. Realistic in the French political sense of having no illusions, thoroughly contemptuous of idealism — aggressively "practical," it now made announcement that it would preach what it had practised and it would practise what it preached. "The end justifies the means" became its four Evangels and its Law and its Prophets; any end, apparently; any means whatsoever. The result was a wave of riding out the current gust of wind that was as shameless and as shortsighted as has ever been known. It was *sauve-qui-peut* and God help him who guessed badly.

The list of alliances and counter-alliances, schemes and counter-schemes, by which various units in Italy sought to employ against other Italian units those very resources which should have been used against a common enemy, is too long to relate and too tragic. But it is no exaggeration to say that there was hardly a secular prince south of the Alps and there was hardly a head of the church, who to gain the most trivial advantage, would balk at anything.

There is no need of turning to a popular "bad man" such as Caesar Borgia for an example. Pope Julius II prided himself on being the most patriotic, even the most chauvinist, of old firebrands. Yet it was at Venice, also Italian, that he hurled the thunderbolts which he had forged in the League of Cambrai, and it was the Duke of Ferrara whom he harried most persistently and not any Frenchman or Spaniard. The same with Il Moro. This swarthy-looking Ludovico Sforza called down the tornado on Italy simply to make sure that the filched duchy of Milan would remain in his hands. He had taken it over from his nephew whom some say he later poisoned. It is pleasant to record that he reaped the whirlwind. The first French invasion — which he had arranged — confirmed him in the possession of his plums; but a second invasion snatched them and him too, and he died, a caged panther, at Loches, having rotted there ten years. Nor was it only the lords lay and spiritual who thus sold themselves. No more sturdy individualists existed than the staunch republicans of the lands between the Romagna and the Venetian *terra firma*, yet when the Pope elbowed Ravenna — just to name one instance — its citizens threatened to put themselves into the hands of the Sultan. The sad truth of the matter was that there was always enough sensational, even if temporary, success in this attitude to justify its continuance. Consequently, so it went on.

In surroundings like that, what was more likely than that similar opportunists should arise in other branches of activity? One of them was Pietro Aretino. Titian rightly called him a *condottiere*—a gangster chief—of literature. Nor was he the one to deny this. The coat fitted him, and he not only put it on, but wore it proudly.

"I too am a captain," he wrote the Duke of Montmorency, "but my soldiery does not rob, cause people to revolt, or betray citadels. Instead, with its regiments of ink bottles and with truth painted on its banners, it brings more honor to the prince it serves than men of arms do."

Here we have the historical justification of his biography. Aretino is a type man of this "great age of human intensity," as much so and as necessary to our understanding of it as any of its more familiar figures.

As to the human justification, it is less complex. Insect or son of the gods, blind worm or fallen angel, the human being is the one hero of our epic, and the one thing that art can write about. It has been said rightly that no person has ever lived whose life did not have a lengthy book in it. It follows as the inevitable corollary that no person need ever apologize for writing a book about any person who has ever lived.

And Aretino was no ordinary human being, but a most extraordinary one, indeed. Two centuries and a half before the technical beginnings of *liberté, egalité,* and *fraternité,* he was born without any opportunities whatsoever, yet so deeply was he imbued with the dynamic potencies of the age that he rose by sheer force of energy to pride of place and universal acknowledgment. His letters went to popes and kings and what is even more important popes and kings answered his letters. He came into the presence of the greatest emperor since Charlemagne, and the greatest emperor since Charlemagne sat him at his right hand. The first universal Italian poet since Dante called him "Divine" and spread abroad his nickname "The Scourge of Princes." I refer to Ariosto. Nor was this all. Noble ladies sent him presents so that his letter of thanks mentioning their name would appear in his next volume. Dukes bid for his praise. Marquises sought his dedications. He called himself a "free man by the grace of God" and it was as true as it could be in those days of fawning and of adulation. He appropriated the title of "The Fifth Evangelist" and it fitted him as well as "The Fourth Estate" fits the modern press. One of his tribe named him "The Secretary of the World" and it was almost an understatement. He was the first blackmailer, and the first journalist, and the first publicity man. And back of all this was a slum in a small city, and the gutters of Italy. Here, therefore, leaving out all else — and there is nearly everything else — is a success story, *par excellence,* one of the most dazzling success stories ever narrated. For no wielder of the pen ever attained quite Aretino's influence before him, and no wielder of the pen has attained it since him but Voltaire.

It is these circumstances that set the limits of my biography, and I do not find them circumscribing. Without falling into the stodgy dullnesses of those two-volume "Life and Times" that are earnestly deplored by all sorts of persons who have neither the patience nor the ability to write them, I would like to narrate the saga of this brilliant man in such a way as to make it, at least by implication, a social history of the age that made him possible. Without too much assistance from fiction — which is all right in its own place, but latterly has taken to invading foreign territory — I would like to tell a vivid story.

But the story is actual and the need for invention, therefore, slight. My task has been largely to set it down.

Greenwich, Connecticut,
December 1939

CHAPTER I

The Son of the Shoemaker

PIETRO ARETINO was born in Arezzo during the night between April 19 and April 20, 1492.

The town gave him his name — Pietro from Arezzo. It was in a sense a nom-de-plume, and living somewhere else he might have been Pierre Parisien or Pedro de Madrid or Peter New Yorker.

The year set him off in time. Lorenzo the Magnificent died in 1492, and it was in 1492 that Christopher Columbus discovered America. Aretino thus came into the world at what could be regarded as the exact point of separation between the modern and the old. Certainly the death of Lorenzo ended the fresh Maytime of the Renaissance with its exquisite if often artificial Botticellis and Polizianos and Pico della Mirandolas — the very syllables of whose names seem to suggest the multifold, delicate flowers and the sudden, cleansing rains of the Florentine spring — just as definitely as it removed from the Italian scene the one Italian who had the insight and the tact and the ability to keep Italy inviolate. And if the finding of a new world was not, literally as well as symbolically, the beginning of a new era, what was?

The only significance of the day was an ironic one. April 19, 1492 was Holy Thursday, and April 20 was Good Friday. Aretino himself laid stress on it.

> On that calm night, most holy and most still,
> Which followed is by Venus' sacred day,
> On which all faithful, pious creatures pray
> Reverently, with gushing tears that spill,
> Nature — to fortune far more good than ill —
> Drew forth and fused my spirit and my clay
> From the maternal cave. So I can say,
> Since I, to bear what comes, have steadfast will.

I

Jesus knew pain his fellow men to save
At that same time when in the womb no more
I lay; and as from prison I was borne,
I did not keep as silent as the grave,
But for His bitter cross I wept full sore:
Christ died for me, and I for Christ was born.

Evidently he had forgotten the legend. It was not one who
"for Christ was born" but Christ's opponent, the anti-Christ,
who was supposed to have come into this world on Good
Friday. But if he forgot, his enemies, who were legion, never
did. They took pleasure in reminding him from time to time.

His father was a poor shoemaker whose Christian name was
Luke. Any other he may have had has been lost forever. It has
been guessed that his last name was de Bura; but that is not
probable, since the de Bura, or the Burali as they were sometimes called, were noble. It has been suggested that it was
Bonamici or Camaiani, but the evidence therefor is tenuous.
More likely he was simply Luca Calzolaio, or Luke the Shoemaker. Especially among the more obscure, the family name
was not yet in all cases definitely established, but was still being formed out of place names and out of occupation names
and out of nicknames. And Luke, father of Pietro, plainly was
obscure. He was not a shoe merchant, but a cobbler. In a small
booth up a dark alley, he worked tirelessly — not making
pointed buskins for la-de-da lordlings who had stepped out of
pictures by Benozzo Gozzoli, or golden slippers for their ladies,
but half-soling or even cutting out of stiff leather and then
putting together heavy boots for artizans and shopkeepers or
useful clogs for peasants. He was industrious, solid, conscien-
tious, and in his own line he had ability — but undoubtedly his
clothes were made of the coarsest wearable material, and his
breath stank of garlic and of cheap wine.

His mother was a woman of the same class. She was a *citta-
dina*, a daughter of the tenements, not a countrywoman. Her
name was Tita, and she lived out her days and perhaps was
born in that same town that gave her son his name. But she

was not Luca's counterpart in any other way. We know that she had great beauty, and we have reason to assume that she was vivacious and intelligent with an oval face and dark hair, and that she gave Pietro his piercing black eyes with which he looked out so seeingly upon this vivid world.

Beyond this, we are informed only that she was regarded by her amazing son with a filial reverence that was at once exquisite and moving. Matteo Lappoli had been commissioned by the town fathers to paint a fresco of the Annunication for the Church of Sant' Agostino, and he chose Tita as the model for his rapt Madonna. Aretino never tired of referring to this fact. "If it were not well enough known without it," he wrote Giorgio Vasari, "this alone would be proof of her modesty and virtue." This he swore to "by the very tender love I have for her memory." Then he begged Messer Vasari, who happened to be in Arezzo at the time, to make him a copy of the picture; and he urged him to "make sure that this image is so life-like that I will be able to take almost the same pleasure from seeing her painted that I did when she was still alive." When it was completed, he showed Vasari's handiwork to Titian, and that shrewd expert of the human countenance told him that in his whole long experience he had "only seen one face less worldly." The "one face" convinced Pietro that the opinion was sincere, not flattery, and he talked about it boastingly to all listeners. For the words meant much to him. Like so many other great rogues, whose relationships with individual women had been on the most cynical plane possible, he still wanted to think loftily about Woman in general and particularly about that representative of Woman who had brought him into the world. And that, Titian made it possible for him to do.

That Aretino had this humble origin was not always known.

"The Aretine," sneered the unknown author of a pamphlet of vituperation, "was born — so that you may know his origin — in a little hamlet about three miles outside of Arezzo. His father was a low villain. His mother was a whore."

It was a chance shot, but though it came near to the mark, it gained little credit. Aretino had his own story of his birth, and he saw to it that it was the accepted one. He was the bastard of an Aretine nobleman. He even picked his supposed father —one Luigi Bacci. Luigi had two sons, Gualtiero and Francesco, and throughout his long life, Aretino always spoke to them and wrote to them as brothers. "We were both kneaded from the same dough," he told one of them with vulgar candor of expression, and when the younger died shortly after old Luigi did, he wrote his friend Albergotti he had had a double loss.

"I do not grieve so greatly for my father's death. He after all had lived out his time. But I do mourn the loss of my brother Cecco Bacci."

The fact that the relationship thus proclaimed cast a doubt upon the virtue of the mother he so loved, did not even enter his considerations. The two Bacci accepted him as their brother. Small-town Walter and small-town Francis, even though of the nobility, did not mind the glamour of connection with the most famous son of the city they lived in. And if they made no objections, who else would? Anyway, bastardy carried no stigma in those days and sometimes much honor. Boccaccio had been a bastard and he was regarded as the glory of Italian literature. Leonardo da Vinci was a bastard, as was Caesar Borgia. The Emperor's bastard daughter was his favorite princess. And before Aretino reached middle manhood, another illegitimate son achieved the high papacy itself, while that baseborn fellow's at least allegedly baseborn son would become Duke of Florence. Better the wrong side of the blanket, if noble, than a mere plebeian. Without any sense of shame, therefore, but, since he was wise, more by implication than by any positive statement, he indicated that the great talents with which in his own estimation he astounded the whole suppliant universe came from the fact that not even by inheritance was he any common being. Castiglione will tell you how important this was. In his estimation—and he speaks in "The Perfect Courtier" for the age's ruling snobbery — there is no real achievement possible except you be nobly born.

But for a hot-headed flare of temper, this pedigree might well be credited still. In the year 1550, one Medoro Nucci descended upon Venice where Pietro then lived, and like all others of his ilk, he knocked on Aretino's famous door. He called himself a painter, which might have meant anything; and an engineer which probably meant nothing; and he was in general one of those vagabond artist jack-of-all-callings, of which Cellini and Leone Leoni were the only successful examples and of which the unsuccessful ones starved in all the courts and hedgerows of Italy. But he had one advantage over his fellows. He was a native of Arezzo, and for one reason or another, Pietro put himself out even more lavishly than usual for such fellow citizens of his as tried to cadge from him. Nucci wanted help. This meant that he expected Aretino to feed him (excellently); to clothe him (like a gentleman); and to provide him with a generous patron. Curiously enough, Aretino attempted this. He took one of his own fine shirts and put it on the scarecrow's back, and he quieted the clamor of his belly with the best wines and the tastiest wild chicken of the Casa Aretino. The patron question was more difficult, for in providing Nucci with a man to sponsor him, he must make sure not to rob himself. But apparently, even here he was successful for soon he was receiving grateful letters from Medoro's wife.

"My dear daughter," he answered one of these, "I have received the tennis balls and the letters which you sent me, and I prize them as coming from the heart and pen of one who wishes me well. Certainly the former are as pleasing to the lover of exercise to whom I gave them, as the latter are to me who only exercise my mind. Indeed, reading them, I am astonished to find a woman who has such intelligence and such grace. I am beginning to think that God must have bestowed the genius which He once used to give the men of Arezzo on its women.

"I hope," he went on, "that Medoro will soon find himself sufficiently settled to bring you on to this city where you can know me as a father."

There was a catch to this altruism, of course. There was always a possibility that Angela Nucci, married to a man young enough to be Pietro's son, might prove on inspection to be as comely as he hoped she was. And the wives of the men he helped out sometimes showed their gratitude in ways their husbands did not dream of. It added to the gaiety of life.

But that wished-for consummation did not come to pass. For a quarrel, not a gay triumvirate, was the next step in the *entente* Nucci-Aretino, and since we find Aretino beating savagely at the Florentine ambassador's door we may assume that whatever libel on the part of rogue Medoro brought it into being, its aim was to get Florence plums that previously had been Pietro's. We do not know, unfortunately.

"Nucci is a rogue," he shouted. "Nucci is an impostor. Nucci is—a bigamist!"

He woke up the following morning to find a letter on his doorstep and he had only to walk as far as the Rialto to be aware that all Venice had read it before he had.

"O villain clown," it began, and it then went on to express marvel that anyone lived—let alone a Florentine diplomat— that still believed Pietro's slanders. "I am surprised too," it continued, "that the world admires you so greatly for the merits of your works. First, that is, for the lewd sonnets which you made under the picture of Raphael of Urbino; second for the *Trentuno* which you composed about Angela Zaffetta; third for your *Puttana Errante;* fourth for the six days of your *Ragionamenti* in which you taught all kinds of persons to do villainies; besides that for many sonnets which I have with me, the large part written in your own hand, and for many other of your faults which I have ways of proving that you know of." Lastly, it challenged Aretino to prove his as-

sertions before the Signory of Venice and threatened legal
retribution.

Aretino flew into a white rage. He must answer immediately, and he must now write the Duke of Florence himself.
He did so with racing pen, the words tumbling in ungram-
matical speed. First, he told Cosimo that he had kept Medoro
— "a gallow's bird predestined to the gallows" — for four costly
months in his own house. Next, he asserted that he had paid
all of Medoro's debts. After that, he said that Medoro was
"more of a book-binder than an engineer"; accused him of
circulating a lying report that Cosimo was giving him a pension of three hundred crowns; and offered to substantiate the
bigamy charges. Then he extenuated the licentious writings
for which he had been upbraided — half of which, incidentally,
were not his own — on the ground that they were youthful
indiscretions, and in proof pointed to his pious lives of Jesus
and the Saints. Last of all, he gave vent to temper. "I laugh,"
he said furiously, "at his calling me a villain clown, for that is
what he is himself."

Then he saw the superscripture.

"To Pietro Aretino," the letter was addressed, "*son of Luca
the shoemaker,* in Venice."

Could he deny this statement?

He could not, he realized, for Medoro not only spoke the
truth but could prove he did.

Better, then, to accept the situation.

"I tell you," his pen dug the paper, "that I glory in the
title which he, to vilify me, has given me; and may it teach the
nobility to procreate sons like the one which a poor cobbler
has begotten in Arezzo."

Elsewhere he repeated this to Danese, the sculptor.

"Indeed, I take honor from being born of base blood in
Arezzo, for none of my line before me were what I am. I give
nobility to others even though I have received it from no one."

Call this bravado if you will; call it making the best, merely,
of a bad situation; and you will still have to concede that there

was something rather admirable about its insolence and fear-
lessness.

And from now on, far from hiding his birth, he traded on it.
Over and over again in his poems and in his letters there is a
proud saying which might almost be the legend on his scutch-
eon. It came to him once, and he repeated it until he believed
in it.

"I was born in a *spedale,* but with the soul of a king."

Hospital is the literal translation of *spedale,* but perhaps
charity ward better gives its meaning.

"I was born in a charity ward, but with the soul of a reigning monarch."

Quite plainly, we are compelled to agree.

Besides Tita and Luca, four of Aretino's near kin have
escaped oblivion. They spent at least part of their life in the
fierce glory of the light of being notable which beat down on
him; and they are today remembered only because he did not
forget them. There were two sisters, and there were two
uncles. The two uncles were Niccolo and Fabiano Bonci, but
whether they were brothers of his mother or his father cannot
be said. A kind of instinct leads us to believe brother of his
mother, but instincts are not always reliable. One sister's
name was Francesca. The other sister's name remains unknown.

The two Bonci seem to have presaged what their nephew
might do. They themselves did not attain any great heights
but at the same time they did not stay in the slums, and the
sympathy they showed young Pietro indicated the hope they
had that the boy would follow them. Fabiano, the elder, was a
priest. Jovial, popular, and a good talker, he never became
a great prelate but he moved on in the world, and anyway
even a *parroco* — unless of a very rustic church — must have
seemed somewhat better than a shoemaker. Niccolo was a
lawyer. He wore no vair robes and like many another small-
time legalist he thumbed his books frequently and hoped he

did not get his precedents wrong. But he knew Latin and had seen the outside world.

Aretino remembered both gratefully.

"Your letter, most honored uncle," he wrote Niccolo many years afterwards, "has mantled my face with the crimson and ruddy colors which the paintbrush of shame always tints it with. For since you are as full of worth and goodness as you are with legal knowledge, I should have been as swift to write to you as, when I was a boy, I was swift to run to you every time you came from Siena. But let the great reverence which I really have for you counterbalance the faults of my pen whose laziness will henceforth change to zeal. Therefore, love me with the same fullness of affection that your elder brother, Messer Fabiano did. O that venerable canon, excellent priest and splendid man! His splendid, excellent, and venerable memory even now brings a flood of tears to my eyes, for he was one of the most loyal friends, pleasant companions and courteous gentlemen that I have ever known."

He had excellent reason to think so of them. In our formative years, we require the stimulus of an elder mind, and that stimulus Aretino got from Messer Niccolo and Father Francesco. Francesco undoubtedly narrated, the boy listening, many of those gusty tales of life in a priest's world that later he incorporated into the first part of the most full-blooded bit of writing which he ever did. Niccolo talked of the more worldly world. He had visited Rome and Siena, and had watched men he had rubbed shoulders with at law school become not only famous lawyers but councillors, secretaries, great writers and even rulers. He told about living by one's wits. He had seen men who had used their talents for their own benefit both honestly and dishonestly, and had profited by either means. The small boy determined to do likewise. He owed, therefore, a large debt to the priest and to the lawyer. He would repay it even if only in words.

As for his sisters, they were sisters and nothing more. They began where Pietro did and they remained there. True, gossip did try to do a job on them, and if you could believe all that was said and written about them they were a bad enough pair. They not only spent their nights and gained their livelihoods in houses of ill-fame, but they supported Pietro with the ill-gotten profits therefrom. This is to laugh at, rather than to be angry. Certainly some fine writers of Rabelaisian fiction strayed from their vocation when Aretino's enemies started publishing pamphlets about him. It is too bad, for they had a flair.

For deplorably — since it would have made a gaudy background — this was absolutely untrue. Aretino's sisters were uninterestingly respectable. Both of them were married. The elder, whose name does not survive, to a certain Scipione. Later Pietro used his influence to get one of her daughters into the convent school of St. Catherine, and this seems to have been their only contact. Francesca, the younger, to a soldier named Orazio Vanotti. Both of them were poor, and for neither of them — despite his almost fantastic generosity to every hanger-on — does he appear to have done much more than offer counsel that poverty was dear to God. Francesca did receive something in hard cash. Though Pietro himself gave her nothing, he at least dunned prince and prelate until the Cardinal of Ravenna paid her dowry for her. Probably Pietro's vanity supplied the reason. She at least had seen his apotheosis and witnessed his grandeur. For she, living in Pietro's childhood home, had been startled one day by a gay retinue in front of her door. It was a prince who came there — dark, negroid, and dissolute-looking, but a prince.

She went to the window.

"Who is it?"

"Alessandro de'Medici."

The Duke of Florence!

Down the stairs she flew, and soon she was kneeling at his feet.

"How can I serve your Highness?"

"Is this —" he smiled ironically — "the house of Aretino?"

"Yes ! your Highness."

"Was Pietro born here ?" he asked.

"No," she answered, "but he dwelt here."

The Duke took off his hat, and bowed politely.

"In this tenement," he told his followers, "a great man and a friend of mine once lived."

Then, tossing her a golden ducat, the dark Medici rode off.

The slow pen of the daughter of the shoemaker set all this on paper and then sent it to Venice.

And thereafter at least one of the family of the satrap of the written word received his benediction and his coin.

CHAPTER II

Student in These Matters and in Painting

THE city of Arezzo is situated on what timetables call the *"linea ferrovia Firenze-Perugia-Napoli"* — the railroad that takes you from Florence to Rome via Perugia rather than the more direct way. It is not far from Terentola where you change cars and wait patiently, looking out over an umber plain rimmed with hazy blue mountains, and hearing the clanking buffers of the carriages as they are shunted back and forth; and perhaps you go into the *ristorante* with its beaded reed curtains (to keep out both the calm heat and a Mosaic plague of flies) and there drink *un vermouth bianco con selz.*

By courtesy it is a "hill town," but actually it is not one of those castellated diadems such as Todi or Terni or Spoleto which crown every strategic eminence of the peninsula from the French border south. It is on the side rather than on the summit of an elevation. Shaped much like an open fan, its handle is grasped firmly by the rugged Apennines that tower two or three thousand feet behind it — azure in summer, and white, veined with indigo, when December brings a wolf's howling even today! Its curved surface faces a green valley which is really a little plateau, formed by the confluence of the Arno and the Chiana. These rivers move toward each other slowly, and there where they finally meet they leave this verdant triangle. For the rest, it is exceedingly similar to half a hundred other cities of north central Italy.

Looking south and westward from the Public Gardens, you can see — through a frame of blue-black cypress trees — the tiled roof and the brown, square belltower of Santa Maria della Pieve. It was founded in 1050, and the last touches were put upon the reserved arches of its dignified facade in 1226. Somewhat closer is the plain Loggia de Vasari and the exquisitely ornate portico of Santa Maria delle Grazie. Besides them, there are straight avenues (modern) and crooked mediæval alleyways. There are plain dwellings whose over-hanging roofs do not indicate whether they were built yester-day or six centuries ago; a town hall that already stood when the young man who later wrote the *Decameron* passed by the city; and at least half a dozen churches from romanesque to baroque, most of which have been pretty badly handled by the Nineteenth Century restorers. There are the ruins of a Roman amphitheatre, and a fragment of the ancient brick walls, and a stern fortress built by the Medici. There is, finally, a museum filled with Etruscan funeral urns and with the famous *vasi Aretini,* those amazing bits of pre-Roman pottery that moved even the sharp-tongued poet Martial to speak praise of them; and an art gallery not so overstocked with masterpieces that you have no time to admire the few fine pictures there.

As in the other cities of its sort, you look down on fields of waving wheat, on twisted olive trees which are a shifting sea of silver, on yellow dust, on slow cream-colored oxen, on gray walls, and on heavy burdened vines that bear as good wine grapes as there are in Italy. Within its limits, there are wide, handsome limes — for shade — and scraggly, drought-browned palms — for decoration. In January, it is raw, gusty and often swept with driven snow. In August, the glaring sun beats down out of a cloudless noonday sky with such a blast-ing heat that even the houses seem dizzy, and as you sit indo-lently at a small table you smell street litter and horse sweat. But its Aprils are amazing dreams.

One quality about Arezzo distinguished it from other little cities of the same sort, and distinguishes it still: the quick, volatile intellect of its inhabitants, their animated, if irascible dispositions.

> The Aretine
> Hath a spirit keen.

Thus the proverb today. And Michelangelo said the same thing four hundred years ago. "Giorgio," he told his biographer, Vasari, "if my wits have any worth to them, it is because I was born in the sharp climate of your Arezzo." To explain this remark, it should be stated that the great Florentine sculptor was born in the tiny mountain hamlet of Caprese where his father at the time of his birth was *podestá*. And Caprese was in the Aretine territory.

"You, my son," Aretino himself wrote to Leone Leoni, the engraver, "would be neither a man of Arezzo nor a man of genius, if you did not have an impetuous nature."

Dante's way of referring to the same qualities was less affable:

> *Botoli . . .*
> *Rhinghiosi píu che chiede lor possa!*
>
> Mongrel curs . . .
> Who snarl more fiercely than their
> lack of teeth allows!

The Arno, he continued, moving downward from the Casentino heights where rude peasants fed on acorns as the swine do, came suddenly upon this city and then turned aside, wrinkling its nose in disgust. But Dante had a reason for disliking the place. Young and full of soaring dreams, he had taken part in the battle of Campaldino; and although there "the light-armed squadrons and fleet foragers" of the Florentine army, led by that haughty aristocrat, Corso de' Donati, routed the men of Arezzo and their Ghibelline allies, Dante had had — by his own confession — a bad scare. There is some possibility, even, that when in the first onslaught certain of the bannered Florentine cavalry broke and fled, he was among the fugitives. And this left a sour taste in his proud mouth.

Every reference to the place we know of bears out the judgment of these observers. What the stone-age inhabitants were like with their handsome, beautifully worked flints, and also the Italic Umbrians with their fine bronzes with geometric decoration, is, of course, lost in prehistory. But the first mention of Arezzo in a written document is as one of the twelve warlike cities of the Etruscan League; and when Lars Porsena, renowned to schoolboys, marched irresistibly upon the then half savage city on the Tiber, and imposed on it his rule and civilization, men from Arretium lent their strength and fierceness to his army. When the Romans turned the tables, it was turbulent. In the days of Marius and Sulla, rioting in the name of civil faction took place at Arezzo; and when Cataline, a left-wing aristocrat who was probably, however, more for himself than for the people, fled the city under the stinging lash of Cicero's grandiloquent oration, Arretium was one of his refuges. Caesar found it necessary to establish military colonies there. When the Empire fell, fierce Longobard kings and Gothic chieftains made it their stronghold. In the Middle Ages, Guelph harrying Ghibelline, and after the Ghibellines had triumphed, one Ghibelline family fighting another, made it as turbulent as Florence, and very nearly as bloody as Perugia. Even after it had fallen into Florentine hands, which it did temporarily in 1336, and permanently in 1384, it was contentious, troublesome and seething. In the modern days of Garibaldi it supplied some of the combativeness that is necessary to a successful revolution, and it did the same again in the more recent revolution of 1922.

As for the wits it produced, this much must be said in preface. Arezzo, though its wealth and fortune have varied, never numbered more than ten to fourteen thousand inhabitants. Then look at the list of those who were born there: Maecenas, patron of Virgil, in Roman days; Guido Monaco, artist and architect, and Fra Guittone, notable primitive poet, in the Middle Ages; Petrarch in the early Fourteenth Century; Leonardo Bruni, anticipator, to some extent, of great da Vinci, in its latter half; Michelangelo, Giorgio Vasari, Leone Leoni, Pope Julius III, Pietro Aretino, Bernardo Accolti, and Vitellozzo Vitelli in the Cinquecento. The last list is particularly impressive. The greatest sculptor since the Greeks; a fine painter who was also the Boswell of Italian painting; an exquisite goldsmith; our scourge of princes; a courtier; and one of the five ablest generals of Renaissance Italy. These men — and the others also — had a common denominator: the energy Arezzo gave to them; its vehemence that took them down their roads.

Aretino was an Aretine of the Aretines. *The* Aretine, he called himself and rightfully. Aretine he was by birth, and Aretine by temperament. His wit and talent were Aretine wit and talent, and he had in full measure the Arezzo turbulence. Even his limitations were the limitations of the place. Arezzo was a small town with great ambitions and with no small esteem of itself. The drive of a nature that realizes its lack of advantages, and will not let this circumscribe it, was Aretino's all his life.

Beyond all this, he loved Arezzo and every man and woman who came from it. We have already seen what he did for one Aretine rogue and the reward he got, but this did not discourage him, and there were a mort of other Aretine rascals and of Aretine fine men and women who were indebted to him. He defended the city in its troubles, and once even successfully used his influence to call off dogs of war that had been unloosed on it. Even in his busiest and most famous days, he wrote almost incessantly to its citizens. Sometimes he seemed to know more of their successes and their failures than they did themselves. He spoke frequently in praise of the city itself.

"If, my brother," he wrote when he was forty-five years old, "any man of merit who desired to rid himself of all cares, were to go back to see his native land once every ten years, there is no question but in the brief space of a fortnight he would experience all the beatitude which souls know when they revisit heaven.

"For look you," he continued, "a smile which reveals to you the true face of your own home city, lifts you up to greater heights than the honors given you by strangers. A 'good-day'

from an old neighbor is worth more than any reward whatsoever from this prince or that one. The soul derives more joy
in glimpsing the smoke from the paternal hearth than it takes
from the flames kindled by the glory of its own virtue."

Elsewhere he became more specific: "Arezzo, no less wise
than it is valorous." "The old time generous spirit of my
fatherland." "The commodious life of Arezzo." "That noble
city that begets geniuses." When he first made the acquaintance of Giorgio Vasari, his principal delight seemed to be to
discover that his natal city had produced so able a painter.
When a certain Aretine, Bernardino Ricco, was imprisoned
in Florence, he sent money to help bail him out. There was
no reason for doing this except to lend aid to an Aretine in
trouble. When he received honors, Arezzo was the first place
to know of it, and the letters of congratulations from the
Aretines were the first answered. In his old age, Arezzo made
him an honorary citizen, and this recognition seemed to have
meant more to him than any other he had ever received. His
answer, literally, was larded with his gratefulness. "Ecstasy of
happiness." "Lifts me to the sky." "Unexpected dignity." He
went further and made a statement which cut right into the
very essence of his being.

"This gracious thing that you have done will be an example
to the young men of Arezzo. It will teach them perseverance.
It will show them to what heights base birth can rise through
application."

He had, as we shall soon see if we have not already, an
exaggerated way of speaking, but this time he was genuine.
This time he was not bombastic. This time he spoke from the
heart.

This being the case, it is too bad that we have only a fragmentary record of his boyhood spent in this town. But shoemaker's brats are scarcely ever recognized as future marvels
of the world by those fellow townspeople who are later so
solicitous of them, and the details of their doings are not frequently set down.

"All that I know—" this is his own account—"my mother taught me in Arezzo where I was born and brought up. I had no school teacher. I did not trouble my head about the art of the Greeks and the Romans. I attended school there, but only long enough to absorb the elements of our holy Religion. These, however, I was made to master thoroughly."

Shakespeare's "little Latin and less Greek" is suggested.

"Hardly—" it is an enemy now speaking—"was he five years old when the young ape commenced reading the pig Latin poetry of Merlin the Mantuan, and to this he applied himself with such zeal that he outdid Alfisibro who studied fifteen hours a day.

"I am obliged to tell you," continued his adversary sarcastically, "that he did this so profitably that at the age of ten he composed a hymn called 'The Seven Joys,' which he said was perfect, and which the blind still sing in church."

When he was between those two ages, copies of Virgil and of Petrarch were placed in front of him on one hand, and of the "Loves" of Lucan and the *Anacroia* on the other.

"Wonderful to relate, he, inspired by that love of poetry which the heavens gave him, took the *Anacroia* and the said dirty dialogues, which was an overweening sign of the greatness of his soul."

He learned also his father's trade of shoemaking.

"He still has in his possession—" this was written in the days of his glory—"a pair of boots made by his own hands. These he keeps with him always. He values them as most people would value a manuscript copy of the unpublished sonnets of Vittoria Colonna."

Piece the two accounts together—his own reticent one, and the venomous barbed arrows of his pamphleteer biographer. Then slowly the true picture comes out. The alert boy, somewhat tall for his age, with short, crinkly, black hair, restless eyes, a quick tongue, and a square, obstinate chin, that had, nevertheless, a slight cleft in it. The father with his modest but successful business which he assumed naturally, if unimaginatively, that his son would carry on. The mother with her higher aspirations. Luca, as a matter of course, made Pietro an apprentice in his little shop, and the boy, being apt, even if not docile, was not a bad one. His mother, equally as a matter of course, taught him how to read and tried to teach him virtue. The last step in his personal development came from within.

It is not easy to explain, but for want of being able to say it exactly, let us call it the famous Aretine air which had bestowed upon him those more intense than the ordinary powers of mental functioning which we call genius. And accident — the chance finding, in his case, of congenial inspiration — showed him the use for it.

It was as indicated by his hostile biographer. He could not, it so happened, have read the macaronic verses of Merlin Coccaeus; for Folengo, the renegade monk who used that as a *nom-de-plume,* was but a year older than Pietro himself and had not yet either scandalized his convent with his untidy clothes and even untidier living, nor invented the device of writing Italian so that it looked like Latin which was to prove such a good medium for rough humor. But some other satiric poet must have fallen into his hands. Lucan would do, or the author of the *Anacroia,* but more probably it was Burchiello. Burchiello was a rhyming barber "whose Muse was a hobo Venus bred among the taverns and the low haunts of vulgar company." With his burlesque allusions and his trenchant popular slang, he was typical of Florentine street wit, but in that city, whose literary tastes were more fastidious now, he was outmoded. He was still quoted in the provinces, however.

One day Aretino picked up a copy of his poems, or perhaps heard them recited at some street corner. He read — or listened —absorbed, then memorized. The next step was to begin to imitate, and soon lines of his own, sentimental or satiric, were reverberating through his brain. He set them down on paper and they seemed good to him. He next showed them to his mother, and she approved. It was a fatal happening. That drug-taking habit, which we call creative writing, and which is far harder to break than cocaine or opium, needs but little encouragement. He began in earnest. Tita smiled. Maybe if she could have seen far enough ahead, she would have done otherwise. Luca grumbled. A rhyming barber might be all right in Florence, but not certainly a rhyming shoemaker in your own family. Disapproval has its uses as an educator, and the growl taught Pietro he would have to fend for himself. The stream running toward the future had begun to flow.

It was not slowed at all by an event in the world of politics which took place at exactly this time. In 1502 — when Pietro was ten years old — a new element was thrust into his experience. New to him, that is; for certainly it was an old element in the life of the peninsula. Civil riots broke out. The citizens of Arezzo rose suddenly against their Florentine masters, and against — even more violently — such of their own townsmen as were pro-Florentine or even supposed to be. For eight and forty hours blood and fire ruled the city. An earthquake would have hardly been as destructive.

The true cause was an act of violence committed against a prominent Aretine. We have already referred to Vitellozzo Vitelli. He had two brothers. One of them, Paolo Vitelli, entered the Florentine service and was made a general. General Vitelli was sent against the Pisans, with whom Florence was in a chronic state of war, but he did not make progress fast enough to suit his employers. Possibly also there was political jobbery involved in which case a charge of treason was a good cover for malfeasance by the city fathers. At any rate, he was seized without warning, and sentenced without trial. His head fell in the small village of Cascina down the Arno. Vitellozzo was likewise in the pay of Florence when he got the tidings, but he resigned by taking flight. His first refuge was the city of the leaning tower, against which he had just ceased to do battle. He was welcomed tumultuously. Then he went to Città di Castello.

Sitting by the Tiber, which is there little more than a brook, he meditated his revenge. Who would help him clip the Florentines? The two Borgias, he felt reasonably sure: Caesar, because he dreamed of his own state in Central Italy, and a strong Florentine republic stood in the way of this; Pope Alexander — Roderigo Borgia — because his son wished him to. The two Medici, because Florence had exiled them. Pandolfo Petrucci, because he was the lord of Siena. Giovan Paolo Baglioni of Perugia, and the whole clawing bear tribe of the Orsini. Last of all, the city of Arezzo.

Certainly, the Aretines, always unruly, would rise up against Florence if encouraged, and that truly would dismay the republic. An important citizen of Arezzo had fallen into Vitellozzo's hands, and other prominent Aretines sought out the captain to negotiate for his release. Vitellozzo received them personally. He broached swiftly his plans, and got instant acceptance of them. On the spot, a conspiracy was formed. Secret names were assigned. Secret signals were agreed upon. The whole thing would have gone off without hitch or even much bloodshed but for the fact that too many whispers make a roar. The roar was overheard, and was reported to Florence, where it was paid for. Florence sent a commissioner. He entered Arezzo, and there arrested the first one of the conspirators he could lay hands upon. Had he arrested every conspirator, the whole thing would have gone up in smoke. But he showed, in this crisis, the usual democratic fault of trying to be legal. He wanted evidence. While he hesitated, one of the men he should have apprehended rode from piazza to piazza.

"The Florentines are seizing our grain supply!"

Their grain — for the soldiers of the oppressor!

The bells started a clangor, and the swallows, startled from the belfries, darted hither and thither. Voices rose. Out of the houses and the tenements, poured the populace. "To the palace!" shouted someone, and the crowd echoed it. It was a Spring day when men are naturally rioters, and the mob began to move. Soon it reached its destination. As it seethed there, the man arrested broke loose from indecisive captors and stood upon a balcony.

"Fellow Aretines!" he cried, "see now to what a pass our poor city has been brought, and we too, its poor citizens. Now are we not only deprived wrongfully of our small food supply, but we cannot even greet our relatives." This should be explained. In the conspiracy, Vitellozzo was always referred to as *cugino* or cousin. The arrested man pretended it was a real cousin he had been writing about. "Rise up for once," he continued, "and show that you are men by defending your liberty. Do not harm the Florentine commissioner or his captain, but strike hard for the free city and for the bread you eat!"

A roar answered him.

"Liberty! Down with the Florentines! Long live the Medici!"

The last, all things considered, was a strange saying to couple with the first.

White of face, and now finally realizing that he was confronted with something truly ugly—a city plebs in revolt—the Florentine commissioner tried to intervene. He stepped out and faced the crowd.

"Citizens," he implored, "lay down your arms and go home. You will all be pardoned."

A surf pounded in answer. It was the jeer, half defiance, half a scornful laughter, of the stirred up people.

Then he lost his temper. He sent out a crier and the crier read an official edict. This time the rioters were not begged but ordered to depart, and the full weight of Florentine wrath was promised those who stayed recalcitrant. There was no mincing of words and the iron step of Florentine soldiery entering the city was promised by its syllables. It had no effect. The mob did not knife the crier and it did not hang him, but it tore him to pieces.

On that signal, the people arose. They laid hands on the commissioner and on the Florentine-appointed captain of justice, but fortunately the captors of those two men carried them to a place of safety. Presumably a later ransom was hoped for. They took the keys to the city gates and strongboxes from the gonfalonier, and seized all the customs money. Then they started in on palaces. A certain Messer Cristofano Francucci, a doctor, harangued the crowd. "That gang has robbed us," he shouted. "Now let us rob them for a change." It was popular oration. The commissioner's palace was the first one entered. Every valuable it contained was flung into the streets, and what was not trampled on was carried off. Then torches were applied and there remained a gutted skeleton. Next came the palace of the captain, the palace of the priors, and the houses of every Aretine who had even vaguely espoused the Florentine cause.

After that, human victims were in order. A certain Bernardino Tondinelli, against whom nothing more could be said than that, being a native of Todi, he was not heart and soul for the Aretine cause, met Bernardo Camaiani, one of the conspirators on the street. Being a relative, he went up to him to congratulate him. Camaiani stabbed him in cold blood. This was a signal to kill every male Tondinelli in the town. Two brothers and four sons were butchered. One of the latter was a priest. He was dragged out of his hiding place in a drain pipe at his monastery and cut to pieces by the crowd. Another son was pitched screaming out of a window to the citizens below. He was not living when he reached the paving stones. The same Camaiani murdered one Francesco Albergotti who had come to him under safe conduct. His excuse was that if he had not stabbed Francesco, the people would have lynched him. There may have been something to it, for when news of Francesco's death spread, the crowd seized his father and the first one of his brothers they could get their hands on, and hanged them from the windows of the palace of the captain of justice. Cocchi Albergotti they were not satisfied with hanging. He was stripped naked and a lighted torch thrust between his buttocks. Thus *"il soddomito,"* as the angry crowd decided to call him, was dragged about the city.

As always in times of violence, men of the losing faction took their own lives rather than fall into the hands of
their adversaries. Last of all, the fortress was torn down — last
only because it took a little time to subdue. The symbol of
Florentine rule, it was carried off stone by stone by the
exultant Aretines much as the men of Paris carried off the
Bastile nearly three centuries later. Only when there were no
more to slay and nothing else to destroy, peace, or maybe it
was stupor, held the city. The ruins ceased to smoke. The
rain washed the smears of blood away.

The small boy with the observant eyes and ears witnessed
all this, whether or not as a pleb ragamuffin he took part in
it. He saw Vitellozzo arrive at the city gates. A revolutionary
committee greeted him.

"Here, great captain," said a spokesman, "are the keys of the
city. They were taken from the Florentine Republic by your
aid and counsel. Now do you defend us from this enemy.
Arezzo freely gives herself into your protection."

"I receive them," answered Vitellozzo, "in obedience to
your will, but I give them back to the citizens and to the liberty of Arezzo. I will protect Arezzo as if she belonged to me."

Aretino witnessed also the troops marching through the
streets to do battle with the hated Florentines. Sturdy foot-
soldiers, men of solid Tuscan blood descended from the
Etruscans and from the legionaries, who wanted only able
leaders and patriotic ones — the last of which, like the rest of
Italy, they never found — to make them as good as any in the
peninsula; active cavalry; and the first "mounted riflemen" in
history.

He may also have seen a certain unbelievably handsome
human being who passed through Arezzo that summer on his
way to join Caesar Borgia, who had appointed him chief engineer. He was a painter, one of the finest of that art the
world has ever known, but he preferred filling his notebooks
with dynamics, hydraulics, and with plans for mechanized
war chariots and machines for rising in the air that presaged

tanks and aeroplanes. He came from Vinci, and his name was Leonardo.

And Aretino shared certainly the small city's anguish when the Pope's son abandoned Vitellozzo at the French King's orders, and when Vitellozzo abandoned Arezzo. The French entered the town but soon handed it over to the Florentines.

"Behold, O Florentines," said General Imbalt who though fierce was not vindictive, "Louis XII, King of France, restores the city of Arezzo to your government. He wishes you to pardon all the conspirators, and all the Aretines. I urge you to do this. Not only in obedience to my lord, but also lest by contending with them longer you destroy both them and yourselves also."

Then he marched out.

This was on September 10.

On September 11, the Florentines sacked such of the city as the Aretines had not sacked themselves, and confiscated the goods of every citizen of Arezzo who had ever known of the plot. As a pledge for future good conduct, they took thirty leading Aretines as hostages. These were maltreated, imprisoned, and on the least suspicion of trouble, put to torture.

Later, too, young Pietro could not have helped hearing fellow Aretines talking over Vitellozzo's end. Vitellozzo had revolted against Caesar Borgia but later they made peace and Caesar thereupon summoned him, with three similarly involved captains, to the town of Sinigaglia by the Adriatic strand. There was to be a grand reconciliation scene. But instead the Pope's son had lured the four men from their bodyguards, and they were prisoners. Two he took to Rome for further anguishes before he had them executed. But the two others, Michelotto, doer of this Caesar's blackest deeds, strangled before sunrise. Vitellozzo was one of them.

"It was a shame. It was a foul deed. It was treachery."

Thus protested some of the Aretines, angered at the mere thought that a bastard and a Spanish one should lay hands upon a fellow citizen.

But others smiled sardonically. They remembered the proud promises the murdered soldier made that he would guard their city, and they remembered equally well that he was comfortably taking the cure at the hot springs of San Casciano when the men of Florence sacked Arezzo.

One further phase of Aretino's education was now complete.

But it still had a long way to go before it made him the complete man. He could write doggerel, and he knew, having seen Caesar Borgia and the Vitelli, what the great were like. This was important, since he was to live by milking them. Arezzo, however, set upon its Apennine slope, was by no means the wide world, and the wide world, as he sensed instinctively, was to be his oyster. Running away from home is neither so unusual nor so complicated that a whole set of special reasons has to be given. Nevertheless, reasons have been given, and profuse ones. A biographer, guessing wildly, says that his father took him, and that the poor shoemaker found his son a position in a mighty Roman household. Poor shoemakers, however, are not usually able to provide even talented sons with places men of influence cannot always get for their scions. A legend says he wrote a sacrilegious sonnet, but that seems to be confusing one episode with another. A scandal monger says he robbed his mother. It is one evil deed we cannot believe of him.

Actually, it was the seething discontent of early manhood. As he reached fourteen years of age, he became restive. He was mature now. For he was at least no longer a boy, as Italy, in those precocious days, saw it. He must make his own way. He must seek his fortune. On a hot summer's day of 1505 or 1506, an eagle, flying in the clear air, might have looked down on the white road that wound toward Cortona and Lake Thrasymene, and seen a tall stripling, plodding slowly southward. On his shoulders was a bundle which contained all his few belongings, and his shoes, hosen and breeches gradually grew gray in the dry Italian dust. At night he slept in ditches, behind wheat stacks, and when lucky in some *contadino's* barn.

He drank water and he lived on what he cadged. It was Pietro, son of Luca Calzolaio, later Pietro Aretino. It was not a long trip he ventured on. His pouch bulging with coin, he would come back in short order to dazzle Luca, Tita, and his fellow townsmen. Actually, it was only once until he was well past fifty that he again trod the Aretine cobblestones, and glittered as he walked. Even his immediate journeys — where he wandered in the next decade only — took him far and wide.

He began as a bookbinder's assistant in Perugia, and he studied art there. Incidentally, his departure from that city was caused by a doing reminiscent of the sacrilegious sonnet. In the principal piazza of that steep city with its narrow streets and overhanging arches was a painting of Mary Magdalene at the feet of Christ. Her arms were widespread, seeking compassion, and her eyes were filled with tears, and she was represented as sorrowing, but her face showed her to be one of those high-hearted buxom citizen's wives so dear to the *Decameron* who would "liefer have two husbands than one," and whose marital imbroglios were so much a part of the tradition of Italian burgher life. The temptation was too much to resist. Aretino went to her one night, and in her hands painted a lute. There she sat, and waited for her lover!

He then went to Rome where he found employment in various households. He lost his job in one because he stole a silver cup, and did so well in the second that when his master, Cardinal San Giovanni, died, he left the young lackey a piece of old fashioned brocade, a chain worth ten ducats, and a velvet cap. He next took to the road again. He became a street singer in Vicenza — reciting, one imagines, long ballads about the Kings of France, and the heroes of chivalry, and the mock heroes such as Margutte and Morgante, while oafs goggled at him. He masqueraded as a wandering friar. He got a place as hostler in the Sheep Inn at Bologna. He became an "Ebrew Jew," a money-lender — though God knows where he got the money to lend, and so probably he was a money-lender's agent; a tax collector, a mule driver, and a hangman's assistant. He

served a term in the galleys. "Because he had to," says our
source of information redundantly. He became a miller, a
courier, a pimp, a mountebank, a swindler, a scholar's groom,
a courtier's lackey, and "the devil and worse." He made a
short side trip to Venice. There, incidentally he brought out,
at twenty, his first book. Like many first books, it gave no indi-
cation of the author's future talents, or even of the direction
they would take. It was not even original. It was a fluent imitation of the works of Serafino Aquilano, that short, ugly little
improviser (he was virtually a dwarf) with the winning and
magnificent voice whose pleasant eclogues and mellifluent
strambotti first captivated Isabella and Beatrice d'Este and
then all the peninsula; and like what Aquilano had written,
the appeal came not from real poetry but from clever images
and fantastic verbal tricks.

One copy still exists.

"New writings of that very talented young man, Pietro
Aretino, the painter. That is, *strambotti*, sonnets, capitoli,
epistles, comic poems, and a lover's lament. Imprinted . . .
by Nicolò Zopino in 1512 on the 22nd of January."

At the head of the sonnets it says also:

"Certain things written by youthful Pietro Aretino, student
in these matters and in painting."

Thus, it at least establishes his art career.

Finally, he entered a monastery at Ravenna. There he
bound books for the library; read such of them as were profane; and saw with his own eyes those doings of the monks
and nuns his priest uncle, Niccolo Bonci, had told him about.
Needless to say, he remembered them. Then he made the
error of imitating. A stern superior taught him in plain words
that what was perhaps something to be condoned in a member
of the order was a grave moral scandal when practised by a
mere servant of theirs. He was told he must depart at once,
and left feeling he was lucky to get off at that. Once more he
packed off, God knows where.

It is a great pity that we have no detailed telling of these

¶ Opera Noua del Fecudissimo Giouene Pietro Pi-
ctore Aretino zoe Stramboti Sonetti
Capitoli Epistole Barzellete &
una Desperata.

Qual par piu miglior pcepto ¶ Che i reo
Se in la dextra el crudel ferro
Tien alchun per suo suplitio
Mal puoi il ciel se io non erro
Vetar questo sacrifitio
Reuochar se uol iudicio
Anchor tor non po erricepto ¶ Che i reo
Non poi ciel al peccatore
Se si mhenda piange e pente
Negar suo deuin splendore
El contrario se consente
Trouar pluto in foco ardente
Gli cede quello ha electo, ¶ Che i reo,
Se mie luce sempre mira
Far lo po che glie concesso
Se intorno il cor regira
Per dispecto il laccio adesso
Se mie lingua il tuo interesso
Manifesta a me e dilecto ¶ Che in reo.
Sha in odio el tanto amare
Per tuo doglia attare intendo
Non mi puoi questo uetare
Per quanto io ueggo e comprendo
Se col mio languire toffendo
Piangero per tuo dispecto
Che in reo en buono effecto
E dogni hom larbitrio francho.
¶ Finis.
¶ Impresso in Venetia per Nicolo Zopino.
Nel. M.CCCC.XII. Adi.XXII.
De Zenaro.

ARETINO'S FIRST BOOK

"Certain things of ours dashed off almost in an instant . . . if the style does not please you
at least the boldness will."—*Aretino.*

days; the rogue's Odyssey of Pietro Aretino would have made
a robustious and a full-blooded tale. For he saw more of the
gutter than Cellini, who moved after all from one patron to
another one, and Aretino reported—when he did report—
far less egotistically and far more honestly. Whom did he
swindle as money lender; and whom else, ground between
the upper and the nether stones of hard necessity and a society
devoid of what we now call social conscience, did he help out?

Against what wolf-like sea dogs of Barbary and Tunis, did
his bronze beaked galley leap the Tyrrhene waves to strike?
Could one of them have been that red-headed son of an Alba-
nian renegade and Christian widow, who, as Keyr-ed-Din,
King of Algiers, wrote him in his days of grandeur?

"The galley slaves," it is said, "were chained six to a bench,
on benches four feet wide covered with sacking over which
sheepskins are thrown. The master of the slaves stays aft with
the captain, but there are two other officers, one amidships,
one at the prow. These men have whips. The slaves row ten,
twelve, and even twenty hours at a stretch. On such occasions,
the officers give them bread soaked with wine. If, in spite of
this, a man faints, he is flogged until he appears dead and then
tossed overboard." What villainies did he see, overhear, or
take part in, in various inn chambers? Of what harlotries was
he sponsor? What poor quaking wretches, physically and psy-
chologically unmade by time spent in the torture chamber,
did he lead trembling to the gallows that at this point must
have been almost welcome? How much of his picturesquely
effective language—the billingsgate he made use of with such
literary fluency—did he learn driving long-eared mules along
some Lombard road?

There are, of course, exceptions. His escapades when he
was an art student he has set down for us, and they are much
like those of many other art students at almost any time in history. When he was nearly fifty years old, he received a letter
from an old friend who had been a fellow student.

"Do you remember our mad youth?" he wanted to know.

Aretino did.

"And certainly," he replied, "I often go back to the mad deeds we then did. For you must not think that I will ever forget the flight of that old woman who decamped in haste, terrified by the villainies we shouted at her from the window. It was broad daylight. You were clad only in your undershirt and I was stark naked. I also remember the fight that I had in the room of Camilla Pisana when you left me there to entertain her. And as I remember it, I seem to see Bagnacavallo who looked at me and said nothing. And as he looked at me and said nothing I could almost hear him saying in astonishment: 'This fellow is good for any evil!' Just because I had overturned a table! At the same time, I have the happy memory of Giustiniano Nelli who fell down for joy at the havoc I had wrought—just as I fell down for sorrow the other day on learning of his death at Piombino. This was a great loss to the whole of Italy and not to Siena alone, for besides possessing excellence of manners and of learning and of goodness he was one of the best physicians that ever cured human ills. So let us honor him with obsequies of praise, since we who were his brothers in some many good times, cannot honor him in any other way."

It is a tone of reminiscence still much indulged in by elderly alumni, holding down deep, cushioned armchairs in the windows of various University Clubs throughout the nation.

"Gad, what a young devil I was!"

His fine letter to the gambler, Gian Manente, evidences such a knowledge of the cogging ways of those plausible frauds then called mountebanks, that it must be autobiographical. Reading it, we see young Pietro standing on a bench in some dusty piazza in north Italy. He harangues the gawking multitude.

"Tickets!" he shouts. "Buy your tickets for the lottery!"

Then those two "ribald sisters, Fate and Hope" who are "like a pair of gypsy wenches at the fair of Foligno or of Lanciano who make a fool of this knave or that" start to do their work. The crowd surges forward, "trampling and suffocating one another in the crush to place their bets."

"And such language! The ugliest, most villainous, silliest, spiciest, dirtiest, and most diabolic of any in the world! And yet all mixed in with words from the Psalms, the Gospels, the Epistles, and the Calendar of the Saints! Half verses and whole verses!"

A poor cripple hobbles up to him and puts down his money for a ticket. To get this, he has sold the bed he lay upon.

A widow addresses a priest:

"Take this chaplet in payment and say the masses of St. Gregory for the salvation of my soul."

"To the devil with masses!" answers his reverence. "In a short time I will have said my last of them!"

Then he explains to the good lady that what he is going to win will keep him in nice indolence for the rest of his life.

Next in line, a country bumpkin appears. The hayseeds still cling to his jerkin, but on being told what a small sum will buy a ticket and what a large prize you can win, he takes a coat he has and pawns it. As far as he is concerned, the ducats are already pocketed. "My last furrow is ploughed," he cries exultantly. "I will never farm a field again as long as I live — not if Christ himself should be a farmer."

A master borrows money from his servant, and the servant bets all the master has not borrowed.

Then when the drawing has been made, it turns out that the winner has already sold his ticket.

"I'm going to hang myself," he wails.

One other part of his life during these years, Aretino chronicled. His days as a servant.

"If your bad luck forces you to enter a servant's hall," says a character in his comedy *La Cortegiana*, "as soon as you enter you will see before your eyes a tomb so damp, so dark, and so horrible that even a sepulchre would have a hundred times more cheer. If you have ever seen the prison of the Corte Savello when it is full of prisoners, you have seen the servant's hall full of servants at meal times. For those who eat in a servant's hall seem like prisoners just as the servant's hall seems like a prison. But prisons are much more comfortable than servant's halls, for prisoners are as warm in winter as in summer, while servant's halls boil in summer, and in winter are so cold that the words freeze in your mouth. And the stench of a prison is less disagreeable than the stink of a servant's hall, for the former comes from prisoners and the latter from the dying.

"And listen. You eat off a table cloth of more colors than a painter's apron. It makes you vomit to think about it. And do you know what they wash the tablecloth with at the end of the meal? With the pig's grease of candles left over from the night before. Yet often enough we eat without light at all. Then we are in luck. For in the dark, our stomachs are not turned by the sight of the foul repasts which they bring us, which since we are starving satisfy us, but satisfying us, drive us to despair.

"For meat we have some ancient bit of beef. And then come the fruits. When the melons, artichokes, figs, grapes, cucumbers and plums are ready to be thrown away, they give them to us as if they were a state's ransom. Sometimes, it is true, in place of the fruit they hand out four slices of buffalo cheese so hard and dry that it gives us a colic that would kill a statue. And if anyone, with a thousand supplications, begs the cook for a platter of thin soup he is offered a platter of lye.

"Indeed the soup they give you is like the soup that friars have. Do you know why so many friars quit their orders every day? It is because of the soup. I mean to say they ruin the soup just as the court destroys the faith of those who serve it. And who could tell of all the false tricks which they play us in Lent when they make us all fast? They do this not for the good of our souls but to save money on us.

"Yes, Lent comes around and, look you, for luncheon you have two anchovies to serve as an antipasto; after that a few Sardinian weeds, burned not cooked, appear. They are accompanied by a certain bean soup, without salt and without oil, which is enough to make anyone curse heaven. Then in the evening we make our supper on ten nettle leaves for a salad, a small loaf of bread, and good appetite to you.

"All this would be a trifle if they only showed us a little consideration in hot weather. At that time, not only must we endure the horrible stench that comes from heaps of offal which are never swept up, and which are open to all the flies of the city, but you are given wine diluted with tepid water to drink. Before you taste it, it has stood settling four hours in a copper vase. All drink out of a single pewter mug which the waters of the Tiber could not clean. And while they are eating, it is a fine sight to see this one wiping his hands on his breeches, this one on his cloak, another on his jerkin and another against the wall.

"And for the greater torment we have to gulp our food down posthaste after the manner of buzzards. For when that respectable man, the reverend steward, has sounded twice with his musical baton a *laetamus genua* we have to rise. It is a shame. We are not only not allowed to have our fill of food, we cannot have our fill of words.

"Once in a lifetime they give us a banquet. If you could see the procession of heads, feet, necks, carcases, bones, and skeletons, you would think you were looking at the procession which goes to San Marco on Master Pasquino's day. Just as on that day, parsons, arch-priests, canons and similar gentry carry in their hands relics of the martyrs and confessors, so lousy officials bring on the remains of that capon or this partridge and having first set aside a portion for themselves and their whores, they toss the rest to us.

"My friend, I saw one yesterday who on hearing the dinner bell which is the ambassador of starvation, began to weep, just as if it were knelling the death of his father. When I asked him why he was weeping, he replied: 'I am weeping because that bell is calling us to eat the bread of sorrow, to drink our own blood, and to feed on our own flesh, cooked in our own sweat.' He was a prelate who told me that; that evening he had four nuts with which to break his fast, while the chamberlain had three, a shield bearer two and myself but one."

Castiglione, in his fine book about Duke Guidobaldo's Urbino, has painted for us a glowing picture of one of those assemblages of lords and ladies which was known as a court. In the rush-strewn great hall with its massive marble fireplace, they sit till dawn makes rosy all the mountain tops while soft music plays and the scent of orris keeps their mind from primitive plumbing fixtures. They talk there. They discuss poetry, manners, the place of women in the world, Plato, the Italian language, and what things go into making a gentleman. The phrases used are ornate and full of compliment. If there is love, it is idyllic love, and if not idyllic, it is hid behind the arrases. So too with crime and violence. Fine wines are served to them in exquisite glass goblets, and costly, delicate foods on silver platters. It is thus usually we visualize the Renaissance. But there is another side, and Aretino is the only one to tell us about it. He can, for he has lived it himself. Every meanness recorded above is meanness he himself endured. Every misery is misery he suffered. Every indignity and each galling humiliation are indignities and humiliations he put up with. The great period he lived in had other qualities than those seen in dialogues about the heart and pictures by the two Bellini. The bright medal we are so bewitched by, had a reverse ugly and sordid. We are indebted to him because he set it down.

CHAPTER III

Rome, Coda Mundi

IN 1516, he made his way once more to Rome. "On foot,"
reported a friend, "and with no other belongings than the rags
that served him for clothes." There is a certain amount of
malice in this description. Though amicable relations between
the two were always preserved, Sperone Speroni, whose words
are quoted, had been the victim of too many Aretine shafts
not to take a certain pleasure in dwelling on the man's less
happy days. But it was basically, if not literally, true.

Clearly, then, his ten years as a rogue of all trades had not
brought him many material rewards. He was still unknown,
and fame was the bright lady he courted even that early in his
career; and if he was not absolutely penniless, in his pockets
clinked very few of all those crowns, ducats, and *giulii* which —
even if but to throw away — seemed to him so desirable and
so necessary. On the other hand, they had not been entirely
wasted. At least they had given him a chance to matriculate
into the great university of Renaissance villainy. During his
wanderings, he had been able to learn the jargon and the ways
of the whole under side of Italy. This made him something
of an authority upon gutter ways — possibly the greatest
authority the world has ever known. François Villon, for example, who had associated only with straightforward Paris
thieves, was a mere tyro in comparison. He had seen something of the upper side too — where it impinged upon the
lower side. It may have been less shabby, but it was made of
the same cloth. He was now twenty-four years old. His black
hair was now wavy, and it flowed back generously from a
broad forehead. His dark eyes, always alert and intelligent,
had a new look of knowing just a little too much that could
have been called cynical if there were not also in it such animal
vitality. We know that he was alert and witty, and he must

35

have been bold or he would still have been in Arezzo sewing shoes. During his adventuring, he had acquired the worldly experience, the knowledge and the beginnings of the self-reliance to make use of these qualities. And this he proceeded to do.

He found a well-nigh ideal setting. Indeed, it is doubtful if ever in the course of history there has been a more perfect field of battle for a literary bravo like Aretino than that resplendent cycle of years which we call the Cinquecento. We have already said something about its exuberance, its astounding vitality, the large scale—whether for good or evil—on which it thought and did. We have discussed likewise its great confusion. We should now mention its reverence for the accomplished fact, its worship of the individual, and its absolute lack of anything that in the ordinary sense of the term could be called moral standards. The man of the Renaissance—even the superior man of the Renaissance—seemed to be willing to condone knife, poison, and even outright, cold-blooded lying treachery when the issue thereof was successful. Machiavelli sets down its opportunistic tone when he makes his famous analysis of Caesar Borgia, and does not blame that symbol of all wickedness for the crimes he committed but for failing to commit the few more crimes that would have permanently established his regime. "Taking the Duke's action all together," he said, "I can find no fault with him. Nay rather, it seems reasonable to me to put him forward, as I have done, as a pattern for all such as rise to power by good fortune and by the help of others. For with his great spirit and his high aims, he could not act otherwise than he did." Obviously, then, the man of the Renaissance would condone also that kind of knifing and of poisoning and of treachery which was done on paper. It would just be another way of reaching a goal.

The city by the Tiber was, equally, during the first two decades of that century a first class starting place for a young man who wished to get on. It was the rest of Italy quintessen-

tialized. It was Renaissance in concentrated form. The head
city of a faith which in theory at least chased the moneylenders
from the temple, it was corrupt, mundane and brilliant. The
wherewithal was plentiful and it was spent with easy hand.
Wit opened all doors; and even genius was not turned away
when it had enough sense to wear the court dress of obsequiousness and the bright plumes of ingenuity. Rome, *caput
mundi* — Rome, head of the world, it had been in the days
when it gave rule to the nations. Now it had become Rome,
coda mundi, which is the vulgar anatomical opposite. Aretino
gave it this title and he knew what he was talking about. The
capital of the successors of the poor fisherman of Lake Galilee
had become a dissolute Vanity Fair.

The exact steps by which this situation was reached are
devious, but well-known. Rome imperial was a mighty metropolis that sprawled far beyond the traditional limits of its
seven celebrated hills. At its greatest, it had more than a million inhabitants. Its palaces and its temples were of marble,
and in spite of the proverb about Augustus, which sounds like
the slogan of some Chamber of Commerce, there were also
plenty of crowded tenements made of brick. It was a great
polyglot melting pot. The ambitious poured into it from
Gaul, Spain, Britain, Egypt and the seething ant-hills of Asia
Minor. Rome of the Middle Ages was a necropolis, a ghost
town, a deserted village. At one time not more than 17,000
people dwelt in it. The aqueducts broken by the barbarians
and the marshes no longer drained, its climate became un-
healthy. Its streets were deep with mud after every Spring
freshet. Horses were stabled in its early Christian churches,
and sheep and cattle had their mangers in the pagan temples.
Robber chieftains — of the later mighty families, such as Orsini, Colonna, Savelli, and Anguillara, — took possession of its
classic ruins, and using these as strongholds, waged savage warfare among themselves and practised brigandage against all
others. Finally, even its popes deserted it, departing to the
greater safety — and civilization — of Avignon. Indeed, but for

the magic of its name and the spell of the Roman church, Rome now would be like Aquilea and Nineveh. It would be known only to excavators.

But this spell was too strong to resist and the turning point came in 1377, when young Pierre Rogier de Beaufort — Pope Gregory XI — had the political acumen to bring back the Papacy to the city founded by Romulus. He realized what alone could keep the pope from being just another bishop. He died a year later longing for *"le beau pays de France,"* but his fortunate work outlasted him. The return from Babylonian exile became permanent. It was inevitable. For even the most France-loving pontiff could not help realizing that for all the discomforts of the city and the bullying of the Roman barons, he was at least — due to internecine quarrels — independent at intervals, whereas in France he must bend always to the strong king.

Then came a series of forceful popes, and the climb back to importance, if slow, was never checked. Nicholas V — born Thomas of Sarzana — was the first of these, and because writers of history are men of letters a lot has been said about his patronage of scholars and the library he founded, but his most important single act was to convert the tomb of Hadrian into the strong fortress of the Castel di Sant' Angelo, whence the popes could do a little dominating themselves. Nicholas was succeeded by Sixtus. This founder of the della Rovere line is now known as the Haussman — the city planner — of the Renaissance, and he built, among other things, the Sistine Chapel, the Capitoline Museum, the Vatican Library, and the great network of roads radiating from his castle's gracious bridge. Of more moment, however, is the fact that the Geno- ese ex-fisherman virtually invented papal nepotism. He had a large family and he placed every member of it in a strategic position. He almost made the papacy hereditary.

Soon afterwards came Alexander VI. Alexander's son was Caesar Borgia and he had also a sharp-tongued minor Pepys for master of ceremonies. Consequently more lurid light has

Raphael   *Florence*

POPE LEO X

"Certainly Leo had a nature that ran from extreme to extreme, and it would not be for everyone to judge which delighted him most, the conversation of the learned or the chatter of buffoons." — *Aretino*.

beat on his career than on any pope before or since. Actually
he only carried on what Sixtus IV had begun, though probably
in a more thorough-going and ruthless manner. Next was
Julius II, who could manage things himself. When he was not
roaring at Michelangelo — or being roared at by the artist, for
they were two hot-tempered giants who were only afraid of
each other — he was fulminating against Venice or thundering
at the French that he would chase them out of Italy. He almost
did. Those who liked a good spectacle were permitted to see
a papal army capture Bologna with the white-bearded pontiff
at the head of it. "Make me with a sword in my hand!" he
told Buonarotti when the latter questioned him about the
statue he was casting. The long uphill journey had reached
the crest. The papacy was made of straw no longer. Even
under Julius, the city on the seven hills did not have the in-
trinsic potency that Rome under the emperors did, but it
was no longer negligible. Once again the tide of human beings
that moved toward it in its prosperity and away when its fortunes declined, changed its direction. It flowed rather than
ebbed.

But now even those vigorous days had gone their way. In
the chair of St. Peter when Aretino arrived was Leo X — erstwhile Cardinal Giovanni de' Medici. He was stout and near-
sighted, and if fussy, was thoroughly amiable. His father was
Lorenzo the Magnificent, and he was what we like to think
of as a typical rich man's son. He commanded a huge fortune,
and he had not made a single *soldo* of it. He wielded great
powers and he had done nothing to build them up. Consequently, though he had inherited much of Lorenzo's ability —
and in any practical sense of the word his father was unquestionably the most able man produced by the Renaissance — he
had little sense of responsibility and no sense of difficulty at
all. Indeed, it would be hard to imagine anyone more different
from the fiery Julius than this stuffed, self-indulgent man with
his puffy bloodless hands, and his bulging, batrachoid eyes.
His physique made him love physical and mental comfort —

though he was an ardent huntsman when there were beaters enough — and this inherent inclination was strengthened by the fact that for a long period of his life any kind of comfort whatsoever was the one thing he could not have. He had been born to influence — Lorenzo, who accomplished what he set out to, had him made a priest at seven and a cardinal at thirteen — and when he was not yet one-and-twenty, the brainlessness of an elder brother who tried to give the volatile Florentines the name of absolute rule instead of just the fact of it, made it necessary for him to skip from the city rigged as a monk. The next eighteen years of his life were spent in exile. He was born to wealth, yet sometimes as he wandered through France, Germany and even England, he was hard put even to find a copper coin to fling the potboy. He was born to an easy life, yet after the battle of Ravenna, he was actually a fugitive from prison and escaped only because he had enough male attractiveness to persuade a great lady, Barbara Rangona, to help him. Then suddenly all he could have wanted fell into his hands. The words he said then were almost the product of a reflex action. "Let us enjoy the Papacy now that God has given it to us." This was to his handsome brother, Giuliano, who loved comfort as he did but was slightly more scrupulous.

What followed, therefore, was inevitable. The age of Leo became the golden age of everything which that pleasant gentleman happened to like. It was in the blood of the Medici to love art; and art, consequently, if somewhat more ornate and somewhat less original than it had been heretofore, flourished brilliantly. Leo's own taste — and his own aptitudes — led him to a fondness for the antique. Classic study and the cult of the antique took on mighty proportions. He was pleased by letters and patronized them generously. So many poets flocked to the city that Paolo Giovio, the historian, felt justified in attributing his advancement by Leo's puritanical successor to the fact that he was the only man of the era who had been immune to the disease of verse-writing. Indeed, it is probably to Leo's patronage of minor writers—for the one great writer who came to him, the poet Ariosto, was sent away empty-handed— that he owes, more than anything, his renown. For they celebrated him in song and story. Why should men of intelligence be held back by any such Pharisee virtue as false modesty? Leo must have had good taste. Didn't he admire their writings? Leo must have been great. Didn't he treat them as his equals? Didn't he treat them well?

But it was not merely by such affable if unpopely mundanities that the character of Leo's reign was made plain. There were other worldlinesses and they were more deplorable. "Certainly," said Aretino, "Leo had a nature that ran from extreme to extreme, and it would not be for anyone to say which delighted him most, the conversation of the learned or the chatter of buffoons." The untampered-with figures of an official census establish that in the capital of Christianity, there were more prostitutes than honest women. Leo must have known of this. High offices—such as that of *Piombatore* or papal Privy Seal which was once held by Bramante and later offered to Titian—were bestowed on such mean favorites as the ex-barber and present buffoon, Fra Mariano, whose greatest claim to fame was that he once ate twenty capons at a sitting. An eye witness reports that Leo took such delight in worldly comedies that he had them staged frequently and at great expense. He sat in a conspicuous place, and motioned with his gold-rimmed eye glasses as to who was to be admitted to the play and who not. He laughed immoderately at the coarse humor. Paris de Grassis, Leo's master of ceremonies, was scandalized by his master's love of the chase and by the unashamed frankness with which he showed it. The Pope, he noted in his diary, received distinguished visitors by hastily donning pontifical robes over his hunting clothes. Under their brocaded folds, you could still see his riding boots.

One is not greatly surprised to learn that it was not the abuses of Alexander VI with his blatant murders and his violent harem intrigues, and not those of the soldier Julius that caused Martin Luther to nail his ninety-five theses to the door of the great church in Wittemburg. Nor was it to either of the two he wrote his scathing letter of denunciation. It was to the easy-going and tolerant Pope Leo de' Medici.

"I must acknowledge," he said, "my total abhorence of your see, the Roman court, which neither you nor any man can deny is more corrupt than Sodom or Babylon; and which, according to the best information I can get, is sunk in the most deplorable and notorious of impiety. Indeed, it is clear as daylight that the Roman church, formerly the most holy of all, has become a licentious den of thieves. It has become a shameless brothel. It has become a kingdom of sin, of death, and of hell, the wickedness of which not even Antichrist himself could conceive."

It was amid such surroundings that the young man from Arezzo found his first congenial place. Evidently his luck was with him for a change. For the great city by the curving, muddy river was filled with future men of genius, and the lavish patrons who help them toward their destiny were limited in number. Yet within a few weeks of his ragged footsore arrival at the massive gates, he was employed in the household of the greatest of them. Just how he accomplished this feat is not now known. But we do know it gave him the opportunity he long sought.

Agostino Chigi was one of the outstanding men of his time. That he is not now one of the really well-known men is partly accidental. History is very often snobbish and Lorenzo excepted, it is the ducal Medici and the two Medici popes who have made the name Medici a symbol. But no Chigi descendants ever wore a grand-ducal or even a ducal coronet, and the only Chigi ever to sit on the throne of St. Peter came a century later. Then it was too late for fame.

He was born in Siena which is notable for shrewd wits, and his career was the exact opposite of so many that we are told of. We are always hearing of the poet who leaves business for art. Chigi left scholarship for business. The change was purely voluntary. He was put to school, but account books had greater attraction for him. By that time his family had moved to Rome, and at twenty he was apprenticed to a certain Ambrogio Spannocchi. The Spannocchi were also Sienese, and their castles still stand in the Maremman Apennines. In a short time, there was a firm of Spannocchi and Chigi, after which Agostino branched out on his own. He set up an office in the Contrada dei Banchi, which was Rome's Wall Street, and when it was not inundated by the Tiber's Spring freshets, he worked busily. His capital was 2000 ducats, and it was borrowed. Twenty years later he had main banks in Rome, Naples, and Porto Ercole, which latter seaport, by the way, he virtually owned. He had branch banks throughout the whole of Italy. He had warehouses in Constantinople, Memphis, Alexandria, London and Lyons. He had a private fleet of one hundred vessels. His employees numbered 20,000. He had contracted the salt works at Cervia, and the papal mint in the Vatican. He owned the fabulously productive alum mines at Tolfa near Civatella, and thus had substantially a world monopoly of this important product. Alexander VI had given him sole right to supply grain to the Papal States.

Julius II made him papal treasurer, notary, familiar and abbreviator, which was almost like being Secretary of the Treasury, and having in addition some of the powers of the Secretary of State and the influence of a member of the kitchen cabinet. His hand and the protection of his interests were seen at the back of a good part of the many wars of the period, and while the public was then, as in other centuries, a little hysterical on the subject of the sinister influence of the bankers, there was doubtless some truth to this. So varied were his activities that he told Leo that he could not say at any given moment exactly what he was worth. It is known that his income from rents alone amounted to 70,000 ducats annually. The comparative values of money are almost impossible to determine, but it would not be safe to set this at less than half a million dollars.

But Agostino Chigi was much more than simply a successful maker of big money. His hawk nose may have indicated shrewdness—Pope Alexander VII, who was a great-nephew, said it did—but his blue eyes looked on and enjoyed the world. In this respect he was a typical man of the period. He happened to prefer simple clothes so his wardrobe was not famous, but he rode only the best of blooded steeds, and he collected dogs of every known rare breed.

His banquets were Lucullan. One of these is particularly famous. On this occasion, he entertained the Pope and a group of cardinals and used a solid gold service. When each course was ended, the plates were thrown into the Tiber. It made a great sensation and Chigi did not see any need to mention the somewhat practical corollary that he had stretched nets beneath the water for them to fall into. Another banquet featured lampreys brought alive from Constantinople and a ragout of parrots' tongues. The Pope said, "We must be good friends since you receive me so informally." His mistress was the famous Roman courtezan Imperia. Do not think of her as any ordinary street-walker. By Renaissance standards, she was a great lady. "She spoke Latin like a humanist; read Plato in Greek; knew Petrarch and Boccaccio by heart; could play the zither and the lute, sang beautifully and composed verses." The novelist Bandello tells an anecdote of the Spanish ambassador calling on her. The grave Don was so impressed by her apartment—furnished by Ser Chigi, incidentally—that having need to expectorate, he let fly in the face of his servant. "It was the only thing of no value around," he said.

Chigi's collection of jewelry and of precious objects was without equal. He had a library of rare books printed specially for him, and he was known to read them. One of them—the poems of Pindar—was the first Greek book ever printed in Rome. One of his two palaces—that today known as the Villa Farnesina—represents just about the height of private building of the time.

Indeed, it is the Villa Farnesina that shows Agostino Chigi

at his best. It is perhaps his most fitting memorial. It was designed by Baldassare Peruzzi who was certainly not the least artist in a period where the average artist was not far from great. Every detail matched the fine exterior. I will not stress the bedsteads carved in ivory and encrusted with gold and precious stones, nor the bathroom fixtures made of solid silver. These have—like the Lucullan banquets—a suggestion of vulgarity. Yet even with their ornateness, they were things a king might envy. The gardens were world famous. There were rare trees from every land, and grottos leading off from the Tiber which were used as bath houses. Except for Michelangelo, virtually every great painter of the day was commissioned to do a room, and even Michelangelo—according to legend—left an unasked-for "calling-card" in the form of a charcoal head of Alexander the Great which he drew upon a wall. Raphael, Giovanni da Udine, Sebastiano del Piombo, Daniele Volterra, Il Sodoma, and Giulio Romano, to name a few of them. Indeed, at one time the very completion of the building was delayed by nothing more than artistic temperament. Raphael was at work there on his great painting of Galatea, and all at once this girlish-looking but in no way effeminate man of genius began to sulk because the task kept him so long from his mistress, La Fornarina. He even threatened not to complete his masterpiece. Word of this was brought to Chigi, and he immediately gave orders to have the dark-eyed baker's daughter whom we still see in so many Raphael Madonnas given apartments in his palace. He was not going to lose a canvas he wanted when the remedy was so easy to find.

Aretino did not enter this magnificent establishment by the front door. That kind of a reception—which he never allowed himself to think of as other than his due—had to wait until later.

"A young man," he insisted, "when he goes into some splendid household is like a pearl on bombazine. He is adorned with grace, filled with politeness and simplicity, is all modesty and purity. He has two sets of clothes, and they are in as good a style as his father's purse and generosity permits. He goes up the long stairway, and as those in front of him and those in back of him look him over from head to foot, he seems like the Lamb of God in innocence. Blushing rosy in his shyness and timidness, he kisses the hand of his new master who gives him a sly leer and then greets him with bawdy laughter. In about three days, he has found his place, and is set to work cleaning privies, polishing chamberpots, lighting candles, sweeping out bedrooms and performing lewd offices for cooks and stewards who soon see to it that he is all pricked out and embroidered with the French disease. In the meantime, his shirt is stained with sweat, but is not laundered. His breeches are reduced to rags, but are not patched. His shoes wear out, and they are not resoled. His now lousy hair is not washed, and a smell of staleness which is musty enough to make ten iron stoves sick takes possession of him. The good youth has become like an apple out of which two bites have been taken and then it is cast into the gutter for the flies to feast on."

With notable exceptions—for Aretino at this stage of his career had neither two sets of clothes nor any look of innocence—he is talking about himself. For he came back to Rome on the same basis on which he left it, and he entered Chigi's household via the servants' hall. It was the old story all over again. For living quarters, "one half of an undersized room" with a hard bed, coarse blankets and a fetid sheet. At meal times, a place "big enough for one buttock" on the rough board that served as bench. For provender, all that sorry fare that has already been described.

"Blood and spittle," he said savagely.

There was one difference, however. He was now a fledged writer with a published book, however juvenile it was, and though a groom or lackey as he described himself—though an under-valet or assistant scullion or a second houseboy—he had moments to himself.

He devoted these to pursuing his career. He found somehow some tranquil corner and he set down rhyming words.

They did not stay hid. He saw to it that the men of talent who took food at Chigi's table and slept in his apartments, found out that their ragouts were passed to them, and their boots polished, by a rising poet. He showed them his effusions.

The wit pleased them — for he had now turned from sentiment to satire — and they said so.

"All I now need," he told himself, "is to find a subject that will entertain all Rome."

Suddenly one fell into his hands.

On March 12, 1514, a magnificent embassy appeared in Rome. It came from King Manuel of Portugal. Its supposed purpose was to pay homage to the Florentine Pope and to urge continuance of the Lateran council to reform the church since "from the time of Alexander VI on, there was, in the Roman court, much license as to way of living and consent was given secretly to every manner of vice." Its actual object was to fish Roman waters for any aids that could be obtained to Portugal's Far Eastern policy, the Portuguese now being established in India and in the East Indies. Tristan da Cunha, the great explorer whose name is preserved by the loneliest inhabited island in the world, was the ambassador. He knew how to impress the Romans and their pope. The show was a magnificent one. Bagpipers in gay Lusitanian costume filled the air with their barbaric music as the long procession wound through the narrow streets. Cardinals marched in brilliant regalia, and there were royal ushers "clad in velvet, wearing scarlet berettas and gold collars." There were two leopards in gaudy cages and behind them a swarthy-skinned huntsman from Hormuz rode a prancing steed, while across his saddle bow lay a tame panther. Last of all, came the ambassador himself. He was "clad in the Portuguese manner in black satin and velvet" and he wore an enormous black hat which was embroidered with pearls. The East seemed to stare from his countenance as he accepted the homage of the crowd.

But the principal attraction was neither the ambassador

nor the ushers nor the cardinals nor the great, snarling spotted cats. The principal attraction was a great elephant named Hanno. The first one of his species to have been seen in Rome since the days of the emperors, he was "as big as three cows and had the tough skin of a buffalo." On his back was "a superb saddle cloth of crimson velvet which reached down to his feet and was embroidered with King Manuel's arms." Resting on this, was a silver howdah. In the howdah, sat a slim native prince of Malabar, who was clad in silk. Around him were rich gifts from the King to the Pope, but the great animal was the richest gift of all. The crowd — still the Roman plebs with its avidity for bread and circuses — howled collective delight. "It's a great spectacle!" shouted one of the by-standers. "It must be," remarked a neighbor grimly. "It cost 70,000 ducats!" Stories about the animal's intelligence flew from mouth to mouth. A favorite one was typically Latin. Hanno, on the point of leaving Portugal, had refused to board the ship. His keeper had a mistress in Lisbon whom he did not wish to leave. Consequently he had filled up the elephant with all sorts of stories as to how rough the Mediterranean could be in winter, and the latter had decided to stay ashore.

But if the Roman populace was enthusiastic, the gay hearted Pontiff was even more so. When the elephant reached his presence, the huge creature lumberously got down on his knees and then, filling his trunk with water, drenched all the spectators. Leo's midriff shook. Indeed, if his brother Giuliano had been made King of Naples — something Leo wanted much more than Giuliano did — or if his nephew, Lorenzino, who was "not quite so able and astute as Caesar Borgia, but very nearly so," had become Duke of Milan, he could hardly have shown greater delight. He forthwith appointed Raphael's friend, Giovanni Battista of Aquila, keeper of the animal and gave him, for its care, a liberal allowance. When, that June, Lorenzino wanted to make use of the creature to help celebrate the great festival of San Giovanni at Florence, Leo refused to allow the beast to go. He was afraid to risk his favorite toy, and he said, therefore, that he had not been asked in time. As a substitute he offered the two leopards and the panther. The Florentines, as a result, were obliged to fall back upon their fireworks and upon their customary mundane revels and masks to celebrate the voice crying in the wilderness. Indeed, virtually the only ceremony in which the elephant was allowed to take part was the mock coronation of Cosimo Baraballo on the steps of the capitol. But Baraballo, a doddering old poet-aster who took this bestowal of Petrarch's and of Dante's laurels in dead seriousness, was a privileged character. His fatuous and smug refusal to see anything but a due honor appropriately bestowed, though the people and the Pope and cardinals howled their merriment, gave him front rank among Leo's buffoons.

Yet in spite of this care and these precautions the great animal soon went the mortal way.

"You have all heard," wrote Ulrich von Hutten, "how the Pope had a great animal which was called an elephant, and how he held him in great honor, and how he loved him greatly. Now, therefore, you should know that this animal is dead. When he was sick, the Pope was filled with woe. He summoned many doctors, and he said: 'If it is possible, cure my elephant!' Then they all did the best they could. They examined the elephant's urine, and they gave him a great purgative which weighted five hundred ounces. But it did not take effect, and so he is dead, and the Pope greatly grieves. They say that he would have given five thousand ducats to anyone who cured the elephant for he was a remarkable animal and he had an enormous nose. And he always knelt down when he came into the Pope's presence, and trumpeted resoundingly: 'Bar, bar, bar!'"

What really did happen was not utterly different from that which the sarcastic Lutheran reported. The Pope actually was very upset. He moved glumly about his apartments. Then he had a thought.

"Send for Raphael," he ordered, and the painter stood before him.

"Make me," he directed, "a picture of the elephant life size upon the wall beneath which I have buried him."

Raphael nodded.

"Underneath it write this epitaph. 'Beneath this enormous mound, I lie buried, the huge elephant. King Manuel, conqueror of the East, sent me a prisoner to the tenth Leo. I was an animal not seen here for a long time, and the young men of the city admired me because in the body of a beast I had a man's intelligence. Fate envied me my home in fair Latium, and would not permit me to serve my master for as long as three years. Therefore, O Gods, add that time which destiny snatched away from me to the life of the great Leo. — He lived to be seven years old, died of angina, and was twelve palms in height. This monument was placed here on June 18, 1516, by Giovanni Battista of Aquila, papal chamberlain and the elephant's head keeper. What nature took away, Raphael has with his art restored.'"

Rome watched the words, and painting take shape. Then Rome was convulsed with laughter. A new "monument" to the elephant appeared, and it was hawked at every street corner. It was a pamphlet, "The Last Will and Testament of the Elephant."

"The elephant of India," it began, "which Manuel, King of Portugal, sent to Pope Leo X, has lived in Rome four years under the care of Zuan Battista of Aquila. But now having fallen sick either because of the temperate Roman air or because of the avarice of the said Zuan Battista, he realizes through his great wisdom that there is nothing more certain than death. Therefore, although sick in body nevertheless sound in mind, he wishes to make final disposition of his worldly affairs. To this purpose has commissioned Mario de' Previchi, a consistorial lawyer, to draw up his last will and testament and to have it duly witnessed. And he has appointed me to make one or more copies of the same."

Two very sure laughs. The Roman climate and the implied grafting of a well-known court official.

Then it went on to the individual bequests.

"Item, to my heir, the workshop of St. Peter, I give the golden covering which I wear on festal occasions—on condition that they do not put the alms of the said workshop to unholy uses. . . .

"Item, to my heir, Cardinal San Giorgio, I give my ivory tusks—so that his thirst, like that of Tantalus, for the papacy may be moderated. . . .

"Item, to my heir, the Cardinal Santa Croce, I give my knees, so that he can imitate my genuflections—on this condition that he tell no lies in council. . . .

"Item, to my heir, Cardinal Volterra, I give my wisdom—if he will promise to be generous for a change. . . .

"Item, to my heir, Cardinal Santi Quattro, I give my jaws —so that he can devour more readily all of Christ's revenues. . . .

"Item, to my heir, Cardinal Medici, I give my ears—so that he can hear the doings of everybody. . . ."

"Item, to Cardinal Grassi . . ."

But it would not be decent to set down just what parts of his anatomy the late lamented Hanno bequeathed to this cardinal whose lubricity, if you could believe gossip, was notable even for the Roman court. This, after all, is not the Sixteenth Century.

The last one of the bequests ended the matter pleasantly.

"Item, to my heirs, the Cardinal of Luxembourg, Cardinal Wolsey, and the Cardinals of Strigonia, Sion, and Toledo, I leave nothing at all, since they are absent from the court. They can hardly be among the living . . ."

Instantly, all tongues began to buzz. Who wrote this scathing masterpiece with its timely wittiness and its keen knowledge of everybody in Rome? This poet and that poet was given the honor. Then, conveniently, a masque appeared—there is some evidence that Aretino wrote it himself, that it was his

first essay in self promotion — and four lines in it gave away
the secret.

> See to it that Aretino is your friend,
> For he is a bad enemy to have.
> His words alone could ruin the high Pope,
> So God guard everybody from his tongue.

He stepped into the dazzling sunlight to hear praise from
all who read or listened. He was the cynosure of all looks and
every conversation. His ears were warmed by phrases of appreciation. He found they played a very pleasant tune.

But it was not only in compliments that he received his reward. Material advancement was also in store for him. And
the person from whom this was to come was none other than
the very one at whom his words had been aimed. The Pope's
grief for his elephant was not long enduring, and once it had
subsided, there was no man in the city better able to appreciate the entertaining squibs that it had provoked. To appreciate this was to wish to give the author his protection.
Leo sent, therefore, forthwith to Chigi, and asked him to release Pietro so that he could enter the Papal service. Naturally
Chigi complied. Thus with a piece of writing which he might
have composed in an afternoon, the son of the shoemaker
made his first lightning march from obscurity. Only a few
years before, he had entered Rome, poor, friendless and nearly
unknown. Now he was in the employ of the titular head of
Christendom, who was also the greatest and the richest prince
in Italy. His wits were beginning their aid to him. His pen
was beginning to work.

It was, of course, true that he was little more than a new
court jester, but in the household of Leo, as we know, a court
jester was a person of no small significance, and Aretino was
aware of this.

Announcing the appointment, Leo summoned him to his
presence.

"Which," he asked jovially, "serving me, would you rather be — Virgil or the poet laureate?"

"The laureate," replied Pietro without hesitating, "for he, drinking by himself in the Castello in July, has more good mulled wine than my lord Virgil could have gotten if he had written two thousand fawning *Aeneids* and a million *Georgics*."

This was an answer after the fat Pope's own heart.

The poet laureate referred to, it might be pointed out, was one Camillo Querno. Like Baraballo, he was one of those semi-illiterate writers of bad verse Leo liked to patronize. His coronation had been with cabbage leaves.

Aretino had then, at last, and at the age of twenty-six, secured an audience. His career was at last fairly started. The next thing he needed was a wider field to work in — an occasion which would allow his words and his ambitions to be attended to by the whole world.

CHAPTER IV

The Chancellor of Master Pasquino

AND such an opportunity soon came, or if not soon at least in due order. To be exact, only three years later. Before either his enthusiasm or his novelty had found time to wane.

In January 1519, the Emperor Maximilian peered for the last time from beneath the wide battered brim of the famous Tyrolese *jaeger's* hat in which he has been immortalized by Albrecht Dürer. He died still dreaming incoherently of being pope as well as emperor, and writing long, rambling letters on the subject of religion to his daughter.

A successor had to be chosen, and though for three generations now, the Hapsburg crown prince had received this honor, the seven imperial electors still had theoretical power of choice. They proceeded to assume that it was actual power. Who wanted the office, and how much was he prepared to bid? Henry VIII of England, Francis of France and Maximilian's young grandson, Charles Hapsburg, all three of them still in the first flush of young manhood, stepped forward. Shrewd tradesman Harry soon saw that he had no chance, and withdrew, having spent much, but not enough to embarrass him; but Francis paid money down, and promised lands, castles, and marriage settlements with a shameless openness. He got just about what he deserved. Three of the electors answered with a silence which he mistakenly took for consent, but the other four accepted his money, pledged him their support, and then gave it to his rival. Young Charles was chosen unanimously. He took the title of Charles V. Charles *chi triche,* instead of Charles d'Autriche, even his fervent admirer Brantôme called him — *"car il a esté un grand trompeur et un peu trop manqueur de foi."* Thus to the nineteen-year-old Caesar's control of Spain, Flanders, Burgundy, Naples, Sicily, and the Americas was added Germany, Austria and a slice of Hungary.

MASTER PASQUINO

"They are going to celebrate Master Pasquino in my name this year, and he will make a fortune. May God protect every faithful Christian from the evil tongue of the poets!" —*Aretino.*

It was, therefore, not only Francis' irritated personal desire, but his plain national duty to oppose him. Italy would be a field of battle, and the Pope, consequently, a man to have for ally. The two princes made open overtures. For a long time, Leo could not make up his mind. Then after attempting to remain neutral, he signed, early in 1521, a preliminary treaty with Francis, but on May 8, reconsidered and calmly concluded an alliance with the young Emperor.

He had some unhappy moments as a result of this. The first successes went to the French. In Lautrec and his brother L'Eclus, they had great marshals, and but for the resourcefulness of the Florentine historian Guicciardini, who displayed a military skill and a diplomatic acumen that not even his admirers had suspected, Reggio Emilia would have fallen and the Pope's power might have been crippled.

At last, however, a Papal and Imperial army was raised and placed under the valiant Prospero Colonna and that famous husband, the Marquis of Pescara. The combination worked. On November 19, they reached the walls of Milan, and the next day that city surrendered.

Four days later, Leo returned to Rome from a hunting expedition at La Magliana down the Tiber. His bag bulged with game, but he was hot and tired.

A messenger approached him.

"The allied army is in possession of Milan, Your Holiness."

Leo's drooping face lighted up at these tidings. Then it became grave. After all, he was Pope too, as well as temporal prince.

"Is it right," he asked suddenly, "for the head of the Christian religion to rejoice publicly when so many Christians have lost their lives?"

The messenger was a diplomat.

"If the Holy See had derived any great advantage therefrom," he replied tactfully.

"We have indeed obtained a great prize," Leo answered.

He then issued orders for a Consistory to be held on November 27. In it, he would consider the implications of the victory.

But it was never convened.

For an hour or so after receiving the news, Leo was his father Lorenzo, and he paced up and down a Vatican balcony, scheming great schemes. He would rebalance Italy. He would end its humiliations. Doing this he would incidentally set up the Medici family as the keystone of the reconstructed edifice. He almost forgot that not counting Cardinal Giulio and his grandniece, Catherine, there were only distant cousins left. So great was his emotion that he continued his pacing long after the sun set, still wearing his unchanged clothes.

They were damp from his exertions, and the Roman night air was, in those days, just about as deadly as the famous Borgia arsenic. The result was that he caught a slight chill. For a few days, this did not seem to be serious. Then suddenly it became pneumonia. That signed his death warrant. Pneumonia is never trivial, but Leo's soft, corpulent body, relaxed by good food and excellent drink, was even less than the average able to put up a hard fight against the malady. Soon he was gasping into unconsciousness. On December 1, he died.

Instantly there was noise and confusion. On one hand, there broke out a veritable fusillade of joy which gave voice to all the stifled hatred "which unfulfilled promises, a ruthless policy, and a faithless political stand had accumulated around the Medicean Pope." The Duke of Ferrara struck a medal: *ex manu leonis*. He had good reason to. One of the few objectives of the easy-going Pope Leo from which he never swerved during the nine years of his papacy was his obstinate attempt to ease Duke Alfonso of his duchy, and the gunsmith d'Este ruler who had now had to stand off the worrying of two popes, felt entitled to resent this. In Venice, Ferrara's ally, there were celebrations just as if there had been an important victory. At Rome, Cardinal Soderini thanked God in an extremely eloquent sermon. He was not unbiased. His brother Piero Soderini ruled Florence until Leo and his kinsmen returned and kicked him out. On the other hand, all those dependent on Leo were overcome with real grief. The bankers who had advanced huge sums to him, feeling safe since he was only forty-five years old; the cardinals and the bishops who had foregone benefices so as to turn the revenues over to him, knowing that they would be repaid later; the men of letters, the artists and clowns all lamented their possessions now vanished forever and their high hopes come to nothing. They liked Leo anyway, and the fact that personal advantage depended on a pontiff they were fond of only made their natural feelings all the stronger.

"Since the church of God was founded," said one man who was in Rome at the time, "never has a Pope died in worse repute. All over Rome they are saying: he took office like a fox, he ruled like a lion — *ut leo* — he died like a dog."

"All mourn the Pope, and his late goodness," testified another. "Nor do they do this wrongly, for they all love him, poor man."

"He died like a cur without confession or communion, and Fra Mariano, the clown, recommended his soul to God."

"He died confessed, and he did not say anything to his household who stood around him except: 'Pray God that I may live.' And then: 'God bless you.' His soul left his body like a butterfly."

De mortuis nisi nil bonum was, however, hardly the Renaissance Roman point of view; and the malice, therefore, outweighed the good feeling. Sonnets, epigrams and verses were pinned on Leo's tomb in increasing numbers. Most of them were scurrilous.

"Here in this court," wrote John Clerk to Cardinal Wolsey, "is now *summa licentia* in saying evil, in jesting and railing, in setting up slanderous verses and rhymes, and that in all languages, especially against the Pope that dead is, and against his nation, and any that hath *dependentium* of them. And there is no cardinal in this court that has any notable spot but he might as good have it written in his forehead. *Haec est romana libertas.* I would not write the specialities, for I know Your Grace would abhor the reading as much as I should the writing."

One wonders just how much the not unwordly Cardinal of York relished this omission on the part of his representative.

An Italian comment was more mordant.

"They have made a St. Peter," Alfonso Facino told Isabella d'Este, "with mitre and triple crown in his hand, and twelve cardinals are asking him to give it to them, but he seems to be in doubt. And that is nothing to what is being said and written in Italian and in Latin. They say so much evil of the cardinals that I do not see how they can help becoming good and holy just from fear. And of Pope Leo more than anyone else they keep saying things that are diabolical."

Many years later Paul III asked the wit Fra Baccio what he considered the finest festival in Rome. "When the old Pope dies and they choose a new one," was his answer. It was more than a humorous retort.

But if the death of Leo carried with it such emphatic sound and fury, the conclave which was to name his successor brought on pandemonium. Two sets of opposing forces drew up their lines of strength and intrigue to do temporal battle for the highest spiritual office in the Christian commonweal. Two desperate conflicts came into being. And since the office of *Pontifex maximus* could only be secured by a vote of two-thirds of the assembled cardinals, Cardinal Giulio de' Medici, bastard son of Leo's handsome uncle Giuliano, who by guile, personal charm and lavished promises had secured control of fifteen votes — more than a third, hence enough to block any other candidate — was the center of them both.

Let us see what they were. The first was a battle royal between the French and the Imperial factions. Leo's broken treaty had made Francis I a permanent enemy, for an ally lost seemed much worse to him that an ally never had, and he said vehemently that "he would gladly spend 1,000,000 gold thalers to have a Pope of his own choosing." It was a question whether

he had 1,000,000 thalers to spare but he liked full-blown figures and the sentiment was a real one. Later he thought matters over, and decided that it was Leo's right-hand man—and
left-hand cousin—who was the schemer. Then he remarked
to the English agent at his court "that if they elected Cardinal de' Medici who was the cause of all this war, neither he
nor any other man in his kingdom would obey the church of
Rome." Charles was too astute a statesman for such sweeping
pronunciamentos. Medici was acceptable to him, he allowed
to be known, but he was not amateur enough to limit his
choice to any one man. Cardinal Farnese would do, for that
sly Roman was a realist and he felt capable of dealing with
realists. So would Cibo, another Medici cousin. So too, he
signified, would Valle, Pucci, Jacobazzi or Campeggio. Beside
them, there was Adrian of Utrecht, who had been his tutor,
and theoretically, though not actually, Cardinal Wolsey. No
one except Wolsey himself, however, who authorized the ex-
penditure of no less than 100,000 ducats on the strength of
his illusion, took the candidacy of the ambitious English
churchman very seriously. Nor was even Adrian pushed forward particularly hard. He too was a foreigner—that is, a non-
Italian—and was not thought to have any real chance.

The second battle was the one waged between the young
and the old cardinals. The young cardinals were united in
favor of Medici. Their elder colleagues, on the other hand,
set it down as a principle that no one under fifty could be
chosen. They remembered how Leo, who was only elected because he was supposed to be dying of a fistula at the time of
the last conclave, had cheated their hopes by living very
blithely for nine years. By this resolution the ambitious Florentine was barred definitely. Their position had one weakness,
however, and that weakness was a fatal one. Medici elimi-
nated, they could not agree upon a substitute, for each of the
elder cardinals had his own individual candidate. That candidate was himself.

The princes of the church did not assemble for nearly a

month. The reason for this delay was that the French in-sisted that enough time be allowed for the cardinals of their faction to arrive, and one of these, Cardinal Ferreri, had been detained by the Imperialists at Pavia. This simple military method of making certain of an election victory had advan-tages, but it also threatened repercussions. Notes were ex-changed, and recrimination countered angry charge, but even the Imperialists could remember Avignon and pope and anti-pope and see the advantages of having a head of the church who would be recognized by everybody. Ferreri, therefore, was released. He came to Rome as fast as horse could carry him. Then on December 27, after the mass of the Holy Ghost, Vincenzo Pimpenella preached the customary sermon. Like most others on similar occasions, it urged conduct that every listener approved of, and few seriously considered for them-selves. That concluded, the cardinals filed into the street.

The Roman mob, always glad of an excuse for being turbu-lent, seethed around them. The press was so thick that life was endangered. Slowly and on foot, thirty-seven members of the College filed toward the Vatican. Two others, Grimani and Cibo, who were ill yet who would not give up their votes, were carried swaying seasickly in litters. Their destination was the Sistine Chapel, where thirty-seven cells, sixteen feet by ten feet in dimension, had been prepared. Each cardinal was al-lowed three servants, and the sick ones a doctor as well. Each one was also allowed his "conclavist," or campaign manager. The little group of men, gaped at by the milling crowd, moved slowly into the great chapel, which was as large as an enormous barn, and in the raw Roman winter must have been as chilly. When the last of them had entered, the doors were locked.

And not only were the doors locked, but the most elaborate precautions were taken to sever those within from the world outside. They were isolated by a triple ring of guards, each one of whom not only watched the cardinals, but each other. The outermost was made up of the "barons and the Lords

Roman." Next came the ambassadors. The third row of guardians consisted of a group of chosen prelates who had the actual keys. Thus the city, the Christian world, and the Church joined together to keep tabs upon its chosen leaders.

"The chief thing," again English Clerk writes Wolsey, "wherein consisteth the orator's and other prelates' charge, is that there be no letters sent out of nor into the conclave, nor other watchwords to and fro, so that we search their meat, their pots and their platters; and if they agree not within three days we may diminish their fare and at last keep them at bread and wine. Their meat and their drink is delivered to them at a round turning wheel made in the wall, as I am sure that your Grace hath seen the like at religious places."

They must see to it, in other words, that no bribes, whether of cash or of promises, trickled through to reach those who were selecting the successor to St. Peter, and conversely that no messages of value to kings or speculators leaked out. Seriously they seemed to take their duties, and so rigorous was the watch they kept, that when, on the third day, the cardinals asked that the doors of the conclave be opened that "they might avoid such filthiness as they had within of fragments of meat and drink, the savor whereof was so great, they said, that they could not abide it," permission was refused them. They were told, Clerk continued to Wolsey, "that they might avoid their leavings and their fragments (saving your grace) into the draughts."

Yet in spite of all these precautions, rumor after rumor reached the city and there is no question either that valuable information filtered in. One day Farnese's servant demanded a bigger pot of wine "because all of the cardinals liked it well." Rome then knew for certain that this was a pre-arranged signal that he was about to be elected. Possibly it was. Similar chance happenings involved Jacobazzi, Egidio and Piccolimini, while hardly a day went by in which Medici—always on the authority of someone who had an infallible source of information—was not just on the point of receiving the tiara.

Consequently the excitement was enormous. "At the banks," said an observer, "there is continuous holiday. No one does any other business except to place wagers on this or that cardinal." It was like the Stock Exchange on a day of wild short selling. Odds were quoted, taken, refused, changed, and then offered again. Clerks and apprentices ran hither and thither upon errands seemingly meaningless. Coins clinked on counters, were poured into and out of bags. Men screamed trying to make themselves heard. Wildest among the bettors were the old Medici partizans. They staked all on Cardinal Giulio. They would make tremendous fortunes, or lose every *soldo* which they had.

And it was not only in this one quarter of the city that a fever flared like running fire. Little knots of people gathered everywhere. Everybody in Rome had an interest in the outcome. There were the courtezans, who had been welcomed or at least tolerated by Leo, and who now wondered whether or not they would have to find some other sanctuary. There were the great ladies, whose husbands backed one or the other candidate. There were the courtiers with pale masks for faces, who wondered if they would be able to change allegiance in time. There were the murderers and the bravos. There were the lawyers hoping for renewed employment whoever won. There were the merchants, and the jester, and the grooms.

From December 29, couriers had their horses saddled in every courtyard, ready to carry the news of the election to the ends of Europe. For there were many who would pay well to know half a day ahead of anyone else who had been chosen. The French king, for example, and the money changers of Augsburg and of Amsterdam. The populace, too, found congenial employment.

It was the disorderly prerogative of the Roman people, when a new pope was finally agreed on, to pillage the palaces which he had occupied before he had been elected. The houses, therefore, of several of the cardinals were in grave danger, as rumor, followed by report, grapevined outward, saying that they had been named. Indeed, Cardinal Farnese's manors without the limits of Rome were "spoiled and ransacked to his damage of two thousand crowns," while his city palace was only saved because he had prudently provided a private army of three or four hundred men and seven or eight pieces of artillery. The crowd roared up to the barricaded gates near what is now the mighty Via Giulia, and then not liking the answer indicated by those shotted brazen mouths, seethed away again. How little out of the ordinary this seemed is shown by a comment made. That perfect courtier, Baldassare Castiglione, was in the city as the Mantuan ambassador. "Rome," he reported, "is full of persons of all sorts, but so far there have been no grave disorders."

In the midst of this wild confusion, suddenly there rang out a new sound. It had the sarcasm of satire, and to some degree the unerringness and the assurance of genius. It was the voice of Pietro Aretino, *"già tenuto libellista,"* and now about to prove that this common report was not a libel itself. For three years he had been fumbling around, seeking for a sequel to his pachydermic will-writing. But he had not been able to find one. Now, however, events gave him what he looked for, and his scathing tongue and facile destructive wit rose to the occasion. Once upon a time the immature would-be poet had become almost overnight the rowdy, disrespectful court jester. Just as swiftly, the court jester now became the satirist of an age.

And what made this all the easier was that along with the subject, he found a means of "breaking into print." In the Piazza Navona—where from 1477 to the days of Pio Nono, pigs squealed, and chickens, and peasant women cackled in the Babel of the public market—stood an ancient statue. It had been found in the gardens of that bon-vivant, Cardinal Oliviero Caraffa, whose grand-nephew, another Caraffa, made the Church's prime interest religion again. It lacked arms and legs and its nose seemed to have been crushed off by a blow from a cestus. It was supposed to be a Hercules; but Rome christened it Pasquino. There was an original Pasquino, but who he was, the doctors — of philosophy — agree not. Some say that "he was a witty and sarcastic man who kept a tailor shop in the Parione quarter of Rome, where he and his assistants used to amuse themselves slandering the Pope and the cardinals." Others — knowing presumably the changeless and unchangeable character of barber shops — state that he was a barber. A third group is certain that he was "a would-be writer, or a school teacher called Pasquino or Pasquillo" but that sounds uncommonly like wish fulfillment, most of the delvers having been one or the other if not both. Only agreement among all of them — Master Pasquino or Pasquillo was a sharp-tongued and an outspoken man.

The statue took on these qualities. As early as 1500, there was a recognized feast of Pasquino, when all wits and would-be wits plastered its pedestal with Latin verses on a chosen subject. But it spoke also on other occasions. For to it, said Castelvetro, with a grave Spanish sounding phrase, came all "the careful courtiers and the cautious poets of Rome, not breaking away from the now old custom of reproving the faults of great men as if divulged by Master Pasquino, to whom they assigned and still do assign sentiments of their mind when they wished to say that which they could not, making themselves authors, without evident danger." In other words, the statue of Master Pasquino became the headquarters for that popular Roman diversion, speaking evil wittily. Anyone having anything scurrilous to say fastened it to Master Pasquino. Indeed, a short scurrilous jibe became known as a "pasquinade."

Aretino made good use of this fact, and the truncated statue became his scandal sheet. He kept it plastered with his sharp effusions. Sonnet after biting sonnet. Each one was filled with acid humor and with well-directed thrusts. They struck out at every cardinal. Nominally he was supporting Giulio de' Medici, but since he knew well enough that what he did outside the conclave would hardly penetrate the three rings of guards, not even Cardinal de' Medici was always immune. For it was his own candidacy that Aretino was really promoting. He wanted to be known as possessor of the most dangerous tongue in Europe. If, at a time when the whole world's attention was concentrated on Rome, he could arouse the cynical amusement of the *Signori* and at the same time again the applause of the populace, he would certainly accomplish this end.

It is not possible to reproduce in full the tremendous effect of these journalistic pieces by rendering them into English. They are too mordantly ephemeral, too packed with contemporary slang. Moreover, to get their significance, it would be necessary to share all of the feelings of the Romans during the tense days of the conclave. And this we can hardly do. Yet not to cite some of them would be to let our man escape us just as he is coming into his powers.

Here, therefore, is one of them:

> Rome has gone mad on bets and wagerings,
> As some Ponzetta want; some Armellino;
> Some the three friars; some Trani; some Orsino;
> And some Farnese with his chatterings.
> Here's one who to Colonna firmly clings;
> This one to Cornar; this to Cesarini,
> These ones to Ivrea; Monte; Soderino;
> This one on Jacobazzi his money flings.
> To cover Medici twenty coins let fall;
> Grassi needs seven; Grimani little more.
> On Santa Croce men don't wager at all,
> And Mantua and Petrucci are out of play.
> Ancona's case is even worse than they
> Though Cesis and Rangone hope to score.
>   The vote no hope can convey
> To Ridolfi and Salviati. They complain
> As this one bets on France and that on Spain.
>   But Ceccotto tells us plain
> He's found a forecast in the Doctrinal
> That chosen Pope will be some cardinal.

The name he would let fall
But that the crowd, louder than trumpet's boast
Had chased from the conclave the Holy Ghost.

Here is another one:

Rome is one vast intrigue of rivalries.
The Jews want Santa Crose to be Pope.
Couriers, Flisco. Grimani, the misers hope.
The swindled, Monte. Farnese, talkers would please.
Rogues, Soderini; as do the Bolognese.
His sons, Ancona, and Trani, his mamma.
Fools, Cornaro and Cibo — ha, ha, ha:
Whores and their pimps, the Cardinal Sienese.
Housebreakers want Ponzetta or Armellino.
The tyrants want Petrucci, and the wrong
Egidio, Santi Quattro, Fraticino.
For their own lustful purposes, the strong,
Mantua or Cortona. Poachers, Orsino.
Colonna, those who others wish to wrong.
            For Como, the dead long.
Vico, cut-purses wish. The duellers,
San Sisto, as do, too, the perfumers.
            Whereas the usurers,
Salviati and Ridolfi think quite fine.
Sion or Ivrea, those who sell good wine.
            Jacobazzi, the herders of kine.
Campeggio, those to fasts who are averse.
Medici, those who fear lest things grow worse.
            Buffoons and clowns rehearse
For Cardinal Rangone their monotone.
But nobody wants Trivulzio on the throne,
            Since it is widely known
That he's a person who is half insane
Who a much bigger rump hath than a brain.
            Since most will wish in vain,
This is the feeling that to me did fall:
It might be well to have no Pope at all!

Here is a third one:

If Flisco's Pope, he'll go for a whole year
Without a lawsuit, and for that same time,

Farnese will not talk, and of all crime,
Colonna, his foe Armellin' will clear.
Mantua to small boys will not go near.
Ponzetta money lavishly will strow.
Campeggio'll be less courteous and more slow,
And Grassi will desert his wife, poor dear.
Ancona'll reign his furious temper in,
And Pucci will draw up no further deeds;
    And though his kind heart bleeds,
Valle'll give up his children, Cesarini his whore,
And Trani his mamma, who loves him sore,
    Cortona, his plots, and more.
Cavaglione, his friends who sing his praise in choirs.
Ridolfi and Salviati, the rogues each hires.
    While the three friars,
Even hypocrisy would throw away
If the high office should but come their way.
    This does Grimani say;
He will wipe out each obstinate miserly trace.
Cornar'll give up — sometimes — his daily chase,
    While with a downcast face,
Sion says good sweet wine, he'll drink no more,
And Monte, Master Pasquin will give o'er.
    Here's Soderini's score,
He'll be baptized on Peter's holy strand
By Vico or by Santa Croce's hand.

Here is a fourth:

We have a pope! And each low hostelry,
Each customs house, each corner butcher store
Blazes with light and sound and trumpet's roar
To see fulfilled Pasquino's prophecy,
As to the bleating, braying hierarchy
Of geldings, sheep, slow oxen, bullocks, cows,
Lord of high-sounding, but of broken vows,
Armellino is Pope on fool's Epiphany.
And though he can't put on his triple crown
Until, like dulling lead instead of rain,
The Holy Ghost descends from the still air;

Yet since his name is vaunted through the town,
It suddenly comes to make his boast more plain,
A hee-hawing donkey instead of the dove fair.
            Then all the tin horns blare,
Proclaiming the new monarch, super-arch,
While only sorrows the Cardinal of the March.

Fifty-odd in all, they left no one untouched and they did not
omit any aspect. A new pope always chose a pontifical name
and this was made the subject of a fleering sonnet. This cardinal would call himself Pope Gomorrah. That one Pope Car-
neval. This cardinal would call himself Pope Midas. That
one Pope Iscariot. The conclavists were brought up for consideration. Monte would have Pasquino for his "campaign
manager"; Flisco, the Law Courts; and of course, Trani his
now famous mother. The conclave was compared to a game of
cards. The character of St. Peter if this cardinal or that were
elected was discussed. The conclusions were always withering
and sometimes ribald but they must have been based on what
was accepted as true. Otherwise no one would have laughed
at them. Over and over again Mantua's interest in small boys
was both hinted at and directly stated. You could hardly con-
vict a man on this evidence, but it shows what Rome believed.
The same with Pucci's women, Cardinal Sion's sweet wine,
and Alessandro Farnese's fondness for making speeches. As
for poor Trani's mother, he indeed lacks imagination who
cannot see plainly that woman, large, Roman and full of
intrigue. Her son was afraid of her and so too were the cardinals. I do not doubt that even Aretino trembled a little as he
penned those lines. He was enough of an anticipator of
Shakespeare with his shrewd seeing, to realize what it is that
hell hath no greater fury than. But he kept on just the same.

Nor did the audacious poet permit what he set down to remain anonymous. As was the custom, these flagrant pieces
were issued without the name of their composer, but as soon
as their popularity was evident he took care to remedy this
trouble.

This was his boast in one sonnet:

> Everyone says: "I am surprised the College
> Can find no way of stilling Aretino."

He was known, he said proudly in another, "as the Chancellor of Master Pasquino."

His inn, said a third, "was the academy of Pietro Aretino."

Even his pretended repentance was a jibe at the cardinals:

> O learned college, *misere me.*
> *Peccavi.* I have sinned. Chastisement's meet.
> Yet where's the cardinal so indiscreet
> Who won't absolve my poems for what they say?

Now all his years in back halls and in servants' quarters, doing the dirty work of the lords, began paying dividends to him. He had all these reverend gentlemen at his mercy, for he knew every weakness of the Curia, and could banter or rail as he chose. He did both. And all listened. Federigo Gonzaga, later to be one of Pietro's most influential friends, wrote his ambassador as follows: "Please send me all the verses that have been fastened to the statue of Pasquino. I want all you can find. Not only this year's but those of years past." Far away in Mantua, he was not going to take any chances of missing anything that brought back the flavor of Rome, and he must, therefore, have fumed no little when the correct Castiglione, to whom such an errand must have been eminently distasteful, told him that they were mere flashes in the pan — *foco di paglia* — and that he could not find any. And it was not only Mantua that wanted them: every prince in Europe did. Pietro's compositions went, in consequence, to every court and to every palace on the whole continent, carrying with them the scandal and the shamelessness of Rome at a time when, with Martin Luther just beginning to thunder, she had more need of being without scandal than ever in her history. They also carried with them the renown of the son of the Aretine shoemaker. Kings thus heard for the first time the name they were shortly to fear.

Chapter V

The Election of 1522

In the meantime, the assembled cardinals were having troubles of their own. Indeed, no description made on the outside of the conclave's riot and confusion could have approached, much less exaggerated, what went on within. Michelangelo's "Last Judgment" had not yet been painted upon the altar wall of the great chapel, but if the physical attitudes of that volcanic masterpiece were not forecast by the contending cardinals, its hopes and fears were. It was reasonable, when you considered the prize.

The first question to be thrashed out with bitterness and intrigue was could Cardinal Medici be blocked? It was answered in the affirmative. Medici fought hard to be chosen—he was, as it was noted at the time, "very strong for himself"—and he was no longer the unobtrusive, sallow young man who had seemed merely Leo's errand boy, but a shrewd politician in his own right. But the odds against him were too great. He had made all the enemies a leading contender is obliged to make, and like all leading contenders he had to win in the first two or three ballots or be beaten permanently. The lines held, and he was beaten. The next question was if not Medici, who? Here Cardinal Giulio's position was stronger. For if he could not be Pope, he could at least, if he played his cards adroitly, choose who would.

The first person for whom he threw his influence was Cardinal Alessandro Farnese. That fox-faced Roman, who had won the purple because of Pope Alexander VI's love for his astonishingly beautiful sister, had enough popularity to add a few votes of his own, and in the first scrutiny in which his name was offered seriously, he polled so high that Cardinal Pucci began shouting: *"Papem habemus*—we have a Pope!" hoping to start a scramble for the bandwagon. It came within an ace

Jan van Scorel   Hanover

POPE ADRIAN VI

"Servant of the servants of God, that master of school,
  Don Adriano, chosen Pope by lot,
    And by divine stupidity . . ."—*Aretino.*

of working. But Cardinal Soderini, leader of the French faction, saw that if he moved quickly he could turn this maneuver against its very users. He cried out that it was irregular. It was—inasmuch as it had not succeeded. Cardinal Colonna supported him. Naturally! For he had his own hopes and interests.

Next Medici advanced Innocenzio Cibo, but the grandson of a corrupt Pope (Sixtus IV) was hardly a desirable candidate, and besides that he was dead Pope Leo's nephew. The French vetoed again. If they did not want a Medici friend, they would hardly accept a Medici kinsman.

Then Valle was put forward, and this time it was the older cardinals who defeated him. The French did not have to waste their resistance.

With equal firmness, the Medici faction opposed either Carvajal or Soderini, the latter almost vindictively. The impasse grew to be a deadlock. The French faction would have no one allied with, or even cordial to Medici, and although they did not command quite a third of the cardinals they always seemed to manage to pick up enough votes to accomplish their purpose. Medici, who did have the necessary fifteen, had an equal right to be obdurate. After two weeks of this, even the most courteous of those on the outside were inclined to sarcasm. "Every morning," wrote Castiglione, "we await the descent of the Holy Ghost. It seems, though, that he has gone out of town."

And then with a dramatic suddenness, the whole thing came to an end. Though most of Italy was content to await, even if impatiently, the outcome of the conclave, there were a few who saw in its prolongation a means of advancing their own ends. One of these was Francesco Maria della Rovere, rightful Duke of Urbino. He had an understandable grievance. On fantastic charges which were nothing but a cover for some plain and fancy stealing, Leo had deposed him from his dukedom. Papal troops enforced the decision, and then Leo gave Urbino—which was not his to give—to his nephew

Lorenzino. Now Francesco Maria saw a chance of winning it back. Hastily, therefore, he concluded an alliance with the Baglioni of Perugia, who had a grievance too. Their leader Gianpaolo Baglioni had been judicially murdered by Leo, who had lured him into Rome by means of a safe-conduct and then beheaded him, making his excuses afterwards. Together they marched on Siena. The news pushed past the watched dishes, and one man in the locked chapel saw its significance. Cardinal Giulio de' Medici. He realized that if some pope — indeed *any* pope — were not chosen immediately he would not only lose the papacy, but there would be a new Florentine Republic. One Florentine Republic was enough for any Medici. The tidings reached him on the tenth of January and on the morning of the eleventh he addressed the conclave.

"I see," he said, and he took pains to be as winning as possible, "that from among us who are here assembled, no pope can be chosen. I have proposed three or four, but they have been rejected; candidates proposed by the other side, I cannot accept for many reasons. Therefore, we must look around us for one against whom nothing can be said, but he must be a cardinal and a man of good character."

This met with general approval, and he was asked whom he would suggest.

"Why not," he said, seeming to weigh each word, "choose Adrian of Utrecht, Cardinal of Tortosa, a venerable man of sixty-three who is generally esteemed for his character?"

He paused to let this thought sink in.

There was just one chance in a thousand that they would do what he hoped they would do, and he was going to take it. Here was a dark horse, someone not even at the conclave, and when all these worldly princes of a heavenly regime saw just what a dark horse could amount to, might they not stampede back to someone known and familiar?

Someone such as Medici for instance.

Anyway this would impress on them that they had to choose a pope.

After that he called for a vote.

One by one the cardinals stepped up and cast their ballots. When the tally was announced it was Carvajal, 15; Adrian, 15; the rest scattering. What had happened was apparent. The French had clung gamely to Carvajal but those of the Imperial faction went to the new candidate.

There was a deathly silence, during the interval of which Medici — who now saw what was going to happen — paced, white and horrified.

After that someone shouted "Vote again" and a new scrutiny was authorized, but it was never taken for the choice was by accession.

First Cardinal Cajetan arose. He was a learned man, a commentator on St. Thomas Aquinas, and he was in no way regarded as a partizan of the Emperor. Rather he was one of the doubtful cardinals. But he could speak eloquently, and he now used his eloquence in praise of the son of a humble ship's carpenter who was risen through application and austerity to be first the tutor and then the counsellor of powerful young Charles V. He announced gravely that he was going to cast his vote for Adrian. Then Cardinal Colonna who had so far supported the French said that he would do the same. You could have heard a pin drop. He was followed by Jacobazzi, Trivulzio, and Ferreri. When Colonna had deserted the French cause, there had not been a word, but as Ferreri followed him, a rally was attempted. It was led by Orsini.

"Blockheads," he shouted, "do you not see that this is the ruin of France?" He was not even heard.

Cardinal after cardinal abandoned every pledge and soon twenty-five had gone over to Adrian. Twenty-six were needed. The twenty-sixth and deciding vote was cast by Cardinal Cupis, a Roman. He made the most of this fact, for it was hard for such a political heeler as a Roman cardinal not to believe that the Pontiff-elect would be grateful to him.

"I also am for the Cardinal of Tortosa," he shouted, "and I make him Pope."

It was the work of a few minutes after the deadlock of three weeks. Cardinal Cornaro, as dean of the Sacred College, went to the balcony and announced to the faces below that Cardinal Adrian of Tortosa had been chosen to the chair of St. Peter. As he had a feeble voice Cardinal Campeggio had to repeat the announcement.

"Who?" shouted the crowd.

"Cardinal Adrian of Tortosa."

Then the Roman populace did at last realize that a stranger and a Dutchman had been chosen to rule over them, incredible though it might seem.

The Venetian ambassador gives us an account of what followed, and like all such accounts by Venetian diplomats it is extremely graphic. He was at some distance from the Vatican, he said, when he heard suddenly a confused medley of cries. "Medici!" shouted some voices. *"Palle!* Medici!" "Cortona!" shouted others. "Cortona! Cortona!" "Colonna!" was flung back by the partizans of that Roman house, and there were likewise shouts of "Valle!" Next he saw people running singly and in groups toward the Piazza of St. Peter's, where the still unfinished church fronted somberly a field of mud. He cried out to find what was the matter, and one galloping citizen told him that a pope had finally been chosen, but like the mob, he could not grasp the name. The second questioned hurrier made it plain to him, and when he realized that it was not even the most hated Italian, but a cardinal who dwelt in Spain, he was "well-nigh dead with astonishment," and could not believe his ears. He rushed to the conclave where he had friends and privileges, only to hear the incredible reiterated and to learn that the impossible was true. Then he walked slowly home. On the way home, he noticed the behavior of Leo's courtiers. One wept. Another uttered lamentations. A third was making preparations for flight.

The cardinals themselves seemed dazed at what they had done. Tebaldeo, the poet, who saw them come out of the conclave, said that they appeared "like ghosts from limbo, so

white and distraught were their faces. Almost all are dissatisfied and repent already of having chosen a stranger, a barbarian, and a tutor of the emperor." As they emerged into the
streets, they were greeted by whistles, jeers and catcalls, the
Roman crowd being noted neither for imperturbability nor
good manners. One indignant citizen did indeed catch Cardinal Minerva by a trailing garment, and spoke to him "strange
words with a Roman effrontery." He told him that he wished
to see the members of the conclave "roasted or boiled or
pounded into jelly." The cardinals were too abashed to protest. Instead, now that it was too late, they were inclined to
agree with the mob. "We deserve," said Cardinal Mantua,
"the most rigorous punishment. I am glad that you do not
avenge your wrongs with stones."

Along with the indignation came an outburst of fierce irony.
Est locanda—"To Let"—was found posted on the doors of
the Vatican. The political cartoon made its debut, and drawings of all sorts, from the ribald to the sarcastic, sprang up like
weeds. One of these showed St. Peter in flight with a bag of
plunder on his shoulders while a Roman street-walker tried to
hold him back. "I have escaped from the hands of the moneylenders and fallen into the hands of the Jews," she cried. An
explanation is perhaps needed. The Florentine bankers were
the "money lenders," and they had handed over to Leo a
king's ransom which they would now never see again. The
"Jews" were the Spaniards. To the Romans, the Spaniards
were always either the "Moors" or the "Jews" because of the
prominent position which—until the conquest of Granada—
both of these races enjoyed in the peninsula. Another cartoon
showed Adrian himself dressed as a school teacher. He had a
ruler in his hands. Several cardinals fled before him on horseback as he flogged their bare behinds. Said the inscription: *En
quo discordia patres peruxit miseros*—through their wrangling they have came to this sorry pass. Master Pasquino—it
was noted—was very busy.

And with Master Pasquino, Messer Pietro Aretino. During

the conclave, as we have noticed, he had been playing his own game. Wit and sarcasm had been his principal weapons. Now, however, he became the mouthpiece of the outraged Roman populace. Wit and sarcasm still found their place, but they were sharpened by anger. Nor was it the half playful anger of the earlier pieces.

> O Cardinals, if you were changed to us —
> And not for anything would we be you —
> And we had done the same bad things as you
> Tell us quite frankly, what would you do to us?
> We are most certain that you would hang us,
> As we would like to hack to pieces you,
> Indeed, had we the same power as you,
> You would be crucified at once by us.
> But since all honors are but shames to you,
> And not yet infamous can you call us,
> We will no longer deign to speak of you.
> You filthy rabble, foe to Christ and us,
> To be buried alive, we'd like to sentence you,
> Now that you've brought to ruin you and us . . .

Even the rhyme does not change. You — us. Us — you. And in Italian the *voi — noi, noi — voi* had an even more savage monotony. It was incredible the fury it conveyed.

Or again:

> Today for the eighth time a day is done,
> Since Christ, the Church, St. Peter were betrayed,
> And even the heavens their protest have displayed
> With hail and rain and snow that blot the sun . . .

Or yet a third time:

> O villain College, who has betrayed Christ's name;
> And given over His earthly heritage,
> The Vatican, to vile Teutonic rage,
> Do not your hearts split open wide with shame? . . .

Indeed only on one occasion did he rise to his old levity.

Servant of the servants of God, that master of school,
Don Adriano, chosen Pope by lot
And by divine stupidity, comes to this spot
Of boastful charlatan and noisy fool.
And here he'll read the Koran, the Bible's rule
Unto Ponzetta who hates subtlety,
And he'll convert to Christianity
Cardinal Santa Croce with his drool . . .

It was entirely natural. No man, even when he is thirty years old, which is where youth begins to get the power of maturity, and even when he is filled with an energy so boundless that it amounts to audacity, likes to see his world go to pieces around him. Aretino had set all his temporal hopes — which were the only hopes he knew — on the continuance of a worldly Roman court. The temporary madness — thus it seemed to him — of some thirty-odd cardinals had signed its death warrent. No wonder he could give voice to Rome's feelings so eloquently. His feelings and Rome's were the same.

Yet neither Aretino nor Rome gave in too incontinently to despair. For one thing, such was not their sanguine nature. But besides that, a whole sequence of rumors came into being just like mushrooms after a rainfall. Adrian was dead. Adrian was not dead, but he would not accept the papacy. Adrian was living and he would accept the papacy, but he would not leave Spain. All tended toward the same solution. There would be a new conclave and never would any new meeting of the cardinals repeat the mistake of the last meeting. As the magnificent galleys, bearing the emissaries sent by the cardinals to their chosen Pontiff, skirted the many promontories of the blue Mediterranean so as to avoid January storms — for even the princes of the church fear shipwreck, and what is worse, seasickness — Rome basked in a false summer. Then her winter recommenced again. The messengers from the cardinals reached the severe Dutchman and he received them with dignity and perhaps sadness, but there was no doubt as to his actions. Indeed, anyone who had doubted them, did not know

Adrian. For he was devout, if unimaginative, and he had a
sense of duty. God's will be done, even if it be a distasteful
will. "We did not either seek nor desire the office," was the
gist of what he told the cardinals, "but we will of course accept
it. We will sail as shortly as possible." These tidings sped with
a seagull's swiftness, and they reached the city by the Tiber
even before the austere Adrian had stepped on board his ship.
Rome was horror-struck. Now swiftly, she realized that there
was no way of putting off the dread tomorrow. The Golden
Age was over, perhaps forever. Only those whose affairs made
it impossible for them to quit the city, stayed within its walls.
All the others fled.

Aretino was among the latter. When the tidings reached
him, he thought uncomfortably about many lines of verse he
had written, and decided not to take a chance. Possibly forgiveness might not be on the long list of Adrian's Christian
virtues. So he went out hurriedly, making a long cast and putting rugged Apennines between his plain-speaking and its consequences. Very shortly he was in Bologna. There he paused a
while, and there presently he received a letter from one Messer
Andrea, a painter and a practical joker, who was one of his
most intimate and most scapegrace friends:

"I have not written sooner, not because I have nothing to
say, thank God, but because I did not know what title to give
you in the superscription. 'Respectable sir' is fitting for
Ghismondo Chigi, because he is a merchant. You say 'Your
Excellency' to soldiers — that is to say, to Ottavio Orsino, and
to my lord Francesco Malatesta de' Medici. 'Egregious' does
very well for one like Moro de' Nobili. I was about to say
'Very Christian and Catholic,' but then I recalled that you are
something of a heretic and never go to mass, and besides I am
saving that for Girolamo Beltrami and the Fiscal himself. I
had it in mind to call you 'Distinguished,' but when did you
ever study law? And besides that is for Lorenzo Lueri. I cannot say 'Most Illustrious' for you are not a prince of the kingdom of Cyprus. Likewise if I call you 'Reverend,' Cristofano

de Rios will have it in for me; and if I say 'Brother in Christ,'
Fra Mariano will take me to task. I wanted to call you
'Prudent Sir' but I would have lied in my throat, because you
have never protected yourself with a written contract so far
as I know of; 'Magnifico' would have seemed true enough,
but you were not a Venetian lout. By the body of Christ, I
was about to call you 'Sir Pietro' but Captain Molinas said
that you were neither a Spaniard or a Neapolitan. I was about
to say 'Most Fair' but the hunchbacks Bibbiena and Sermoneta
took it very ill. I was going to, nay I actually did address you
as 'Sheep' or 'Ox,' but Simon Tornabuoni menaced me. So
I am in a bad way to know what the devil dignity is really
yours. 'Egregious' belongs to Cordiale. 'Very Excellent' and
'Very Learned' to Pattolo who composed *L'Orchessa*. 'Singular, and 'Son of the Muses' to the lord of Nepi, that is to say,
to the other — to the one and only Aretine. 'Very Noble' to the
sons of Fra Egidio. I thought that 'Renowned and Laurel-
Crowned Poet' would suit you well, but it was the Abbot of
Gaetá who rode upon the elephant. If I said 'Speaker of
Good,' Soderino, Colonna, and Cornaro would crucify me.
If I said 'Speaker of Evil' the illustrious Cardinal Medici, our
common patron, would call me a great liar. And it is this
bedevilment that has kept me from writing up till now. Now
with the aid of God and of Master Pasquino I have found a
superscription of a kind that no one can blame me for, and
that will satisfy you, and that will be enough for the first part.

"Dear man of Arezzo, my greeting to you! How much your
departure has increased the sorrows of Rome, Master Pasquino
knows. He has not spoken since you left, and he is wearing
mourning."

It was addressed "to that Aretino who made so many fine
sonnets when the papal seat was vacant, to the praise of the
sacred college wise and good." It was dated from "dirty Rome
in the last of hangman July in the cutpurse and traitor year of
1522."

First of all, it gives us a little glimpse into Aretino's personal philosophy in his high-hearted and young-spirited days. He "did not go to mass" and he "was something of a heretic." Later on we shall want to think back on this. Second, it confirmed his identity with Master Pasquino. Third, it showed that Pietro was now so well-known that he, quite as much as Accolti famed in "The Perfect Courtier," was *the* Aretine. Next, it showed that he had imitators, this letter being something that he could have written himself. That too is an evidence of prestige. Last of all, it showed that he and Cardinal Giulio's partizans were not alone in deploring the election. Rome's "Greenwich Village," represented by Andrea, the hack painter, joined with the court of Leo and with the Roman populace in sharing the regret.

When Adrian arrived, the worst fears of all were confirmed. He was not only a good man but—and this was worse—both a sincere and an unsophisticated man. And his tastes were such simple ones. He knew nothing of courts, and had so little idea of the state popes habitually kept, and so naïve—as Rome would have put it—a conception of what was fitting to his office, that he wrote ahead asking that "a small house with a garden" be rented for him. Apparently, he had never heard of the Vatican. When he saw it, he lived in it as if it were a small house. Leo kept a hundred household servants, and Adrian dismissed all of these but four. For his viands, he spent only a single ducat a day, and this he took out of his own pocket with his own hand every evening, and gave to his personal steward. Gone were the Chigi banquets and the Lucullan food. The new Pope adhered strictly to church rules. He ate only veal, boiled beef, capon, and a platter of soup. On fast days, his whole diet consisted of fish. His cooking was done, his bed made, and his linen washed by a gaunt Dutchwoman, whom he had brought from Flanders. Her uncouth language, and her informal attitude toward the Pope—she being in looks plain and unappealing—scandalized a city that would have both applauded and approved, if he had slept openly with a Tullia d'Aragona or a fair Imperia. Rome also was

scandalized by the fact that he did not take for himself a
sounding papal name but called himself Adrian VI. Had he
no conception of papal grandeur? Would there be no more
Calixtus' and Gregorys?

Even more dismaying, he showed absolutely no appreciation
of the great treasuries of art which made Rome the world's
cynosure. He was taken through the Vatican.

"This is not a dwelling for the successors of St. Peter, but
for those of Constantine," he said.

He was asked to admire the Laocoön as the most distinguished example of ancient sculpture. He turned away in
horror.

"A heathen idol!" he cried.

He never even entered the famous Belvedere gallery which
contained the finest collection of great sculpture in all Europe.

"Let it be walled up," he directed.

Last of all, he turned his attention to Master Pasquino.

Shown the head and torso to which had been affixed so many
gibes rankling to himself and disgraceful to the Papacy, he
commanded that it be thrown into the Tiber.

"You cannot do that!" cried the Duke of Sessa who knew
Rome.

"Why not?"

"Under the water, he would croak like a frog."

"Let him be burned then," said Adrian.

"No, for a burned poet will not lack adherents, who will
crown the ashes of their Maestro with malicious songs, and
will hold solemn commemorations on the place of his martyr-
dom."

Adrian felt constrained to accede to this logic. He did not
forgive, however.

"Let us hope then," he said, "that every possible effort will
be made to arrest all who have slandered me or others, and
that when they have been taken they will be punished severely."

Probably they would have been, but they were gone.

CHAPTER VI

At the Camp of 'Il Gran Diavolo'

AND so once again Aretino had come to a dead end. He had been obscure, and by the use of his wits and by the force of sheer boldness, he had bludgeoned his way into prominence. Now he was a nobody once more. Worse than that, he was a somewhat discredited nobody. Any number of motives had actuated his hasty removal from the scene of his first notable triumphs—confusion, discouragement, simply instinct—but it is quite evident that cowardice was the principal one. To be sure, it was physical cowardice rather than moral cowardice —for that Aretino never had—and knowing the age in which he lived there was reasonable justification for being nervous, but the flaw shows there just the same. Let him believe reverently, as he always tried to do, that it was nothing but common sense. Let him announce over and over, as he did, that he who fights and runs away is on most occasions simply using good judgment. It is, nevertheless, plain even to his partizans that it was stark belly-clutching apprehension of what the Pope's sombre hangman or the Pope's grim-jawed torturer might do to him, that sent him off so speedily. "Thou clay-brained guts!"—Prince Hal's words about Falstaff apply to him. "Thou knotty-pated fool! Thou whoreson, obscene, greasy tallow-catch! You carried away your guts as nimbly, with as quick dexterity, and roared for mercy, and still ran and roared, as ever I heard bull calf!"

Nine men out of ten would have dropped out of the picture forever after this. But Aretino was the tenth man. And here we encounter for the first time that one of his characteristics which is perhaps most important of all in the shaping of his career: his absolute resiliency. It was impossible to down the fellow. I once heard it said of a later writer that he had all the advantages of not being quite a gentleman. In a similar sense, you could state concerning Aretino that he had all the advantages of not knowing the meaning of the word shame. In his categories, there was only one sin, which was not getting on, and that sin he proposed not to commit any more frequently than necessary. He also either guessed or thought out what a majority of those successful in a worldly way have known since — that memory almost always works only in the present tense, if given half a chance. Until the biographers arrive and often afterwards, what a man is, not what he has been, is important.

The small river, on which Bologna stands, brattled beneath his window as it had for many million years; and the square buildings and the two brown, leaning towers kept their secrets of young Dante, who had also been obscure there. Gowned scholars paced gravely in the streets, or drank as scholars do in the too-many taverns. In the classroom, learned jurisconsults droned their theories, and then retired to their studies to belabor each other in fierce Latin which may have been Ciceronian in grammar but which was bawdy-house in vocabulary and tone. But Aretino paid attention to none of this. He was possibly hungry, and probably cold, and certainly disheartened. But his wits still did their work for him, and his purpose still was strong. He had been kicked down the stairs at the commands of fickle fate, and the bolts had been drawn in his face. But he was not one kept out thus easily. He picked himself up from the gutter, and wiped off the muck from his clothes. Then he looked about for ways to mount anew.

It was Cardinal Giulio de' Medici who again opened the door. Not advertently, to be sure, for despite all Pietro had done and risked for this Medici cousin at the last and lamented conclave, nothing even faintly resembling a banished satirist with his present troubles and his future aspirations occupied the forefront of this churchman's mind. But Aretino never waited for people to want to help him. He tried instead to fabricate a situation where they had no choice in the matter. And this is what he did now.

Things a-plenty had happened to the one-time right-hand man of Pope Leo, since he made that short speech which precipitated the election of Dutch Adrian, and thus lost his own cause.

To begin with, he discovered how ungrateful righteousness can be. A pope chosen, Giulio took in hand the pressing business which had made him use his weight to close the conclave. He moved well-trained soldiers to a point where they could guard Siena. By the cardinal committee that now governed until Adrian arrived, they were ordered out of papal territory. Giulio was not disturbed. The new Pope would appear and would pay for his election by rescinding this. But he measured incorrectly both the Dutchman's innocence and virtue. Adrian did not know papal elections were bought, and he did know that private cardinals had no right to public armies. He supported the committee.

Then Florence itself began to seethe. The second Medici rule was not oppressive, but the independent burghers of the city were by nature shy of harness and they obstinately valued labels of freedom even more than actual freedom or efficient government. A wide movement came into being, having for its public purpose a new order which would govern in the name of the people, but actually aiming at its own members' rule and power; and the French clothes, trimmed and perfumed beards, royal wives and sounding titles of the younger Medici gave it food to feed upon. Giuliano, Duc de Nemours; Lorenzino, Duca d'Urbino. Il Magnifico had been a simple citizen.

Last of all Michelangelo, who was now in Medici employ, was in a customary contrary mood where he wanted to do anything except what he was asked to do, and to get him to complete the Medici tombs he had already started, it was necessary to let him spoil good (and expensive) white Carrara marble by carving it into that breath-taking Mother and Child which is now known as the Pietá.

Why not, thought the harassed nephew of the late Pope,

who saw that his representative, Cardinal Cortona, had lost control, go to the seat of troubles and take charge myself?

He would keep out of the Pope's sight—which was a good thing in his present frame of mind—and he might also, being an experienced disentangler of snarled affairs, accomplish something.

Why not, thought Aretino, go to Florence, now that Cardinal Medici is there? He may remember Rome and have a place for me, or he may simply want to get rid of me. Either course will cost him something.

Galliardly he set out.

It turned out that he had reasoned correctly. Seated in the Riccardi Palace (as it is now known) with its massive walls, and its fine paintings of the elder Medici, Giulio was in a mood to realize that to employ Aretino would not help him any in his new schemes of gaining Adrian's tolerance. At the same time, he did not wish to antagonize Pietro. For one thing, he had read too many of his sonnets, and for another, he might need his help again.

"Seek out Messer Pietro Aretino," he said to a secretary, "and tell him we are honored he has come to Florence. Tell him we wish we could receive him, but it is impossible. Tell him that we are consumed with affairs. Mention to him the conspiracy of Messer Diaceto; the unrest of the city; the sad need we had of executing two noble youths; and say also that we are obliged to keep to business night and day. Point out to him that it is now winter, and that it will be blazing summer before we find the pleasant opportunity of talking to him."

"I can understand His Excellency's difficulties," replied Aretino, "but for my part, I am prepared to wait days, weeks, nay even months if need be, for His Lordship's convenience. Anyway I have been ill, and I dare not travel yet."

Then Cardinal de' Medici tried another plan.

"Send for him at once," he directed.

Aretino was conducted to his presence.

"Would God," cried the Cardinal, "that there was something I could do for you, but unfortunately there is not. I will take you into my confidence. Even my own position is not secure. I rule only by the Pope's sufferance. I have to be careful."

After that, he appeared to think.

"Why not," he asked suddenly, "go to Mantua?"

"Mantua?" exclaimed Pietro.

"Yes—Mantua," repeated the Cardinal. "The Marquis of Mantua has long been your ardent admirer. I could show you a letter he wrote Count Baldassare Castiglione during the conclave asking him to secure all your writings for him. He treasures them greatly, I assure you. Now he and his court would like to meet you in person."

After that, he called for paper.

"Cardinal Giulio de' Medici to the Lord Marquis of Mantua," he put down in slanting characters.

Then he gazed off into space as if seeking for words, and his smooth cheeks, as he did this, were blue as gunmetal with the dark beard he had not grown yet.

At last they came to him.

"Messer Pietro Aretino," he began, "the bearer of this epistle, is a person so pleasing and acceptable to me because of his great talent——"

Then he scratched the last words out.

"—because of his great *genius,* that I would not have consented to deprive myself of him for anybody other than Your Excellency. However—" looking at Aretino—"since he has asked my permission to come to you, I have freely given it. And now,"—with the twinkle of a grim smile—"I must excuse both him and myself if his coming seems late. Neither he nor I is to blame, but two serious illnesses which he had in Florence, as he himself will tell you with his own words.

"I will bear witness," he continued, "that the said Messer Pietro is no less desirous to serve you than to serve me. However, besides the great love which he will bring to you, I my-

THE MARQUIS OF MANTUA

"After this he will make a hundred herds of swine citizens, and having offered up his sword in the temple of Venus, the pleasure-giver, he will announce that the greatest good is Petrarch's 'sloth, gluttony, and lazy lassitude!' "—*Aretino.*

self recommend him to you. May you long take pleasure in him."

Then he signed it.

"Here," he said, handing the paper to Pietro, "will this serve your purpose?"

Aretino looked at it.

It was the best — his common sense told him — that he could obtain at the moment and certainly it was an improvement on Bologna.

"Your Lordship has been good to me," said he.

"I will have it sealed for you," the Cardinal said, "and give it to you tomorrow."

Under date of February 3, 1523, it was handed to him. Immediately he was on his way.

The city toward which he directed himself was about the only one, all things considered, in which at this moment he could have stayed with any satisfaction. It was not Rome but it was at least a substitute. And with Rome in the hands of a Puritan Dutchman, it would have to do.

The native town of the poet Virgil, and likewise the final resting place of his sybil Manto who had founded it, did seem, if you wished to wax poetical, to have taken something magical from both of them. There was an elusive beauty to the place. Though set in the flattest and most monotonous part of Italy — the wide, wheat growing plain of Lombardy — it was ethereally fair. The outlying countryside was nothing much, to be sure; but the city, moated by its river, rose graciously beside a quicksilver-colored body of water that was at once a lake and a marsh, where large water birds waded on long stilts and whence mighty clouds of ducks arose. At dawn, the marsh character was most evident. Paludine mists, faintly tinted with lavender and old rose, lifted from the waters, wreathing the brick towers and the solid stone edifices. The long bridge seemed a work of fairyland. That much for the aesthetic appeal, and that much only because, as we will later explicitly find out, such charms meant a great deal to Aretino. More objectively, it was the capital of a strong race of round-headed, Alpine-appearing soldiers, who had supplied most of north Italy with generals, and who, so doing, had amassed fortunes, which made Mantua—and their house of Gonzaga—rich, prosperous, and important. The last of these warriors before the present Marquis, was Francesco Gonzaga who commanded the Italians at Fornovo when they hurried "wittold Charles" VIII of France out of Italy. Francesco was notable for three things. First of all, he actually was an able soldier. Second, he was one of the first prominent men to die of syphilis, and this sickness of his had political consequences. Thirdly, he married Isabella d'Este. This alone would have guaranteed his renown.

It was Isabella d'Este who made Mantua really great. Before her, it had been merely noteworthy. She had wit. She had skill. She had judgment. She was an extremely good-looking woman, and yet she had a man's steel of purpose. Francesco, as the nature of his death signified, had been thoroughly unfaithful to her, and yet she was able to realize that her destinies were inextricably entangled with his, and she aided him at every turn. She kept Mantegna working for her, against the bids of Rome, until in "The Triumph of Caesar," he had painted one of the most amazing series of masterpieces that even Italy had ever seen. She was cold-blooded enough to think only— when Caesar Borgia had taken over the Duchy of Urbino— of how she could persuade Caesar to give her, or let her buy cheaply, the art treasures of her brother-in-law, the expelled Duke; and yet she was warm-hearted enough to protect the Duke and his poor wife, even at, knowing Caesar Borgia, not uncertain risk. She schemed for her son Federigo, who later succeeded his father, and for her son Ercole, who almost became Pope. She collected paintings, statues, *objets d'art,* and cameos. She collected poets, playwrights, dwarfs—particularly dwarfs, for whom she had built a whole set of miniature apartments—and philosophers. She put both her son and her husband in a position to collect blooded horses, until they had the finest stables out of Turkey. Buildings rose at her command, and the Reggio, or Palace of the Marquises — which was already in existence — became under her remodelling almost a city in itself. Her little "Paradise" — her own private suite to which she often retired — was both jewel-work and incomparable art. And she danced country dances at the wedding of Lucrezia Borgia, when that stupid yet not altogether unlovable flaxen-haired victim of slander married her brother Alfonso d'Este, thus rounding out the circle of the Renaissance sense of being alive.

It was to her eldest offspring that Aretino carried his letter. He was the son of both his father and his mother.

"Today in Italy," Baldassare Castiglione made Count Lodovico da Conossa say in "The Perfect Courtier," "you can find certain sons of illustrious lords who, if they do not have the power of their forbears, make up for it in talent. And of these, the one that shows the greatest promise is Signor Federigo Gonzaga, eldest son of the Marquis of Mantua. Besides his well-bred manners and the discretion which at so tender an age he shows, those who have charge of him say marvels regarding his wit, his desire for honor, his courtesy and his love of justice, so that from such a beginning you could not expect other than some very excellent end."

Even granting this to be one side of the truth, he was also a perfect product of the Renaissance disintegration. Sent to Rome when he was ten years old as hostage for his father who, taken prisoner by the Venetians, had been released at the instance of Pope Julius, he did manage to put on at least the surface of refinement. But it was only skin deep. He admired the Laocoön, as was fitting, and desired to have the goldsmith Caradosso make a relief of it to wear in his cap. Dark haired and handsome, he was painted by Raphael in "The School of Athens," and as the heir spiritual of his mother and the descendant of men who had at any rate been taught wisdom and goodness by Vittoriano da Feltre, he could not have failed to display some interest in beauty and culture. But he was taken to the Pope's bawdy comedies and to shows of lewd buffoons and Spanish courtezans and these seem to have made a deeper impression on him.

He was avaricious, unprincipled and a sensualist.

"Sardanapulus — I mean to say Frederick," wrote Aretino at a later date when a quarrel had unloosed his tongue.

He added:

"Because all his honors have in the ascendant shame, *coram populi,* he will appoint Abram, Isaac, and Jacob senators in full synagogue. After this, he will make a hundred herds of swine citizens, and having offered up his sword in the temple of Venus, the pleasure-giver, he will announce that the greatest good is Petrarch's 'sloth, gluttony, and lazy lassitude.' Master Abraham, his doctor, finds it in the ducal constellations that he is in danger of going to the Antipodes, because of some gravel in his kidneys which has been aggravated by his drunkeness and his continual relation with both men and women."

Federigo carried Roman finesse back to his city on the reedy Mincio. But he carried Roman corruption as well.

He received Aretino with gusto.

"I am now in Mantua in the house of the Lord Marquis," Pietro wrote exultantly to his supposed brother, Gualtiero Bacci, "and so much in that Lord's graces that he gives up eating and sleeping to talk to me, and he says that he has no other real pleasure. He has written things about me to the Cardinal de' Medici which truly and honorably give me great joy, and he promises that if I stay with him, I will have an income of 300 scudi a year. He has given me the very apartment occupied by Francesco Maria, Duke of Urbino, when he was driven from his state, and has assigned me a personal steward to take charge of my meals. At my table, there are always great gentlemen, and in short, he could not have done more for me even if I had been some important Lord.

"As a result, all his court now bows down before me, and any member of it who can get even one of my verses calls himself lucky. And as fast as I make any, the Lord Marquis has them copied. Already I have composed several singing his praise.

"In this manner I live here, and each day he makes me presents, fine things that I will show to you in Arezzo. But even as I repassed through Bologna they commenced to give me gifts. The Bishop of Pisa gave me a fine cassock of black satin broidered with gold — there never was a more magnificent one. And so, like a prince, and in what for once could be called royal state, I came to Mantua. Amazzino accompanied me that far. And everybody addressed me as 'Messer' or as 'My Lord'.

"God willing, I think that this Easter I will be at Loreto, where the Marquis is going, so as to carry out a vow. And in that journey I will fulfill the wishes of the Duke of Ferrara and of the Duke of Urbino, both of whom desire to know me. The Marquis will present me to them."

"Our Pietro Aretino," the Marquis wrote Cardinal de' Medici from his country place at Marmirolo, "is like a festival of joy and pleasure to me. The fact that I am away from Mantua hardly irks me at all, for being with him is like being in a whole crowd, and his conversation takes the place of many talented men. Indeed, if it were not for the reverence and the obligations which I feel toward Your Reverend Lordship, and the loyalty which is second to no-one's, which Messer Pietro has for you, I would attempt to decorate my court permanently with this precious jewel. Forbidden this by the two above mentioned reasons, I am not forbidden, however, to enjoy his presence for a certain amount of time. I hope this will content you. I know that to a person as busy as Your Excellency is, such a man must be the greatest recreation and pleasure. Therefore I will restore him to you soon. And if this *soon* seems late to you, to me it seems very early indeed. If I did not wish to close the door with your illustrious Lordship to having him again with your good wishes at some other time, I would keep him even longer than this."

Incidentally, Cardinal Medici's reply to this deserves also to be noted. He expressed delight that "the good qualities of Messer Pietro Aretino" were pleasing to the Marquis.

Then he went on as follows:

"I wish Your Excellency to keep him and to enjoy his services as long as you see fit and as you wish to. And I assure you that I could have no greater pleasure than hearing that Your Excellency was satisfied with anything I can do for you. Nor do I think it will displease Messer Pietro to stay with you; I have always known him to be desirous and eager to serve you. If he does this, he will give me more pleasure than if he were serving my own person, and besides that I regard it as serving me. And if there is any other way in which I can serve Your Excellency, do you advise me of it. For I will always be most ready to carry out every wish of yours."

Though he was too crafty to say this in so many words, it is obvious that the subtle Giulio was well pleased to see his plans working. He was well pleased to have Pietro off his hands.

Yet in spite of his reception there — and though we know Aretino liked to make a generous story, the letter of the Marquis shows that it was exactly as indicated — Messer Pietro soon grew restive at the Gonzaga court.

It was not that he did not have a good time. On the contrary, he glowed with well-being, for at no previous period of his existence had his needs and his pleasures been so well provided for. In the morning, there was a ride or a hunt. Even before the mists had dissolved, he and the Marquis vaulted into their heavily-tooled saddles upon two of the famous Gonzaga steeds, and went off at a gallop over the interminable ploughed fields, which were smoking as the sun finally slanted over distant poplars, or between the hedgerows and the olive trees, while groups of *contadini* gaped at them curiously but saluted them respectfully, and their curs, having the same interest but not the manners, strained ferociously at their chains and barked. A series of ditches taken at full tilt would but add to the exhilaration. Then, as the sun mounted toward the blue, a falcon was cast, and soared till it was a black speck, only to dive suddenly as if flung from a sling and drive its sharp talons into a plump partridge which they would later feast on. Perhaps hunting dogs—not improbably "Spanish poynters"—would be set down and would nose into likely-looking thickets with their tails busy and their flapping ears. The Gonzaga kennels were very nearly as well-known as the Gonzaga stables. Or the merits of that new-fangled German device, the "wheel lock" or primitive fowling piece, would be tried out. Being March, the air was still chilly and sometimes even raw, but it was stimulating indeed after the miasmas of the Tiber valley, and Aretino flourished. His muscles hardened—something that would stand him in good stead very shortly—and the color came flooding into his face. Then, in the early afternoon, a gay luncheon, frequently *al fresco,* followed by a siesta. And in the evening, dancing, banquets, love-making, sometimes plays, and conversation.

At this time of the day, Aretino shone. The men wanted to hear what he had to say, and the women, led by Isabella Boschetta, Federigo's beautiful and intelligent mistress, swarmed around him like a flock of tantalizing butterflies. It was the witty Aretino, the learned Aretino, Messer Aretino this, and Messer Aretino that. For he had not only seen, but lived in that Rome where they all wished they could be, and he would tell them about it from the inside. Raffishly too, and with a fine full-flooded humanness so that it was theatre to listen to him as his words flowed and glowed and brought to life. Salty stories about this court official or that cardinal. The jests played on such and such a poet or such and such a philosopher. Politics, Politics, Politics—salted with personalities as Latin politics always are. Chat. Gossip. And tittle-tattle. "In short" —as he once said of someone else—"he would serve just as well for a scandal sheet as a monument." He, who wanted not to be unnoticed, was the cynosure of every Mantuan eye.

Nor was it likely that some delay in the payment of his 300 scudi caused him to cast about for somewhere else to go. To begin with, there is no evidence that payment of his installments on this salary was in any way delayed. But even if it was delayed, Aretino knew the ways of the great well enough not to be discouraged in a few short months. And while he was at Mantua, he was being fed, clothed, fêted, and cared for.

What happened was that he suddenly realized that he had been led off into another backwater, pleasanter than Bologna certainly, but not any more likely to carry him toward his goal. He told this to Federigo.

"I must leave your court," he announced.

"To go where?" Gonzaga asked.

"To go to Rome," Pietro answered.

"It is sheer madness," Gonzaga said.

"At least," persisted Aretino, "I must go to Florence."

"Wait, at any rate," implored the Marquis, "until I write L'Abbatino and ask him to sound out Cardinal Medici."

L'Abbatino was the Mantuan ambassador. Aretino agreed.

Not more than a week later the reply came back.

"I have spoken to His Reverend Lordship regarding Messer Pietro—that is, that Your Excellency could not keep him in Mantua because he wished to return to Florence at all costs, and that he had already asked your permission time and time again. The Cardinal's answer was that Aretino was a loud-mouthed and unreliable trouble-maker, and he said nothing more. It seems to me, therefore, that he knows very well that you cannot manage Aretino, and that as far as he is concerned, you can dismiss him at any time you see fit. Nevertheless you should tell him the following, which is true: Master Paul of Arezzo told me that certain new writings against the Pope and against some of the Cardinals have been passed about from hand to hand in Rome, and because of these the Pope has sent Cardinal Medici a brief ordering him to arrest Aretino and to deliver him into his hands. Therefore, even if he should only come as far as Florence, I doubt if the Cardinal could protect him."

With slow fingers Aretino drummed the table as he read

this, and then suddenly he flushed with anger. But he bridled it, and did not thunder.

"I must go all the more urgently," he said icily.

"Very well," answered the Marquis. "I will write His Lordship."

He sat down at a writing table and began slowly.

"If I desired the excellent Messer Pietro Aretino before Your Reverend Lordship granted him to me, I will do so even more after his departure which is to be shortly. This is because I have enjoyed so thoroughly during these days—which to me, however, have been but a moment—his engaging virtues and the pleasantness of his most happy wit. Indeed, I would never have been able to give him his dismissal which he asked for over and over again—if it were not that he returns to Your Reverend Lordship. For I know under what obligations to you I am, since, through your love for me, you deprived yourself for so long of the company of one who deserves to be desired always. For that much, I thank you infinitely. In fact, I place this grace among the greatest favors I have ever received. Furthermore, although it seems impertinent to recommend to anyone his own property, yet since Pietro has become mine also, I pray you that he be recommended. If I had anything of equal worth, I would offer it to Your Lordship in exchange. But since this is a matter for which I can make no fair exchange, I am that much more indebted to you."

Evidentally the Marquis had his own share of diplomacy—and his own faith in Aretino also.

He handed the letter to Pietro who took it.

"I am grateful to Your Excellency," he said. "I will always remember this."

The pear blossoms made Lombardy a maze of lighted candelabra as he rode off.

They were not snow on the ground as he entered Florence by the Prato gate. It was Spring and it was Tuscany. Poppies had been growing in every wheatfield and the grape vines put out their pale green tendrils. He jounced in through the animated, narrow streets and the activity heartened him. The quick Florentine speech was tonic to him after Lombard Mantua. He rode to the Medici palace and dismounted there.

"Cardinal Giulio de' Medici."

"The Cardinal is engaged, Messer."

"I am Pietro Aretino."

There was no lackey who could keep out his confidence and he strode, following one, down the gloomy coolness of a long corridor.

He was led into a rich chamber and there was Medici.

"Your Lordship," he began.

Cardinal Medici looked at him and was frankly disturbed. He had been walking the tightrope of Roman politics which is no mean feat, and had not only not fallen, but had almost reached the other side. At any rate, Adrian had become not hostile to him, and friendship was the obvious next step. Yet here looking across the table at him — and looking very coolly — was the man with the sharp pen whom Adrian had ordered taken and delivered to him. At the same time, he could not get it out of his head that Aretino one day might be useful to his machinations.

He took refuge in procrastination.

"You did not like Mantua?"

"On the contrary, I was delighted there."

"Why did you leave, then?"

"It is you — not even the Marquis of Mantua — that my heart wishes to serve, Your Lordship."

Then once again the Cardinal's wits began to work for him.

In the north, at Reggio Emilia, was a distant relative of his, Giovanni de' Medici who was known as Giovanni delle Bande Nere or, in other words, John of the Black Bands. Like Aretino he was straight-forward and of a single purpose, though his purpose did not happen to be the same one as Pietro's was. Like Aretino, he was wild and dissolute. So much so in fact, that he was known as *Il Gran Diavolo* or "The Great Devil." Like Aretino, moreover, he was kept from

Rome partly because his presence might be embarrassing there.

"I still," he said gravely, "cannot favor you openly but I still wish to help you. I have a kinsman. How would you like to go to him?"

"Who is he?" asked Aretino.

"Giovanni de' Medici — Giovanni delle Bande Nere."

Aretino gave a start.

"John of the Black Bands?"

"Yes, Messer Pen-wielder."

But it was not politic to seem too eager.

"Since he is your kinsman, I will go to him."

But this time he had chosen well and wisely. This time he had hitched his wagon to a star, and not to a fickle planet. This time he had begun an attachment that would last.

Even if you discount all that is said by a nation of hero-worshippers seeking for a military hero at a time when there were few in Italy, Giovanni delle Bande Nere was an extraordinary man. He was extraordinary for the peninsula, but he was even extraordinary for the age. For he believed that to be a good soldier it was necessary to fight better than your opponents, to have better disciplined troops, to have more resource in planning and to be more impetuous and bold in action, rather than to be more tricky in drawing up treasonable agreements, which was the usual form of generalship. And he almost proved that he was right.

He had a curious pedigree. His father was another Giovanni de' Medici, belonging to that elder if up to then less distinguished branch of the family which hoed its own garden, and for a long time kept out of politics, but which made up for this seeming aberration by amassing money and encouraging art. For him, for example, Botticelli did his lovely "Birth of Venus" and his bewitching "Springtime" which are among the most exquisite if not the greatest paintings of the Renaissance. This elder Giovanni was a handsome fellow, pleasant, perhaps a little weak, and popular; and he died a millionaire.

His mother was Caterina da Forlì, bastard grand-daughter of the great Duke Francesco Sforza who had sprung of peasant stock but who had hammered his way upward to greatness and had become ruler of one of the five largest Italian states. She had met Giovanni during one of her periodical intervals of widowhood when he had been sent to her as Ambassador by the Florentine Republic, and had first loved him and then married him, much to the scandal of his at-the-moment straight-laced fellow-citizens. Like her grandfather, she was a fighter and even when she was carrying her children — among them the future Delle Bande Nere — she rode at the head of her troops in full armor. Generally she was victorious, and but for treachery, she would always have been, but she fell finally before Caesar Borgia, who made her prisoner, but was afraid to murder her. Giovanni took after her. His half-brothers and half-sisters — all those Feos and Riarios who move like wan shadows across the contemporary scene — were typical men and women of the decaying Renaissance, selfish, treacherous and cowardly, but the young Medici was direct and valorous. He was, even as a small boy.

It is not possible to know exactly how he looked. There is a great portrait of a mustached young man by Titian, and it gives Giovanni delle Bande Nere the keen eyes and the restless aquiline profile of a young aristocrat, and there is a photographic miniature by Bronzino which could be passed off as a picture of Napoleon. A marble statue, however, shows the drill-sergeant jaws, and the hard mouth of a Roman emperor.

In some ways he had all of these qualities. Rich enough to do anything he wanted to, the only thing that attracted him was to become a mighty soldier. When he was eleven, he started preparations. His mother died, and he retired to his hereditary stronghold of Castello overlooking the Mugello, where he took up the anachronistic life of a predatory mediaeval baron. The conservative Medici gasped, but there was nothing they could do about it. For the most part, he rode wildly from dawn to dusk; swam ice-cold rivers; or followed his bird dogs on foot; but once or twice he participated in traditional deeds of robbery and rapine, and once or twice he figured in bloody brawls. At twelve, he had visited his first brothel and at twelve he had already killed a man. Yet he had enough poise to receive Giulio de Medici with dignity and enough wisdom to do it hospitably. When he was sixteen, his distant cousin became Pope Leo. Then he went to Rome. He went there to get a commission, and he was given one. A band of Corsicans was placed under his command. At seventeen, he won his first war. He was sent under Lorenzino de' Medici to the taking of Urbino and he supplied just the military skill that Lorenzino lacked. At twenty, he was known as a fine captain throughout the whole breadth of the land.

Then followed an interlude of peace in which his enormous vitality, which was like the rise and fall of tides or like the shock of earthquake, having no outlet, got him into one scrape after another. An attempted duel with a prominent poltroon, in which his conduct was correct but hardly wise, obliged him to quit Florence for Ferrara whence he roared new challenges and defied law and order to keep him still.

After this, there was a series of women, for women of all sorts seemed to come to him. Sluts out of the gutter. Learned and affected courtezans such as Niccolosa Pinta who read Petrarch and Boccaccio, and quoted Virgil and Horace. Professional gold-diggers like Lucrezia Mother-won't-let-me, whom Aretino himself claimed to have named and made famous. Wives of citizens and burghers. Even noble ladies. I am afraid that the sluts out of the gutter were the most numerous, for Giovanni delle Bande Nere had inherited his mother's coarseness with her courage, and it was Caterina who had defied her enemies when they threatened to murder her children with her ribald answer that she could make more. Poor Maria Salviati, his pale childhood sweetheart who had married him and who loved him loyally if futilely, had to pawn jewels to raise money not only for his armies, but for his mistresses as well.

But now, when he was twenty-five, new wars broke out, and once more he was a captain. He guarded Italy from the north. His camp fronted the barbarians — as by the Italians all those beyond the Alps were regarded — and he was the shield of Italy. As long as he stood stoutly, neither foreign nor domestic foes could menace her. France and Spain might bid against each other for Milan, and they could divide up the peninsula by sword or treaty but as long as the young warrior remained there, their traced lines would have to stay on paper. The pitched tents of his soldiers were the last stronghold of a vanished mighty nation, miraculously revived centuries later. If luck held, they might be the first tents of a new Rome.

Aretino, on his arrival there, was greeted by the sounds of turmoil.

"Joy filled the hearts of all," he wrote, "for the young leader had just given his soldiers a night of liberty. Torches were blazing everywhere, and the easy-virtued beauties of the city had come thither in great numbers. Some of his men were leaping off their horses. They had just returned from a foraging party, and bottles of wine, well-cured hams, baskets of fruit, and even bleating lambs were slung across their saddle-bows. These had cost them nothing, for everybody for ten miles around who had anything fit to eat had been robbed. A few of the women wept and tore their hair, while peasants clamored and argued and begged for their wives and daughters and for their livestock, and were beaten back with the flats of daggers and of partizans. Enormous campfires blazed under a stand of oak trees, and the shadows of men drinking, gambling, or love-making were flung hither and thither by the ruddy light of cressets."

There had been an interlude in the days of fighting, and Giovanni delle Bande Nere was making use of it to allow his soldiery to engage in those relaxations which the professional fighting man has always sought.

Among the rioters, Aretino saw a tall man dressed as a common soldier who moved among the others with an air both of comradery and command. He seemed at ease among the men, one of their number, yet at the same time they deferred to him. It was the young general himself, and Pietro moved toward him. Having reached him, he halted, hesitant, but Giovanni delle Bande Nere turned and saw him.

"Messer Pietro Aretino?" he asked.

"At the service of Your Excellency."

The soldiers saw their leader clasp the handsome stranger's hand and a few heard the name he said.

"Evviva Aretino!" they shouted. "Evviva Il Gran Diavolo!"

"Viva!" shouted back the echoes.

Aretino joined with them.

A few minutes later he was led into the huge tent where Giovanni delle Bande Nere was feasting with his favorites, his light-of-loves, his captains. A new phase of his life had begun.

It was perhaps the happiest and it was certainly the most high-hearted that he ever knew. And he remembered every vivid detail of it until the end of his days.

"On the arrival of your letter, O illustrious lady," he wrote twenty years later to Girolama Fontanella, wife of the Cavallerotto Fontanella, one of Giovanni's ablest lieutenants, "I was occupied in setting down certain humble words with which to thank the Queen of Poland. By a gift, Her Majesty had showed she thought me worthy of her courtesy. And perhaps I would have found in my mind a spirit of gratitude and would have repaid with the words it gave me, the thing I received from the serene Bona, if hearing your name did not snatch this subject from my fantasy, and snatching it, did not take away, too, the thought of her goodness and affection, carrying me to where you are.

"Then Time dropped away, and it seemed to me that I stood once again in that place where a long while ago I darted hither and thither about the city on the back of my palfrey which in whiteness surpasses the snow—head over heels in love with Laura to keep company with the love affairs of that often easy-going often temperamental Giovanni de' Medici.

In those days, my beard was ebony not ivory. In those days, I had wings, not feet of lead.

"Did you ever see a more continent or a more timid lover? Don't you remember how for three days he ate nothing and then was like some engine in his new ferocity? Often enough Orlando wished to carry away Angelica, but our youthful grandee never even thought of eloping with his lady love. Owing to the greatness of his soul, he was able to quench the fire, which was truly burning up his heart, in festivals, in banquets, and in jousts, when he shattered, with incontinent blows of his lance, even the columns which supported her portico. I used to think that heavens and earth would be riven asunder when he hitched his furious chargers to their chariot, and drove madly about the streets with an outcry more diabolical than amorous. And what place in your ladyship's house has not received him, all done in and beside himself, and like a man possessed?

"His having loved not only modestly, but with a reverent mind can be watched with any miracle that has ever come from the rule of Cupid, the more so since that act is the most praiseworthy which is done the least. In short, God permitted this to happen, so that the good Paola who inflamed him with her divine graces could take glory from his respecting her chastity.

"But all these things are resolved into the air that carries away the sound of voices. They pass like a dream. It seems to me only a short while ago that I saw the leader of that unparagoned soldiery embraced by your husband, the Cavalerotto, who was more to him than a brother or a friend. It seems to be that I still hear them, and still see them talking and jesting together.

"And now let us speak of myself. Certainly my eyes are filled with tears when I remember how affectionately, in church and in the streets, the dear, sweet, and lovely little Countess Madrina used to kiss me. Every comedy re-enacts the mischance which made me sleep beside her when I found her

ill. Having talked a while by her bed, and being nearly overcome by heat and fatigue, I lay my head on the pillow and
there I snored until that idiot, the Count of Casal Po, her
husband, shook me furiously. 'Undress yourself,' he cried,
'and get into bed!' How the learned Messer Aurelio da la
Fossa nearly split his jaws laughing when some great ladies or
other told him the story. And that by the way is what I did
when the same lady, having read a letter which I brought to
her from Milan, turned to me and said: 'My husband writes
to me that I am to treat you just as I would him. Will you
sleep with me tonight?'

"And where is that Martha who, recounting the mad deed
of him, who, when she was still a girl loved her so utterly,
said: 'Pardon me, husband, for since the poor fellow lived
here I was obliged to do him some kindness.' I remember the
blushes of a man from Modena who once danced with her.
He asked her what her name was and thought she answered:
Merde! What she had really said was: Martha! But he
dropped her like a hot cake.

"But now let us make an end of chatter. Let us give our attention to living. And putting aside tales of the past time, let us
imitate that gallant fellow who came with the Duke of Ferrara
to this paradise. The Duke put twenty *soldi* into his hands,
saying: 'So much shall you have every day, that you may eat
when you wish to!' He answered: 'Keep them, then, yourself,
for since I have come here to serve Your Excellency, and have
nothing to do but wait until you have eaten, I don't expect to
lose a mouthful.'

"For although jests will not keep us from growing old or
from dying, it is indeed true that thinking continually about
the madcap recklessnesses of youth makes Time walk with a
slow pace. Thus the memory of these things drives away without pity the thought of the death sentence which every man
living carries over his head. And I, in spite of it, will use '*I
will*' instead of '*If I am able.*' For no living man has been able

to escape love entirely, and as long as there is beauty and there
are eyes to see it, no man ever will.

"I salute the grace of Reggio, bait and birdlime of the
bestial and the gentle bands. If Ercole" — naming a typical
Renaissance lord — "had stayed here even a short time, he
would have made bread, washed pots, and turned the roast.
But lo Mars de' Medici hurled in breastplate, sword and
spurs, and if it had not been for the Imperial and the royal
war, he would have been Castellan of Ruolo.

"O good Reggio, O courteous Reggio, I have the same desire to see you as I have memory to exalt you, nor do I know
which holds more of my good will, Reggio or Arezzo, where I
was born. Reggio is affable. Her advantages are free to all. She
is almost such as to make me change my swearing that I will
never leave these mighty and renowned waters. Will it ever be
that you and I and the Cavalerotto sit together and spend a
month talking about the things that have happened since we
last saw each other?"

But it was not merely a congenial and a protected life that
Aretino acquired from sharing the tent and table, and becoming the left eye — while Captain Lucantonio Cuppano became
the right eye — of "the immortal Giovanni de' Medici, high
inventor of a strenuous warfare." Something definite was
added to his stature.

"But now let us leave priests alone," he wrote the Marquis
of Mantua, "and talk of the *armorum*. What a fine comedy I
saw in this siege! By God, my lord, every annoyance would fly
from you, if I could only spend an hour telling you of the
things done in the war! I would make you laugh most of all
about the doings of the Sforza whelp. As the Devil wished it,
one day in his absence his company took as woebegone a
Frenchman as possible, and he came to Milan with trumpets
and went round and round the whole place as if he had routed
the entire French Army. All the women rushed to the windows with lights in their hands and cried: 'Victory, victory!'
The next morning they preached his prowess in the cathedral,

and then the people, robed in white, made a solemn and villainous procession, and Sforzino perambulated through the city in a triumphal chariot drawn by four lanzknechts with the prisoner in front of him and with a sign saying: *Veni, vidi, vici.* And a thousand other things of which I could not say which was best."

Please note very carefully the tone of these amusing sentences, and make certain deductions therefrom. "The Testament of the Elephant" was the strained effort of an immature though witty young man, who was trying to attract attention by clown tricks and parody. The sonnets of Master Pasquino, though swelled up with god-given insolence, still bore the tags of someone not established. Though Aretino did not hide their authorship but rather boasted of it, the fact that they were issued anonymously showed that he was not ready to stand on his own feet. The letter describing his reception at Mantua had a certain assurance, but it was written to an old friend.

This epistle, however, came from one man of the world to another man of the world; and since the writer was the son of the shoemaker, the man who received it one of the first lords of Italy, the inferences are obvious. Already, as we have seen, Pietro was no longer a man seeking to advance himself, but a person whom people wanted to know. But he had passed even this. The menial who had become one of the Pope's literary courtiers was now the associate — on terms as near equality as was possible in that age of etiquette and punctilio — of at least two great aristocrats. If from now on we note a certain swagger in all that this tall fellow with black hair and beard says and does, it is pardonable. It is not so much bravado as an ease come from reliance on himself. And he will need it before long.

CHAPTER VII

Pope Chameleon

THE reign of the unfortunate Adrian did not last for long. He died on September 14, 1523 — after a pontificate of less than two years. His death was due to natural causes. He was worn out by over-work — for he had honestly, if not too capably, tried to reform the Church — and when a summer outburst of the plague swept Rome, he not only refused to seek refuge at Tivoli or among the cool, vine-fragrant Alban hills, but he did not even take ordinary precautions. The jubilant Romans decided, however, that the Dutch pontiff had been poisoned, and they proceeded blissfully to fête his private physician. They garlanded the house of this gentleman, hanging it with wreaths which they had inscribed: "to the Savior of his Country." Clearly virtue was neither popular nor very much believed in, in the city where Christ's Vicar was Lord.

In November of the same year, Cardinal Giulio de' Medici was chosen to succeed him. The methods by which he achieved this election are illuminating. He had entered the conclave with sixteen votes which was only one more than he had commanded in 1522, but this time he did not repeat his former tactics. Cardinal Colonna was his principal rival. He went therefore to Cardinal Colonna, and purchased his support with the promise of high offices. The French were his most obstinate opponents. Without letting the Imperialists even hear a rumor of it, he came to a secret understanding with the French. Finally elected, he told his friends that he would become Pope Julius, but they convinced him, using Adrian as an example, that it was bad luck for a pope to assume office under his own name, so he adopted the title of Clement VII. All of Rome rejoiced. Cardinal Medici had been Leo X's right-hand man, and now as Pope himself he would bring the golden days again. But they had counted their chickens before the eggs which would produce them had even been laid, and they had reckoned without at least one important element of the new Pope's character. The truth was, as Aretino diagnosed correctly at a later time that Clement was like a chameleon. He took his color from those who surrounded him. With whom he was going to surround himself remained to be seen.

When Aretino received word of the election, he was still in Milan. But he was as exultant as the Romans were.

"I, my Lord," he wrote very exuberantly to the Marquis of Mantua, "set out very shortly for Rome, and great is my delight to realize that in spite of all Ponzetta could do I will find my patron has become Pope, though he was only a cardinal when I departed. But God forgive me, for I no longer wish to speak the truth about the cardinals since they have conducted themselves so well! What a good man Colonna is! I would like to murder Pasquino who called him a base rogue and who accused old Del Monte of practising magic arts, and who said even worse things of the other sage and sainted *monsignori*. But now to change the subject, I would like to send you the epitaph of poor Master Adrian, by the grace of God a friend of ours. I know that he was very dear to you, because you loved him while he was living."

The "epitaph" was in the best manner of Master Pasquino.

> Here lies poor Adrian, made by wine divine:
> That is a Dutchman, a shipbuilder's son.
> To be a Cardinal he surely won
> By teaching Charles the alphabet to whine.
> He was a pedant, and he used to hold
> A school for janitors. This makes me weep:
> He was named Shepherd though but a poor sheep,
> And he chased Soderini from his fold. . . .

That, however, was no more than a beginning. Warming to his subject, Aretino—as he usually did when his ideas were fluent—elongated the sonnet into far more than the fourteen traditional lines, and each neatly-forged added link of verse presented a sarcastic or a stinging epithet. Cardinal Enckfort, closest friend of the late Pope and fellow Nordic Aryan, came in for mention. He was referred to as Cardinal *Trincaforte,* or Drinkhard. The Italians, whose vices were of another sort, found this eminently amusing. Adrian's economy was the subject of a line or so. Those who admired Leo — who had not only squandered the large fortune he had inherited from Lorenzo the Magnificent, but had taken over and scattered the 700,000 golden crowns Julius had accumulated in the papal treasury — thought the mere label of living within one's income a supreme and witty insult. And the poor shabby Dutchwoman was made a harlot again — Adrian's "psalm-singing, religious washerwoman" being once more set in rhyme as his mistress. Apparently the loquacious statue was like the Bourbon kings of France. It had learned nothing — and forgotten nothing. But apparently also, Messer Pietro from Arezzo who wrote the statue's pieces for it, knew his public. For the new effort was greeted with applause.

As soon as he had dashed this off, Aretino went, not as he had announced he would, to the capital of the Catholic world, but back to Reggio. The explanation which he gave was a high-hearted one. He was in love with a cook there. All summer long, if we can believe him, she kept him dancing in attendance on her in the hot kitchen. As he turned the spit for her, sweat poured from his huge limbs just as grease dripped from the sizzling roasts. Truly, he was burned up by love. And yet not even a chucked chin or a stolen kiss would she permit to him, to say nothing of more substantial tokens.

"But now in the crisp autumn she gives me hope at last."

The truth seems to be, however, that while his cook lady-love made him pick Reggio to go to, it was not Laura who kept him out of Rome. After all, as we shall see later, there were cooks in Rome too — as well as other ladies — and they were all amenable. What kept him out of Rome was that he felt that it was too soon to venture there. Clement's favor was not only his best card, but, with his soaring ambitions, his only one. He did not wish to play it until he knew that it would take the trick.

His new caution was not ill advised. Clement, the Pope, was not quite the same person as Giulio, the Cardinal. Or perhaps he really was the same person. As a cardinal who aspired further, he may have realized that it was well to create the impression that he would be a new edition of his cousin, Leo, but that elected, something else was called for. "His Holiness," wrote a Venetian ambassador, "is temperate in every human action, particularly in eating and drinking. And he gives such an example of continence that nowadays (I will not vouch for the past) nobody can say anything against him." The diplomat from the Adriatic city protected himself by adding that whether this was truly the Pope's way of life or whether Clement was simply careful, he was not prepared to say. "He indulges in no sort of vice," said another Venetian emissary. "He does not spend anybody else's money. He will not sell any benefices and he does not bestow them out of simony. He gives much to charity. Since his election, he has not been to Leo's hunting lodge more than twice. He does not care for music or buffoons." The prospects did not look exceedingly good for one whose chief hope of prospering lay in a new corrupt and worldly court.

But it was not merely the unfamiliar spectacle of the new Pope's virtue or pretended virtue that turned Aretino into a cautious fellow. If that was disconcerting, it was at least something he could measure, and hence cope with. The uncertain, however, was added to the unpalatable. A fierce battle of intrigue to gain influence over Clement was now being fought out in the complicated chambers of the Vatican, for like it or not, this last scion of the elder line of the Medici was prince temporal as well as prince spiritual, and the two forces which opposed each other with armies in north Italy, in Naples, in the Low Countries and along the Pyrenees, each tried to win him as their ally. And so equally divided seemed the chances of victory that an opportunist could not tell the way to jump.

When he did jump, Aretino jumped the wrong way. Giovanmatteo Giberti was the head of the French faction, and the level-headed persistence of this determined illegitimate son of an ex-sea captain made his star seem the one to follow. He was the man for the new era. He loved art which kept some of the old regime loyal to him, but neither so passionately nor so extravagantly as to fall into the bad graces of the current asceticism. He was good personally, but he knew also the stage he played on, and did not let this interfere with him. He was a politician of the first order. While others sought cardinal's robes and wealthy benefices, he had more practical aims. His office of choice was papal datary, which was not so much an office in itself as the supervisor of all other offices. Before you were appointed, the papal datary passed on you and approved or disapproved. His thin lips did not indicate a starved character but resourcefulness and patient obstinacy.

Thinking this over in his Lombard sanctuary, Aretino decided Giberti was his man. He left Reggio in the latter part of November, and as the first snows of December whitened the encircling hills, he was in Rome again. There, busily, he set to work. New sonnet after new sonnet; poem, ode and *capitolo* were scratched on sheets of foolscap. Spring blossomed on the Campagna, and he had a batch of them. He sent them to Vittoria Colonna, and she did what he expected her to. "I have," she wrote Giovanmatteo, "a whole sheaf of writing by Pietro Aretino, and they are all in praise of you."

Then suddenly he shifted from the man to the idea. Fra Nicholas Schomberg, a German who had come to Italy as a dissolute student and had been won to the life of religion by Savonarola, and Girolamo Schio, Italian bishop of French Vaison, did not have between them enough talents and ability to make half a Giberti, but they convinced Aretino that their cause, which was the Imperial one, was the one the Pope must ultimately follow.

Aretino thought to beat the gun. Without mentioning either France or Empire, he made preparations for an about-face by starting to write fulsome praises of Fra Nicholas and of Bishop Schio, while at the same time he attacked the Datary. It was a ghastly error. In the first place, Giovanmatteo really had the papal ear, and logic or no logic, he would decide the issue. In the second place, he was an unforgiving enemy.

Turned on by an old supporter, he was doubly this.

"That lewd speaker can praise the German and Girolamo," he said icily, "but he has dared to snarl at me, and he will have me to reckon with."

Rome, waiting eagerly, waited only to see what form the vengeance would take. It came suddenly, but in an unexpected way.

During the summer of Aretino's unfortunate decision, Giulio Romano, who was working in the Vatican on the rooms left unfinished by young Raphael, turned aside from murals for a while, and set his talented hands to a gay jape. He left off painting saints for the moment, and started in on sinners. Mainly to amuse his friends, he slapped boldly on canvas sixteen bawdy pictures. They do not survive, but we know all about them. They were an illustrated guide to lechery, showing — in magnificent colors, no doubt — what Vasari describes as "the various manners, attitudes and postures in which lewd men have dealings with lewd women." Had this been the end of them, a great many illustrious men would have laughed ribaldly behind closed doors, and the episode would have been closed. But it was not. In Rome at the time was a new artist with a new art. Marcantonio Raimondi was his name and he came from Bologna. Recently he had invented — or more probably had stolen from some German followers of Dürer — the process of engraving, and could make many pictures from one. At first he had contented him with forging Dürers, and was praised greatly because connoisseurs were fooled by them, but latterly he had sailed under his own colors and made "copies" instead. He needed subjects. Giulio Romano persuaded him to use the sixteen paintings.

"They will circulate, and you at the same time will become both rich and famous."

And, of course, they did.

But with results which were not those he had anticipated. Even in Rome *coda mundi,* there was outcry and scandal. Nothing could be done to the painter, for he was in Mantua where he had recently taken service with the Marquis. Marcantonio was on hand, however, and he was seized and thrown into prison. It was Giovanmatteo Giberti who accomplished this. But Marcantonio had one ally, and he was a potent one: Aretino. The engraver had already done Pietro's portrait and that was a sure way of winning his affection. Besides here was a chance of scoring against his enemy. Aretino went to the Pope. What he said is not reported, but Raimondi was set free immediately. Then, in his triumph, Pietro suffered a brainstorm. He went to his room, and he wrote sixteen filthy sonnets. One for each of the engravings. They spread even faster than the pictures did.

They gave Giovanmatteo the opportunity he had been waiting for, and he wasted no time in using it. He set into motion the same machinery of justice he had employed against Marcantonio. Aretino realized that he had blundered. He launched one brief, defiant defense of what he had done, which was later published as a letter to the physician Battista Zatti.

"When I obtained from Pope Clement the release of Marcantonio who had been imprisoned on account of his engravings, there came over me a wish to see the figures which has caused busybody Giberti to exclaim that the good craftsman should be hanged and drawn. Seeing them, I was inspired by the same spirit which had caused Giulio Romano to paint them. And since it is well known that the poets and sculptors, ancient and modern, have seen no harm in entertainingly allowing their genius to write or to carve out once in a while such lewd trifles as the marble satyr trying to violate a boy which is in the Chigi palace, I amused myself by writing the

sonnets which you can now see under each picture. Their
indecent memory, I dedicate to all hypocrites, for I am all out
of patience with their scurvy strictures, and with that dirty
custom which tells eyes they cannot look on that they most
delight to see. What harm is there in beholding a man possess
a woman, and are the very beasts more free than we are? It
seems to me that that thing which nature gives us for our
preservation ought to be worn around the neck as a pendant
and in the hat for a medal. It is that which has made you, who
are the first of physicians. It is that which has produced the
Bembos, the Molzas, the Fortunios, the Varchis, the Ugolini
Martellis, the Lorenzo Lenzis, the Fra Sebastianos, the Sansovinos, the Titians, the Michelangelos, and after them the
Popes, Emperors and Kings. It has begotten the loveliest of
children, the most beautiful women, the holiest of saints. The
hands might well be hidden for they gamble away money, witness false oaths, lend at usury, make insulting gestures, pull
and tear, give fisticuffs, wound, and slay. As for the mouth, it
spits in the face, gluttonizes, makes you drunk, and vomits."

Thus far, either arrant boldness or incredible effrontery,
which was coupled, however, with a sort of bawdy logic.

Then on his strong wrists and ankles, he felt in imagination
heavy iron shackles and he breathed in the noisome dampness
of the rat-infested papal prison. Giovanmatteo Giberti was
quite capable of letting him rot in one. Consequently, he
decamped.

He did not this time, however, go quite as far as he had gone
before. For he was now an expert at these unpremeditated
exits and, a quick learner, he knew reassuringly that if the
law's arm was drastic in the things it did to you, its reach was
limited. Crossing the Campagna, which had been burnt
golden by the sun of August, he looked over his shoulder
from time to time to see if between him and the hazy roofs
and towers, there were any pursuers. But when, finally, he
had reached the other side, he breathed easily. The Tiber now
ran — such of it as had survived the summer drought — be-

tween rough and craggy hills, and there were no more meadow
larks. He paused at Spoleto with its strong castle and the graceful arches of its slender, Roman aqueduct, and refreshed himself with tasty amber wine. Then he rode on again. He passed
Assisi without stopping; and a few miles further, having
crossed a lesser valley, he looked up as he rode north to see
above him the crouched griffon of the place in which he
studied art. The huge stones of its Etruscan walls made a
grim precipice. Finally, he reached Arezzo. It was the first
time since he had run away that he had stood on native soil,
and he dawdled hopefully, waiting for his fellow citizens to
recognize him as a famous son of the place. They paid little
attention to him. Then as he twiddled thumbs, wondering
what to do next, a messenger accosted him.

"Messer Pietro Aretino?"

"Yes," he answered.

"Here is a missive for you."

His heart leapt as he beheld the now familiar handwriting.
He opened it.

"On receipt of these lines," he read eagerly, "I beg you to
leave Arezzo and to come to me. This is something I desire
greatly. I admit I should not do this, but should really be
annoyed with you; for in turning to the party of Fra Nicholas
and Vaison, you have lost Giovanmatteo, and consequently
also lost the Pope. So doing, you who could give laws to the
world, have ruined your own prospects. You have harmed me
too, for while you were at the Roman court, I had one who
would defend with whole heart the rightness of what I was
doing, what I had already done, and what I might do in the
future. However, I do wish to see you and very much. Here
is probably the reason. The very foolish thing you have done
was done through bad judgment but in sincere good faith.
For I am able to give you this praise — that while everybody
is calculating from time to time, you never are."

His face flushed with pleasure at this compliment.

Then he asked a question.

"Where is Lord Giovanni?"

"At Fano, *messere.*"

Down by the blue Adriatic with its tepid waters and its long and topaz strands!

Oh yes; he recollected now. The Roman gossip mongers had talked of these new doings of the warlike Medici. He was now a pirate. His cautious employers having failed to provide him with enough revenue to maintain his armies, and booty being scarce these days, he had marched suddenly into this little town, and had become a corsair chief. His swift ships now rivalled those of Tunis and Algiers, and there were some even who said — behind his back — that he was not always careful that the boat he captured was an enemy.

Aretino rode across the mountains to join him there. They had a gay month like the time spent in Reggio, and then moved on again.

Pavia was the destination.

"My both-ends-against-the middle cousin," said Giovanni delle Bande Nere, "has consented that I take service with the French King. This leaves him free to dicker with the Emperor and still have two baskets to put his precious eggs in. And my new employer wishes me and my army."

"May I ride with you?" requested Aretino.

"I expected it and hoped it," said the soldier.

It was October when they arrived there, galloping with their joint impetuosity so that they arrived far ahead of the accompanying soldiery. But the autumn comes late in Lombardy and they were hot as they dismounted from their horses and they were choked with gray and stinging dust.

It turned out to be fortunate for Aretino and for his reputation that he had made this trip. When Giovanni delle Bande Nere had his first interview with the French monarch he took Messer Pietro with him. Then he called upon the King alone.

"Where is Messer Aretino?" asked Francis.

"He stayed back. He did not wish to intrude upon your Majesty."

"Send for him immediately."

The first monarch he had ever met was as taken with his personality as the first marquis, first noble general, and first pope. They sat late, as the king's brocaded servitors brought them delicacies and fine French wine; and as Aretino held forth before the other two, it was easy to see why. For he was a man's man, *par excellence*. He was entertaining, outgoing, human, and always at ease. He knew how to act. Though full of egotism, he was never pompous, and though anxious to advance himself, he was rarely obsequious. He saved those two qualities for some of his writings. And he was almost always genuine. Whatever his faults may have been, he had almost always that rare virtue. At any rate with those he liked.

Yet in spite of this promising episode, Aretino still felt drawn toward the city by the Tiber. It was not, as Giovanni delle Bande Nere had suggested to the young and gallant King, that Pietro preferred courts to camps. At the moment quite the reverse was true. But courts were still necessary for the schemes which he had laid out for his advancement, and camps — even when they held Giovanni delle Bande Neres and François *Premiers* of France — were not. Accordingly he began to cast about for a means of making his peace with Rome.

It was not long before he found one. It was to use his pen in praise of that very man he had attacked. Two fulsome *canzoni* celebrating Pope Clement were followed by a third one honoring the Datary. It was not published until February of the next year, but it must have reached Giberti, for by November he was high in favor again.

"To our great pleasure and content," the Marquis of Mantua wrote him, "we have been informed by persons worthy of credit, and likewise we have learned from the letters of Messer Francesco Gonzaga, our very dear ambassador, that you have been talking so honorably of us that it seems there is nothing that you do so freely. You have done this in the most frequented places of Rome and — which is more important — in the presence of the Pope himself. Because of his benignity,

His Holiness has listened freely. For this reason, we acknowledge ourselves to be greatly obliged to you. We cannot deny that it delights us to be praised by men of letters. It seems to us that theirs is the one true and solid praise. It delights us especially to be praised by you, for we know that we did not urge you into any study of adulation. That vice is alien to your character."

He went on to say that since so great a merit called for a recompense, Aretino was to call on him when he wanted some favor, and the Marquis would do it willingly.

Then he added in his own hand:

"Please let us see something that you have written."

On the same day, Isabella d'Este received the following:

"Your Excellency can give this news to Gianozzo. The Pope has made Pietro Aretino a Knight of Rhodes."

Even Messer Berni, Giovanmatteo's secretary, who never quite forgets to be spiteful about Pietro, adds his evidence.

"He now walks through Rome dressed like a duke. He takes part in all the wild doings of the lords. He pays his way with insults couched in tricked-up words. He talks well, and he knows every libellous anecdote in the city. The Estes and the Gonzagas walk arm in arm with him, and listen to his prattle. He treats them with respect, and is haughty to everyone else. He lives on what they give him. His gifts as a satirist make people afraid of him, and he revels in hearing himself called a cynical, impudent slanderer. All that he needed was a fixed pension. He got one by dedicating to the Pope a second-rate poem."

The episode of the sonnets was closed.

The first thing that Pietro now did was to attempt to do a service for the lord who had befriended him.

"Today," Francesco Gonzaga, Mantuan ambassador to Rome wrote to his cousin the Marquis, "I transacted the business that you put upon me. I thanked His Holiness, kissing his feet in your name, for the affectionate and humane terms he used of you when he spoke of the protection His Beatitude

has taken of Your Excellency and of your state. I also thanked
Messer Pietro Aretino for his kind offices in praising Your
Excellency, as in your letter of the 5th you asked me to. When
I told him how pleased you were to be praised by learned persons like himself, and how cordially he was beloved by you,
he replied that he felt himself obliged to Your Lordship for
the potent demonstrations you had made for him after you
made his acquaintance. He said that he would never forget
them, nor would he ever forget to bear witness to your worth
and excellence in whatever place he found himself. He added
that while talking to the Pope three evenings ago, he informed
His Holiness that not long ago you had expressed a keen desire to have that picture by Raphael of Urbino which is now in
Florence, in which the late and happily-remembered Pope
Leo, together with His Holiness and others, are represented,
life-size. He said that the Pope was sorry that he had not
learned of your desires sooner, because you would have then
been satisfied many days ago. But that the things which had
not been done, would be done. Therefore the Pope ordered
the said picture to be sent to you in Mantua, saying that this
was but a small favor compared to what he would gladly do
to give you pleasure."

The next thing that he did was to seek a favor for himself.

The picture was not immediately forthcoming, and the
Marquis wrote his ambassador, directing him to tell Pietro
that he awaited it "with the greatest anxiety in the world."
Francesco summoned Aretino and delivered the message.
Pietro promised to investigate immediately, and in two weeks
he brought back a reply.

"Messer Pietro Aretino," reported Francesco, "said to me
that he has spoken to the Pope in regard to the painting which
was to be sent to Your Excellency. He said that His Holiness
has sent orders to Florence to have a certain excellent painter
there make a copy of it, so that he could keep this in memory
of Pope Leo. As soon as this is finished, the one done by
Raphael of Urbino will be sent to Your Excellency. He, Mes-

POPE CLEMENT VII

"The Pope . . . is like a chameleon that takes its color from what it is touching."—*Aretino.*

ser Pietro, also wishes to say to you that he will arrange to send you the promised *canzone* as soon as it is printed. According to what he told me, it will have a short letter in front of it, in which it is dedicated to you. Besides this, he insistently begged me that I would pray Your Excellency to have him sent two pairs of shirts worked with gold in the style that they use at present, and two other pairs of shirts worked in silk, together with two golden caps. He said that you would be doing him a singular favor. And he begs you to excuse him if he takes too much liberty with you. The demonstrations of friendliness and the offers made to him by Your Excellency, together with his devoted service of you, give him the heart to have recourse to you in his needs with every confidence. And the sooner he can have the said garments, the more grateful he will be. I, indeed, said to him that in this matter he should write to Your Excellency himself. Nevertheless he insisted so firmly that I do this office that, to satisfy him, I was unable to refuse."

The story of these controversial garments merits being told in full. The Marquis never got his Raphael, for the Pope sent him the copy, slyly keeping the original in his own hands, though whether Lord Gonzaga ever suspected this is something the learned still debate about. But Aretino did get his fine linen (worked with gold or silken thread) and how he did this makes a merry story. It is also an important one. For it shows Aretino and how he worked.

As soon as the Marquis of Mantua received this letter, he wrote Francesco Gonzaga, saying that they would be ordered immediately. Gonzaga told Aretino, who was delighted. He said that he was the Marquis' "servant" and his "slave" and he "promised to compose a *canzone*" — so Gonzaga told his lord — "in your praise, in which he will strive — so as to come at the truth — to put no less study and diligence that he had put into others of his that had preceded it." The shirts and the caps "when he has them, will be exceedingly pleasing to him." He "kisses Your Excellency's hand, and to your good graces recommends himself." Aretino even sent a few samples of his writing—on credit, as it were. Their splendor was as good as on his back.

However a month passed, and no shirts had arrived, so he began to grow restless. He spoke to Francesco Gonzaga, and Gonzaga said that he would see what he could do about it. The result was an epistle to Jacopo Calandra, the Marquis' secretary. "In reply to the other parts of your letter, I say that Your Lordship cannot do wrong in soliciting the shirts of Messer Pietro Aretino, because in his letters he urges me in this matter, saying that he wants them made in a certain design which to him is a matter of no small importance, and the delay in the matter annoys him."

Then six weeks, and this time the ambassador wrote to the Marquis direct.

Aretino, he said, had given him a poem which he had written in praise of the Datary, and it was sent here enclosed. He now promised to attend to one in praise of Mantua. He also said that he would like to send the Marquis a life-sized plaster reproduction of the Laocoön, as well as some antique heads. Last of all, he had asked Francesco Gonzaga "to remind Your Excellency of the shirts and caps you promised him. He is awaiting them with great eagerness."

That long Pietro's patience held out, but no longer. Two days later he burst into Gonzaga's apartments.

"He denied Heaven because he has not received the shirts," Gonzaga told the Marquis. "In a great rage, he swore to me today that he did not want them any more, so thoroughly was he dissatisfied with the business. I tried to quiet him by telling him the sincere desire Your Excellency has to do him pleasure, and the urgent orders given to make them diligently. I said that the negligence of the women, or their many tasks, to put it better, was responsible for the delay. I said many other things to calm him down. To the last he remained obstinate, saying that he knew well the fault was not Your Excellency's but your ministers. Certainly the matter has taken somewhat too long. He complained about it in many ways."

A week later, Francesco referred to the tardiness again.

"Regarding the shirts of Aretino," he wrote, "Your Excellency has seen how much I have written about them. In conclusion, he does not want to make peace, since the Carnival has passed without his having had them. Your Excellency knows his tongue, therefore I will say no more."

This very plain threat seemed to have the desired effect, for soon the shirts were on their way.

"We send you by Paolo Bondi, our familiar," the Marquis wrote his ambassador, "the shirts and the caps which we have had made for Messer Pietro Aretino. There are four shirts worked in gold and four of silk; and a pair of gold caps and a pair of silk ones. Have them brought to him as coming from us, and excuse the delay as best you know how. Certainly we are greatly displeased that the matter has taken so long, but we have had to deal with persons whom we could not command and make obey us, even though they were payed. That is to say, holy sisters. They will not work except at their own hours and own convenience."

It was a plausible and a convincing excuse, and any desire Aretino may have had to find out whether it was true or not was dissipated by the fact that what he wanted now was actually here. And there were two silken caps he had not even asked for. Francesco Gonzaga delivered them himself.

"Aretino is entirely satisfied," he wrote Calandra. "He does penitence for the angry words he spoke about the delay. He goes about everywhere preaching the worth, goodness, and liberality of your Lordship. He has asked a thousand pardons. He says that he was wrong."

Pietro's own letter does not, however, show any large amount of contrition.

"Excellent prince," he addressed the Marquis, "I kiss your hands, and I thank you for the present. It deserved being given to a much greater person than myself. I will enjoy it on account of you, and I am only grieved that the bringer could not, on account of the ornament not being finished, carry back to you a little work which I am sending Your Excellency in token of my servitude. I have had the ancient Laocoön of the Belvedere copied in stucco. It is a *braccio* in height, and in the opinion of the Pope and of all the sculptors of Rome, nothing was ever better copied. It was done by a certain Jacopo Sansovino. Your painter Giulio can tell you who he is. It took him all winter to do, and the Pope often went to the Belvedere to see him work. In short, I will send it to you within ten days, accompanied by many other new things. By the way, the Pope told me yesterday that the painting by Raphael is almost copied, and that he will send it to Your Excellency soon. They are going to celebrate Master Pasquino in my name this year, and he will make a fortune. May God protect every faithful Christian from the evil tongue of the poets! I, my lord, will send you all he talks about."

But the barbed reminder of what might have happened which was contained in the last sentences was at best a statement of his independence, and the whole letter was a gracious one. It was more than that. Having gotten from the Marquis what he wanted to get, he wished to show him his good will was worth the trouble. That he was not simply a gaping maw and grasping hand. That he could do as well as be done for. That he was a useful and potent friend.

It turned out to be fortunate that he had taken this attitude. For he soon needed the patronage of the Marquis more than ever. Having just extricated himself from one serious scrape, he now found himself involved in another one. And this time it was even more ugly than the one before.

The person responsible for his new predicament was his old enemy, Giberti. With what compunctions Aretino had persuaded himself to make peace with this fellow, it can well be imagined. But it was necessary if he wished to stay in Rome, so he drank down the nauseating medicine without a face.

At last, however, something happened which appeared to

change the situation. For some time Francis I of France had frittered away his time by laying futile siege to Pavia when he might have been destroying the Imperial army. His generals —notably the handsome but incompetent Bonnivet, whose mistress Francis' own sister had so nearly become—persuaded him to do this. Now when the Imperials had assembled a new army, they persuaded him to attack. He laid seige at the wrong time, and he did battle at the wrong time. But still dreaming of that flushed day of Marignano when he had been knighted on the field of battle by the Chevalier Bayard *"sans peur et sans reproche,"* he deemed fondly that he was invincible. And to cap the climax, like a boy playing soldiers, he rode joyously at the head of a premature charge, thus blocking his own artillery.

What happened was but inevitable. The French army was routed, and the French monarch barely saved his own skin. He was no coward—he was not a general who would die in bed—and when he saw the catastrophe he spurred madly into the thickest of the mêlée. There he ringed himself with dead foes. The engagement had begun literally at daybreak when the white mists still wreathed the yet untramped-on meadow, and at nine o'clock of that February morning he was at last at bay. A Spanish captain found him thus. Thrusting into one of the few groups of men still fighting, he saw a harassed Frenchman who would neither yield nor run. He had no helmet, and his hands and bearded face were bleeding.

It was the King of France.

"Your Majesty, you must yield to me!" he cried.

Francis looked up. This was no common soldier—he would have died rather than surrender to such—but an officer, a *caballero,* a brave gentleman like himself.

Slowly and with head erect, he brought down his reddened blade, handed it over. Then they led him to the camp of the Imperials. In a tent there, he asked for pen and paper. Long and steadily the former scratched the latter until the whole tale of catastrophe was told. The letter was addressed to his mother.

"All is lost save honor," he concluded it.

Then he had a realistic afterthought.

"And my body which is safe," he added.

But that phrase, French historians, for reasons which are fairly obvious, usually leave out.

Tidings of this disaster reached Rome in short order, and Aretino was among the first to hear them. They told him two things. First, that the master of his friend Giovanni de' Medici had been taken prisoner. This was bad news. Second, that Messer Giovanmatteo Giberti, who had maneuvered the French alliance, would have his wings clipped. This was good.

He took care of the first aspect in a characteristic manner. He wrote a long glowing letter to the fallen monarch. What was more important he made it public.

Then, having showed that he would not desert a friend, he set to work to attack an enemy.

As he had written the Marquis of Mantua, Master Pasquino's day was to be celebrated this year with him as high priest, and he made use of this fact to turn it once again into a festival of abuse.

But there was but a single victim.

Giovanmatteo Giberti.

This was toward the end of April, and throughout the Spring and early Summer, Aretino continued his attacks. That long the seacaptain's patient bastard bided his time. He wanted to give Aretino enough rope to hang himself, and he wanted also Pavia to have faded a little from people's—and from the Pope's—memory. But when he did strike, he struck hard.

"You will have heard," wrote the Bishop of Vaison to the Marquis of Mantua on July 20, "of the strange thing which happened the other night to our Messer Pietro Aretino. At two o'clock, he being on horseback, he was wounded by a man on foot, who stabbed him twice in the chest. One of these wounds may be mortal. However, with the aid of God, I hope that we will save him. May God, who can, give us this grace. If it turns out otherwise, Your Excellency will lose a good and devoted servitor. It is not yet known who is responsible for this misfortune. He who did it fled, and he must have acted this part at the instance of others. But already there are nine persons in prison on account of it, and I believe that all will be known and that the Pope will make that sort of a demonstration which is due to such a man."

Thus far gossip — then the authorized version.

Aretino's assailant had been one Achille della Volta, a Bolognese poet. He and Aretino had both been in love with a young lady employed in Giberti's kitchen. Aretino had written a sonnet to her, and it had come into Achille's hands. This, though he could have written a sonnet himself, was his answer to it.

No one, it must be added, was taken in by this explanation — least of all, Pietro himself. Though his assailant had been masked, he was willing to accept Achille as the physical wielder of the blade, even though the latter, under orders from Giberti, called on him frequently to see how he got on. But he was not willing to accept the motive assigned. It was a hired assassination, not a passionate one, of which he was to have been the victim. It was the Datary himself, and not the Datary's kitchen maid that had supplied the motive. In plain words, he ordered Aretino to be killed.

He lay at death's door for many weeks. Then thanks to a "miraculous oil which is absolutely perfect for wounds" he was cured.

The first thing that he then did was to clamor loudly that the criminals be punished. This brought no results. Then he threatened to make public their names. Still no action. Then he published them. Even at that, neither Achille nor the Datary were hailed before some Roman magistrate and thrown into prison. What should he try next?

He sat long in his room, and brooded.

He had already, staying at Rome, written the first draft of his first brilliant comedy, *La Cortegiana,* and there is much reason to believe that he now started, as he fumed and convalesced there, its famous second draft.

Therein is interpolated a new character, Flaminio. And Flaminio is believed to represent himself.

If so, there are one or two exchanges of dialogue that have distinct bearing on the present situation.

"Let your son stay with you," Flaminio tells Sempronio. "You don't want to send him to Court to become a rogue."

"How rogue?" asks Sempronio.

"Rogue is an old story," answers Flaminio, "but after rogue comes treacherous villain. What more? With incurable hypocrisy even murder is not proceeded against."

Pope Clement. Giovanmatteo Giberti.

A little later on, Flaminio tells another character that he is going somewhere else to die.

"But where will you go?"

He reflects.

"The world is large," he answers.

"Yes, but where will you go?"

"I will go," he says finally, "to Mantua where the goodness of the Marchese Federigo denies bread to nobody."

Though he had once tried Mantua and had found it lacking, it now seemed an excellent idea. Achille being at large and Giovanmatteo still prospering, his skin hardly would be safe, and, even personal tremors aside, a dead libellist — or satirist — is not exactly a successful one. Nearly as bad, his prestige had now spent itself at the court of that Pontiff in whose cause he had once fought so strenuously and so outrageously. His enemies were in the seats of power. Every failure having redounded to his glory, his first success — that of seeing Cardinal Medici in the chair of St. Peter — turned against him.

He quit Rome on October 13, and curiously enough carried with him papal blessings.

"Messer Pietro Aretino has left here," Schomberg wrote the Marquis of Mantua, "and I believe that he has gone to pay his respects to Your Excellency. The Pope has asked me to recommend him to you very strongly, and since he holds him for his servant, he loves him the more, the more he knows him given over to Your Excellency. I would say even more in carrying out this commission of His Beatitude if I did not know that Your Excellency loves this very great servitor of his. The Pope could not more warmly beg Your Excellency, nor more warmly urge me to write you about him."

Nobody, at any rate, could say that Pope Chameleon was not consistent. Having no colors of his own, he could hardly be true to them. But he would be true to his change of colors to the last.

CHAPTER VIII

The Death of a Hero

BUT although Mantua was eager to receive him, Aretino did not plan to make it his permanent abode. He sought merely for a temporary refuge. He wanted only to pause and look around.

It was not that "this most sweet Paradise, this *domicilium Venerum et Charitum"* — as schoolmaster Tom Coryat called it, that first one of the description-writing travelling Englishmen — appealed to him any less than before. Indeed, it should have been more attractive than ever. Giulio Romano was there — his good friend and his partner-in-crime in the old scandal of the lewd pictures and the filthy sonnets — demonstrating that he too, like most Renaissance artists, was a jack of all trades. At Rome he had been a painter, little more than one of Raphael's many assistants, but here he was an architect, and on a grassy meadow outside of the city walls he tore down old stables to build out of their ruins one of the most handsome edifices of the Cinquecento. It is called the Palazzo del Te. It is a warm, golden brown, classically grave, and has stately chambers, dignified columns, realistic pictures of giants, goddesses and thoroughbred steeds; and it is still worth traversing the ocean to look at.

The Marquis himself was at his most affable. Isabella d'Este had gone to Rome. There that Renaissance paragon but somewhat exacting mother watched pig races; was made much of by cardinals (who wanted money from her) ; and posed as the neglected dowager. Isabella Boschetta came into the open. She had been mistress, now she was unlegalized wife. And with one Isabella no longer there to hold him in check, the other Isabella eager to urge him on, lavishness was lord and master. He gave painter Giulio a stallion: Ruggiero, from his own famous stud farm. You can still see him with strong shoulders and arching neck among the five others painted on the walls of the *Sala dei Cavalli.* Then he gave him a house. Last of all, he appointed him Chief Engineer and assigned to him a princely salary. Five hundred unclipped golden ducats! It was five thousand dollars in modern equivalents. In buying power it was vastly more.

If Aretino had been willing to join the staff of the young nobleman, he might well have been awarded just as much. But joining staffs was the last thing he thought about that autumn, and he was through with courts, at any rate for the time being. The mere idea made his eyes darkle with insolence. "Courts," he would have snarled, "for *courtiers!*" And with good reason. Three times he had attempted the most important court in Italy, and three times, just when success seemed in his hands, he had been repulsed. A new course of action was indicated — or else honest admission that he was defeated. But the last, given his temperament, was impossible. The only thing that kept Pietro from the first was that he had not quite decided what the new course ought to be.

It was a king's broken promise that showed him how to make up his mind. And that king was none other than the gallant French Francis, whose sad plight we have just beheld.

Until Pavia, this impetuous young monarch had seemed nobody's second; and indeed, after Marignano where he defeated 40,000 of the hitherto untameable Swiss in a battle which was twice definitely lost, he appeared to many to be the first soldier in Europe. At any rate, he and the phlegmatic Charles Hapsburg fought as equals. But the chances of a single, quite avoidable conflict sent him crumbling, not the loser of a battle but an actual prisoner. At the famous Certosa, where they took him to spend safely the first night after his defeat, he was almost desperate. Then they carried him to Pizzeghettone on the river Adda. There behind somber walls and a deep moat, he regained his courage. He met the Spanish ambassador. "Before yielding an inch of French ground, I will die a prisoner." Next Spain. En route to the port of Valencia where they

disembarked him, he became even gayer. He would meet
Charles and with his great magnetism he would win back all
that he had lost. Charles refused to see him. That started a
battle between two wills.

Charles ordered Francis treated with great show of consideration but actually maltreated him with subtle fiendishness;
for he shut him in a castle near Madrid; kept the athlete, who
loved hunting better than his dinner, from all exercise save a
daily jog on mule back; and deprived the great amorist of
nearly all consort with women. Francis countered by falling
desperately ill. This was serious, for as a corpse, the French
king had no value whatsoever. Charles relaxed a little. He
called on Francis and was polite to him, but he said that he
would not trouble an invalid with discussions of affairs of
state. Francis sent for Marguerite of Navarre. Instead, however, of being gullibly persuaded by the charms of Francis's
sister, Charles, certainly his own master, made his terms a
little harder. Then Francis capitulated—probably not many
hours before Charles, harassed by treason on the part of the
Duke of Milan, would have capitulated himself.

On February 14, he agreed to give Charles Burgundy,
Milan, Naples and practically every other bit of land Charles
could think of; to marry Charles' own sister; to pardon
Charles' ally, the Duke of Bourbon; to pay Charles 200,000
crowns; to swear perpetual friendship with him; to support
him on land and sea; and to give Charles his two eldest sons
as hostages: He promised further to return into captivity if he
broke even one article of the treaty and he swore "on his faith
as a gentleman and a king" to observe it faithfully.

On March 18, he reached the border. The Bidassoa divides
France and Spain, and in midstream a raft was anchored. On
this raft, Francis and his two sons changed places. Francis
then was rowed ashore, and once landed, he leaped onto a
horse, and galloped to St. Jean-de-Luz. He ate hastily there,
and was on his way again. By nightfall he had reached Bay-

onne where his court awaited him, and then the next day they moved to Cognac.

At Cognac, the hidden became apparent. Lannoy, the Spanish ambassador, asked him when he would turn over the lands agreed on.

"As soon as possible," he replied, "but you must realize that I face difficulties. My subjects resent strongly that I have alienated French territory, and I need a short while to pacify them."

It was an alibi—and it was also a deliberate lie. For even when in Spain, he had consulted lawyers lay and canon, and they had advised him that an oath made under compulsion was not binding. Instantly he had summoned the French Ambassador to his cell. "I am acting under vile duress, and I pledge to you that I am no king of yours if I sacrifice one right of France."

It took two months to be able to live up to this. French ambassadors tossed on hard beds and complained loudly as they rode muleback over snow-choked Alpine passes. They were ferried over the stormy English Channel. They crossed over the Venetian lagoon in cockle gondolas. They shivered in some damp Roman inn.

One even went to Madrid.

"The gold indemnity will be paid in full immediately if Francis may but break the treaty to the extent of holding Burgundy. But that land is French and it must stay French."

"Francis is a scoundrel!" cried Charles.

Then, half forgetting himself, he blurted out a challenge to a personal combat.

"I will give up my land to the devil," he continued, "or to Sforza who is his servant, before I dot another *i* or cross another *t* with the false Frenchman!"

It should be pointed out that there were rumors, later confirmed, that this Duke of Milan was listening to the Emperor's enemies.

Then Charles turned to one of his officers.

"See to it that the French princes are treated as common prisoners."

Word went north—as Charles intended it to do—that the Dauphin and his pitiable brother (both, it so happened, future kings of France) were dragged from stern fortress to stern fortress, shut in behind barred windows, and cut off from all consort with any Frenchman.

But instead of frightening Francis, it stiffened him, and on the eighteenth of May he put aside all hesitation over signing a document which he himself had engineered. It was the high sounding and solemn-purposed League of Cognac.

"To protect the peace of Christendom"—and to secure other more material benefits—Francis, Sforza, Venice, and the Pope bound themselves to act together. To maintain the high tone, and to ensure at least English neutrality, Henry VIII was invited to "adhere," and since that "friend of humanists" and also of the ladies was already casting amorous eyes toward a certain comely Anne Boleyn, and still hoped that the Pope might coöperate in his divorce problem, he did eagerly. As a crowning irony, the very man it was directed against was offered a place in it. The Emperor of Germany—the Holy Roman Emperor, to give to him his true, trumpery title— was requested, in a word, to make war upon the King of Spain and Naples, and to help filch Milan and Burgundy from him. The difficulty was that they were the same person.

Naturally he refused.

"It does not," he said, smiling like a great gentleman, "comport quite with my dignity to enter a confederation made principally against my own states."

War blazed at his quiet sarcasm.

Venice had an army back of the Oglio, and she went through the motions of moving it forward toward the Adda under that stocky murderer and good general when he chose to be, the Duke of Urbino. Money was paid into the hands of the Bishop of Lodi and the Castellan of Mus, and those two rogues—one of them a soldier churchman, but the other a

frank brigand—departed separately in the direction of the
Cantons, where they would waste precious time seeing how
little of it they need spend to get an acceptable amount of
fighting men, and how much they could retain for themselves.
Even the Pope acted decisively a second time. Count Guido
Rangone—whose mother had been so helpful to Pope Leo—
had long since been dispatched to Piacenza with 6,000 papal
soldiers. Now Clement sent re-enforcements, 4,000 chosen foot-
soldiers, it was said. Giovanni delle Bande Nere was their cap-
tain-general. It was a sure guarantee that there would be a
fight.

Aretino received these tidings after a dull winter by the
Mincio, and if his patron was disturbed by them—the Marquis being a paid general of the papacy who at the same time
held his title from the Emperor—he most definitely was not.
Now at last he saw a chance for action. Things were happening in the great world. Italy was being re-carved, and the one
man whom he genuinely loved (and who fortunately loved
him also) would do the carving. He must sit in at the ensuing
banquet. Those who make history or even live significant lives
—unless they happen to be Cellinis—are usually negligent
about writing down details, while the paid chroniclers have
an irritating if a practical way of confining their remarks to
dukes, marquises, barons, bishops and kings and others of
the rich or powerful. Consequently, we cannot give an exact
date. But one day toward the middle of June, he leapt upon
a spirited steed. Jauntily upon his head there sat a gay beretta
with a golden clasp, such as we see in Marcantonio Raimondi's
famous engraving of him. He wore an embroidered shirt—
possibly one of those finally given him by the Marquis. His
beard crinkled, neatly curled, and his eyes were animated. He
came forth from the mighty Reggia, and his mount caracoled
as he did not let it have its head crossing the hard earth of the
wide drill ground in front of it. He turned toward the Porto
Pradella. Nobody noticed him, for he often took a morning
canter across the flowered meadows outside the city.

But this time he did not canter straightway back. He continued riding. He rode southward and eastward. Just how he went we do not know. Bozzolo to Piadena to Cremona and from there, via Monticelli and Caorso (crossing the wide Po) to Piacenza would be logical under ordinary circumstances, but now there were objections. Lombardy was a blasted inferno.

"I rode across its whole length," reported Nicholas Carew, Henry VIII's ambassador to Venice, "and saw no laborers in the fields, no dwellers in the villages, and whose families were reduced to beggary." The chimneys and the walls of what had once been houses stood like skeletons. The grain was not harvested in the fields. When it did not stand in burnt and blackened rows, it had been left to go to seed. The pigs, rooting further and further way from home, had become wild swine. If you did see human beings they darted away from you with the wild eyes of frightened animals. Furthermore, all the key cities were in Imperial hands. Cremona, blasted by the relentless sun, lay at the ingenious mercies of a band of mercenaries and it is not likely that their sportive torturing of the unfortunate townsfolk would have kept them too busy to have given a reception he would not enjoy to so warm and so well-known a partizan of their great adversary. At Carpi was a band of thirty Spaniards. They had left their native land as foot-soldiers, but they had stolen horses, and mounted on them, they were sowing terror. For the few ducats and the letters he probably carried (to say nothing of his Gonzaga steed), they would have toasted Aretino.

Most compelling of all, however, he had just gotten word that Giovanni delle Bande Nere would not be at Piacenza when he reached there. He would be at Lodi Vecchia. The Duke of Urbino had set this small city which was safely behind the Adda as the rendezvous of the two armies, and since the young Medici was junior general of the two, he had no choice but to comply with this. On June 28, he and Urbino met there.

Bronzino   *Florence*

GIOVANNI DELLE BANDE NERE

"The great Giovanni de' Medici who was gifted from the cradle with as much largeness of soul as any man that ever lived . . . I can already hear the Pope's shouts of joy. He thinks that he is better off for having lost such a man."—*Aretino.*

"Ten thousand Swiss mercenaries—those being hired by the Bishop of Lodi and the Castellan of Mus—are expected instantly," said Francesco Maria, "and we will be safe here until they reach us."

It took that day and the next one for Giovanni to convince his colleague that they would lose valuable time also.

"We must advance toward Milan and we must do so instantly."

On June 30—after threatening to withdraw and fight alone —he won the argument. The joint army started forward. Marignano, now, as eleven years earlier, a key village, was the destination.

Every bit of circumstantial evidence—and there is no other —indicates that Aretino joined it at this point.

There is no reason to suppose that the third meeting between Aretino and Giovanni delle Bande Nere was any less enthusiastic than the two before.

The young leader grasped his friend so firmly in his warrior grip that the writer, whose scars had not yet whitened, gave an exclamation.

"Careful, Excellency," he cried.

"Oh yes, I forgot that they had cut you."

Reminiscences next.

"Martha?"

"That was four summers ago!"

"And the Countess Madrina?"

"Oh! So you remember her!"

Gossip after that, and politics. Separately—upon those rare occasions when they could be disentangled. Otherwise together—which was almost all the time.

"Rome?" Giovanni delle Bande Nere wanted to know.

Aretino reflected. Telling all the latest doing at the Tiberine sink, he must be careful to be accurate, for it was important for Giovanni delle Bande Nere to know every shift of Roman breezes. Rome was his employer now.

"Schomberg says this," he said. "Bishop Schio that. Just

now archmule Giberti's influence is thus and so. But it may
be later——"

"Cousin Clement?" asked the young de' Medici.

Aretino replied in verse.

> A papacy made up of compliment,
> Debate, yielding the point, and hesitance;
> Of "furthermore," "then," "but," "yet," "well,"
>   "perchance,"
> "Haply," and such like terms inconsequent;
> Of thought, conjecture, counsel, argument;
> Thin guesses to keep up bold countenance;
> Fine words and shifts, expenses to prevent;
> Of sluggard feet, of tame neutrality,
> Of patience and parade to outward view. . . .

Giovanni delle Bande Nere interrupted him.

"Did you write that?"

"No. Old woman Berni did. But it is your cousin, my Lord.
For to lean against Clement is to lean against a weathervane."

Then outright scandal. Stories about the various courtiers
and their doings. Mirthful stories. For the most part, bawdy
stories. Giovanni delle Bande Nere laughed at them. Suddenly
his laugh became a scowl.

"We have courtiers here too," he said in explanation.

"Courtiers? Who?" asked Aretino.

"The great Duke of Urbino!"

"He? Impossible!"

"Well, then, how else account for him? For mark you, Pietro, he is neither a poltroon nor a fool yet he acts much like
both of them."

That much he voiced his feelings, and then seething with
puzzlement and irritation, he grumbled inwardly.

"*Duke,* by the Lord! *Urbino!* . . . By God," he cried suddenly, "you could just as well be Marquis."

It came to him like an illuminating idea.

"And you will be Marquis!" he said.

"Marquis?" stammered Aretino.

"It is the thing," he said. "Pietro," he added, "if I live through this year's campaign, I will make you one."

"Marquis of what?" asked Aretino.

"Of Arezzo," said the young de' Medici.

> Under Milan, "Pietro, if good luck,"
> He said to me a hundred times, not one,
> "And God's grace bring me safely through this war,
> I'll make you sovereign lord of your own town."

Thus, many years afterwards, he remembered the incident, when it was but one of his not-attained dreams, and he wrote these four lines in a *capitolo* — or *terza-rima,* but very prose-like poem — to Cosimo, the Grand Duke of Tuscany, who was straightforward Giovanni delle Bande Nere's very tortuous but no less able son. Possibly he thought that pale Cosimo might, somehow or other, be persuaded to redeem this alleged promissary note given by his father. Probably — since he knew Cosimo — he only faintly hoped so. But in late June of the year 1526, it was a soon-to-happen reality. "Pietro Aretino, Marquis of Arezzo!" It was the tune beat by his horse's hoofs on the roads of Italy as they moved toward the city of the plain.

But there were no marquisates won either by Pietro or by anyone else in the flurried skirmishes — they were not battles — fought without the sprawling metropolis in the days that followed. For despite his high hopefulness, and Giovanni delle Bande Nere's resolute and forceful ability, it turned out to be an *opera buffa* campaign.

"The King of France," thus runs the nursery jingle, "he had ten thousand men. He marched them in, and marched them out again." Francesco Maria della Rovere, Duke of Urbino and generalissimo of the allied armies, had more than double this provision of soldiers. His infantry — "the backbone," as Machiavelli puts it, "of any army" — numbered, counting Medici's well-trained and seasoned troopers, 20,000; and he had besides those men-at-arms, light and heavy cavalry, good artillery and full supply of food and ammunition. The Imperials, whom he now almost surrounded, and who, in turn, had to use up a good part of their forces in bottling up the Duke of Milan in his own castle, could scarcely muster half that number. They were unpaid. They lacked provision. They were further quartered in a city, the walls of which were notably weak (being in many places merely the walls of dwellings) and most of whose inhabitants, ground under by their arrogant oppression, would have risen up and rioted at the least encouragement. But the beetle-browed nephew of Pope Julius not only emulated His Mother Goose Majesty, but went him one better. For when he marched right in, he crawled, arguing and bickering every step of the way. And when he marched right out again, he ran.

The excuse given was the dilatory Swiss. For they were still missing, not being — one supposes — as chuckle-headed bargainers as the grafting purposes of the envoys of the allies required.

Francesco Maria reached Marignano with no more opposition than that offered by the dikes and ditches of this cut-up section of Italy, and then he noticed this fact. He sat down like a spoiled child who, not able to get his way, suddenly goes limp in the middle of his nursery.

"Our troops are inexperienced," he said. "This is an important enterprise. It is not wise to go further without re-enforcements."

It took three days of arguing even to budge him.

Then a messenger arrived.

"The first thousand from the Cantons have reached Bergamo."

"We may then advance a little."

And thus halting and then moving onward and halting and moving onward again, they crept slowly forward. On July 6, the roofs and towers of Milan at last were visible. In eight days, they had advanced eight miles.

It was as far as they ever got. Historians differ, but the

consensus is that the Duke of Urbino was playing a two-faced game. Should the Imperials threaten Venice, he must in duty block them, but there was no reason not to let them trouble Clement whose family had filched his lands from him. And now suddenly he had a chance to do more than be dilatory. During his snail-like progress, re-enforcements had reached the men he marched against. They were not many: 800 Spanish footsoldiers. But their leader was the Duke of Bourbon—first nobleman of France, but now a turncoat—and they brought with them 10,000 ducats. Spirits rose. If Charles sent them this money, he had not forgotten them. When it was still black on the morning of July 7, the long range bombards of the allied armies found the gates of Milan and hammered them, but instead of flying or surrendering, those inside them made a sortie. They marched boldly to the allied lines where they opened fire.

Urbino took advantage of the moment of confusion this brought. "Our troops are in disorder!" he shouted.

Certain officers rode up. "Your Excellency, they stand firm," they told him.

"Sound retreat!" he ordered.

A retreat still left his army covering Venice, fulfilled what he was hired for.

A Swiss colonel appeared and he was furious. "Five thousand from the Cantons hold your flank, and we have never fled from a battlefield. Our national honor is at stake!"

"Order a withdrawal!" said Urbino.

Struck dumb, but thus far still in rank, the best army in north Italy turned its back upon a desperate handful. But they did not stay in order long. Night retreat is always dangerous, and it is doubly so when unprepared for, when reasons for it are unknown. No foe being seen, imagination did its work. Panic started harrying the stragglers. Arms were thrown aside and baggage, cannons, food and munitions left behind. From the field of battle on which no battle had been more than begun, disciplined withdrawal turned to rout.

Giovanni delle Bande Nere alone stood firm.

"Dolts and idiots," he shouted, "will you flee by night from a battle which you could have won by day?"

His own troops supported him.

Aretino stayed with him too. Bullets whistled past his head, but though he did not believe in heroism, he kept unruffled.

"The new Caesar!" he sneered. "I came, I saw, I—ran away!"

Then as the dawn broke and Giovanni's troops withdrew in order, another scathing thing to say about Urbino came into his head. He took off the helmet one of Giovanni's officers had given him, and using it to write upon, set down a sentence.

"The Duke for breastplate wants a city wall!"

Why, it was in meter! It was the first line of a sonnet!

One after another, he composed swiftly the subsequent thirteen lines, and it is a pity they no longer survive, for judging from the way this bit of writing irritated the Duke, and delighted everybody else, it must have been one of his best ones. He handed it to Giovanni. The young general took it, and his face reddened as he shook with laughter. He looked at Aretino, but in a different way. He had always liked the fellow, but he had also always slightly suspected him. These writers were not soldiers quite. They were just a shade too plausible. They said they did things, but you always half suspected a good story. But now he had to modify his ideas. For here certainly was a man after his own heart. Even under fire, he could still ply his trade calmly and efficiently. There was a new warmth as he shook him by the hand.

But it was not merely in an old friendship, freshly cemented, and indeed made stronger than ever, during the morning after that disastrous night before, that Aretino found the weeks that followed pleasant and profitable. He had, of course, accomplished that. His unruffled humor and his witty presence of mind had swept away all reticences and reserves, and the men of action now accepted him not merely as someone that they liked, but as one of their number.

But he did other things that summer than capitalizing on that relationship and riding confidently with Giovanni and his captains, as he watched the young leader of guerrillas forge himself slowly on the anvil of experience into the first great Italian strategist since Rome fell.

"Giovanni delle Bande Nere," said Guiccardini, "fought many engagements that year which brought glory to the Italian infantry, but likewise hurt our cause because so many needless lives were lost."

But that is a politician's view, and gentlemen of that devious profession regard any victory as suspect which is not won through their tortuous negotiations.

He took part in the life of the soldiers.

There was a *gaudeamus* — as he so aptly put it — on the packed earth of one of the few Lombard barnyards that still flourished. The rough soldiery of the unequalled leader burst in upon an unhappy farmer. They laughed raucously as he ran hither and thither, trying frantically (while good-natured sword points pricked his unappreciative buttocks) to save clucking hens, squealing porkers and the one calf he still had left, from being roasts and fricassees. They flung back at him the not consoling reminder that since he had become commissary to the army they would now protect him: they would guard — in other words — that which no longer remained from anyone who tried to take it.

Aretino was one of them.

There was a military hanging. A young footsoldier of Rangone's army had taken comprehendible liberties with a peasant girl, and in her first reasonable reluctance to admit cooperation — and perhaps urged by her parents who thought money might forthcome — she had cried rape as loudly and convincingly as possible. Count Rangone grimly sentenced him. Then girl and father and mother who did not want any half orphan child or grandchild changed their tune. They wept and begged forgiveness for him, but the unconvinced general sat obdurately in his saddle and said discipline was discipline.

Aretino saw him kick his heels on Lombard air.

There was the jape played on Niccolo Machiavelli. That sallow civil servant with the thin lips of a shrewd and calculating fellow and the bulging forehead of a man from Mars, was the failure at politics who had written the most famous treatise on the subject ever penned. He was also, though not a soldier, author of a volume on the art of war. He came to the camp upon some pettifogging mission or other, and Giovanni delle Bande Nere asked him if he would like to drill the army.

Would a cat eat fish!

Then, for three long hours, march and countermarch were executed at his shrill command, and more and more complicated grew the formations, until at last even the confident theorist realized that by no method out of any book that he had ever written or read, could he hope to disentangle them.

By then it was high noon.

"Would you now like me to relieve you?" Giovanni suggested.

Machiavelli yielded to him.

There were no more than two or three orders and the maze became an ordered column.

Aretino was among those who bit their lips grimly so as not to spoil the joke by laughing at it, and who drank gulps of the extra ration of wine Giovanni delle Bande Nere issued to his soldiers to make up for the bad morning they had put in.

He plied also his own trade, never letting himself forget that galloping with the young Medici was but a pleasant interlude. In his saddlebags was the unfinished manuscript of *La Cortegiana* which he had started rewriting in Rome, and now with a cresset for illumination, and with a widened cynical appreciation of the flagrant lack of honesty of courts and curias, he concluded it. It was the first really authentic product in more than fifteen centuries of that smilingly detached, if also usually sarcastically malicious way, of regarding man's humanness, which alone can beget true comedy. Since they buried the Carthaginian émigré, Publius Terence, to be exact!

He prepared finally, a raft to get ashore with, should the floods come.

Watching these happenings and indeed — as has been pointed out — taking part in most of them, polishing his comedy, and riding galliardly with the active young Giovanni, Aretino prepared for all contingencies by his contacts with Mantua. He wrote to Federigo Gonzaga every chance he had. On the surface, there was no ulterior motive. One friend living an active and an interesting life corresponded with another who was chafing in inactive boredom. But actually, his letters were a bid to be remembered — a bid to be remembered with good will.

Evidently, they achieved their purpose.

"For some days," wrote the Marquis on July 25, "I have wanted to have word from you, and to learn where you were. Three days ago I discovered that you were at the camp, and since then it has been my intention to write you by the first courier who went that way, and to ask you to give me some news of how the war is going and to send me something that you had written. You can imagine, therefore, how delighted I was with your letter of the eighteenth. I want to thank you for it as much as possible. The three sonnets which you sent me pleased me as much as possible. I read them and re-read them, and I enjoyed them as I do all the products of your skillful pen. I am also looking forward with the greatest antici-pation to your fine comedy, and the sooner you send it to me the better pleased I will be. Indeed if you wish to delight me and have me always in your debt you will see to it that no one sees it before I do."

Second paragraph:

"I will be glad to give you a good horse, but unfortunately all my horses — on account of having changed their stables and gone into new ones — have taken cold, and they are now being treated for this. But yours will soon be in good health and the week after next I will send him to you."

Two weeks later:

"I have today received your most elegant epistle, and I lack words to thank you for it. The bearer who carries my answer rides the Turkish steed I promised you."

Toward the end of August:

"I beg you to continue the office you have undertaken, writing me now of one thing and now of another. And when your very witty letters are accompanied by, and adorned with, the addition of some fine sonnet or madrigal, they bring me all the greater pleasure, and increase my debt to you. Incidentally, your learned comedy has now arrived, and is filling me with delight. It is the true mirror of the modern court and of present day life."

Early in September:

"You will be presented on my behalf with a jerkin and a vest of mine. I send them to you, not because they are what your merits deserve, because those deserve great presents and this is a small one, nor to match my willingness to do you favors, because I wish to do you greater favors than this. I send them to you because you asked for them."

To Count Guido Rangone:

"Our Messer Pietro Aretino will ask of Your Lordship a favor which he desires of you regarding a certain matter having to do with a friend of his, as you will better be able to understand from his own mouth. And although I know that without my intercessions he will be able to obtain from Your Lordship all that he demands, both because this matter is entirely just and worthy, and because Your Lordship loves Messer Pietro deservedly by reason of his many virtues, none the less to satisfy myself I do wish to pray Your Lordship that you will content him for my love also. And I assure Your Lordship that in this you will do me the very greatest pleasure on account of the singular love that I have for the said Messer Pietro who is my chiefest and best friend."

To Aretino again — who had apparently raised questions on this subject:

"I want you to know that I have an extraordinary fondness for you, as much as for anyone who lives in this world, and that the demonstrations of friendliness which you have made toward me have left me very satisfied. Nevertheless your doubt pleased me if only since it has given you the subject for so fine and so beautiful a letter."

With such unmistakable evidences of good will supplementing his close comradeship with Giovanni delle Bande Nere, Aretino rode the crest of the wave.

The trough followed in due order.

Francesco Maria della Rovere was again responsible. "The folly and the delay of the vacillating Duke of Urbino" — or the calculating and treachery of the vindictive one — did not end upon that night of July 7. He made a summer's and an autumn's job of it. He advanced only when he found it wise or necessary to make a show of valor, and the gains of each slow move forward were more than nullified by the subsequent and swift withdrawal. He left his army, and he came back to it. He gave to the enemies of Italy the precious gift of time.

Charles did not fail to take the fullest advantage of it, and since man power was his most pressing need, he sent emissaries to Germany. They faced George Frundsberg, a Protestant and a free soldier.

"What terms for raising an army?"

"Right to harry the Pope!" was Frundsberg's answer.

"Agreed to," said Catholic Charles' negotiators.

On the last day of October, consequently, frightened fugitives arrived breathlessly at the allied headquarters. Red faced *lanzknechts*, they panted, are gathering between Bolzano and Merano in the lower Tyrol!

"How many?" they were asked incredulously.

Thirteen thousand, was the answer — some said fourteen thousand. They are all followers of Martin Luther's heresies. George Frundsberg is their leader, and indeed paying them from his own pocket. New Babylon is their destination, and a golden chain to bind Pope Clement with is part of their equipment.

"They march now on Salo on the Lago di Garda!" came a second message.

This was hardly credible, Salo being actually in Italy.

Next a swift horseman rode up, and bore even more disastrous tidings.

"They have reached Castiglione delle Stivere in the territories of Mantua!"

They had crossed the mountain ramparts, in other words, and they now stood upon a rolling hilltop with nothing between them and the Po valley but gently sloping vineyards, wheat-fields and perhaps a handful of ditches.

The sun gleamed on blond or ruddy hair, and was reflected sullenly from dinted helms and habergeons as history turned back a thousand years.

"A new Alaric or Attila!" the poets warned.

Though it shone also on the locks and barrels of modern arquebuses, a thick column of black smoke rising grimly to the northward from burned villages that had been the scenes of violence and butchery, seemed to bear out the classic reference.

Giovanni delle Bande Nere was the one person on the peninsula with the ability—and with the courage and impetuosity—to stop these new barbarians. And this time he did not either have to await orders that never came, or else march on his own initiative. Even the Duke of Urbino was now anxious for action, realizing that the unloosed German army would not only bring discomfort to Pope Clement, but might also, marching toward the Eternal City, deflect far enough to the east of the direct course to wreak havoc on his own domains as well. But he had no time to reorganize his now demoralized army. With the ducal blessing, therefore—with the Duke's admonition to do what should have been the Duke's own job—and with 600 men-at-arms, a troop of light cavalry and 9000 well trained infantry, the captain of the black bands flung himself north-eastward. Aretino went with him. A great moment in his career was about to arrive. He would see the young leader, to whose destiny he had now linked his own, prove himself to be the man of Italy's hour. He would see Rome's still disunited daughter save herself as she ought to be saved — by her own strong hand.

But for "that thief, fortune," nothing could have kept this from coming to pass, and God knows how many pages of humiliating history would never have been written down in Italy's from then on tragic book. That thief, fortune, and its light of love, self-seeking treachery! For if facing two ways started the sad story, facing two ways completed it. This time it was Alfonso d'Este, Duke of Ferrara. Making cannon was his chosen hobby, and this time he combined business with pleasure. Not wishing to join the Germans openly, yet at the same time — and for much the same reasons as Urbino — not reluctant to see Clement in difficulties, he sent four of them to General Frundsberg. One would have been enough.

Guessing rightly — by the simple process of imagining what he himself would do under like circumstances — the hurrying Medici discarded the two obvious routes for the invaders and marched straight to Governolo. It was a small town eight miles southeast of Mantua, and situated in the V made by the conjunction of the great Po with the little Mincio, it was protected on two sides. The third side was covered by a line of lime-kilns.

There he found the Germans entrenched.

"Forward march!" he ordered.

For if the two rivers protected them, they also cut off retreat.

Step by hard-fought step, the Italians advanced, and victory was in their hands when a chance shot from a Ferrara field-piece found its mark. Giovanni delle Bande Nere. He sank helpless to the ground, and his troops, after picking him up, withdrew uncertainly. They carried him, as the dusk deepened, to Mantua. Two days later he was dead.

Aretino was at his side in that hour, and for two weeks thereafter he was as good as dead himself in his deep gloom. Then suddenly his resilience reasserted itself. His pen still was sharp and facile and there were ink and paper in the world. He made use of both of them. Sitting in his small chamber where he had taken temporary refuge, he wrote swiftly a vivid composition which was like nothing he had ever penned before. He addressed it to Francesco degli Albizzi, now Giovanni's son Cosimo's secretary. But he saw to it that the whole world would read it, and he put into its 2000-odd words the full measure of his love and admiration. It was an *in memoriam* that has not been often even equalled. So doing, he paid a debt of gratitude he genuinely acknowledged. But he also served himself. For he added a positive to his negative, demonstrating to the glory-loving princes whom he wished to be his paymasters that he could praise as well as blame.

"When the time drew near," thus it ran, "which the Fates under God's approval had appointed for the death of our commander, His Highness moved with his accustomed fierceness against the town of Governolo. There the enemy had fortified themselves. And while he was attacking their position near some furnaces, a shot struck him in the leg. It was the same leg that once before had been wounded by an arquebus.

"And no sooner did this happen than fear and dismay ran through the army. Ardor and joy died in the hearts of all. Not a man but complained bitterly that Destiny should have slain blindly so great a leader: one indeed whose equal no one could remember; and at a time like this, on the eve of such great and portentous happenings, and in Italy's hour of dire need.

"The captains, who had followed him out of love and veneration, blamed Fortune and his own great rashness for their loss. They spoke of his age which was just ripe for mighty undertakings. They spoke of his capacity in every difficulty. They sighed, for they remembered the largeness of his ideas and the greatness of his valor. They could not refrain from recalling his comradeship. He had shared everything with them—even to his cloak. They could not keep from speaking of the providential acuteness of his genius. They kept themselves warm with their warm-hearted lamentations. In the meantime, the snow fell in blinding swirls about them, as he was borne in a litter to the house of Lord Luigi Gonzaga.

"There that same evening—" this was the one calculating touch—"the Duke of Urbino came to visit him. For the Duke loved Giovanni. Indeed, he reverenced him so greatly that, nobleman though he was, he was afraid almost to speak in his presence, which was greatly to his credit. And, as soon as the wounded man saw the Duke, he showed that he was deeply touched.

"Then, seeing the condition he was in, the Duke said to him with great emotion:

" 'It is not enough for you to be renowned and glorious in war. You must also preserve your good name by observing the rites of your religion. Those rites brought you into the world !'

"Giovanni realized that he was talking about the confession. 'I have done my duty in all things,' he replied. 'I will do it in this matter too.'

"When the Duke had left, he began to talk to me. He spoke of Lucantonio"—this was Lucantonio Cuppano, his right eye—"with the greatest affection.

"I said, 'We will send for him.'

" 'Do you wish,' he answered, 'to have a captain of his importance leave the fighting to talk to a wounded man?'

"He recalled also the Count of San Secondo, saying: 'At least if he were here, there would be someone who could take my place !'

"Sometimes he scratched his head, and then savagely bit his nails.

" 'What is going to happen to me?' he wondered.

"Then, as if he answered his own question: 'I have never been a coward in my life !'

"But I, being urged by the doctors, went to him and spoke as follows:

" 'I would wrong your immortal soul if I lied to you and told you that death is the cure of all ills, and that it is more feared than it deserves. For there is a way of saving you, and it is best you agree to it willingly. Give, then, these sawbones your consent to cut away the wreckage made by that field-piece. In a week you can make Italy queen again. She is now a slave. And your lost leg will be a medal of valor in place of the one given you by the King, which you would never wear. Wounds and the loss of limbs are the honorable badges of those who serve the god of war.'

" 'Let them get to work immediately,' he replied.

"At this, the doctors came in. They praised the courage of his decision, and set to work. Before dark they had finished their preparations. Then they gave him some drugs, and went out to make ready their instruments.

"At about supper time, he was seized suddenly with vomiting. 'The omens of Caesar!' he said to me. 'I must now think of things other than this life.' Then he folded his hands, and made a vow to go on a pilgrimage to St. James at Compostella.

"Time passed, and presently the worthy surgeons returned. They had in their hands their saws, and they asked for eight or ten people to hold him during the agony of cutting.

" 'Not even twenty could hold me,' he told them smiling. Then he sat up with face as resolute as could be, and held in his own hands the candle that gave light for his operation.

"I fled, and putting my hands into my ears, I heard two cries only, and then I heard him calling to me. 'I am cured,' he said when I had reached him. He turned this way and that way, and seemed filled with great joy. Indeed, if the Duke of Urbino had not forbidden it, he would have had them bring forward the foot with the piece of the leg still hanging to it. As it was, he laughed at us because we could not even bear to see what he had suffered.

"His sufferings were worse than those of Alexander and of Trajan. Yet one of these kept a cheerful face while he pulled out a small arrowhead and the other laughed when he severed his own nerve. Indeed his pain, which had worn off, came back about two hours before dawn. It brought every kind of torment. I heard him beat against the wall in frenzy and was stabbed to the heart. I dressed in an instant and ran to him. As soon as he saw me he began to chide me, saying that the thought of cowards caused him more anguish than his wound. He talked with me in this manner, hoping that if he refused even to think of his misfortune, he could outwit death in the ambush it had laid for his soul.

"But as day dawned, things grew so much worse that he made his will. He dispensed many thousands of *scudi* in money and in goods among those who had served him, but he set aside only four *giulii* for his funeral. The Duke of Urbino was named executor. Then he came to confession most Christianly, and seeing his confessor, said to him:

"'Father, inasmuch as I have followed the profession of arms, I have lived according to the customs of a soldier; just as, had I put on the habit you wear, I would have lived like a man of religion. If it were not that it is not lawful, I would willingly confess myself in the presence of everybody. For I have never done anything unworthy of myself!'

"It was after Vespers when the Marquis of Mantua came to his bedside. He was moved to do this by his own innate goodness, and also because I begged him to. He kissed the wounded man tenderly and spoke words which I never would have believed any prince except Francesco Maria would have known how to utter. His Excellency ended with this saying:

"'Since your fierce pride never allowed you to make use of anything that was mine lest it be said that you had yielded to my will, ask me now one favor that is worthy of us both.'

"'Love me when I am dead,' replied Giovanni.

"'The heroism with which you have acquired so much glory,' said the Marquis, 'will make you not merely loved, but adored, by me and by all others.'

"When the Marquis had concluded, Giovanni turned to me and directed me to have Madonna Maria send his son, Cosimo, to him. At which Death who had already cited him to the place underground, began to renew his agonies.

"Already the members of his household were crowding around his bed. Inferiors mingled with their superiors without any respect to rank. All were burdened down by cold misery as they wept for the bread, the hopes and the service which they were losing with their master. Each one tried to catch the dying man's eye with his own in order to show how great his affection was.

"Thus surrounded, he took the hand of the Marquis, saying: 'You are today losing the greatest friend and the best servant you ever had.' But His Most Illustrious Lordship, putting on a false mask of joy and changing the tone of his voice, tried to make him believe that he was going to get well. Then Giovanni, for whom death had no terrors even when he knew he was going to die, started to talk about how to carry on the war. He proposed things that would have been stupendous even if he were going to live, instead of being on his death bed. Thus he continued his struggle until the ninth hour of the night. It was the even of the feast of St. Andrew.

"But at last his agony became more than he could bear, and he asked me to put him to sleep by reading to him. I did this, and he seemed to pass from doze to doze.

"After he had slept for a quarter of an hour, he awoke.

"'I dreamed that I was making my will,' he said, 'and now look, I am cured. I will teach the Germans how to fight, and that I can avenge myself!'

"But when he had said that, the light failed him. It gave place to eternal darkness. Then he himself asked for the extreme unction, and having received that sacrament, he said: 'I do not wish to die among all these bandages.' So we brought a camp bed for him and laid him upon it. And while his mind slept, he was taken captive by death.

"In this way met his end the great Giovanni de' Medici, who was gifted from the cradle with as much largeness of soul as any man that ever lived.

"The vigor of his spirit was incredible. Liberality meant more to him than power. He gave more to his soldiers than he kept for himself though he was a soldier too. He endured hardships with a patient graciousness. His anger never got control of him. And everything that he said he was going to do, he did.

"He valued brave men more than he did riches and indeed only desired the latter to keep the valiant, who served him, from going hungry. There was nothing about his men's lodgings or their conduct in action that he did not know about, for in battle he fought side by side with privates in the ranks and in peace-time he made no distinction between himself and others. Indeed, the very clothes he wore proved he was himself a fighting man. They were worn and shabby and they had armor stains upon the legs, and arms, and chest. Above all things, he was eager to win praise and glory. He pretended to despise them, but he really coveted them. But what more than anything else won the hearts of his followers was that he said 'Follow me!' instead of 'Go ahead of me!' in time of peril.

"His virtues were his own, his faults those of his youth, and God knows that if he had lived out his days everybody would have known his bounty just as I already knew it, for certainly he was the most outgoing friend there ever was. He sought only honor and not his own interest, and what proves I speak truth instead of flattery is that he sold all his possessions to his own son to get money to pay the army's overdue salaries. He was always the first to bestride his steed, and always the last one to dismount. His bold nature loved playing a single hand, and he could plan as well as execute, yet in counsels of war he did not haughtily say that those of a known reputation should have charge of things. But he did try to see to it that those who sat around the table knew the trade of war.

"He had marvelous skill at patching up the quarrels of his men, and he knew just when to keep his mastery over them by love or fear or punishment or reward. No one knew better than he when to use deception and when strength in an attack, and he never dinned the ears of his soldiers with lying braggadocio, but exhorted them with the stupendous sayings of his innate valiancy. Laziness was his prime enemy. He was the first man to use Turkish steeds. He was the first man to insist on comfortable clothing for the soldiers and he was best pleased when they ate and drank well.

"As for himself, he cared for none of these things, and he quenched his own thirst with water merely colored with wine.

"In short, all had to envy him and none knew how to imitate him."

Then Aretino remembered where he was, and what the circumstances were. The bells, tolling on the damp and frosty air the new day of December 10, 1526, came from the church towers of a Mantua that was already—though it was not molested thus far—behind the German lines; and the large halls of the enormous Reggia were filled with the agitated followers of the dead general, who could not decide, as they tried futilely to get a little warmth from huge fireplaces that were still inadequate, whether to hope against hope that the Duke of Urbino would now rally an army in which they could serve their country, or to go over to the enemy and at least be paid. Italy had been betrayed to Germany.

And one man was responsible—even more so than Francesco Maria della Rovere if only because he made Francesco Marias possible. Pope Clement VII, that yea-and-nay pontiff who had tried desperately to be all things to all men and who now ended by being very little to very few of them. The Pope also, who had employed Giberti, who had hired Achille della Volta.

Even as Giovanni was fighting for him, he was suddenly become neutral again, and so doing he had destroyed all confidence.

Aretino decided to add this to his letter.

"Would God that I lied," he concluded, "but Florence and Rome will soon find out what it means not to have this man among the living. Yet I can already hear the Pope's shout of joy. He thinks that he is better off for having lost such a man."

It did not take one jot away from the effectiveness of the praising paragraphs. In fact, it heightened it.

And it reminded certain people that he had not forgotten what they had done.

CHAPTER IX

The Fifth Evangelist

IN THE meantime he had his own life to reorganize. The death of the young de' Medici was, as far as Italy was concerned, like the breaking of a strong dam that holds back an inundation. Temporary disasters could be expected. But to Aretino it was far more serious. High waters, after all, recede—if you give them time. But while a peninsula, which has two thousand years of history behind it, and as many more ahead, can afford to wait, an individual cannot. Particularly if he has Aretino's egocentric temperament. Like all persons of an impatient vitality who approach middle years without having yet attained the goal aspired to, he had become acutely conscious of the flight of time. For he had, as he realized very clearly, but his short hour to strut and fret upon the stage, or to posture vainly there, and besides that the prizes that he wished for would not, probably, appeal to him when he was older. A new island rising above the waters must be found immediately. The new island, was, however, one he had rejected earlier. The letters he had exchanged with Federigo Gonzaga while at Giovanni delle Bande Nere's camp had made him realize that at Mantua he would at least have bed and salary. And bed and salary were singularly desirable to him now that hopes of greater things were gone.

He went, consequently, to the Marquis with his cap in his hand and he asked courteously, even if an inner skepticism still teased him, for two favors.

"What are they?" asked Gonzaga.

"First—employment at your court."

"Granted."

"Next—a letter to His Holiness asking him for but a gesture that he is no longer wroth with me."

Federigo Gonzaga sent for paper.

"To the Lord Lieutenant who is like a dear brother to me," he set down.

Then he looked up.

"I am writing to Francesco Guicciardini rather than to Pope Clement, for it seems more politic."

After that, his pen continued scratching.

"I would be very ungrateful to the devotion which Messer Pietro Aretino has always shown to me, and I would play the part of one little friendly to genius, if I did not in every way try to make the world pleasant for this unique man. Indeed, I myself have seen him do miracles. In a month, he has composed more things in verse and in prose than all the talents of Italy have in ten years. For that reason, and because he is an excellent man, and because he has used up half his life in serving two popes—and with what affection and faith everybody knows—I feel obliged to aid him. Moreover if the Pope does not listen to me in this very proper matter, I will hold it certain that I am in no way pleasing to him. Likewise, if Messer Pietro were not the Pope's humble servitor, far from helping him, I would chase him away from me as an evil fellow.

"Now what I want is this: I want His Holiness to restore Pietro to his good graces, and to those of the Reverend Datary. This is as important to me as to have my brother made a cardinal. Messer Pietro does not ask to return to Rome, but only that some demonstration be made that will show that his servitude has not been wasted. Indeed, it is no honor to the Pope and to the Datary not to quiet him. These are times when praise is worth more than blame, and the offense against him was an ugly one and is known to everybody. For my part, I would rather fail my own interests than those of Messer Pietro, but what I do is as much for the honor of His Holiness as for his advantage. I wish to write to Rome on this matter, and both to the Pope and to the Datary, and I beg you to write of it also in that manner which your wisdom suggests. I will be glad to hear from you as to how the matter is disposed of, and when I hear from you I will act accordingly."

It seemed a small favor to ask, and the reasons given for granting it were both convincing ones, and offered very tactfully. A return letter from the former Medici cardinal, indicating at least technical forgiveness for the man, who, after all, had fought so many battles for him, seemed the least that the Marquis could expect.

Such a letter did not come, however, and Guicciardini in his answer gave the reason.

"I will do as Your Excellency asks me," he told Gonzaga, "knowing that the fact that you have commanded me will excuse my presumption. Yet I tell you that I will accomplish nothing by it, for the mere memory of one of Aretino's offenses will outweigh any arguments that I can offer."

The Datary was still the Datary in other words, and he was still stubbornly vindictive. Down through the Apennine passes moved ultimate disaster to the Pope, and the hour was at hand when he would need, just as Mantua had pointed out, every friend that he could find. But Giovanmatteo Giberti still kept him in his fool's paradise, where he could think more of pinpricks not to be condoned than of decisive matters. Not only in respect to Aretino, Giberti would cost Clement and the Medici things that never could be regained.

Yet at that, if Pietro had been willing to accept temporary rebuke, he could at least have kept a hostile peace. But he could not. He must be either friend or enemy, and that choice the Pope and his manipulator had made for him.

First of all, he wrote a sonnet, therefore.

> Seven false and futile years I've flung away:
> Four with Pope Leo, with Messer Clement three,
> And if I thus made many an enemy,
> Their fault it surely was, not mine I say.
> And for all this I've so little pay
> That poor as threadbare mountebank I be —

Yea, just as so much wind have blown away
All hopes I had of any papacy.
True, I have scars upon my hands and face
Because five times a day I did defend
The honor of my patrons and their fame.
But salary and benefice, rank and place
Are given only the bastards and men of shame.
To be rewarded by Clement you must Clement rend.

Then he wrote a *disperata*, "The Complaint of Pietro Aretino." Evidently he complained of many things. But he did not forget Pope Clement among them.

A sorrier wretch he is than Adrian.

Last of all, his abusive *giudizio* for the year of 1527, "The Prophesy of Master Pasquino, the Fifth Evangelist." Since the *giudizio* was the straw that broke the camel's back, definitely embroiling him with Pope Clement and forcing the latter to take positive action, it is here necessary to do a little investigation. Just what was a *giudizio?* Just how did it get its effect?

The Renaissance was, like all ages in which the mind makes great progress, still burdened with superstitions which it had inherited. One of these was a belief in astrology. The saints with their mediæval intercessions may have been taken with a grain of salt, but there was hardly a prince so sophisticated that he did not wish to have his fortune told. Would his wars be successful? Would his treaties turn out well? Would his *mal francese* yield to treatment? Would he beget a young marquis or young duke?

The result was the rise of a class of men who combined the supposed prophetic powers of the Delphic oracle and the Roman sybils with the most fantastic clap-trap of a gypsy at a country fair. Once a year—sometimes oftener—they issued their almanacs and their so-called *giudizii* or prognostications. Venus being in conjunction with Mars, this would happen. Pisces being in the ascendant, that would happen. They were gibberish, but they were sought for with avidity. Possibly they owed their success to a quality, which they had in common with Delphi—and with nearly every other oracle—that they were so vaguely worded that it was impossible for them not to be right. At any rate, they had a vogue.

But, of course, there were some persons who did not take them seriously. Rabelais—almost Pietro's exact contemporary —was one. Aretino was another. Once a year from 1526 to 1534, and often in the intervals, he issued his own *giudizii*. They were at once parodies of the more serious prophecies, and vehicles for his fierce sarcasms and satire. It was in one of these—the one written that winter in Mantua—in which he took his sharp flings at the Pope.

Unfortunately this document no longer exists, or rather, it exists only in fragments. Another does, however: that of 1534. It shows Aretino when he was most unbridled, most effective, most scathing, and most outspoken. It explains why what he wrote was so eagerly sought after. It also shows why it was feared.

This is its proem:

"If God almighty had not rained down His grace upon the idiotic Prophets and the Sybils, the Prophets and the Sybils would have conjured up the same kind of chimeric clap-trap about His coming, as their successors did about what was going to happen at the meeting at Marseilles." Parenthetically, the meeting at Marseilles was a Cinquecento Munich where the high and mighty of the earth arranged for a perpetual peace until the next fighting should begin—and it was just about as lastingly successful. "But they forecast right even to His birth in a manger, because the Holy Spirit descended on them from above—just as French friendship did upon Clement, so that from a poor silly sheep, 'behold a man was made.'

"Now what I want to get across to you is this. This cow Gaurico—with those other oxen of wandering astrologers— since nothing rained on them from heaven but fol-de-rol—predicts everything the wrong way. When they announce peace to Milan, war breaks out. When they foretell liberty to Genoa, she is enslaved. When they say the Pope will die, he looks younger every day. And so forth and so on, guessing incorrectly about both riches and lack with their own lean astrology.

"Moved by the same frenzy which inspired me to forecast the ruin of Rome, *coda mundi*, I have calculated — by the leave of that rascal Tolomeo and of that rogue Albumasare — from the venerable life of princes, a prophecy for the present year. And since Your Majesty —" King Francis I, to whom this particular *giudizio* was dedicated — "with your common sense has put a yoke on the neck of the traitor stars, the highwaymen planets and the drunken influences — wherefore all have begun to tremble before your worth — I have sent it unto you. I am certain that Cancer, Scorpio, Libra and Gemini, with the rest of the Scribes and Pharisees of the Zodiac, will pour down on me the secrets of the universe, just as they have drenched that herd of cattle, the Lords, with meanness, poltroonery, ingratitude, ignorance, villainy, evil thinking and heresy, only to make you generous, worthy, grateful, skillful, courteous, good and most Christian.

"And since it is the sky that has made them asses, low-born, and scoundrels, why do Ferrara, Milan, Mantua, Florence and Savoy, who are Dukes in name only, blame me? What fault have I in the close-lipped avarice of the Emperor? Have I inclined England to seek a new bed-mate? If Mars abandons the soldiery of Frederick Gonzaga, why say I am responsible? If Pisces incites Alfonso d'Este to salt eels, get angry with him, not with Aretino! If Gemini conjugates Cardinal Cibo with his sister-in-law, why does the hardy Lord Lorenzo threaten me? If Capricorn puts his device on the forehead of this Count, that Marquis, this Duke and that Prince, am I the villain of the story? And if Cancer —" syphilis — "eats the bones of Antonio de Leyva, it is his fault not mine.

"Here you have the Voivode saying 'I renounce Thee' to Christ, and I am sure that he will say to anyone who asks him that 'Thus it was decreed by Fate.' Ferdinand is going to turn

Lutheran, and if anyone wants to know the reason, he will say 'So Destiny wished it.' The Pope has broken with the Emperor and being demanded why, he will reply 'We were impelled by Fate.' The great lords do a great wrong in being clumsy fools from birth, and then blaming me, because I declare before all people what they do before all people.

"And if the King of France erred in the fault of avarice and stupidity as the others err, neither his having gilded my tongue nor his having bound me with chains of gold, could keep me from saying of His Majesty—whose wide open hands I kiss—that which I have said of all lords and prelates, who imitate the Catholic and Apostolic stinginess instead of the liberality of Lorraine and de' Medici, who are the shame of the Cardinals as a result of being too good for this hangdog century, which is as worthy of the Duke of Ferrara, as the Golden Age was of Saturn."

Then it went on to its prophecies:

"In the present year of 1534, the Marquis of Vasto being Lord of the Ascendant and sitting in the center of the Zodiac between Fabrizio Maramaldo and Tomasso Tucca, one of the erstwhile buffoon and the other the former falconer of the Duke of Mantua, many renowned soldiers—as for example, the Duke of Malfi, stallion-in-chief to the women of Siena—will take to perfumes and embroidery. . . .

"In autumn, Taurus, according to the Bishop of Lodi, al-chemist and wizard, and according to Taccuino, the Heavenly Goat, will break loose from their tethers, and with their horns they will gore and bring to earth part of the useless tribe, the Cardinals: namely, louse-ridden Trani, rascally Gaddi, boor Cesis, blockhead Spinola, thief Bari, pot-bellied Valle, beast Santi Quattro, idiot Accolti, luckless Palmieri, drunkard Trinkaforte, and good-for-nothing Mantua. . . .

"Because the direction of the sun will light up all the heavenly bodies through the quadrature of the moon, the winter will be colder than the flowery springtime and the musty fall; as a result of which, all the Lords of Lombardy will bed themselves with their cousins, their sisters-in-law, and their sisters, according to the custom of the country and so they will not die of cold. And they will cite to those who blame them the law of the Emperor who in Bologna made love to his sister-in-law, with the consent of the Pope. . . .

"Pope Chimente, to name him courtierwise—" this was a play on words, changing *Clemente*, merciful, to *Chi mente*, he who lies—"who from sheep has been made a shepherd. . . ."

"He who triumphed over the Turks he never saw—" Charles the Emperor—"having been left in the lurch by Fortune in the same way the Voivode abandoned the Church, will rage to hear the loss of Genoa, of Milan, and of the Kingdom of Naples. As a result of this, following the advice of Covos, an ass rich in brocade, he will change the reverse of his medal, and setting there in place of the Pillars of Hercules two German stoves, will make the device *plus ultra* read *non plus ultra*. And sitting himself down in an inn, thus imitating Maximilian, his predecessor, who was born, lived, and died in a tavern, he will accept the rules of Martin Luther and with that man's favor will arm the Council, which is as much feared by us as King Ferdinand is by King John Zapolya . . .

"The King of England who has given way to *omnia vincit amor* (as has not only the Duke of Mantua, but with *utriusque sexus*, the priests and friars) will end, since the Church is in closer conjunction with France than the two Gemini in the Zodiac, by consummating his marriage with his new wife with Apostolic benediction. But as God himself might well say, His Holiness was in the wrong, as I have many times averred, in not giving permission to discard an old wife, when he gave it to a Duke, who in Mantua refused two young ones. And if I had not taken a vow to speak nothing more of His Holiness, I would cite the example of the Pope himself who has refused Madonna Giovanmattea—" his old enemy Giberti thus made a woman of— "her consort who is in a monastery in Verona. . . .

"The Cardinals *viso, verbo et opere* are more safe from

every evil thing which may happen through the influence of the stars than is genius from poverty, thanks to King Francis; because there is no star so rascally that it would even think of a Cardinal. . . ."

Even his friends were not entirely safe from irony.

"The Lord God," he predicted, "with the consent of all the stars, all the planets, all the signs, and all the heavens, has resolved that this year the sons of King Francis,—on whom have been rained so many virtues that Paradise is running short of them—will be healthy, happy and consoled; and that the Dauphin, since he has followed his father's footsteps in goodness, courtesy and valor (so that he will not abandon them in love), will this year have dealings with women."

This, however, was all in the best of humor. King Francis was as proud of his feats in the kingdom of Venus as he was of his military exploits, and indeed, taking them all in all, they were perhaps more notable. We can imagine that he laughed loudest of all.

The few fragments of the 1527 *giudizio* show that it was written in the same mordant vein and with the same devastating knowledge of what was widely believed to be true. Its strictures against the Pope, however, were more vehement. Among other things—as far as we can deduce both from Aretino's own words, and from the comments of the Marquis of Mantua—it predicted the Sack of Rome, which it anticipated joyously. Copies spread abroad as if on wings, and soon they were in the Eternal City where they fell into the hands of Pope Clement. Clement did not laugh. Instead, he spoke to one of his priests, and the priest sought out Mantua's ambassador.

"Yesterday," the latter wrote the Marquis, "a Franciscan Friar who is the Pope's confessor came to see me. He said that the matter which brought him was of no small importance to Your Lordship. A little book of Pietro Aretino's has just appeared in Rome. It is full of slander, and it deals principally with the Pope, and the cardinals, and the other prelates of this court. It is dedicated to Your Lordship. This fact has caused

a great deal of scandal among the persons concerned. It is
thought strange that, in view of your relations with the Pope
and the reverend cardinals—" Mantua was Captain General
of the church—"you should allow such a book to be brought
out in Mantua under your auspices and your name. For that
reason, and urged to do so by a person who loves Your Lordship's honor and who wishes Your Lordship to remain in favor
with His Holiness, he came to tell me this confidentially. He
wanted me to write Your Excellency and beg you to dismiss
this Aretino from Mantua, and deprive him of your grace.
Then His Holiness and these other lords will have no reason
to believe that Your Excellency knew of, and was accomplice
to, such villainies, which you may rest assured they despise
thoroughly, and will reward as befits those who esteem their
honor."

Mantua's answer showed him to be a true prince of the
Renaissance. He ordered his chancellor to instruct his ambassador to inform anyone who broached the matter, that when
Lord Giovanni de' Medici came there to die, he had been
begged by "this Aretino" to give him shelter for six or eight
days. He did not know how to deny this, especially as he
thought him to be in the good graces of the Pope since he was
a servant of Giovanni delle Bande Nere. It was true that both
now and formerly Aretino had tried to enter the service of
Mantua, but he had not permitted this "as that kind of an
animal was never pleasing to him." Certain of Aretino's writings had pleased the Marquis, he admitted, but never when
they said evil of the Pope and his cardinals. Moreover, since
he had come to know Aretino's true nature, he had so detested
him that he had refused to receive him, and finally he had
told him "in God's name to go." When he had said this to
Aretino, the latter had defied him and had threatened to write
more slander of him than he had ever done, but His Excellency had so answered him that he became meek as a lamb,
and went off like a whipped dog. It was true that the Marquis

had not wished to alter from his accustomed liberality, so he had given him one hundred crowns and some other presents.

"Of the fact that Aretino dedicated the book to the Marquis, His Excellency knows nothing. Your Lordship can realize then, and make known, whether or not His Excellency consented to the said maledictions. Likewise, the Marquis says that if His Holiness does not think it is enough that he has dismissed Aretino from his court, let Clement inform the Marquis what else he wants. If he has escaped from the hands of others, he will not escape the Marquis. And the Marquis will do this in such a way that no one will know at whose instance it was done."

The last sentence carried the plain implication that if the Pope wanted Aretino murdered, Federigo would arrange it for him. For that reason it is a pity that we do not have his answer. It seems reasonably certain that Pope Yes-and-No would not possibly have asked directly for Pietro's death, but did he even hint at it? To what degree would Clement emulate Giberti? How far had Papal scruples advanced since old Pope Borgia?

Whatever the reply was—and this writer personally believes in Clement's virtue even while doubting some of his other qualities—Aretino was not even remotely near his end. For the good reason that my lord Mantua did not have the least idea of killing him; and for the better reason that he had made certain, on this account, to have him out of reach. About a month earlier, he had guessed the consequences of Pietro's latest writing and advised him to begone. And he had made sure that he would do so.

One hundred golden crowns were counted out and put into Pietro's hands on condition he would leave the city.

"Where will you go?" the Marquis asked.

Aretino's decision had already been made.

"I will go to Venice," says Flaminio in the same revised version of *La Cortegiana* to which we have already referred, "where I have already been, and enrich my poverty with her liberty; for there at least, poor men are not ruined at the whim of any male or female favorite. Only in Venice does justice hold the scales with an even balance. There only, fear of disgrace does not force you to adore someone who was in the gutter only yesterday. Surely she is a Holy City and the Earthly Paradise."

He set out immediately. He went on horseback to the Po river, and then drifted down it in a lazy barge. He went past Ferrara, seeing its brown towers across waving reeds, and thinking bitterly of its Duke and its Duke's cannon. Needless to say, he did not find it in his heart to halt there. He went on to Adria. At Adria (or thereabouts), he disembarked and jog-jogged on horseback to Chioggia at the feet of the lagoon.

There he found a boat, and it crawled northward, wafted by a spring wind, past the sixteen miles of narrow sand dunes, which shields limpid water from the Adriatic. There were small towns with pastel-colored houses. There were nets drying. And there were fishing craft. Pellestrina. Alberoni. Malamocco. At last, in the far distance he saw something taking form. A jewel box upon a pewter platter. He drew nearer to it. The jewel box became palaces and towers; the blue roof and red brick gracefulness of the Campanile; the Doge's palace like a pink and white confectionery; the ornate and eastern tracery of St. Mark's.

Presently he could make out the people. Handsome women with hair golden as cornsilk walked upon *cioppini* or shoes with fantastically high heels. Prosperous men with their crimson fur-trimmed robes. Gondolas plied hither and thither, and sailors shouted in half a dozen languages. There was a smell of salt marsh, and of spiles grown with seaweed, and perhaps — though it was early — of oleanders. The breeze began to freshen, and along the Riva the many colored sails of all the vessels moored there, flapped and shivered.

His boat grated against the Molo, and he stepped ashore, between the two columns with the Lion of St. Mark and with the statue of San Todero slaying the crocodile. It was March

27, 1527, one of the few dates we can establish definitely in his whole life. He was now at the high peak of his full manhood. In one month — lacking four days if you wish exactitude — he would be thirty-five years old.

CHAPTER X

Venice, Lady Pope of Cities

THE arrival in Venice set a period to the first phase of Aretino's life. Up to then his had been the typical career of a Renaissance literary adventurer. Bolder, of course, he had been than his fellows, and likewise more original. But the main scheme of his days had run true to the accepted pattern. First there was the long, difficult struggle to make himself known. The name is the thing—if you are a writer who seeks to make your fortune with your pen. And though the encyclopedias contain enough articles upon unrecognized geniuses, who blazed forth in subsequent glory, to hearten every springtime literally legions of predestined failures, Aretino had neither the futility of character to play literary solitaire nor the unworldly altruism to starve picturesquely in a garret. Nor did he intend to do so. Next—now that he had attracted attention—came the studied search for a patron. We have just finished our story of the results of this.

Here, however, by the small bridges and the olive green canals, he made suddenly a startling discovery. He could go further and could speak louder on his own authority.

He was the first person—at any rate, in the western world—to realize this important fact, and we now have in consequence a new character to add to the *dramatis personae* of that fascinating tragi-comedy of the written and the recited word which began all those millenniums ago when the first witch doctor of our Stone Age ancestors improvised certain rhythmic sequences of words to placate or to summon or to exorcise the dark spirits which were supposed to rule this world.

"I am a free man by the grace of God," he said, and liked the sound of it.

He began uttering, if not always what he believed, at least what he wanted to. He strutted the proscenium, haranguing a growing audience in what amounted to a long monologue and no man dictated the words of it. Indeed, he improvised it as he spoke it. In it the farsighted could have read a forecast of both the power and the danger of the press.

The back-drop in front of which he did this talking was a brilliant one; in fact—it should be stated at the outset—for another time in his amazing career he had found surroundings that seemed made to order. Venice was in the heyday of her glory. Standing upon her immemorial piles of water-resistant larch, she may slowly have been sinking at the rate of half an inch a century, but in the realms of richness and magnificence, she still towered toward the sky. The historians—who, like Aretino's astrologers, are such good "prophets after the event"—today tell you that she had already passed her apex, and if you read only in the light of what we now know to have happened, there is much in what they say. The League of Cambrai, called into being by Pope Julius II—who as a man of Genoa may have felt a certain vindictiveness about the ruthless, thoroughgoing way in which Venice had removed his home city from her first place in the carrying trade—and made up of half Europe and all of Italy, had ringed her savagely as a proud stag is ringed by the hounds; and in 1509, in the fierce rout of the Agnadello, she learned bitterly the still applicable lesson that one power, however resolute, cannot stand off a continent. Her mainland possessions dropped away from her, and though shortly afterwards Andrea Gritti, later doge but then prisoner in France, who, like all thin-lipped, square-jawed men, fought most ably when he was cornered, schemed her back into lordship over them, it was never quite the same. The Turk had taken to the sea. Off the Morea, in the Sea of Marmora, off Cyprus and Candia, a new marshalling of swell-sailed vessels, this time flying the star and crescent, menaced the proud empire of the sea's own bridegroom. One by one, colonies of Venice, and Venetian trading posts and "spheres of influence," fell into his hands, and although he would know setbacks, and although there would

VENICE

"In my opinion, if the Earthly Paradise where Adam dwelt with Eve were like Venice, Eve would have had a hard time to tempt him out of it with any fig." — *Aretino.*

be battles like Lepanto, he would soon rule the Eastern Mediterranean. Worst of all, the proud seed sown by Prince Henry the Navigator came to fruit. The Senegal reached and the hot beaches of the gold and ivory coasts long since passed, Diaz, in 1487, saw the white tablecloth laid upon the mountain overlooking the Cape of Good Hope. Ten years later, Vasco da Gama rounded it. He sped on to Calicut. A new trade route to India was opened up, and since it obviated the dangerous land passage of the Isthmus of Suez with its Arab raiders who exacted tribute, the fate of Venice thereby was sealed. She was now shut in her inland sea. In 1504, ships arrived from Alexandria and Beyrut without fragrant cargoes of cinnamon and pepper. There was a *"mene, mene, tekel, upharsin,"* in the words in which this was set down by a shrewd merchant of Venice, for they seemed to indicate that the great handsome *mappamondo* with its etched lines of Venetian trade routes, which was set on a column in the Rialto, had become an anachronism. "This was something," he said very dolefully, "that I had never seen before!"

Yet you cannot measure history by such literal calipers, and outwardly she was far more splendid than ever. It is the period of Venice that was celebrated by the great Elizabethans, and guide-booked by almost any of the English writers, who have a modest little national pride of their own, you cannot even today walk across the animated city without imagining Desdemona leaning from her balcony—indeed, plausible gondoliers will today show you the house of Desdemona, just as cabmen in Verona will point out to you the horse-trough which they call the tomb of Juliet. Iago also beetles villainous brows down dark alleyways; Volpone outwits his sycophants; and fair Portia makes pretty speeches in the best of blank verse and uses points of law that are distinctly feminine.

But the reality needs no such dressing up. Had you walked from the Merceria which runs—something like a crooked canyon—from the blue and gold clocktower on the Piazza de San Marco to the Grand Canal near San Salvatore, you might

(at any rate, a few years earlier) have seen handsome Giorgione and the two Bellinis, and you would certainly have seen
grave-eyed Titian and ugly Jacopo Sansovino. By the Doge's
palace, you would have seen burnoused Moors, Turks in turbans, Slavs in smocks embroidered with red and blue, sallow
Italians, mincing Frenchmen. In the piazza, a juggler or a
fortune-teller would be plying his trade. Off the Dogana half a
dozen round ships might be lying at anchor. Her private
dwelling places—such as the Ca d'Oro with its façade like
lace from Burano—were the most gorgeous in the world. Her
magnificos were the most opulent. Her women, the most
handsome. Her private feasts, the most lavish. Her public
festivals, the most glittering.

Figures and statistics are but the whited skeleton beneath
the living flesh of truth, yet I cannot resist a few. Even after
the opening of the new Portuguese routes, the value of her foreign trade was set at 10,000,000 ducats a year, with 2,000,000
of these profit. She had 1,000 citizens worth from 700 to 4,000
ducats a year. The assessed valuation of her houses was
7,000,000 ducats and their annual rental amounted to 500,000.
Her shipbuilding industry, her lace industry, her cloth industry, her glass industry and her making of gilt leather were
still the most important in Europe. And her wealth was reflected in her private habits and morals. 10,000 gondolas, vio-
lating all sumptuary laws in the golden decorations on their
prows and their brilliant *felze,* darted hither and thither in
the shallow canals. 11,000 courtezans—some of whom, immortalized as saints or goddesses by the greatest painters of
surface that the world has ever known, now hang in galleries
in Vienna, London, Madrid, and even New York—entertained citizen and stranger. Only those who lacked protectors
with influence took the trouble to wear the yellow veil required by ordinance, or to live in such segregated districts as
the one aptly named the Calle de' Tetti.

Venice had climbed far since those days of the Romans
when her mudflats and sand *lidos* had been the abode of rude

saltmakers, fishermen, fowlers, market gardeners and boatmen who, clad in skins and furs, had served the cities of the
prosperous mainland. First she had been a refuge for the
frightened citizens who fled before Mongol Attila and red-
headed Long-beard Albuin. Next she had dominated the
Adriatic. The Doge of Venice had become also the Duke of
Dalmatia. By mid-Fifteenth Century she was the most important commercial power in Europe. Now, if she was on the
downslide, she did not know it. She still acted like the metropolis of the world.

But it was not Venice's still-bright robes of potency that al-
lured Aretino, nor was it her great opulence. Her potency was
only interesting to him insofar as it gave him a safe refuge,
and his treasury lay elsewhere. A robber baron of the written
word—and like all robber barons his chief victims were fat
prelates and well-clothed princes—a literary racketeer, if you
like, Aretino did not regard the city of the canals as his source
of income but as his hideout. She was his castle in the Apennines, from which swiftly he could swoop down to do his
brigandry. What, therefore, was important about her was that
she had not yet lapsed into her Eighteenth Century moral
timidness, but still held free speech a thing of moment. You
could say what you wanted to in Venice, and this privilege was
extended, incidentally—as were nearly all other Venetian
privileges—quite as freely to foreigners as it was to native
citizens. There was only one restriction. You could not slander
Venice nor even take her lightly. But with that rule it was
easy to comply.

It would have been extraordinary if this prince of self-
promoters with his eyes sharpened to see anything that might
redound to his advantage, had not taken this in and reacted
accordingly. He did so. Venice became his second fatherland.
He was born in Arezzo when he was too young, as he used to
point out, to have any say in the matter. But he chose Venice
freely in his maturity. We have already read things he said

about her before he got there. But they were only a mild foretaste.

"You may believe me," he wrote Francesco Bacci, "that those who have never seen Rome or Venice have missed two things that are marvelous sights. But in entirely different ways! For in Rome, the insolence of undeserved fortune struts up and down, whereas here you have the grave demeanor of just dominion. It is a strange thing to view the confusion of the Roman curia, and a fine thing to see the single purpose of this republic. Even if you should let your imagination, so to speak, soar to Heaven, you would never be able to picture in your mind the evasions of one, and the tranquil comings and goings of the other. For they are immense edifices of turmoil and quiet. I do not remember what man of Mantua it was who, wishing to show the way this city stands in the sea, filled a basin of water with half shells of walnuts, and said: 'There it is!' But on the other hand, there was once a preacher who did not want to wear his voice out describing the Roman court, so he simply showed his congregation a painting of Hell. You certainly should visit Venice if you want other cities to seem like poorhouses."

"Here," he addressed the Doge, "treason has no place. Here favor in high places does no wrong to right. Here the cruelty of mistresses does not reign. Here the insolence of the effeminate gives no commands. Here there is no robbery. Here no one is coerced. Here no one murders. O inn of all the dispersed people, how much greater would be the woes of Italy if your bounty were any the less! Here is a refuge for her nations. Here is a security for her wealth. Here safety for her honors. Venice receives you with open arms; others shun you. She elevates you; others abase you. She takes you in; others hunt you down. And while she cheers you in your sorrows, she preserves you with charity and in love. And so I rightly bow to her. She is Rome's reproach."

But perhaps the most characteristic tribute comes from a letter to Vergerio.

"But to leave fact," he told that worthy churchman, "and to go into fantasy, I am now in carefree, liberal and just Venice, where neither sickness, death, hunger nor war has any jurisdiction. And in my opinion, if the Earthly Paradise where Adam dwelt with Eve were like Venice, Eve would have had a hard time to tempt him out of it with any fig. For it would have been another matter to lose Venice where there are so many lovely things than to lose that place where there were nothing but figs, melons and grapes. For my part, as I have already said, when I die, I would like God to have me changed into a gondola; or into its canopy; or, if that is too much, into an oar or a thole-pin or a mopping rag; or at least into that scoop with which they bale out the boat; or — to name something more appropriate — a sponge; or even — just so that I would not have to leave Venice — into one of those small copper coins they pay the ferrymen. And it would seem to me that I was one of Heaven's cherubim, if I became one of those rats that live in the Treasury. Nor would I change my state for that which popes have in Paradise — if there are any popes in Paradise, which I doubt — if I could only be the entrance to the campanile of San Marco. For, in fine, Venice which is more eternal, or to speak correctly, as eternal as the world, is the refuge, the delight, and consolation of all people."

He added that he thought anyone who left Venice was like one of those poor, foolish animals who refused to enter Noah's ark when the flood was threatening. He had a gift for the effective phrase.

But it was not in phrases alone that he made his acknowledgments to the place which had received him and had sheltered him. He put his whole destiny into her hands. In March, 1527, only the remnants of the 100 *scudi* given to him by the Marquis of Mantua jingled in his pockets, but two years later he was a man of affluence. He had already established himself in the parish of the Santi Apostoli. Where we do not know. Possibly in an inn. Possibly in the apartments of some women who kept the fellow. Now he took a long lease on a splendid palace. It stands still on the corner of the Grand Canal and the Rio San Giovanni Crisostomo and though no plaque indicates it in a city where they almost have a marker even for noted tourists, we can go to it even today. He began living in magnificent extravagance. In Venice, he spent the money that he brought to Venice. He had served princes all of his life and the taste left in his mouth was not a pleasant one. Now he would wipe this out by living like a prince himself.

We have a description of this abode in a letter written to Domenico Bolani, his landlord. Alessandro Luzio shrewdly guesses that Aretino hoped to pay his rent thereby. If so, Bishop Domenico received a coinage that was unique. Letters to landlords are not notable for their literary qualities though they are often eloquent. But this letter was an exception. It contains some of the finest descriptive writing you are likely to see. I will wager you that it is the most immortal letter to a landlord ever penned.

"It seems to me, honored sir, that I would commit the sin of ingratitude if I did not repay with praises some part of the debt which I owe to the heavenly situation of your house. I now dwell in it with the greatest pleasure that I have ever had in my life. For it is so placed that neither above it nor below it, neither here nor there, could you find the slightest improvement. As a result, I am almost as afraid to begin upon its merits as I would be to begin upon those of the Emperor. Certainly its builder gave it the pre-eminence of the finest place upon the Grand Canal. And since that canal is the patriarch of all others, and since Venice is the Lady Pope of cities, I can truthfully say that I enjoy both the fairest highway and the most joyous view in the world.

"I never look out of my windows at that time when the merchants foregather that I do not see a thousand persons in as many gondolas. The piazzas on my right hand are those of the butchers and of the fishmongers; what I look on, upon the left, is the Bridge and the warehouse of the German traders; in the middle, is the Rialto, tramped upon by men of affairs.

There are grapes in the barges, game and pheasants in the shops, vegetables laid out upon the pavements. Nor do I long for meadows watered by streams when at dawn I marvel at waters covered with every sort of different thing, each one in its season.

"It is good sport to watch those who bring great quantities of fruit and vegetables handing them out to those who carry them to their appointed places. All is hurly-burly except the sight of twenty or twenty-five sailboats laden with melons, which drawn up together make a sort of island to which the crowd hurries to count, to sniff and to weigh, so as find out whether or not they are in good condition. Of the good wives, gleaming in silk and gold and jewels, I will not speak, so as not to spread abroad such pomp and circumstance. But I will say that I split my sides laughing at the whistles, catcalls and clamor with which the boatmen followed those who were rowed about by servants without scarlet hose.

"And who would not laugh until he cried if he had seen a boatload of Germans who had just reeled out of a tavern capsize into the cold waters of the canal, as that good fellow Giulio Camillo and I did? He is the same one who pleasantly used to say that the land entrance of this habitation of mine —since it is dark, badly designed, and has a bestial stairway— is like the terrifying name I have gotten by spewing forth the truth, and then added that he who persisted in dealing with me would find, in my disinterested, straight-forward and natural friendship, the same tranquil contentment that one does in passing through the portico and coming out upon the balcony above.

"And then so that nothing is lacking to delight my eyes, I am able to gaze, on one side, on the orange trees that gild the base of the Palazzo de' Camerlinghi, and on the other, on the rio and on the bridge of San Giovanni Crisostomo. Even the winter sun never rises burning that it does not first send word to my bedroom, to my study, to my chambers, and to my great hall.

"But what I esteem more than anything else is the nobility
of my neighbors. Opposite me dwells His Eloquent Magnificence, the honored Maffeo Lioni, whose supreme virtue has
nurtured learning, knowledge and good manners in the sub-
lime intellects of Girolamo, Pietro and Luigi, his admirable
sons. Near at hand, tóo, lives la Sirena, life and spirit of my
studies; and the magnifico Francesco Mocenigo, whose splendidness gives continual feasts to knights and gentlemen. Next
door is the good Messer Giambatta Spinelli whose paternal
dwelling place sheltered my friends, the Cavorlini — may God
pardon Fortune for the wrongs done to them by Fate. Nor do
I hold least among its blessings the dear and pleasant propin-
quity of Monna Jacopa.

"In short, if I could nourish my touch and other senses as I
can my sense of vision, the room which I praise would be
paradise, since I am able to satisfy it with all the pleasures
which these objects give it.

"And what of the lights, which, after nightfall, seem like
stars scattered on the places where they sell things necessary for
our feasts and banquets? Or the music which in the dark
reaches my ears with its soothing harmonies?

"And I must not forget the great foreign lords of the earth
who frequently pass me at my entrance, nor the pride that
lifts me up to heaven when I see the Bucentaur ply hither and
thither, nor the regattas, nor the fiestas which triumph continually in that canal which is lorded over by my view.

"I could more easily express the profound judgment that
you have in things literary and in affairs of state than I could
come to the end of the delights which I see before me.

"For that reason if any breath of genius breathes in the
trifles which I have written, it comes not from the light, not
from the shade, not from the violet, nor from the verdant, but
from the grace which I receive from the airy happiness of this
your mansion, in which may God grant that I live out in
health and vigor those years which a man of good deeds ought
to have."

THE CASA ARETINO

"Certainly its builder gave it the pre-eminence of the finest place upon the Grand Canal. And since that canal is the patriarch of all others, and since Venice is the Lady Pope of cities, I can truthfully say that I enjoy both the fairest highway and the most joyous view in the world."—*Aretino*.

The interior of this house matched, certainly, its resplendent view. The sycophancy of the mighty and the affluent, and the good will of the great artists worked together to make it a veritable treasure house. An "Apollo and Marsyas" and an "Argus and Mercury" had been daubed floridly upon the ceiling of his private apartments by the stormy and irascible Jacopo Tintoretto. Certainly the first subject was suited to the rash temperament of the dyer's son, who smeared on his pigments so furiously that he could not take the time to let the underpainting dry before he put on the finishing touches, and hence arranged for a turgid, muddy future so as to gain a swift and vivid present. And Aretino must have liked it too. The idea of Marsyas, a mortal shepherd, daring to enter competition with the god of poetry himself was one, surely, to appeal to his arrogance and boldness. Only he would have found a way to beat Apollo. He would not have lost the wager. He would not have been flayed alive.

There were likewise certain paintings by Titian hung on the walls. Some of them were permanent possessions. Others — like the famous portrait of Giovanni delle Bande Nere, now in the Uffizi, like Pietro himself with his grave forehead and thoughtful eyes, now in the Pitti, like the St. John given to Luigi Anichini and the Magdalene sent to the Marquis of Mantua — merely paused there while in transit. Sebastiano del Piombo, Giovanni da Udine (who looked still like a mountaineer peasant, and when not painting for Popes — and for their gadflies — was a passionate huntsman who bred his own bird-dogs) and Giorgio Vasari also contributed to the matchless gallery. There were statues by Sansovino and medallions by Lione Lioni and Alessandro Vittoria on display in every room. At the front door, on a pedestal, was a fine, marble bust of a strong, robust man with a flowing beard. It was Aretino himself, who did not ever hide his light under a bushel.

The main salon was lighted by a magnificent glass dome. Under it stood a handsome ebony cabinet, which held all the letters which he had received from the renowned. They were classified according to their senders. One compartment held those written to him by princes, another those by prelates; the rest, those by captains, those by painters, those by poets, those by musicians, those by great ladies, those by gentleman and merchants. It was the embryo of the modern filing system, but its purpose, in this instance, was not order but display. The other chambers had the rich hangings, the noble gowns and robes, the carved chests, the handsome walnut beds, the dignified *prie-Dieu* and the ample chairs sent from all over the world. These were the gifts given or the tribute exacted, as you chose to label them. There were, if you could believe Aretino, only a few books. Pietro prided himself on knowing little or nothing of literature, which was, of course, very far from true.

As to his way of living, let his friend, Marcolini, the printer, describe it. This would be eminently appropriate. For the first modern writer deserves a modern publisher. Let us call this the forerunner of those biographical blurbs that are now sent out so industriously in mimeograph. Let us acknowledge, though, that if exaggerated, it was also basically true.

"If a poor man or poor woman of your acquaintance falls sick, you send a doctor to him at once, and you pay for his medicines, sending enough food both for the invalid and for whoever takes care of him. Often you even pay the rent of his house. Even if you don't know him, but he is recommended to you, you do the same. If a brat is born in poverty, they come to you for help, both for the child and for the mother too. If some wretch dies in your street, or even elsewhere, needs be you must bury him in charity. I will not speak of the prisoners. I know too many who have been aided by you and by your money. For example, the worthy Cavorlini will never stop praising your deed. To bail him out of jail, in two days you raised fifty ducats, making Don Diego de Mendoza, Cardinal Ravenna, Signor Girolamo Martinengo and the ambassador Benedetto Agnello all contribute.

"And that which you force others to do, when you cannot

do anything yourself, is nothing to what you take out of your own tower of necessity. You send men on voyages, aid disgraced women with babies, help girls unhappily married, and put orphans into orphan asylums. For if somebody comes to you naked, you take the hose off your legs, the shirt off your back, and give away your very doublet to aid his neediness. You even bestow your shoes if need be. Indeed Dragoncino told me that you did not give him an old pair, but new ones, and that you took these off your own feet.

"Even the poor gondoliers are helped by you. I do not lie when I say that I know fifty to whose children you have stood as godfather, giving them not a handful of coppers but of silver *scudi* as alms. So loud is the fame of this that when you pass by in your gondola, the embankments and the bridges are filled with boys and girls and with old men and old women to whom you give something for their daily bread.

"What more can I say? The report of your generosity has brought into being a whole tribe of impostors. Without cap and barefoot, they come to your house. They pretend that they are dying of hunger, and their tears make you give as you know how to. I can't help being amused at the jest played on your goodness by one of these rogues. He emptied your purse of its money by telling you that a good girl who used to be your neighbor had just died and that he wanted to bury her. A few days later her brother came to you to ask you for money to marry her with, but before he could open his mouth, you went to him with arms outspread, and then embraced him and offered him your condolences on the death of his sister. The youth was astounded. 'Signor,' he replied, 'if she has not died in the last half hour, she is alive and healthy.' When you refused to believe this, he had to go for her. He brought her to your house almost naked. She went away with a pretty dress and with the promise that you would pay her dowry. You did this, and besides acted as godfather to her first son. I firmly believe that God will repay you all this.

"Another episode which I laugh at quite as much, is now

very famous. The continual hospitality of your house, which is open to everybody, made it no marvel that on May Day in 1533, a band of foreigners, passing by, thought that it was a tavern, especially as they saw a great crowd of men come out, saying that they had just tasted the best wine in Venice. So they mounted the stairs and sat down at a table. 'Serve us with some salad,' they cried. And when they had been served with that and with many other things which they ordered, and wished to depart, they noticed your servant Mazzone, and because he was youthful, handsome, fair-complexioned, tall, fat, gay and pleasant, they thought that he was the host. So one of their number asked him what the meal would cost. Mazzone, seeing that they treated him like an innkeeper, thought that they were making fun of him, so he gave them the reckoning with his fists. At which, from the cursing which you bestowed on him and the four blows which you struck, the gallant revellers realized that you were the master of the house, and not just some noble guest as they had thought. And when it dawned on them that they had eaten like emperors and that it would cost them nothing but 'Thanks' and 'Good luck to you,' they departed, laughing heartily. But they bowed to you and gave you their compliments."

Aretino himself relates another instance and it tells to us the same story.

"It is not more than two months ago," he wrote Don Lope de Soria, "that a young man was wounded not far from my house, so they carried him into one of my chambers. Hearing the uproar and seeing the man half dead, I said: 'I know how to be a host, but not how to be a hospital attendant.' So you can see why it is that I am always crying: 'I die of hunger.'"

We have also as a further commentary on his lavish way of living, the information from his own lips that, during his first ten years in Venice, he had spent ten thousand golden crowns, "not to speak of the cloth of gold and silk worn out upon my back and on the backs of others." In present day money, this is perhaps a hundred thousand dollars, and in buying power, it was very certainly a great deal more. And all this "with a pen and a sheet of paper," he "had drawn out of the heart of avarice."

Small wonder then — when you add to this the world-wide fame or notoriety that his utterances had already won him — that he became one of the sights of the city, and that a stranger who visited Venice without seeing him, felt — as one of them said — like Tantalus. Small wonder, either, that he received a constant stream of donations from those who either wanted his favor or hoped to attract his attention. Money — all those ten thousand *scudi* that he flung around — rich garments, silk stockings for his women, coifs of gold and turquoise silk to round their pretty faces, handworked handkerchiefs, snuff boxes, tarot cards, a mirror with two faces, chains of gold, turquoises, fish, melons, the first strawberries of the season, the first figs, the first cucumbers, grapes, olives, mushrooms, bergamot pears from the lady poet Veronica Gambara, thrushes, quail, partridges and casks of wine. The list is an interminable one and his effulgent letters of thanks were addressed quite as often to obscure priests, humble soldiers and small gentlemen as they were to great princes and important prelates.

Incidentally, he was nearly always grateful.

"Certainly the liberality which you wear as a ring upon your hand," he told one donor, "surpasses all the jewels that are worn in the crowns of others."

"Surely I shall drown in the deluge of your courtesy," he told another.

"You are as generous as all others are avaricious," is the theme of a thousand.

One letter is an exception.

"The Thursday after Carnival there was presented to me a leg of veal which was as miserable as possible. I gave it to a dog to break his fast on, and if he could speak as well as he can bark, he would give you fit thanks for so lean a gift."

But that morning he must have had a headache.

He refers to his headaches in a letter to Francesco Alunno. They were given to him by the great lords and little lordlings who visited and revisited him until his stairs were "worn out with the tramping of their feet, even as the pavement of the Roman capital was worn out by the wheels of triumphal chariots."

"I do not believe," he added, "that Rome, to use a figure of speech, ever saw such a great mixture of nations as come to my house. To me come Turks, Jews, Hindus, Frenchmen and Spaniards. You can imagine what our Italians do. Of the rabble, I do not speak, but at that it would be easier to draw you from the imperial cause than to see me even an instant without scholars, friars, and priests around me. It must be that I have become an oracle of truth since everybody comes to me to tell me the wrong done to me by such and such a prince or by such and such a prelate."

As a matter of fact, often the pressure became so great that to have a little quiet he was obliged to flee to the house of Titian or of Marcolini. Only in the distant garden of the Birri quarter where the great painter lived nearly anonymously, only by the printing presses near San Ternitá, could he find tranquillity.

Even his name was now a label.

"I am at Mantua," a friend wrote him, "and behold there is a fine race of horses known as the Aretines. They are much in demand and are descended from your palfrey. I go to Murano and am presented with some handsome vases. They are of crystal and in the latest style. They are known as Aretines. If some one asks one of your retinue where he lives, he replies: 'In the Casa Aretino. It stands in the Calle del'Aretino, on the Rio dell'Aretino.' Many beautiful women call themselves Aretines. The other night I met one and when I asked her her name she replied: 'The Aretine.' 'I'm an Aretine, too,' I replied, 'we'll get on together.'"

He had been born a person and had made himself a personality. Now he was an institution.

Chapter XI

A Knight without Revenue

But this happy, if untranquil, eminence was not reached by Messer Aretino right away. He had a long ladder to clamber up before he sat there. And this, obviously, he could not do in a day.

In the meantime, he put the best face possible on his present situation.

"You may have my horse," he wrote cheerfully to Gonzaga's abbot cousin in whose stable he had left the fine animal, "for in this city which I love so well, I need a steed of wood."

"The streets are made of water here," he explained.

It was a gay way of letting Mantua know his stay in Venice was to be permanent and that he was happy so. Yet at the same time he did at least two things that gave the lie to this. He kept up his friendly correspondence with the Marquis and he threw out broad hints he wished to keep his patronage. Even more strenuously he made efforts to regain the good will of the former Cardinal Giulio. Almost as if his pride and self-esteem were at stake in the matter, this writer of such bitter papal libels sought the favor of the Pope.

A world disaster of the very gravest nature almost brought it to him.

"The year 1527," wrote Guicciardini, "was to be filled with atrocious events—and ones of a sort not even heard of for many a long year before. There were to be revolutions in the various states. Cities were to be looted amid scenes of frightfulness. There was to be famine. There was to be pestilence. Death, flight for safety, and rapine of the most bestial sort were to be the order of the day." And for one time in the history of reporting, a participant, and a biased one, did not exaggerate. He could not for the language did not have the words.

One single event was crown and culmination of the whole. The Sack of Rome. It alone would justify the writer's phrases. For not since the Visigoths had burst upon the dying Roman empire—and not often afterwards—had the plain artizans and small shopkeepers of a great metropolis been subjected to such ruin. It was, in its unprecedentedness, as if a green hill had split suddenly as Vesuvius once did, and had become an active volcano. The damage wrought by it was comparable. Even if you leave out the indignity to the human spirit, which is not measurable yet which should be measured, it was certainly no less.

The death of Giovanni delle Bande Nere was what let it come to pass. With him among the living, not even doughty Frundsberg would have dared move south from Lombardy. Now it was another story, however. With no one to block their way, not even the captains of the Spanish-German horde could hold back their men longer than the plunder lasted. After that, even Frundsberg found himself in the position of the French colonel in the famous anecdote.

"Why shouldn't I follow my men? I am their leader!"

On February 22, they reached Borgo San Donnino and by March 17 they had approached Bologna. There an accident befell them. Certain German soldiers mutinied—apparently because their swift march was still too slow—and gruff Frundsberg roared at them in gutturals. He was trying to subdue them. Instead, he roared himself into an apoplexy, and he died two hours later. Bourbon was now named commander-in-chief, and the army—if you can call it that—liked it better, for Frundsberg had at least a soldier's principles.

By April they were in the jagged Apennines and a week later they emerged beneath Arezzo. Then their goal became apparent. It was not Florence—from which Bourbon pretended to be turned aside by bribes—and it was not Urbino, fear of which had made the Duke act resolute for a change. It was Rome Eternal.

Ugo de Moncada, Viceroy of Naples and Imperial representative, rode to meet them.

"You must turn aside," he cried, "I have just signed a treaty
with Clement and it guarantees the city."

"I would not be obeyed by my men," said Bourbon.

On April 26, with the birds caroling and the olive trees a
sea of silver, they started south again, and on May 2 they
poured out onto the Campagna.

On May 4, they were at the gates of the city. Here Bourbon
sent an insolent message to the Roman commander.

"Provisions for my army and a free passage to the kingdom
of Naples!"

"No!" cried Renzo da Ceri.

He knew that it was too late for compromise and he preferred, all else lost, to keep his honor.

It was now May 5. Suddenly, through a wreathing morning
mist, came the trumpets ordering attack. The first onslaught
was near the Vatican. Ladders were thrust upward, and at
last they reached the top of the walls. Bourbon mounted one.
He was the first one to reach the summit, and likewise the first
one to topple back again.

"*Ha, Notre Dame, je suis mort!*" he cried.

But the battle raged without him. It was won almost before
begun. By noon, the Imperials had not only occupied the
Vatican side of the river, but had fought their way across the
river. By half past five, the fighting was over.

Then the outrages began.

Aretino tells us all about them. He does so in a fine passage
in his great dialogue, the *Ragionamenti*. Nanna, a Roman
harlot, is talking to her friend Pippa. It is a tribute to his
powers as a journalist that this catastrophe he merely heard
about is related quite as vividly as the death of Giovanni delle
Bande Nere which he witnessed with his own eyes.

"A baron of the Roman *campagna*, not a citizen of Rome
herself, having escaped from the sack of Rome through some
rat-hole like a rat, was cast ashore with his companions by the

villainy of mad gales on the strand of a mighty city, the mistress of which was a lady whose name I cannot tell you. She, taking a walk, came upon the poor man. He had been tossed upon the beach, drenched, bruised, pale as death, and dishevelled, and he looked more like the image of fear, than even modern courts do like that of roguery. What was worse, the peasants, thinking that he was some great Spaniard, stood around him, planning to do to him what, on a tree, highwaymen do to some poor wretch who, without arms, has wandered from his road. She saved him from the noose, restored his ship to him and entertained him in her palace. Then she prepared to listen to his tale.

"It was of treacherous men, lying men, false men, and while the poor lady listened to the talk of her guest, it seemed that she lived only for his conversation.

"At last he began to speak of the Pope and the Cardinals. So she asked him to tell her how it was that priestly craftiness ever fell into such evil hands. At this, the baron, anxious to obey the commands of his suppliant, heaved just such a sigh as comes from the bosom of a prostitute when she sees a well-filled purse.

" 'My lady,' he said, 'since your highness wishes me to remember that which makes me hate the fact that I can remember, I will tell you how the empress of the world became slave to the Spaniards, and I will recount to you what woes I saw. But who could be so stony hearted as to relate them without bursting into tears?'

"Then he added:

" 'My lady, it is the hour for sleep, and already the stars are disappearing, yet if it is your wish to hear about our misfortunes, even though the telling of them renews my sorrows, I will begin.'

"So saying, he began about the people who, to save ten ducats, were destroyed. Next he spoke about the *lanzknechts* and the oaths they swore when they came to make her *coda mundi*.

" 'Thereupon,' quoth he, 'everybody said: "Take your goods and fly with them!" And certainly all would have scattered if that band had not come too swiftly with their: "Your money or your life!" '

"He told how, after these tidings, the people in a panic, began to hide their money, all their silverware, their jewels, their necklaces and collars, and everything of value. He told how little groups of men scattered, and then gathered again, some here and some there, and how they gave as a reason for their fear that which they believed likely to befall.

" 'In the meanwhile, in the wards and boroughs, the leaders and that pestilential tribe that followed them began swarming after the files of infantry, and certainly if there had been valor in fine doublets and handsome hosen and gilded swords, the Spaniards and the Germans would have had a warm welcome.'

"Then the baron told how a certain hermit went crying through the streets, 'Do penance, priests; do penance, you gang of thieves, and beg mercy of God, for the hour of your chastisement is at hand!' But their pride had no ears. Yet when the hostile army appeared at the cross roads like a swelling tide, and when the sun shone on their arms, the villainous light which gleamed forth frightened those blackbirds gathered on the walls even more than if it had been the crash of thunder.

" 'It had now come to such a pass that no one any longer thought of how to beat back those who were advancing, but all looked for some hole to hide in. At this point an uproar arose at the Monte di San Spirito, and our fine fellows in the piazza carried themselves in the first assault like someone who extends himself to do a feat that he will never again do as well. I tell you that they slew Bourbon himself, and having captured I don't know how many standards, they carried them back to the palazzo with a *"Viva, viva!"* that deafened heaven and earth. Yet when it appeared that they had gained the day, the barricades of the Monte were broken, and after

having cut to pieces many who had nothing to do at all with
the war, the enemy ran on into the Borgo.

" 'From there some of them crossed the bridge, but having
gone as far as the banking quarter, soon came back, and it was
said that the good Castel di Sant' Angelo into which the Pope
had escaped did not bombard them for two reasons: first because it would have been a shame to waste powder and can-
nonballs; and second, because they did not wish to stir up the
enemy any more, just as they were lowering down ropes to
joist up into sacred ground a whole batch of fat pedants who
could already feel bullets boring into their rear ends.

"But when the night came, the pot-bellies who guarded the
Sistine Bridge took fright, and the army overflowed from the
Trastevere into Rome itself. Then you heard outcries. The
gates crashed to the ground. Everyone fled. Everyone hid himself. Everyone wept. Soon blood drenched the ground, people
were butchered right and left, the tortured were screaming
out, prisoners were begging for mercy, women were tearing
their hair, old men were quaking, the city was turned upside
down. Happy was he who was killed by the first blow, or who
in his agony found someone to dispatch him. But who can tell
of the woes of such a night? Friars, monks, chaplains, and the
rest of that tribe, armed or unarmed, hid themselves in the
sepulchres, more dead than alive, and there was not a cave nor
a hole in the ground nor a bell-tower nor a wine cellar nor any
secret place which was not filled with all sorts of persons. Respectable men were mocked and with the clothes torn off their
backs, were thrown down and searched and spat on. Neither
churches nor hospitals nor private houses were regarded.
They even entered those sanctuaries where men are not allowed to enter, and chased women, out of maliciousness, into
those places where women are excommunicated for going. It
was pitiful to see fire consuming the gilded loggias and the
painted palaces, and it wrung your heart to hear husbands,
red from the blood of their own wounds, crying for their lost

wives in a voice that would have made the Colosseum weep, and that is a block of solid marble.'

"The baron told the lady all this I have related to you, and when he went on to hold forth about the sad fate of Clement, and what he did in the Castello, cursing I don't know whom who had broken faith with him, so many tears fell from his eyes that he nearly drowned in them, and not being able to utter another word, he was dumb."

Though few of them were as vivid, every eye-witness narration of what happened bears Pietro out. Benvenuto Cellini, who served one of the papal guns during the seige, tells virtually the same story, adding only the flamboyant detail that it was his shot that killed the Duc de Bourbon. Guicciardini does the same—and he also throws light on Aretino's "people who to save ten ducats were destroyed." A certain Domenico, he says, who was very wealthy, contributed only 100 crowns to the defense of the city. His daughter was violated by the soldiery, and he and his sons also were imprisoned and tortured. Isabella d'Este, forewarned by her son Federigo that the "pretty rabble" was headed southward, fortified herself in the strong Palazzo Colonna, yet at that she was obliged to write him that it took 60,000 ducats and the stout loyalty of a German captain named Johann, who had been hired to guard her, to keep her safe.

The plague set in, and decimating friend and foe alike, completed the disaster.

In a few weeks, Medicean Rome was wiped out as thoroughly as if her buildings had been razed to the ground. Most of her men of letters—even such aging and inoffensive ones as the Greek scholar, John of Goritz, who was the last link with the age of Lorenzo the Magnificent and with Pico della Mirandola—were either murdered or in destitute exile. Her artists had fled to Venice or Mantua or they too had been slain—even such innocent and unimportant ones as Aretino's happy-go-lucky painter-buffoon friend, Messer Andrea, who had been pig-stuck by the Spaniards, probably to hear him

squeal. Her great ladies and her nuns had been obliged to
satisfy the lust of soldiers. Her wealthy churchman-patrons
were either ruined or dead. Her palaces had been either
burned or looted. Except for a few in the Vatican which were
saved because the Prince of Orange camped there, her art
treasures were either stolen or destroyed. It was as if any
angry and vengeful Jehovah were chastising her—as in Bibli-
cal story, He had chastised Sodom and Gomorrah—for her
light-hearted iniquity. And indeed many believed so. For if
Rome with some justice could be called the head of the Christian ethical-religious system, it could with equal justice be
stated that she had not quite lived up to her trust. By not
doing, as well as by doing, she had greatly sinned.

One of the principal victims was the man who was most
responsible. Though his skin was unharmed, the long weeks
when Pope Clement was shut up in the round fortress crested
with its bronze archangel, left a scar upon his soul. He "ate
the bread of sorrow rather than the viands of magnificence."
He paced nightly and daily his circumscribed chambers, boring into with his eyes, and yet not seeing, the frescoes on their
walls and ceiling. Covered by a courtier's purple robe so that
the enemy would not recognize him, he stood on the high bat-
tlements and looked out upon the red roof tops and the still
snow-covered distant blue hills. He could hear the cries of the
victims, but he could not do a thing to aid them. He feared
momently for his own safety, but was unable to take a step to
assure it. Most of all, he looked into his own heart, and saw
bitterly how abject it had become. The last traces of his soaring optimism, and the sanguine dream of a potent Medici
state (perhaps, even, based on a hereditary papacy), carved
out of central Italy, dissolved into a poor shabby hope of
merely not being himself deposed. If they would but let him
continue to be Pope in name—he who, shut up not only by
the Lutherans, but by his co-religionists, was no longer Pope
in power! This showed in the way he acted. Though he never,
as long as he lived, ceased shifting and scheming—for if

a leopard cannot change his spots, a chameleon cannot help changing them—from henceforward, he schemed and shifted in a more or less fawning manner. At the time of the Sack, he grew a long beard as a symbol of mourning. He never shaved it off. How could he, since the cause was never removed?

An early manifestation of this new papal attitude was the changed way in which Clement regarded Aretino. He who had so firmly indicated to the Marquis of Mantua that it would be a good move—if he valued papal good will—to send Messer Aretino to some other sanctuary, now publicly regretted that he had broken with him.

"If Pietro Aretino had only been with us," he told painter Sebastiano del Piombo, wringing his hands, "we would perhaps not be here in what is worse than a prison."

The reason: Aretino would have said openly what all Rome was whispering in secret about the iniquitous treaty which had put him in this position.

A little later, he had occasion to repeat these sentiments. He wanted to draw up a letter calling on Charles to protect Rome from new outrages which were threatening her daily, and he commissioned the poet Tebaldeo and others to write one for him. When they brought him what they had done, he read only the first three or four lines. Then he threw the paper to the ground in disgust.

"Aretino alone could pen what we desire," he cried ruefully.

The extent to which his contrition was carried is further indicated by the fact that when Pietro supplemented a stirring ode on the disasters which had befallen the city with a bit of ribald doggerel in which he flayed most of the Papal favorites, Clement was sad rather than resentful.

"We confess the wrong we did to Aretino," he admitted.

He even went so far as to blame Giovanmatteo Giberti whom he held responsible. His change of front was complete.

Word of this crossed the Apennines—for, of course, Aretino had communicative friends—and it reached him in his room in Venice. Was it to be wondered that he jumped at the opportunity thus offered? The Pope wanted a letter—well, he would write him one. Pen in hand was the swift sequel to impulse in his brain.

"To the Emperor," he began simply.

After which, he started scratching. One parchment sheet was covered; two sheets, three, and even four. They fell to the floor as he drove the last stroke of his quill into each of them, wafted thither by the animated fresh breeze that came gaily across the dancing lagoon, cooling the city but not certainly putting any chill upon his impetuosity. Yet impetuous as he was, he did not forget his aim. What he wrote was living, animated and eloquent, but it was also tactful, logical and persuasive. It had to be a good letter, for it was his bid for editorial, as he had already won satirical, importance. It was addressed to a mighty monarch, but the real reader desired was the public opinion of Europe. He wished to show that he could mould the thinking of his day.

It was indeed true, he told Charles, that good luck soon outgrew its modest beginning, and where could you find a better example of this than in His Majesty's case? Hardly had he released the French King, when Fortune and his own merits had placed the Pope in his hands. But in truth everybody acknowledged that there was something of God about him, and this was shown not only in his power but in his clemency. Who else except him would have conceived the desire to free an enemy? Who else would have rested his faith "on the promises, the instability, and the pride of a vanquished prince, since it is the characteristic of those princes who have been defeated to devote soul and body, not to say wealth and people, to revenge?" Now, however, he had a chance to win another crown of generosity.

"And so put into operation that blessed clemency of which I have spoken. Without it, fame has no wing feathers, and glory is burnt out. Mercy is the triumphal crown of him who triumphs, and the reasons which lead him to grant pardon are of greater worth than the virtues to which he owes his conquest. Indeed that victory may be called a defeat which is not accompanied by mercy."

In the hands of Charles lay the disposal of the Pope.

"Release him. Give back to Christ His Vicar in return for the favor of conquering that He granted you. Do not consent that the joy of victory should change you from your god-like custom. Then certainly, among all the prizes which you have already acquired, and which God and the Fates owe you during the remainder of your illustrious life, none other will be more worthy of admiration. But who would not place his hope in the excellent, courteous, and religious Majesty of Charles V? He is always Caesar and always august."

If he had let matters rest at that, he would certainly have gained his aims. Clement could hardly have avoided publicly acknowledging his services, might even have restored him to his court.

But his wise letter was followed by an exceedingly foolish one. To demonstrate that he had power to mould the minds of men, he had written a sane, generous letter to the mighty Charles. His big side went into this. Now he showed his petty side. To prove somewhat vindictively that he was not someone you could trifle with or lightly injure, he followed it with a humiliating one to Clement. It undid all that the other letter had accomplished.

For although on the surface, it was tolerant and Christian, its hypocrisy was entirely evident.

"Put your faith in prayers rather than arms," it began. "You are simply paying for the sins of others."

Then Aretino warmed up. He reminded Clement that he would at least have this consolation in his adversity that he could now at the same time make trial of both human and divine clemency. He pointed out what great glory the Pope could gain by suffering in patience what the will of God had bestowed on him. But what, he continued, must be sincere and not feigned was to have the thoughts of the papal mind turned toward pardon and not toward revenge, for what was more likely "to enlarge the limits of the name of Most Holy and Most Beatific than to conquer hatred with piety, and perfidy with being generous."

To this course, he should be led by his troubles. "The grindstone sharpens steel, and similarly adversity whets generous souls in such a way that they make a mock of fortune." He did not deny, to be sure, that Fortune had done Clement a cruel turn, and that the Pope, had found "obstinancy in his dominions, fraud among his friends, fear among his soldiers, ingratitude among those he had benefited, faithlessness and envy among the rulers." However, this much had been gained: his misfortunes had taught him to serve as well as to rule.

"Therefore, to Him who has power over all things, yield all things, and yielding them, thank Him that since the Emperor is the foundation of that Faith of which you are the father, he has delivered you into his hands. For you can now make the Papal and the Imperial wishes agree and as a result of this, great increase to your glory will shine out through the whole universe. Behold the good Charles who with kindness restores you to your former estate. See him standing before you in that humility which is due him who occupies the seat of Christ, and befits him who holds the rank of Caesar. In his majesty, there is no haughty pride. Hold him, therefore, with the arms of that power which comes from above, and turning the Catholic sword against the breast of the East, transforms him into the agent of your designs. Thus from the sorry state in which you were placed by the sins of the clergy will come a reward for that patience with which you have suffered."

The result was inevitable. As long as Clement stayed in the Castello a close prisoner, he did not risk angering his insulter. But he did not remain besieged there forever. A new treaty signed with the Emperor augmented for the moment the rigors of his fate, for its clauses duly initialed, Captain Alarcon —the same Spaniard who had been jail-keeper to King Francis — took him into what was later called "protective custody."

Free theoretically, the Pontiff and a number of his cardinals were restricted to — "for their own safety" — almost cell-like quarters. Then the theoretical freedom became actual freedom. After months it became evident that the other conditions could not be carried out as long as the Pope was shut up. A second treaty was drawn up, and this treaty provided for the Pope's release. Clement took no chances. He was to be turned loose December 9, but during the night of December 8, he escaped. Escorted by Imperial soldiers whom he supposed that he had bribed, he reached Viterbo. There he discovered that his escape was regarded by the Emperor as a lucky happening, and indeed, almost certainly had been arranged by him, for he had not found it an unmixed blessing to have the Pope stand before the world as too closely dependent on him. But the main thing was the prisoner was free.

He took immediate advantage of it, and one of the first things he did was to signify to certain of his followers that they could now speak out again. One of them did. A sonnet appeared, and it was addressed to Messer Pietro Aretino. It was what technically is called a *sonetto codato* — or tail-bearing one. And the tail, just like a scorpion's, carried venom in its sting.

> You say so much and do so many things
> With your foul tongue that has no salt of wit,
> That in the end a blade will silence it
> Sharper than that of Achille, and with more stings.
> The Pope's still Pope and you are a vile thief,
> Nourished by others' bread and words of scorn.
> You live in a brothel, in the slums were born,
> You cripple, ignorant and arrogant beyond belief!
> Giovanmatteo and those men, his friends,
> Who, thanks to God, are living sound and sane,
> One day in a deep cesspool will drown you,
> Unless, O scoundrel, you change your foul ends.
> If you must chatter, of yourself complain,
> And look at your chest and head and your hands too!

But you do as dogs do,
Which, beaten sharply with most strong endeavor,
Cringe and then, whining, behave better than ever.
Will you shame never,
You puffed-up swine, monster by fame unsung,
At whom is fierce abuse and hunger flung?
Know then: a pile of dung
Awaits you, hangdog wretch, whom scourges chide,
When you die with your sisters at your side,
Those two, who are the pride
Of an Arezzo brothel, where they gain
Applause, sporting to a lewd song's refrain.
Of these, I tell you plain
Should be your filthy sonnets and low tales,
And not of Sanga who no sister bewails.
From them, when your wit fails
Comes that with which you live in style so grand,
And not from my lord Mantua's generous hand.
Since every place and land
You have polluted, each man, each beast makes prayer,
God and the devil too, that ill's your share.
These ducal robes you wear—
Or ducal thefts or ducal charities—
Upon your back with such unhappy ease
To hard blows' melodies
Will be snatched off your shoulders 'ere you die
By Reverend Father Hangman, as swung high,
To our great jollity,
Upon a gallows you sway to and fro
While those who'll draw and quarter you wait below,
And the lickspittles you know
Chant for their friend the "May he rest in peace!"
So live, and your filth cease
Until one day a knife or well or noose
Binds your vile tongue and will not let it loose.

The writer of these lines was Francesco Berni, a native of
Lamporecchio, a small town in the Florentine hills which was
otherwise noted as the home of one of Boccaccio's most simi-

anly shrewd ribald characters; the secretary of Giovanmatteo
Giberti, a comic poet rather than a satiric one; a quiet fellow
whose real idea of a good time was, by his own admission, to
lie late abed and count the designs upon his ceiling; and who
now stood before the whole of Italy as the one man who could
pay Aretino in his own coin. But the important thing is where
and how the lines were written. They were sent down in
Clement's own court and they may actually have been composed in a papal antechamber. After that, they were circulated abroad with the Pope's acquiescence, and perhaps even
at his order. That gave them their significance. For what better
way could Clement have chosen to serve notice upon Pietro
that his first effort to get back into good graces had utterly,
and through his own doing, come to grief?

The next bid for papal favor was in connection with his
poem, the *Marfisa*.

For the satirist had decided to become an epic poet; the
Chancellor of Master Pasquino a devotee of the most lofty of
the nine Muses, driven to it by that irrepressible vital urge
toward greatness that made him suddenly—and quite un-
necessarily—have a certain contempt for all the very striking
things he had already done. "What are my letters—" by which,
incidentally, he is now most deservedly if not chiefly remembered—he seemed to reason, "but the hack writing of a too
facile journalist? What are my comedies—" which are among
the most vivid of the Renaissance, if not of the whole Italian
theatre—"but easy trifles?" It was as if he had been persuaded
by the false logic of his own fluent eloquence which he turned
on or off at will when some prince had benefited him or
failed to benefit him. Charles V, a new Augustus Caesar—why
not Pietro Aretino, a reborn Virgil? For the second time in
his life, the man whose great forte was in being his own self,
became derivative. The first time was when he was a mere
stripling, and at that age virtually all artists are. It is the embryo stage of not only talent but even genius, and has that, at
least, for an excuse.

But if Aretino was derivative, he was derivative in his customary bold way. He set himself no mean or petty task. He turned to Ariosto who was then generally regarded as the greatest living poet, if not the greatest Italian poet of all times, and undertook to continue his work. The *Marfisa* takes up the story of the *Orlando Furioso* where the restrained poet-aristocrat of Ferrara broke it off. Unfortunately he had no qualification for doing this but his enthusiasm, and the result, therefore, was a lot of misspent energy. Aretino wanted to make his steed a Pegasus. But you cannot turn even the most mettled earthborn charger into a heavenly prancer merely by pasting upon his shoulders fine-seeming, but synthetic wings.

Yet by 1529, if he had not produced a work of genius, he had at least set on paper enough stanzas to make a little book. Thereupon he started to cash in on it. He wrote to the Marquis of Mantua and reminded him that the volume, which was to be dedicated to him, contained praises both of himself and of his ancestors. Then he asked him if he could secure a brief from the Pope and a privilege from the Emperor forbidding anyone to print the book in their territories for a period of ten years. This was a sort of rudimentary copyright. Aretino would bring out the book in Venice and since no one else could publish it in at least half of Europe, he would have the profits of selling it.

"Since I expect the printing press rather than the princes to regard me," he added sarcastically, "please be willing to obtain for me this small but important favor." They should be glad to do so, he argued, since it would give them a measure of control over his writings. "But if it so happens that they are not willing, I will write twenty stanzas in the manner of Master Pasquino in which I will speak so scandalously that anyone who prints them will be excommunicated. And for that I will not need brief or privilege." It was the Aretine method which was gradually, as it was more and more often successful, growing to be automatic. He alternately frowned and was menacing. He wagged his tail and growled.

But in this instance it had no results at all. The moment was not well-chosen. Charles V had not yet seen any reason why he should need Aretino's good will, and Clement, basking in the pleasant sunshine of the unctuous deference tactfully bestowed on him by the calculating Hapsburg who was really his master, felt no need to cringe. Mantua did his best, to be sure. It was eminently to his advantage to do so. He wrote strenuously to Giovan Battista Malatesta, his ambassador at Bologna where the two sovereigns were now foregathered so that Clement could crown Charles Holy Roman Emperor, and so that Charles could make face-saving gestures for the benefit of Clement. He urged Malatesta to press the matter.

It was a waste of effort, Malatesta reported. "Aretino is in worse grace than ever, for besides what he has done, he has just written a 'Last Will and Testament' in which he speaks very scornfully of Charles and Clement."

How did Aretino receive this news?

"I never repented more of anything I did," he wrote the Marquis, "than of asking you that favor. Your ambassador will testify that hardly had I sent the letter than I wanted to re-call it. I do not deny that I have written of the Pope with little affection, but had I a good reason or not? As to the 'Testament,' I never saw it, nor has anyone here. You can tell your *nuncio* that it is not mine. Instead I made eight sonnets on the coming of the Emperor to Italy, and this year's *giudizio* is in the Pope's favor and in favor of the Emperor. However, I want no brief or privilege from anybody. Soon enough they will see who Aretino is. The works of genius are not subject to the favors and disfavors of princes. The Pope does not think that I deserve gratitude, but the world does. But he does know that when I was with him, I pleased him, and that I am an un-usual and straightforward man. One day he will open his eyes to my glory."

The spoiled child who cannot have his plaything says wil-fully that he did not want it anyway, yet so forcefully did Aretino make this statement that it rings proudly like the haughty declaration of a man who must be independent, no matter what. But the fact is that he was bilked again.

But it would have taken more than a pope to keep Aretino out of papal good favor. For he was not only persistent but versatile. First he had tried a frontal attack (the letter to the Emperor), then conquest by negotiation (his request to Mantua), now he would attempt an encircling move. Not having been able to penetrate the main defenses, he would now essay the wings.

And the ripe opportunity for this soon came. Having once more semblance of power, Clement VII shortly proceeded to use it, by rewarding his tried friends. Giovanmatteo Giberti was the first of them. The Datary of the Roman curia was made Bishop of Verona. En route to his hill-girdled new official residence with its Roman bridge and amphitheatre, and its austere mediæval, Dante-trodden palaces and churches, he stopped very naturally at Venice. Aretino hastened to the palace where he was staying, and so far forgot his arrogance as to throw himself at Giovanmatteo's feet.

Yet he did this exultantly.

"I must tell you," he wrote the Marquis, "that moved by almost divine inspiration, I have made peace with the Reverend Datary. If I read his face correctly, he received me cordially and with affection. I am as pleased as possible, and I now dream that his goodness will restore what he took away from me. And for that reason I hope that Your Excellency — who are like a god to me — will write him a letter telling him what pleasure you have in learning that I have returned to his service, and how much greater pleasure you will have when you learn that he has rewarded me for this."

He was a hard man to keep down.

Obviously, the Marquis complied with his request, but in so doing he used a tactless phrase that almost spoiled the whole business. He could not do other than love Pietro Aretino, he said — if for no other reason than because he had so honored him with his writings. On that account, he was delighted he was restored to favor again. But it was something, quite frankly, that he had always expected Giberti to do. "For even though I felt sure that you had good reasons for doing that which you did to him, I relied on your goodness and humanity."

Giovanmatteo took him up. He was glad that he had pleased His Excellency.

"But there is one phrase in your letter that I cannot allow to pass. I beg you to be as certain as you are sure that I am your humble servant, that if anything was done against Messer Pietro, it was done without my orders, and without my knowledge. Also it displeased me so greatly that only repeated prayers kept me from making a more forcible demonstration than I did make."

But he did not press the matter further. He was a glib and straight-faced falsifier—this seacaptain's natural son who had now climbed to important office and who hoped probably to climb higher. He had to be to get on in the world. But he also knew his politics. And Aretino now, and unexpectedly, had a new ally. Andrea Gritti, Doge of the Serene Republic. That tight-lipped patrician with his cold steel-gray eyes and almost boundless will had just come to realize how useful to his city in the battles she could not escape would be the voice of Aretino—to Venice ringed by wolf and lion, menaced by France and Emperor.

Consequently he sent for the writer, and the latter climbed ponderously the long Stairway of the Giants and stood cautiously and with his haughty deference in the Doge's little inner room.

"I am anxious for your friendship," Gritti began.

"Yes?" said Aretino.

"Yet I find that your lack of wise discretion makes it hard for me to bid for it."

"Oh, indeed?" said Aretino.

"Would you help me end this difficulty?"

"How?" said Aretino.

"Remove from your excellent books all those things you say in dispraise of the Pope and in their place set things in praise of him."

"After which?" asked Aretino.

"After which," answered the Doge, "I will pledge to use all the influence I have to get His Holiness to do those things you ask of him."

Aretino agreed.

He celebrated this triumph in a wild burst of pagan joyousness. It was the time of the Carnival, and he plunged into that gay span of riotousness with whole heart. He was now in his new palace overlooking the Grand Canal. He "gave bread" to five servants—and also very splendid liveries. And his gifts were beginning to pour in. Claudio Rangone had sent him some masks made in Modena, and there were presents of damask robes and velvet jerkins, to say nothing of a fat hogshead of wine and gifts of game and food which he shared with his scapegrace companions. He joined the noisy crowds, revelled in the streets, ate, drank and was merry. Then he took cognizance of the nature of the promise which he had made. Lent came, and he made another sort of demonstration.

"Yesterday," reported the Mantuan ambassador, "I saw Messer Pietro Aretino. He had a confession in his hands and tears in his eyes. He told me that he knew God would not forsake him, but would treat him better than he deserved, though up to now he had been a great sinner. He said that he was determined to live another sort of life than he had so far done. He said that he was going to lay aside rancor and hate and all the rest of the wicked life he was supposed to live. He said that he repented and was going to confess and to go to mass with his whole household, something he had not done for many years."

Evidently some strolling band of players lost a very histrionically promising recruit when the son of the Arezzo shoemaker took up writing as his trade.

And it had obviously its reward. In May, 1530, Aretino

received a letter from Rome saying that the Pope was sending him 500 *scudi,* and would shortly draw up the privilege.

In September, the latter arrived.

This is his acknowledgment:

"Your majordomo, Monsignor Girolamo da Vicenza, Bishop of Vaison, has placed your brief into my hands. He did this in the house of the Queen of Cyprus. And since you told him to do so, he said that neither your rise from a simple knight of Rhodes to being Pope, nor your change from Pope to prisoner, had astonished you as much as my having attacked you with my writings — especially since I knew why you did not punish anyone for the attempt made upon my life! Holy Father, in everything I have ever said or written, my words always expressed what I felt, and in regard to attacking your honor, my loyalty has always protested that I was not to blame for reproving you. Yet I do repent, and am ashamed of two things. I repent of having blamed that Pope whose glory I have held dearer than my life; I am ashamed that, since I had to blame you, I did so in the worse depths of your misfortune. As it is, I thank God that He has taken from your mind the harshness of contempt, and from my pen the sweetness of revenge. From now on, I shall be the good servant I was when my talents, fed by your praise, armed themselves against all Rome during the vacancy of the seat of Leo."

The courtesies are observed, but he has not become exactly humble.

Less so even were his words to Vaison himself. This old friend, who had fought Pietro's battles so often, brought the writer a gold collar from the Pope, possibly to make up for the 500 crowns which never materialized. He also brought him a promise of knighthood from the Emperor.

Aretino smiled at him.

"I accept the collar," he said affably if patronizingly, "but not this idea of being made a knight by an Imperial privilege. Didn't you read what I said in my comedy, the *Marescalco?* A knight without revenue is like a wall without 'forbidden' signs. Everybody commits nuisances there."

Then he put his arm upon his old friend's shoulder.

"Leave such vain dignities to young fops who are puffed up with them," he said, "and never miss a chance of coming in with 'We knights.' I myself am content to be what I am.

"Though I would like something over and above my honors to maintain them with," he added.

Even knowing the reasons for it, Vaison must have marvelled at this assurance. He was used to arrogance on the part of Aretino. But Aretino's arrogance had deepened into something different during the past five years. Aretino now was confidently calm.

CHAPTER XII

Worship of the Pashas and the Janissaries

BUT the good will of the Pope was not—as has already been stated—the only target at which Aretino shot his arrows. If he wanted papal favor, it was merely because it would give him a certain status. But the smiles of Clement would not take care of any of his spendthrift expenditures, and the kindly inclinations of the Medici pontiff were not likely to assume a more useful form. Even in his good days Clement was a cautious unloosener of pursestrings, a man who promised readily but who did not often honor his verbal drafts when the day for redemption came. And just now he was close to bankruptcy. Much nearer at hand however—and still friendly to Aretino, despite the fact that he had expelled him from Mantua and had even offered to have him murdered— was one of the most lavish young men of the Renaissance, Federigo Gonzaga. How to keep his lavishness directed toward the right quarters was the Aretino's problem. We have already suggested his solution. It was to let the young Marquis know that the satirist was transforming himself into an epic poet; to tell him that he was at work on that wordy carrying along of Ariosto which was to be known as the *Marfisa desperata;* to indicate that it was to contain long passages setting forth in detail, and also glorifying, the purely fictive genealogy of the Gonzaga whose own town captain-gangster genealogy would be now carried back to some brawling hero of the Trojan fable; to hint—without stating so specifically—that the honor of the dedication would go to Federigo: that is, if he paid the price.

A new trend in the history of men's attitudes made this an eminently sensible attack. The Renaissance has been celebrated as the mother of poetry, painting, sculpture, architecture, classic humanism and that reawakening of curiosity and question-asking which is the basis of the modern scientific mind. It brought also the rebirth of the sense of the individual. The Middle Ages were the great era of the anonymous artizan. Here and there names do survive, but Chartres rose out of collective small activities just as certainly as the marvel of a coral atoll is built up out of the immolation of the individual polyps; the *Chanson de Roland* grew from unknown hand to hand; and no record preserves for us the names of the designer who conceived — if there was an individual designer — or the workmen who set piece by piece the gold and black mosaics of the dark lady of Torcello. But with the past discovered came also the corollary discovery that certain names endured. Homer may not, as Boccaccio's money-minded father pointed out, have "left any great fortune" but his reputation seemed likely to last forever. Men still spoke of Vetruvius. No picture by Apelles, no comedy by Menander still existed, yet their names you still could conjure by. This knowledge was an epidemic virus.

There is no more fundamental human desire than that the ego or personality — that small, obstinate flame at the core of our material bodies that not only burns but is aware that it burns — shall endure. The various conceptions of heaven are one method of attempting to satisfy this desire. Immortality — so called — in the minds of one's fellow ephemerids is another. This last method now became the one in fashion. Dante, who was certainly mediæval enough in the structure of his thought, became Renaissance-ly modern in his desire for glory. Petrarch wrote a letter to posterity. Even the almost psychopathically modest author of the *Decameron* told Jacopo Pizzinghe that he hoped to make his name last forever. The motives that men worked for changed. In the Twelfth Century a good job had been done for the inherent joyousness in the work itself, or as a hymn of glory to the Artizan who made both work and worker. Now it was but a vehicle — a vehicle that would take you to undying fame.

But in the high Renaissance, there was still further evolution. A favorite story among the cultured brigands who ruled Mantua, Ferrara, Imola, Urbino, and Forlí during the florid gusty days of the Sixteenth Century, was of Alexander the Great sighing after his conquests because Homer did not live to celebrate them. The truth or lack of truth of this story is of secondary importance, though it can be pointed out in passing that the blond, shock-headed barbarian, whose brilliant raid from the central Balkans to the outposts of India toppled a mighty empire, was a pupil of Aristotle, and a great lover of the blind Greek poet. What is important is the moral that it seemed to point out. As a man is written down by his contemporaries, so is he likely to be known to the ages. It is not so important to achieve, as to have what you are supposed to have achieved duly touted. This problem the lords of the Renaissance met in their customary direct fashion. When they wished a man to be killed, they paid somebody to kill him for them. When they needed soldiers, they did not drill them, but got them in the open market. When they wanted a Homer they did not sigh like Alexander in the story, but they hired one.

Aretino was a Homer of a sort — at least in his own estimation — and he was definitely for hire. The question was to find someone to hire him. The poem settled this problem for him. He sat down in his first Venetian summer, and scratched out the opening lines. He sent them in the Fall to Mantua. Federigo acknowledged them. "I have read," he wrote glowingly, "the fine stanzas you have sent me, and I know that you have completed them in less time than most people would have begun them, yet they could not be more beautiful or learned if they had taken you twenty-five years. I have the greatest desire in the world to see them finished. I thank you infinitely for the great honor you have done me in writing these things for me specially, and for the kind things you say about me in them."

The answer is significant. Sentence number one indicates that what literary standards Gonzaga had were amply satisfied. In other words, that one of the most cultured gentlemen of the Renaissance was willing to go on record as considering all this verbose imitativeness good literature. Sentence number two gave an order to continue. Sentence number three more or less implicitly accepted the dedication. But you did not accept dedications unless you meant to pay for them. Aretino had, therefore, what he could regard as a "contract." He set out to work. For five years we shall follow him as he grinds out his uninspired stanzas, sending batches of them to the Marquis, getting back, very incomprehensibly, praise. We have definite record of 3500 of them, and that may not be the whole story. Eight lines to a stanza makes 28,000 lines. Then by God's grace, Fate released him, and he could do less ambitious, but far abler things.

But it was not merely with bad poetry, highly seasoned with a kind of grandiloquent flattery, that Pietro from Arezzo tried to keep in a state of outgoing benevolence Federigo Gonzaga's affable regard. Any poetaster could have done this. And have won a poetaster's reward, which was a court sinecure or a nice pension to be paid out at such moments when the prince's latest war, or latest mistress or catamite, or even latest court jester, did not make too exorbitant demands. And which lasted until a newer and more fashionable poetaster was found. But Aretino, without even consciously realizing it, was shooting at a higher goal. His quilled pen was to make him not some prince's highest-paid hireling, but the human equal of whatever man that lived. What better way of demonstrating this than the way that he instinctively chose? Not to sell his verses, but to offer them as free gifts. Not merely to accept presents from the tribe of rulers, but to make them presents of an equal princely nature. The fact that the princes later so repaid these gifts—as indeed they were expected to—as to make them virtually purchases did not change the situation. For if you accept a gift you more or less imply the giver's equality. Aretino decided to make Mantua acknowledge his equality by plying him with gifts.

A chance meeting in the ant-hill swarming of some crowded thoroughfare made it possible for him to do this with un-dreamed-of magnificence. That is, if he did not deliberately seek out Sansovino, in whatever was his refuge — for he had not yet been given the dusty, stone-flaked studio in the shadow of San Marco — when he first lit upon the shores of Venice after his wild flight from Rome's destruction. At any rate, the tall, handsome blackbeard, with his keen eyes of a predator, and his wide, ample forehead, met the squat Neanderthal with an ape nose, and a face and body covered with heavy orange hair, sometime before sultry July had made smooth and glassy the still rippled lagoons.

Sansovino, who had known Aretino in the old days of the Chigi palace, and in those slightly newer ones when Pietro, who was angling then for Clement's favor, dwelt in the Via de' Banchi Nuovi, asked him if he knew the painter Titian.

"No," said Aretino.

"Would you care to meet him?"

"There are some matters in which we could be helpful to each other."

When the meeting was arranged, he broached them.

"Why not," he suggested, "let me make presents of some of your work to Federigo Gonzaga? We will ask him no payment for them, but the expressions of his pleasure which you will certainly receive will count up to as much as you would possibly demand from him. And besides that you will gain his good will and a new audience.

"What have you on hand?" he continued.

"A portrait of Hieronimo Adorno."

"Good — he was beloved by the Marquis."

"I could do also one of yourself for him."

Sansovino entered now the conversation.

"I," he said, "am working on the statue of a Venus. It should do for your Marquis. It is so lifelike that it would fill anyone who looked on it with carnal desire."

Aretino slapped his thigh delightedly.

"You know well Gonzaga!"

Then he amplified.

"He wants no hypocrisies—he wants no stigmatas and nails!"

Gone, in other words, was any real market for emaciated-looking St. Francis', Lorenzos toasting on their griddles, St. Sebastians looking much like dying pincushions. The great lords of the Renaissance had other tastes. They wanted Leda with her swan, luscious Europa; or Danaë waiting for the golden shower that brought down her god seducer.

These three would supply them.

Ten days later there came evidence that his plan was a successful one.

"I have just received the two handsome works by Titian, which were brought to me," wrote the Marquis. "They are dear to me not only because I have always wanted to have a picture by that excellent painter, but also because one of them is a portrait of your talented self, and the other of Signor Hieronimo Adorno, whom I loved greatly while he was alive.

"Please thank the said Titian in my name as cordially as you can, and tell him that I will shortly make him such a present that he will realize how grateful I am. I would not want to accept the pictures without giving him the reward they deserve."

There is no letter in regard to Sansovino, but we have other evidence that the statue was as well received as the pictures were. It appeared that Pietro's first skirmish in the campaign of earning lavishness by at least seeming to be lavish was well on the way toward being won.

But it was not possible for Aretino to provide masterpieces for his Marquis every day. To have done this would have taxed even his mighty resourcefulness. There were, however, other things to send to Mantua and they were also acceptable. Venice was a center of handicraft as well as art. East and West met by her canals, the first bringing gorgeousness and love of brilliant color, the second artistry at its most exquisite. Glass making had flourished on the lagoons since the Dark Ages, and now at Murano—whither the glass works had been removed in 1292 to end hazard of fire — black smoke rose from white-hot furnaces, and lumps of molten silicates were blown into orbs like soap bubbles by leather-lunged artizans, who looked just like Father Satan's servitors. They were then shaped by wheel and pincers into cups of fragile delicacy, intricate candelabra, and flagons of incredible loveliness. By the tideless canals of the main city, seventy-one shops, doing 100,-000 ducats worth of annual business, turned out gilded leather for chairs, bookbinding and a hundred other things. They fused Spanish influence, North African influence, Oriental and Turkish influence, Florentine and Frankish influence into something absolutely that of Venice. There was also a Street of the Sword Makers, where steel was fashioned into swords and daggers.

Aretino made his drafts on all of these.

"I today have your letter," wrote the Marquis not hiding his enthusiasm, "and some glass that you sent with it. The glass pleased me greatly. For it is in truth very beautiful and well made and in the latest style."

One is glad he placed the beauty first, and one is also slightly envious. Cinquencento Venetian glass fresh from the foundry! It would be worth its weight in gold now, if you can judge anything of such opaline rarity on so mercenary a basis.

Aretino also had a saddle made for Gonzaga by the famous leather makers. And a dagger by Valerio of Vicenza.

Here, however, Aretino did two favors at the same time — which was characteristic. The son-in-law of Valerio, coming from Brescia with a large shipment of wool, had been seized by one of Federigo's tipstaves, and cast into jail in Mantua until he could pay a 100 ducat fine. Aretino promptly wrote the Marquis that the dagger, which he was having made for him, had been delayed because Valerio was so upset. He thus gained the liberation of the son-in-law, and the good will of the artizan. Then he sent the dagger to Gonzaga. According to the Mantuan ambassador who was not anxious to be pleased by Pietro, it was "a work of art of great rarity and worthy for a

great king to carry." Thus with a dagger that probably cost
him nothing—because of Valerio's gratitude—he gained the
Marquis' good will too.

Federigo Gonzaga acknowledged these gifts—and the steady
stream of completed sections of the *Marfisa* which accompanied them—with a score or so of glowing letters—and
whenever it did not too greatly inconvenience him with more
tangible returns also. It has already been related how valiantly
he worked to obtain for Master Pietro the desired privilege of
printing his lengthy epic, but this was natural, for he was in
effect asking for a copyright on his own passport to immortality. But his acts of friendship also extended to matters that
were not quite so definitely connected with his own obvious
self-interest. Of course, the self-interest was in the background,
as it always is. Aretino was doing something for him that he
wanted done. He tried to keep him in the suitable frame of
mind.

A certain Taddeo Boccacci of Fano, an old soldier of Giovanni delle Bande Nere and hence an old friend of Pietro's,
had accidentally killed one of his fellows while they were scuf-
fling over an arquebus which, of course, like all others that do
similar damage, they knew "was not loaded." When he woke
up the next morning—with a bad head one assumes—he not
only found himself in a cell but also that he had been charged
with homicide. He wrote Aretino, and Aretino, having de-
ciphered the soldier's rude scrawl, wrote to Mantua.

"Concerning your Taddeo," replied Federigo, "I hope that
the letter which I sent will satisfy you, and also that it will accomplish its purpose."

The Imperial army which was to attack Florence in accordance with a somewhat "dirty deal" with Charles, menaced
Arezzo as well. The Priors of the city wrote their one-time
street urchin, asking his assistance. Aretino turned to Gonzaga. The Marquis—now become Duke, incidentally—wrote
his brother Ferrante who was with the Imperials.

"So that Pietro Aretino can have the necessary peace of

mind to go on with his writings and studies, I beg you to free the Aretines from any of the inconveniences of war, and to give them the same protection that you would if they were part of my state. And I wish you to let the Aretines know that any favor you do them comes from my intercession, and that I was urged to this by Messer Pietro."

Aretino—it was a chronic affliction—needed more money, and he begged Federigo for a patent to start a lottery.

"I will be glad to give it to you," answered the Marquis.

But before doing so he felt it necessary to warn Pietro that it would probably not raise the money that he required.

"You want 4000 ducats you say. Others have tried it and have scarcely raised 600 or 700."

Federigo even went so far as to aid Aretino in two love affairs.

While at Mantua during that February before coming to Venice when he had not been sure whether the Marquis would keep him at his court or would send him packing again, he had whiled away dragging hours by plunging into a passionate interlude with a lady named Isabella Sforza. She was presumably a noblewoman, but that did not keep her from succumbing to the charms of the good-looking adventurer who could make himself so attractive. They sang together, talked together, and presumably had other and more intimate delights, while he wrote obscene sonnets—partly to amuse the Marquis, and partly because it was part of his stock in trade to boast how wicked he was—saying that she had kept him from worse things than adultery. Now in Venice he thought about her, and he wrote avid letters to the Marquis asking him to press his case for him. What his case was has not been stated, nor whether he wanted her to come to Venice with him or wished merely to keep in her good graces against a possible return to Mantua.

"I will be glad to help you out in any way I can," the Marquis wrote him.

The next affair was not so savory. For besides Isabella,

Aretino had carried on another amorous intrigue, and this time his darling was a certain "son of Bianchino." Once again he wrote to Federigo but now young Gonzaga could do nothing for him.

"I wish that I could help you in this matter of Bianchino," he said, "but when I heard his stubborn attitude when Roberto spoke to him on your behalf, and when I thought how little honor there was in the business, I concluded there was nothing I could do. I could not command him, for in such matters, to command is neither right nor decent."

It is illuminating that he even tried. When a great lord of the Renaissance, when the cultivated son of the most cultured and most notable lady of a great era, calmly and with scarcely even any implication of criticism plays the pander — or at least does his best in his attempt to play the pander — in a business of so very sorry a nature, we have a sudden and disturbing insight into the morals of the day. Remember Federigo thought it "neither right nor decent" to command, but he saw no objections to persuading. There is much about this period that was simply bestial. It is for philosophers to decide whether or not the bestiality was necessary. In other words, do ages have to go by extremes? Must ages of great art and mighty intellect be ages of extravagant wickedness too?

It throws light also on Aretino himself and the light thrown is most important. Malevolently and in a language far too foul for billingsgate, his enemies, in their poems and pamphlets, accused him of all sorts of unnatural practices which but began with sodomy. They still do today — and worse even, so do a certain type of his admirers. Conversely his friends defended him. But now by his own admission he stands convicted and there is little more to say. Yet we must not jump to conclusions too far reaching. Aretino was at times irregular but he must not be thought of as either a pervert or effeminate. In fact — as you need nothing more than to look upon the portraits of him — he was definitely masculine. We should not condone him, but we must attempt to comprehend him, through the *mores* of the age in which he lived. For not only writers such as he was, and artists such as — also by his own admission — Benevenuto Cellini, but soldiers, statesmen, great lords and in some cases even churchmen approached life on a front so broad that we have now scarcely a basis for judging it. Theoretically, they had laws and measures. Actually there was nothing that life offered them that the love of new experience would not tempt them to essay.

But there was one matter of moment in which the Marquis of Mantua did not dare even to attempt to keep pace with Aretino's expansive ideas. That was where they dealt with money. Flattery Federigo would repay with flattery, actually reading Aretino's endless poem — as is proved by his explicit references such as to the two descriptions of tempests, "one on land, the other at sea" — and interlarding his comments thereon with such adjectives as "ingenious," "clever," "talented," and "pleasing." Favors he was willing to do, even when, as we have just seen, they were most degrading. He made presents also — a robe of black velvet fringed with gold braid and lined with yellow silk; a doublet; a brocade greatcoat — and he supplemented the 100 *scudi* with which he had made easier Pietro's departure for Venice with a new gift of 50 more of those golden unguents at the time Titian's two portraits arrived. They were paid over to Messer Mazzone — Master Mullet, literally — Aretino's strapping majordomo whose duties apparently included everything from collecting overdue blackmail to waiting on the writer's always crowded table. But he was not willing to turn the Mantuan treasury into an unlimited drawing account from which Pietro could siphon, as he wanted to, the large funds required to finance his spendthrift habits, and there was not even a hint of a regular pension. And since the none too anemic egotism of Aretino had nourished itself into believing that the sole function of the great and of the affluent was to keep him provided so that he could live life on the same scale of magnificence that they did, this led, in the long run to a rift.

It began gradually, as was of course natural when you consider the circumstances under which his new relationship — and to break relations you must first make them — with the young horse-racing Marquis arose. At the outset, Aretino had no way of knowing just what interest Federigo Gonzaga would have in this long telling of a windy tale which was offered to him unsolicited by a satirist turned epic poet. The *Marfisa desperata* was a lure cast before the plump trout of Mantua by one who had never practiced that kind of fishing before, and the adjective in the title would have applied equally to the writer of it. But when the fish rose, he felt differently. At first Aretino had hoped rather than expected, and for each token of esteem that reached him, he was duly appreciative. Now he demanded. And when no answer was made — or to be fair to Federigo — when the rewards sent him were less large than what the writer's waxing sense of what was due to him expected, he grew furious.

"Tell your Marquis — " and he wore, as he set down these words, the robe trimmed with gold braid that Gonzaga had given him — "that I will not write a work in honor of a man who lets me starve to death !"

It had no results.

Then he bethought him of his *giudizios*.

The prognostication of 1529 — which was a worthy companion piece to the one of 1527 which enraged the Pope, to the one of 1534 of which we have already spoken in detail — did not go so far as to lay the stinging whiplash on the shoulders of the Marquis himself but it did make some scathing remarks about certain of the Gonzaga servitors. They were true remarks, even if exaggerated, and they were likewise ribald ones.

He saw to it that Malatesta, who was Mantuan ambassador, received a copy and Malatesta reacted in the way he thought he would.

He went hastily to Aretino's palace. "My master," he said trying to smooth things over, "still loves you and he certainly admires your poem. The reason that you have received no recent gifts from him is because he could not make them. He had had no revenues from his states for the past eight months." After which he gave the reasons for this situation, telling Aretino confidentially matters that were public knowledge—diplomats even then having hallucinations about the gullibility of all those not diplomats.

The bad times had made a poorhouse of the marquisate. The long wars had wasted it, even though it was an outsider in those long wars. You could not collect many taxes when there were neither crops nor money to pay them with. He did not bring up, however, the fact that the Marquis, who was still living—hard times or no hard times—in his usual lavishness, had perhaps other ways in which to spend his money.

Aretino smiled at him, affecting sorrow.

"The excuse certainly is a good one," he replied, "and I suppose, truly, I should believe it. Yet I still think that the Marquis is angry with me. For I have not had a word from him in some time. Formerly he used to beg me to write to him. Now he does not even answer my letters."

In the first verbal set-to, he seemed to have won.

But if it was a victory, it was a moral victory only, for not even a scrawled "good luck to you" came to him from the Lord of Mantua.

Consequently he unloosed another arrow.

An informant—and well coached by the man he talked about—sat in Malatesta's chambers.

"Messer Pietro Aretino is about to leave Italy."

He took a sip of Mantuan wine.

"'And after I have left,' he says, 'I will take my revenge upon those high and mighty ones who would not give any help to me. I will tell the truth about them.'"

Such as Malatesta, for instance, wondered the ambassador.

"Such as the Marquis of Mantua?" he asked.

"He will not slander the Marquis of Mantua," said the informant. "So he says at any rate. The Marquis, he says, is a man of virtue. Not in any case — this is my opinion — until he knows certainly that he can get no more from him."

Not more than a handful of days later, Aretino must have decided this to be the case. For Malatesta, happening to go into the palace of the French ambassador, heard, as he entered it, the sound of laughter. It came from the main salon. He strode into it without waiting to be announced and there facing him the writer stood; he was talking loudly to Count Guido Rangone and to the Florentine ambassador.

"Have you heard this that I wrote about the Marquis?" he roared. "Have you heard that?"

And he read excerpts from them. They were in his most sarcastic manner.

Then suddenly he looked up and saw the intruder. Here was an opportunity for him.

"That quarrel," he said bending over toward the Florentine ambassador as if asking for and getting agreement, "between the envoys of Urbino and Mantua as to which one of the two baboons should have the precedence?"

"Yes?"

"Ho! Ho! You know I stirred it up, don't you?"

And he looked at Malatesta.

Diplomatic tactfulness went flying.

"Why, you huge liar!" the ambassador cried. "You arranged that quarrel? You, whom Urbino himself will one day murder because of the sonnet you wrote upon him?"

After that he got control of himself. His words now were clear and deliberate.

"As long as you spoke honorably of my master," he said, "he honored you and wished you well. At first I thought all this talk against him came from your over-jealous love of him, but since you have persisted I know it comes from what you truly feel. Beware, then!"

Aretino was completely taken by surprise.

"I have told the truth about the Marquis' servants and I

will say of the Marquis himself what I choose to," he blurted
out trying to maintain a manner of bravado.

Then Malatesta lost his temper.

"If anyone offends against the Marquis' honor, he knows
how to answer him," he said angrily. "So if you do not show
the respect you owe to him you may find yourself worse treated
than you imagine. And you would not be safe from him if you
were in Paradise. His Excellency knows how to resent an injury whether it comes from you or from someone greater than
you."

His knees shook with contained fury; for if he spoke his
anger, he did not act upon it: that would have been a breach
of diplomatic etiquette for one ambassador in the house of another ambassador, however he might have settled the issue if
he had met Aretino down some lonely side street. But it accomplished what he wished to accomplish.

Aretino found himself threatened on two sides by the two
horns of a most difficult dilemma. If he advanced, there was no
mistaking that he would lose out for good with Mantua. If he
retreated, Guido and the Florentine would know him for an
empty windbag.

He tried roaring lustily, hoping that by saying nothing noisily he would give out the impression of standing his ground
while he was really running away.

Malatesta turned his back on him.

He walked lightly to the French ambassador — who was a
fifth person in the little scene — and talked gaily of irrelevant
matters.

But he looked at Aretino covertly.

The self-sure large fellow was obviously quite taken aback
and likewise thoroughly frightened by the sharp words the
ambassador had spoken to him.

After a due interval, Malatesta went out of the room.

Aretino followed him, and there, making sure that no one
listened to him, he poured out his profuse apologies.

"I beg of you," he implored the ambassador, "to write not

a word of all I said unto His Excellency. It came merely from my great affection for him and for the great eagerness I have to be honored by his hand. I swear to you that neither in writing nor in speech will I ever more utter anything that is not honorable about him. When he sees the book that I am composing about him, he will believe this."

Malatesta thanked him ironically.

"Keep acting in such a fashion and you will every day be more satisfied," he told the writer.

Then he turned away.

That, at any rate, is how the ambassador relates the incident, but Aretino himself more or less confirms the truth of it. For not many days later, he wrote thus to Lord Gonzaga:

"For ten years and with the greatest ardor, I have preached, exalted and celebrated the name of Your Excellency, and for one hour moved by over-impetuous friendship, I have offended against things dear to you. And if I have not been rewarded for the good according to the royal manner of your great soul, surely I do not merit being punished for the bad by something that will cast a stain upon your honor.

"I am Pietro Aretino, at your service from true affection and not from false design; your friend in warm regard and not in cold servitude. And I remind you that if tongues could weary, mine would be entirely worn out with praising you, and if your angelic goodness hates me and outrages me, it hates and outrages its own glory.

"For it is not King or Emperor or the Pope, but the Marquis of Mantua, dear to my heart, who makes me humiliate myself. And this not because I fear for my life, but for the love I bear his merits.

"And I kiss your hands if I am worthy of it."

It looks as if he had advanced, storming the ambassador, to positions which he was not able to maintain in face of pressure. He found that he was obliged to retreat.

But I have not indicated clearly Aretino's character if you imagine even for a moment that this sudden marching back-

ward was a rout. It was rather merely one of his strategic with-
drawals. When the time came, he was ready to resume the
attack.

For the moment, however, this was unnecessary, his gesture
of abasing himself having regained the Marquis' good will.

"I have your stanzas," the latter wrote, evidently referring
to further episodes of the *Marfisa* which accompanied the letter of apology, "and I have to tell you that I read them with the
greatest pleasure for I cannot conceal the fact that it pleases
me to have me and mine praised by such a cultivated and
lofty genius as you are. It seems to me that you have few equals
as a writer and no superiors."

He then added unspecifically, in the best manner of a rich
nobleman who was not, however, rich enough not to promise
many people many times what he could possibly perform, that
he would "keep a full account" of all that Aretino had ever
done for him and that the latter would not "ever have to repent" of the good will that he had shown to Federigo.

That was April 24.

May, and Pietro was working busily, not writing letters and
satires but adding line after line to his epic.

June, the same. July also. August and September.

As September ended, the pile of manuscript was a respectable one, and October 2, therefore, he again wrote to Lord
Gonzaga.

"By Christmas," he wrote, "I hope to have finished the book
and indeed would have done so before this if my rascally fever
had not laid me low."

Then he threw out a broad hint. It might help him to get
well if the Marquis in his gracious generosity should see fit to
make him a present of "a robe lined with fur or even a cast-off
jerkin."

There was no answer. The poem was not finished and cash
on delivery was Gonzaga's present attitude.

Fall. Then winter.

December 24 arrived—Christmas Eve—and the poem still was incomplete and there was still no word from Mantua.

Aretino wrote another letter and this time it was a complaining one.

"Most honored Lord, can it be possible that you who have been so courteous, not to say prodigal toward all men, should be avaricious only to me who do adore you? When have I had a crust of bread from you? After I am dead you will regret that you let a work celebrating the glory of your house be pawned for a paltry 200 crowns. If you were anxious to punish me for two words spoken against you, why will you not reward me for a whole book which does nothing but praise you? By the body of St. Francis, if the book were now in my possession—which it is not since you have not sent me enough money to keep it—I would burn it! Yet even now I do not suppose that I will ever get a shirt from you! . . ."

January 5, 1530. This time he addressed Malatesta:

"I beg you for the love I bear you to have the kind courtesy to write the Marquis and implore him to send me fifty crowns." His demands were coming down. "By God, I will be forever grateful for them."

Postscript: "Tell Messer Calandra—" Federigo's Secretary of State—"that I am sending him my comedy, the *Marescalco*, which has been begged from me by many gentlemen."

This was a lewd skit in play form, about a certain woman-hating courtier of the Marquis who was tricked into thinking he was going to be obliged to marry. The dénouement—and alas, happy ending—is when he discovers that his supposed wife is really a boy. It must have brought great merriment to all but Marescalco, who was a real person.

At this Gonzaga relented a little. With something written by Pietro in his hands, he wrote his ambassador saying he was sending fifty ducats.

"Give these on my behalf to Messer Aretino and tell him that I love him very greatly."

Three weeks later, they were paid over.

"I give unto your excellency," wrote Pietro, "that same thanks for the money sent me as one does unto God for prayers answered."

He had a most marvelous faculty of being able to think if he wished to that what he got at any given moment was all he ever wanted. And it was — until he wanted something more.

And in this instance the wanting something more occurred quite soon. For the next eight or ten weeks he was occupied trying to patch up his quarrel with the Datary and since the Marquis was helping him in this, he did not bother him.

Then he started asking again.

"For ten years," he whined, "I have adored you and in proof of this the world can now see that work which the world most desires. Yet I have never received even a jerkin or a vest. And what makes this seem even more distressing is that the Marquis of Montferrat, who has scarcely known me except during his visit to Venice, has already given me more than six hundred crowns and has invited me to come and live with him."

Exaggeration number one — Aretino had not served the Marquis for ten years. He had not even known him that long.

Exaggeration number two — Aretino had not only received both a jerkin and a vest from Federigo but many other things beside.

Exaggeration number three — the Marquis of Montferrat had not given him 600 crowns, or even half of it. By his own and explicit statement to the Mantuan ambassador, Montferrat had given him a collar worth 100 crowns and raiment worth 150.

But he did follow these lies to gain his purpose with the stanzas celebrating Gonzaga's genealogy, and the Marquis — now the Duke — acknowledged them. He sent a robe of night-hued velvet.

"Thank you and I want more," the answer seemed to say.

The thanks were genuine, and so too was the insatiability. It was the insatiability that led to a break.

For not very long afterwards, Federigo was obliged to refuse one of Pietro's requests, a benefice he had asked for having already been given to another.

Aretino voiced his irritation.

"My tongue is now free," he warned.

"Tell Messer Aretino," came back the answer, "that if he cracks open his maw from now on to say even the least thing not only against the Court but against anyone in Mantua, His Excellency will be as offended as if it were against himself. In fact, he swears by the Lord Jesus Christ that he will have him murdered in the middle of the Rialto."

But the threat came too late and a last sentence which was more ingratiating convinced him that Gonzaga was weakening. Besides he now had the papal privilege and the protection of the Doge.

"He threatened me with violence—then I will answer him in the same language."

Which he did.

It is the Mantuan ambassador who reports the incident. A certain Mantuan nobleman named Mainardo, he reports, was passing through the narrow side streets of the San Cassano quarter on his way to the house of Valerio of Vicenza—that same artizan who made the dagger for the Marquis—where he was about to take back certain money and valuables which he had loaned Valerio. Suddenly he was set upon by armed men, carried to a bridge, and pitched swiftly into the slimy water. He escaped drowning—though he could not swim—and slunk somehow or other to his little inn. There, as he was changing his wet clothes, his door was burst open by the same men. They stripped him, beat him, and robbed him of his purse and of a medallion that he wore. Then fleeing, they called back that they had done this at the orders of Pietro Aretino.

A courtier of Federigo was trying to get money from one of Aretino's favorite artizans. What better way of showing his contempt for the courtier's master—for Federigo Gonzaga himself?

Yet at that—such is the tenacious, stubborn obtuseness of trained diplomats—Gonzaga's emissary tried to pretend Aretino regretted the breach.

"He complains greatly," he maundered writing his report, "and blames Messer Titian and myself."

But where did Titian come in?

It was all the sheerest face-saving fabrication. For the moment, at any rate, Aretino was quite content to demonstrate to all who noticed him with what a glib lightness he could cast off the favor of a reigning Duke. If, somewhat later, he tried to win it back again, that was another thing.

But, at that, two of his largest problems still remained unsolved.

The *Marfisa* lay in front of him with its dedication waiting for someone to pay tribute to, if his price could be met. And he still thought he needed a patron.

The poem he offered to the Duke of Florence.

"Just as Alexander the Great would not have anyone but Apelles paint him, so I am sure Alessandro de' Medici will want only Pietro to celebrate his high deeds. In these stanzas I sing the genealogy of the Medici not without dispraise of Mantua, and my new efforts should testify to the world my loving servitude of him.

"But I will not come to serve you in person until the poem is printed," he added.

Right about face? No, merely business necessity.

But the offer was declined. Though Aretino's old friend, the Bishop of Vaison, had encouraged him at the time that the news of his rupture with Gonzaga was becoming public property, by saying that Duke Alexander "would gladly see a sample of his work" and urging him to copy out a canto, it was one thing to accept a few thousand lines, tossing out therefor some small scraps of largesse, but another to buy the whole poem at Pietro's swollen idea of what it was worth, and the half Moorish ruler of Florence—whom gossip called the son of Clement—could think of more congenial ways to spend his coin. Corrupting wives of Florentines, for instance, when they needed corruption, and when they did not, making husbands complacent.

Then Aretino tried the Marquis of Vasto. He was a vain, pompous, young man, with unhappy eyes, however, and a not unintelligent forehead—whom Aretino had insulted for the malicious fun of doing so, with some of his most sarcastic sonnets, squibs, and ribald pasquinades. He was the nephew of that sad rogue—though very noble one—the Marquis of Pescara whose tangled web of treasons, counter-treasons, betrayals and plots cannot even now be unravelled with certainty; and therefore, also by marriage, nephew of the unco-virtuous Vittoria Colonna. But so anxious was he to have his name recorded that he accepted the pasquinades without anger and even seemed to encourage them.

"If you know anything about me that is not worthy of praise," he wrote Aretino, "remember not to desist in reproving me, so that, being advised of my error, I can avoid it as I wish to, and become better."

A grandee of Spain—for Davalos, though a Neapolitan nobleman was by blood Castilian—was speaking to the self-made pleb of Arezzo! Veronica Gambara, writing fulsomely to "the very virtuous and honorable Pietro" just after he had referred to her in writing as a "prostitute laureate" is hardly more extraordinary, hardly more eloquent of the temper of the times.

The Marquis was only too glad to have the dedication and to pay for it. In 1532, the *Marfisa* came out in his name.

For patron, he essayed the King of France. There were many reasons for doing this, and they were all good ones. First of all—as the case of Leonardo da Vinci before him, of Cellini and of Luigi Alamanni after him, demonstrated beyond cavil—an Italian artist or writer fared well in what was one time Gaul.

Secondly, he knew King Francis personally. Giovanni delle Bande Nere—you will recollect—had introduced him to the

French monarch more than fifteen years previously, and Francis had been entertained by him, and would certainly remember him. Then too he had espoused Francis' cause — if only with a letter — after the black night in the park before Pavia when most friends, feeling the cold winds rising and howling, slunk away.

Aretino made his first overtures as far back as 1528 when he followed his praises of the Emperor in the *giudizio* for the ensuing year, with a long poem in which Italy called upon the French King to save her from the ruin wrought by Spain. This brought no immediate results, but two years later, he was well-established in French favor, and in his first quarrel with Mantua it was from the French embassy, as we have seen, that he launched his words. When his rupture with Federigo Gonzaga became final, he went over definitely to the French cause.

Even at that it took him three years more to receive any real mark of King Francis' favor. Then Francis made him a present, the first one he had ever received from a reigning monarch, and it was a princely one. It was a massive gold chain weighing five pounds and valued at six hundred *scudi*. Hung on it as pendants were a series of little tongues enameled in vermilion bearing an inscription taken from the Bible. *Lingua eius loquitur mendacium* — "his tongue uttereth great lies."

There were two ways of taking this: as a royal if good-natured rebuke — and supplemented by a large gift that indicated that they would no longer be necessary — to Aretino's supposed thriving upon the slanders he made up; as a modest deprecation of Aretino's lavish praises of the king as mere untruthful flatteries.

Aretino accepted it as meaning both of them.

"By God," he said stoutly, "a lie from my tongue is just as likely as a truth from the mouth of a clergyman!"

Then he met the modesty with irony.

"I suppose," he went on, "that if I told you that you are to your people what God is to the world, and what a father is to his sons, I should be telling you a lie? And if I informed you that you have all rare virtues, courage, justice, clemency, magnanimity and knowledge, I should be a liar? And if I said to you that you know how to rule your own passions so that all are amazed, I should not be speaking the truth? And if I stated that your subjects feel your potency more in the benefits they receive than in the injuries they endure, I should be speaking evil? And if I said that you were the father of virtue and the eldest son of faith, I would not be speaking well? And if I say that love of others makes you the inheritor of your kingdom, you would deny me?

"It is true," he continued, "that if I should brag of the 'present' of this collar, I would lie, because that cannot be called a gift which the hope of ever seeing it has devoured, and which is sold almost before it has been seen. For that reason, if I did not know that your kindness is without measure and had no part in the delay, I would tear out all these linked tongues and make them ring so that the ministers of the royal treasury would hear them for days to come. Then they might learn to send in haste what the king gives quickly. But since there is no deceit in your loyal character, I ought not to keep on being contemptuous with my talents, but use them to be always the humble recounter of the ineffable benignity of Your Majesty, in whose favor may Christ always keep me."

The gold chain — said Aretino in these sentences — is a good beginning. But the King, knowing it to have cost what would have been a good year's pension, thought it end and middle also. He sent nothing further. Aretino, therefore, turned toward something else.

"Pietro Aretino," he added as a conclusion to his 1534 *giudizo,* "who has in the ascendant Luke, John, Matthew and Mark, as a result of which the Arctic and the Antarctic stars give him the same liberty of speech that all foreigners have in this blessed Venice, will turn — since he has broken with all lords, whether of the Church or the anti-Church party, and since in the latter part of December appears to him the liber-

ality of the great Luigi Gritti in the farthest part of the zodiac,
—his steps toward Constantinople to the discredit of their
Most Excellent and Most Reverend Lordships. And at every
step will he preach the charity of Christian princes who, to
exalt the seven deadly sins, constrain poor men of merit to go
to Turkey where they will find more courtesy and more piety
than they find cruelty and asininities here. Thus the Pietro
Aretinos of the world are forced to worship Pashas and Janis-
saries."

It was not so lunatic, and it was something Leonardo and
Michelangelo had both thought of. The Doge's illegitimate
son—that Gritti named above—was Venetian ambassador
to the Turk and he had already urged him to come, sending
him money, telling him to bring as big a retinue as he chose,
and promising to provide him with clothes, horses, and living
expenses. The Grand Vizier Ibrahim—who a few years later
was to be strangled with a silken cord for not having the wisdom to flatter (probably with physical attentions) the Sultan's
favorite slave, Roxanna—had heard of him. Seeing Aretino's
portrait, he had asked of what country he was king. Keyr-ed-
Din, better known as Barbarossa, the corsair terrorizer of the
south Italian seacoast, was a correspondent. "Certainly you
have the face more of a soldier than of a writer," he told Aretino. Besides that, it is credibly related that he was the only
westerner known at Teheran and at Cairo. He was an Arabian
Nights character, in many of his aspects. He would have been
welcomed in the Arabian Nights' Near East.

Yet somehow he never went. His only motive in leaving
Venice would have been to find protection and a place of
vantage such as Europe could not afford. Bit by bit, he came
to realize that he had the second of these by the Rialto, and
that the first he did not need. If he had quarreled with Mantua, if Francis refused a regular pension, there were others
glad enough to take their place. We have already noticed the
Marquises of Vasto and of Montferrat. But there were many
more. The Marquis of Musso sent 100 crowns, the Cardinal

of Lorraine 100 crowns, Count Massimiliano Stampa 100 crowns, Monsignor di Prelormo 50 crowns, and Lorenzo Salviati 40. (These all within a very short space of time.) And presently there were others: Cesare Fregoso—he of Castiglione's volume; Count Guido Rangone, the Duke of Ferrara, the Duke of Urbino, Henry VIII of England. Even Alessandro de' Medici, who would not take up the dedication of the *Marfisa*, offered him the gloomy stronghold of the Palazzo Strozzi which stills stands on the Via Tornabuoni. (Aretino's enemies said this was to take further revenge on that rebel family by giving over their proud mansion to so notable a great beast, but it is not likely that Alessandro reasoned that way.) And when Aretino would not accept this house, sent money like the rest of them. In this moment, he discovered that no patron was needed since all were his patrons. "The princes," he had struck on a medal, "who are paid tribute by the people, pay tribute to their slave." Strictly speaking, this was true, for he still kept the forms of humbleness and servitude. But instead of one master, he had many masters, with the result that no one of their number was important to him. And since this was so, he did not have to keep the good will of any of them. He could dismiss his employers, instead of being dismissed by them. That way he gained his independence. By playing off one master against another master, he was master of them all.

Chapter XIII

Aretino Innamorato

In 1534, Angelo Firenzuola, old art student friend of Aretino, went to the small city of Prato to live, and—it so happens—nine years later to die. It was to him, it might be pointed out, that Pietro had addressed the gay, ebullient letter which described their mutual, rowdy escapades in the side streets and the steep, overhung alleys of Perugia. His good luck had left him, and he took the only step that seemed to be left.

His beginnings had not been bad. On his father's side, the ill-favored, sallow, involuntary churchman with the proboscoid nose—his nurse, according to his own somewhat sour statement, had pulled it too hard when he was a baby—was a member of a reasonably prominent mercantile family which had emigrated in the days of Cosimo Vecchio to the city by the Arno from the small, ancient, eyrie-like hamlet which gave him his name. Even during Angelo's own maturity, his sire, Bastiano Firenzuola, held a fiscal office under Duke Alessandro. His maternal grandfather was a noted humanist: the great Ficino had praised Alessandro Braccio. Both temperamentally, and in the career he pursued, Angelo showed his double inheritance, but, as is apt to be the case, this made him something of a dilettante. Not rich, he was still well enough off to follow an aesthetic career. But having been entirely sheltered during his formative years, he lacked the iron to make something really great of himself. As a concession to his father, he became a law student at Siena, and there for nine years, "with the utmost boredom and without any pleasure at all" he "half-heartedly" applied himself to codes and precedents. Then he rebelled one day. He threw down his law books, crossed to Umbria, marched into the city of the griffon, and took up painting under one of the numerous disciples of Pietro Perugino who then thronged the place.

233

He "ground colors" there and practiced at the elements of design.

But not even art was to be his ultimate career and soon he spoiled paper in another fashion. Unfussily prolific, he filled one after another "his unhappy bits of foolscap" with his "crude lyrics, his awkward rhymes." They were instantly popular, for even the most clumsy of metrics were in huge demand during those early decades of the flamboyant Cinquecento, particularly when they were barbed humor in *terza rima* — to such purposes had Dante's instrument been brought down — dealing with thirst, chamberpots, the death of an owl and that "wood of India" which was reputed to be a sure cure for the French disease. (Or Naples disease, if you happened to be a Frenchman.)

Rome was an inevitable consequence. All wits went to Rome — possibly that is why all roads now lead there. There a clever attack upon the proposed addition of the letter *omega* to the Italian alphabet — the said proposal emanating from Trissino, a "minor poet," which places him at least on the level of those various major poets of the present which our critics are discovering in every other book review — won him papal attention. Leo gave him a benefice or two. Good living resulted from the means to spend a little more. But there was also some reputation involved. This led to a literary life.

He took to it as a duck takes to water — or as a man thirsting does to a spring in an oasis. He became a close friend of the very man he had attacked, Trissino not resenting in any way witty sentences which, while assailing certain theories of his, also called attention to the fact he lived and wrote. He became a friend of Berni, of Pietro Bembo, of Molza, of Giudiccione, of Antonio Broccardo. A nice log-rolling group gathered together, and behaved just as such groups always have and always will. They discussed literature, and they nurtured mutually the illusion that they created it. (Maybe Bembo did, certainly none of the others.) But there is some evidence that they considered even more important the red wines sold in the cool cavern of the Comet Inn, where Angelo left and nearly lost his manuscripts one morning; and that while talking about what the philosophers had written and what they themselves were going to write, they also found it amusing to engage in very unphilosophical pastimes with those full-blooded handsome Roman women, who became, instantly a man of letters carried on an intrigue with them, great courtezans.

Firenzuola paid the price. One of his "games of backgammon" cost him a severe case of syphilis.

Almost at the same time, the golden age started to lose some of its lustre. The Sack of Rome led to the gradually increasing timidness of Clement who grew old and cautious simultaneously, and the Medicean splendors started ending slowly through the natural processes of rust. Besides that, a financial depression set in. Though there were still benefices, the returns from them shriveled and sometimes even disappeared. Thus Firenzuola's shrinking income added its arguments to those of health and of general despondency. What was left except retreat? He left the Tiber, and poised, just as if contemplating staying there, by the Arno. But Florence under its dusky Duke was at low ebb, and anyway—the true rich man's litterateur son—he had always hated money-minded Florentines. At Vaiano, outside the "far and smiling town" close to the Pistoian Appenines to which he now withdrew, was the abbey of San Salvatore from which he still got an income, and of which he was still theoretically the head. The well-like coolness of its cloisters now attracted him. In a small city, and, besides that, near his sources of supply, he could perhaps live in at least part of the style to which he was accustomed. There were, of course, misgivings, but he put them aside by saying to himself all sorts of pleasant things about his refuge. He praised its rident disposition. He eulogized its good air. After Rome's miasmas almost any air must have seemed good. He even made some lines about its women in his poetry.

She hath been, of beautiful and virtuous ladies,
Always in Tuscany the most favored abode.

Hope sprang in him at the sound of his own being hopeful.
Such are poets. It did happen to be true that the women of
Prato were reputed to be comely indeed, and perhaps, listening to his persuasive speech, they would disclose other qualities. For he was a "passionate, tolerant, troubled, diffident,
haughty, satirical, and yet warm-hearted and tender" man,
and such are apt to go far with the opposite sex. As he rode
into the cobbled streets, and looked up at the exterior pulpit
of the Duomo, which had been carved exquisitely from marble
by the mighty Donatello, and not harmed by the Spaniards in
their brutal onslaught of the city twenty-two years ago, he may
even have been glad.

This high-hearted optimism did not, however, last long.
That there were ladies in Prato, and that in accordance with
their reputation, they were lovely enough to attract even a
jaded poet is born out by all the Mona Amelia delle Torres,
Mona Lampiadas, Mona Amorroriscas, Mona Selvaggias and
Mona Verdespinas that he soon was writing about. They were
the real ladies of the place in which he now lived. Nor is there
any doubt that he received amorous favors from more than
one of them. That also — as much as exceeding beauty — was in
the Prato tradition. For you must remember that Boccaccio's
Madonna Filippa came from Prato, and it was she who anticipated what we call the point of view of the new woman by at
least 600 years. Accused of adultery, she admitted her guilt
and then asked the judge to demand of her husband if she
had not always contented him. The husband replied in the
affirmative. "Then what," said Madonna Filippa, "should I
do with what was left over?"

There is even a certain amount of evidence that the Selvag-
gia of these Prato days was that same mistress he celebrated in
his poetry. But there are shades and subtleties even to a time-
passing amour, and this small town philandering seemed very
trivial indeed to the man who had spent splendid evenings with

Roman *hetaerae* who could quote Greek and write — when their lovers gave them enough help with rhymes and similes — good Italian poetry. Though in the works he himself printed, he never said anything about his new home that did not glow in its praise, he spoke very differently in a letter. He was "in Prato, a ghastly little village of Tuscany," he said candidly. He first attempted to allay the horrors of this exile by writing a series of short tales in the manner of Boccaccio, but so brutal — for all their vividness and animation — so cynical, and so cruelly indecent, that they might even shock someone who did not know that they were written by a churchman. Then — possibly he had shocked himself — he shifted toward a sort of sublimation. A new book followed, of an entirely different character. In that long list of immortal creations which have been born out of boredom and ennui, Firenzuola's "Of the Beauty of Women" is not certainly the greatest. But it is not likely to be forgotten. It will go down with Castiglione's "The Perfect Courtier" which sketched in the portrait of a Renaissance gentleman, and with Leo Battista Alberti's "Of the Conduct of a Family" and with Della Casa's *Galateo* and perhaps even with Lord Chesterfield's letters to his son, as inimitable of its own kind.

It was a piece of writing that flashed. I am aware that this is contrary to the common opinion, but how many who set it down as dull have actually read the little volume? How could it possibly be dull, since it had for its subject that which has obsessed all truly masculine minds ever since Eve with the help of a serpent first persuaded one of the opposite sex to trade in his lovely and enduring place in the country for some highly perishable fruit? It was a guide book to the charms of the more fragile yet more fascinating sex written by a man who, though bound by priestly vows, certainly had the experience to know just exactly what he was talking about. To its own age it dealt with a subject that was just as important as that of Machiavelli's "Prince." If our age considers it less so, that may be our loss.

Like every good guide book, it was both general and specific. Firenzuola did not leave much to the imagination or to variance of taste. Of his "perfect woman," he set down dogmatically every single detail, circumscribing each, in general, with an almost mathematical exactitude.

Her hair—to start off with an example—should be fine and blond—sometimes golden, sometimes the color of honey, sometimes like sunlight. It should be thick, wavy and long. Her eyebrows, on the contrary, should be ebony. Except for the iris and the pupils, the eyes should be pure white with perhaps just a suggestion of the hue of flax blossoms. They should not be black—despite the Greek and Latin poets—not even heavenly blue, but rather a deep brown. And they should be round, like those of Homer's ox-eyed Juno, but eyes the shape of almonds are allowable. The ears should be like clambering roses. At the edges, they should be faintly transparent. The cheeks should be white, tinged with a rich carmine, just like a little hill whose summit is flushed by the last glow of the sunset. The nose should be small and well-cut, the bridge slightly elevated but not aquiline. The teeth should be small, but not tiny; they should be square, even, and white as ivory. The chin should be round. It should glow warmly. A dimple should divide it into two parts. The shoulders should be large and somewhat square. The neck, shoulders and arms should join much as in an antique vase. The breasts should be full and soft. The legs should be long, slender and well-formed. The feet should be small and slim. Silver-hued, according to Homer, Firenzuola pointed out; but for his part white as alabaster would do. That is when they were bare. He, however, was content to see them slippered, Firenzuola having the idea that woman clothed was fully as alluring as woman in her nudity; "even more so, for attractive clothing adds a little to her beauty." The slippers should be slender, narrow, neat and cut in the most stylish manner. If anyone is interested in knowing how he drew up these specifications, he used the approved method of his day and age. He turned back to the classics for a precedent. Just as Zeuxis, when he wanted to paint Helen of Troy, chose for models the five most beautiful women of Croton, using the most attractive features of each, so Celso, who is Firenzuola, did with the four young Prato women who listened to him, making a composite that out-shone each part.

When he came to the more general, Firenzuola ran into difficulties. Who can write a definition for the indefinable? *Leggiadría*—"that beauty," saith the dictionary, "which is derived from the relations of well-proportioned parts." *Vag-hezza*—loveliness; *Venustá*—Venus-likeness, the true beauty; *Grazia; Aria; Maestá.* Who can compass them within the limit of a phrase?

Nevertheless, he tried manfully.

"*Leggiadría* is none other, as the very word should show us, than the observation of a tacit law given to you women by nature that you must carry your whole body with grace, with measure, with distinction, just as you carry each individual part of it, so that no gesture you make is without rule, man-ner, measure or design. Everything you do should be thought out, ruled, planned, yet graceful."

"*Vaghezza* is that loveliness which has in it all those aspects which compel anyone who sees it to long for it. It is a magnetic beauty which calls forth the desire to look at it and to possess it."

"*Venustá,* in a woman is, then, a noble, chaste, virtuous, reverend and admirable appearance that makes every move-ment have a modest greatness."

Aria and *grazia* are less elusive. We all know what is meant when we say a woman has a certain air, a certain grace about her. So too with *maestá.*

"When a woman is tall, well-formed, has a good carriage, seats herself with dignity, speaks gravely, laughs modestly, and has finally almost the atmosphere a queen about her, we then say she has a sort of majesty."

Thus the background for the specific was sketched in.

But it was not even the general and particular considerations upon feminine loveliness that give Firenzuola's book its major interest. If you were writing a historical novel about Rome, Florence, or those sallow gangsters who were lords paramount of Milan, it might be important to know just what kind of and how many dimples a beauty of the first half of the Sixteenth Century was supposed to have, just as probably in the Twenty-third Century, costume romancers about the age we live in will be thumbing through old newspaper and magazines to find out about rose-tinted fingernails and platinum blonds. But the spirit, not the surface, is of moment when you seriously consider an age. How, therefore, Firenzuola expressed the new spirit of his amazing period in its relation to one subject is what makes us still read his volume four centuries after it was written. Just wherefore he thought what color tresses were preferable, and whether languishing eyes ought to be round or almond-shaped, was worth all this almost pedantic consideration; this is why we look at it today.

And the reason was a very modern one. He rationalized — as the psychologists might put it — a necessity. Having seen what he wanted to do, he did not — as the men of the Middle Ages might have — either pretend that he did not want to do it or put the blame upon the Tempter. He tried to justify it. Plato gave him the text he used. Emerging from the dark centuries whose somber Passavanti's with their "Mirror of True Repentances" had regarded woman, along with every other lovely thing — remember even the affable and not narrow-minded author of the *Decameron* had had his moments when he felt this — as the hiding place of evil and the cause of all our woes, the men of Firenzuola's period had found somewhere in the writing of the Greek sage something they had been able to twist into seeming to identify love of woman with the Love that made and moves the world. Consequently, lute scarcely could play soft tune, or ardent youth in bright crimson or canary yellow hosen hide in arras without indicating that he had secured his license to do so from Socrates' most eminent follower, or at least what he thought was license. For it was not Plato himself who gave out all these permits but what the subtilizers of the courts and courtlets had made out of him. Plato remodeled; Plato, Cinquencento style.

Bembo was the first of them.

"I say, then," so Castiglione reported him, "that according to the ancient sages, love is naught but a certain desire to enjoy beauty."

The ancient sages. Plato, that is; the broad-shouldered one.

But the tall, aristocratic Venetian with his lean, strong, good-looking, intellectual face, who had not lacked courage — gossip says — to undertake the dangerous rôle of lover to Lucrezia Borgia when that flaxen-haired subject of all evil legends had for her third husband the Duke of Ferrara whose race was famous for its ways of avenging such things, drew back from pursuing this thesis to its logical conclusion.

There are two kinds of love, he hedged. (It was thus Bembo rather than Plato, who gave us that concept which we now call Platonic friendship, my guess being that it would have very much surprised its alleged pagan author and inventor.) Love of the senses and love of the intellect. "Being by nature rational, man can," he elaborated, "at pleasure turn his desires now in one direction and now in the other, and in these two ways desire beauty, which universal name applies to all things, whether natural or artificial, that are formed in due measure and in good proportion, according to their nature."

Then he took his stand for what he called the higher of these. "Therefore let him—" i.e. the lover—"shun the blind judgment of sense, and with his eyes enjoy the splendor of his lady, her grace, her amorous sparkle, the laughs, the ways, and all the pleasant ornaments of her beauty. Likewise with his hearing let him enjoy the sweetness of her voice, the concord of her words, the harmony of her music (if his beloved be a musician). Thus he will feed his soul on the sweetest food by means of these two senses — which have little of the corporal and are ministers of reason—without passing in his desire for the body to any appetite that is less than seemly.

"Next let him obey, please and honor his lady with all reverence, and hold her dearer than himself, and prefer her convenience and pleasure to his own, and love in her not less the beauty of mind than of body. Therefore let him take care not to lead her to fall into any kind of error, but by admonition and good advice let him always seek to lead her on to modesty, to temperance, to true chastity, and see to it that no thoughts find place in her except those that are pure and free from every stain of vice; and by thus sowing virtue in the garden of her fair mind, he will gather fruits of fairest behavior too, and will taste them with wonderful delight. And this will be the true engendering and manifesting of beauty in beauty, which by some is said to be the end of love."

He had seen a pleasant pathway open before him, but he did not take it.

Firenzuola did not exercise such self-restraint. He had no fears of consequences—or maybe he was simply more honest with himself. Like Bembo—and his familiarity with the older man's views is indicated by the fact that he used almost his exact words—he agreed that "according to Plato" true love was this "desire to enjoy beauty." But he did not leave the matter suspended there.

"For loving," he went on, "we must perforce seek. And seeking we must surely find. And finding, we will, of course, regard. And regarding, we will naturally enjoy. And enjoying we will receive incomparable delight. For delight is the ultimate goal of every human action. It is the *summum bonum* sought by all philosophers."

But seek what? Find what? Enjoy what?

Why, the beauty of beautiful women, of course, answered the man who had spent many hours of pondering and more of pen scratching as he wrote his treatise on the subject.

"For beauty and fair women, and fair women and beauty should be praised and held dear by all; for a lovely woman is the loveliest object one can admire, and beauty is the greatest gift that God has given to man. It has been called the seat and nest and hostelry of Love. And love, I tell you, is the origin and fount of every human blessing."

Then a cry fluttered from the heart of the unwilling Abate —not to anyone in particular, but to Beautiful Woman.

"I want to look at you. I want to love you. I want to speak of you. I want to write of you. I want to serve you. I want to adore you."

I want also to have you in the ultimate way, to possess all your loveliness and charm!

The "metamorphosis not in Ovid" was now complete. The Greek wise man who had hinted to the grave Venetian that there are two kinds of love, and that at worst even the lower of these proceeded from the same urges as the higher one, had been taken over by Angelo Firenzuola as a sort of literary pander. Such are the facts of the case. And if somehow they seem a little strange, if it seems curious that a man, who had such small compunctions about going down whatever paths he chose to, should need what he misread into an ancient philosopher to justify him, you must remember that this is the usual human way. For we are conservatives as far as appearances are concerned, and when we modernize our interiors, we cling generally to the old-style façades. The first skyscrapers had express elevators, but they were pulled-up Gothic as far as looks were concerned. It is only when time takes the boldness out of innovation that we become new throughout.

But there are some people who are bold at the start. Aretino was one of them.

"I, who am no philosopher," he wrote Sperone Speroni, "have again seen the discourse which you have philosophically composed on the subject of how harmful it is to do what we wish to do, and as far as it concerns the case of love, I will answer it. To those who assert that in following your appetite you hasten death, I make answer that a man just so much prolongs his life as he satisfied his desires."

Then he paused a moment before digging his pen into paper for an incisive final sentence.

"And I say that, and not Plato!" he concluded.

Not Plato! It was that march toward the future, it was that casting aside of duly constituted authority that makes the story of Pietro's various love affairs significant and worth recording. For there are other lovers whose love chronicles are more entertaining and more intimately set down. Casanova, to take a compatriot. But just as Firenzuola said the final word of the Renaissance (as far as attitude toward woman was concerned) so Messer Pietro said the first word of today. In one sentence, he cleared a path toward his objective, and was the first person to base his morals on nothing but his own needs and his own experience. He became a precursor even there.

His own needs gave him ample leeway. How many times, he told Bernardo Tasso, had he laughed, and at the same time been absolutely wonderstruck at the amorous affairs of his old friend, the poetaster Molza. But now that he too found the ladies responsive to him, he laughed less. "Here is a second affair following the first, and a fourth the third — one being added to another just like my mounting debts," he concluded indulgently. "It is certainly true that in my eyes dwells a tender fury that draws every fair thing to it, and cannot ever be satisfied."

"Worthy Signor Gianbattista," he wrote Fossa, "Titian, who is as much our brother as we are his, told you the truth when he said that I am living as gay a life as if the locks of my beard sprouted from my chin black just as they hang from my temples pure white. I realize that the philosophical bigwigs say that I lack both decorum and prudence. Tell them they are wrong. For it seems to me that every hour which I spend in youthful feats takes ten hundredweight off the burden of my years. I do not deny that there are Platonic steers —" Plato lashed out at again — "who cannot have more than one affair a year, but for my part if I did not have forty a month, I would worry lest a decline had set in."

Elsewhere he became even more intimately specific, but the language is too crude for reproduction. As an amorist, if you can believe his own very sounding statements, he was quite a man.

There is testimony to bear him out. Not only from his own announcements, where we might suspect exaggeration, but from the words of others do we realize that not even the Grand Turk — whose service Pietro did not enter — could have gathered together from the slave markets of Byzantium and the East a more striking harem. The Casa Aretino, looking down upon the stagnant, sombre-colored little canal of the same name, held within its rust-hued walls an assemblage of fair ladies that Suleiman the Magnificent — or even Solomon in all his glory — might have envied. Madonna Pocofila, Madonna Cecilia, Madonna Tina, Maria Basciadonna, Lucretia Squarcia, Franceschina, Paolina, Cassandra, Julia, Marietta d'Oro. La Zufolina — which means Chatterbox — pretty, animated, talkative, as boyish as a Florentine page. Her conversation was "like marchpane and honey on the comb and pine-cone tartlets," and Aretino assured her that Duke Alessandro de' Medici carried on an affair with her simply to discover whether she were a man or a woman. Angela Sara, who he first saw as she passed under his balcony in her gondola, and was "burned by her beauty, splendidly lascivious, proud and passionate." She was always "handsome as the moon, and genial as the warming sun." Angela Zaffetta, one of Titian's models and reputedly the most beautiful woman in Venice. "I give you the palm among all those who have lived your sort of life. License with you wears the mask of decency. You do not make use of your wiles to betray men as most harlots do, but in such way that he who spends his money on you swears he is the gainer. You distribute so skilfully your kisses, the caresses of your hands, and your nocturnal rendezvous that no one is jealous, and quarrels and complaints never come near you."

These were but a few of them, for Aretino's physical and

sentimental needs were quite unbounded. They were dark tigresses of the side *calli* —wives of gondoliers and boatmen, like the two hellcats whose violent quarrels and tempestuous moods, used (during the intervals of actual love-making) to divert George Gordon, Lord Byron, three centuries later, making him for a moment forget his own inner turbulance. They were "servant girls of twenty-five carats," which is his own phrase. They were street walkers. They were lawful spouses of respectable citizens. They were great courtezans. In some cases, they were even noblewomen. They filled up his magnificent chambers. They overflowed onto the seething embankment—there by the German warehouse, where Turks, Greeks, Slavonians, men of the Hansa towns, and Levantines made a colorful mélange. They cared for his rich furnishings; cooked his food—all those plump partridges, tasty reed birds, toothsome pheasants, long-legged hares which were sent to him —served his wine; made love; produced children of which he was not necessarily the father; and quarreled noisily while he was trying to write. (Curiously enough, this did not cut down on his production, but then who can stop an erupting hot-spring?) Narcissus-like, they admired their own beauties and grew green-eyed at the beauties of their rivals. Simply by looking at them, he became an authority on hairdressing, and cosmetics, and on various creams and ointments, which is one reason, perhaps, that he was able to write of women with such insight. His repayment for this was to give those who required such things chains and ornaments of gold, pretty dresses and the bon-bons and the crimson stockings sent him by the princes. To the others—to the spouses of staid citizens and the wives of noblemen, for instance—he paid in glamor; in the titillation of being known to go around with him. For there was—even in Sixteenth Century Venice—the moral equivalent of a café society, and a great rogue and successful scoundrel who had a world-wide reputation for his bold talent was a definite asset to it then just as he would be today. On their part, they fed his vanity and the needs of the flesh.

But there were three other women not yet named who played even more important parts in Aretino's full-blooded life: Caterina Sandella, blond and shapely, with red-gold hair like an Eve by Tintoretto or like Titian's Danae; Perina Riccia; Angela Serena. These three women Aretino loved. And sincerely. And with depth. And with something like altruism. For he was far too exuberant an extrovert to take always and never to give. He might lecher in his spacious bedchamber with its inciting ceiling paintings of the carnal love adventures of the high gods; he might even re-enact in the halls and on the stairways those lewd scenes which are so enviously described — and to some extent also imagined — by his enemies; but he craved also that richer experience that comes when desire has for its handmaidens tenderness and affection. This is easy to understand. That he should have wished this experience threefold; that he should have loved three women, and at (more or less) the same time, is more complicated. "Once," said a lyric idealist, "and only once and for one only," can we pour out that full measure of flooding fondness which is known as love. But lyric idealists, even when called Robert Browning, sometimes find the labyrinth of human emotions too much for them. There is a Russian who understood better. N. N. Yevreinov once wrote a strange play, "The Theatre of the Soul," and its main characters are not three persons, but three aspects of the same man. The author calls them "M^1 — the rational entity of the soul"; "M^2 — the emotional entity of the soul"; and "M^3 — the subliminal entity of the soul." Less grandiloquently, man practical, man romantic, and man spiritual. They fit Messer Pietro perfectly. He was a complete man and needed a wife, and a sweetheart, and what is rather unattractively known as a soul mate. One woman of the three he fell in love with filled each rôle.

Caterina Sandella was the wife. To be sure, Aretino never married her. Against that legal and ecclesiastical step — either with her or with any woman — he had bronze-bound and immovable prejudices. He drew back from it as a cautious bird does from the spread lime.

"When it comes to marrying," he told Messer Ambrogio Eusebii, and he was only partly being cynical and witty to impress one of the bright young men of his following, "the lucky fellow is the one who does it by saying he has done it and not the one who does it in fact. Do you know who ought to have wives? Those who wish to learn to be as patient as Job. If your wife is as beautiful as you say she is, you will have a hard time to be sure of her. If she is a scarecrow, you will be sorry you picked her. Leave a wife's nagging to the ears of tradesmen. Leave her whims and notions to someone who does not mind beating her. Come and go from your house without having to say: 'To whom am I handing her over now, and with whom will I find her when I get back?' Be able to appear in church and in the public squares without fear of that whispering which goes on behind the back of every husband of every wife that ever lived. And if you want a son and heir, beget him out of someone else's wife."

Elsewhere he felt a need to be sententious.

"I have not taken a wife in my old age," he wrote Serlio, "for the same reason I did not take one in my youth. Because the very day I was born, Heaven married me to Genius, from which marriage I brought forth that Progeny the whole world knows of."

Michelangelo — with a few bombastic improvements!

But the truth is he wanted to be free.

But if he never married Caterina, he lived with her as wife, treated her with the good manners due from a good husband, and set her up as undisputed queen consort of his seraglio. "The affection that I have for you," he wrote long after passion had faded into a calm mutual regard, "is so truly engraved in my heart, I love you so boundlessly, and so whole-heartedly do I wish you well that as I write you now that you are absent I do not know how to address you. Anything I say will seem little when compared with my fondness." *Essendo io te, e tu*

me — since I am you and you are me. That was another phrase
Aretino had for la Sandella. Banal? Platitudinous? What
every lover says to every other lover? Yea, verily. Yet coming
from the lips of Messer Pietro the words carry with them
freshness and sincerity. This is perhaps because their simple
utterance contrasts so strongly with his usual overdecorated
baroque braggadocio. One feels that he must have meant what
he said since he took so little trouble to dress it up.

The exact details of their long relationship have not anywhere been set down. Aretino was no Rousseau or no Sten-
dhal who found it necessary to bolster up self-confidence by
putting into writing every minute detail of his life. Such
egotists — thunder as they sometimes do — are really tortured
inwardly by an acute inferiority complex, and when they
record every oscillation of their feelings on an autobiographical seismograph, they are trying to compensate for it. That is
the basis for their exhibitionism. Aretino's masculine and
swelling self-assurance needed no such assistance. But he did,
in his letters, set down a statement here or a hint there out of
which we can build up the outlines.

La Sandella was the daughter of an aristocrat. And she was
married to a man of the same class. Polo Bartolo, according to
the man who stole his wife from him, was "a worthy young
man of noble blood and related to many gentlemen." He was
also wealthy, or at least had great prospects of wealth. Two
hundred years previously an ancestor had come from Lucca,
thrust among the marble mountains, where silk mills spun
busily and prosperously, but where there were not opportunities enough for a young man who not only wanted financial
rewards but position and prestige. Lucca was too small to hold
him and Venice was the big city he chose.

He brought with him 200,000 gold ducats which made
him a millionaire in any language and which caused even the
Venetians to take notice. Presently his sons found themselves
married to the daughters of magnificos. Unlike the products of
most such coolly calculated combinations, the family did not

decline. Uncle Luigi Bartolo, ninety years old, and his not so
youthful son, Marcantonio, now controlled a pleasant fortune
that was not less and was probably more than that brought to
Venice in the Fourteenth Century. And on their death, Polo
would inherit it. He had been, therefore, what is known as a
good catch. But he was also a fast-living young man with a
taste for the three tempters of the moral preachments: wine,
women, and song. All led him to the house of Aretino, and,
once welcome there, he brought his wife with him. It was
fatal, though he did not know it. Caterina saw Aretino was a
man of heart and she told her troubles to him.

"Use your influence with Polo," she implored.

Not he the person to reject a pretty woman, and he went to
Bartolo.

"You are well married," he said, "and acting foolishly.
There is no need on your part for this traffic with courtezans."

Polo laughed at him.

"We pick wives," he said, "and you well should know it, to
make a good marriage and not for amorous disport with them.
That, thank God, we still find elsewhere."

"You must not get upset about this," Pietro told the weeping Sandella, "but should close your eyes to what cannot be
avoided. You are not a jealous girl any longer, and must act
like a sensible and modest wife."

From counselling a neglected woman to stepping into her
husband's place is but a short step and an almost inevitable
one. It was a good start for their incipient affair.

Aretino was drawn also to la Sandella by her position, for
the man risen from the gutter, straight-forward though he be,
is always dazzled by inherited rank. Soon he was referring to
the "magnificent gowns, rich collars and honorable rings in
which she appeared" and "which did not silence envy." He
had given them to her. Soon he was reproving her for the
"servant's duties" which she did for him and reminding her
he did not ask them of her. Soon — thus completely about face
had the worm turned — he was warning her not to be dis-

turbed about her husband's jealousies. "Do not let yourself get worked up about the fact that he snatched a necklace off your shoulders, or by his noisy talk of sending around the officers of the law. It is not wise to make a serious matter out of something that should be taken lightly." The implications are obvious. Aretino did not casually bestow valuable jewelry, and it was a chain he had given that Bartolo snatched away. The consolation Messer Pietro gave the lady by being attentive to her while her husband went about his sordid business, and the flattery she gave him, being noble, by seeming to desire this, led to a liaison. Caterina was now Pietro's mistress. The fact that this relationship established itself is not surprising, nor is it surprising that it established itself soon. What does surprise a little is the length of its duration. Calmly and profoundly Aretino loved Sandella for at least as long as ten years.

But he had a reason for this, and as far as he was concerned, it was cogent one. A house built upon sand shall perish, but this house was built upon a rock.

"Although, Father," he wrote in 1537 to his old friend Sebastiano del Piombo, "our fraternal affection needs no chains, I would like to bind it with those of godfather. In this way your good and holy life will be an ornament to our eternal friendship.

"It has pleased God that my child should be a girl. Like most fathers, I had hoped for a son. Yet is it not the truth that daughters — unless there is some doubt as to their virtue which we must guard carefully — are the greater consolation?

"For it is like this. At about his twelfth or thirteenth year, a boy begins to strain at the parental bit. He runs away from school, refuses to obey, and makes those who begot him sorry for it. His father and mother are lucky if the mischief and the threats of mischief with which he assails them night and day end at that. Sometimes his conduct is such that they fear lest the punishments of the law and of heaven will ensue. But a daughter is a couch on which those who brought her into the world can take their repose when their hair is turning white.

Never an hour passes in which she does not bring pleasure to her parents with her gentle ways and with her gentle and affectionate care for their needs.

"For that reason, as soon as I saw the child which had been created in my own image, I put aside all disappointment that she was not something else, and was so overcome by natural tenderness that I experienced to the full the joys of fatherhood.

"I had her baptized in the house because we were afraid that she might die before she had lived many days. A gentleman acted as your proxy, and held her in his arms in accordance with the Christian custom. The affair was contrived rather hastily since from hour to hour we thought that she might fly to Paradise. But Christ has preserved her to be the pleasure of my later years, and to be a symbol of that life which I received from others, and which in turn I pass on to her. For this I give Him thanks, praying only that I live to see her married.

"In the meantime I must submit to being her plaything, for what are we fathers but our children's clowns? The little innocents trample us under foot, pull at our beards, beat our faces with their tiny fists, and rumple our hair. It is for such coin that they sell us the kisses and the embraces which bind us to them. No delight, either, could be compared to the pleasure this gives us, if only the fear that some misfortune might happen to them did not constantly keep our minds uneasy.

"Every childish tear they shed, every cry they give, every sigh that escapes their mouth, disturbs our very souls. Not a leaf falls, nor a piece of down floats through the air, that does not seem a leaden weight that might fall on their heads and crush them. The ordinary ailments of nature do not make them sleep restlessly or lose their appetite without our trembling for their well-being.

"Thus, sweet is compounded with bitter. And the prettier they are, the greater is our jealous fear of losing them.

"So God preserve to me my little daughter. She is the most engaging creature in the world, and I would die if she even felt pain, let alone suffered real harm. Adria is her name, and she is well-called, for was she not, by divine grace, born close to Adriatic waves?"

Caterina was the mother of this baby, as she was also of another daughter, Austria, born in 1547. And for some reason no other of his women bore him a child—or at any rate one he was sure enough to recognize as his. She thus made a great gift to his expansive personality which was eager to have every human experience. He was bound to her by chains of gratitude. There is no evidence they were ever broken.

Incidentally, the love Aretino had for these babies of his was exquisite, but it was also firm, wise and durable. He loved all that was light and gay about them. Doni, the writer, came to his house one morning "with a friend of mine who wanted to see this great man," and bursting into the living room unannounced, found him romping on the floor with a small daughter. He held back the stranger, slightly embarrassed, telling him he must not come in.

"Let him enter," laughed Aretino.

"No," Doni said, "for he has no children of his own, and will think you have gone mad."

"I have," roared Aretino, "and am glad of it. That is the best thing our children do for us fathers. They make us not afraid to be silly."

"My little daughter, Adria," he wrote Fausto Longiano, "yesterday said two witty things which so amused the gay company I was dining with that I cannot help repeating them to you. We were talking about Fame, and the dear little baby intent on hearing what we said, finally yawned, and then turned to me with a radiant laugh, saying: 'Father, your *Fame* has made me so *famished* that we'd better start eating.' After we had eaten a while, I happened to remark that the flesh with which we were being served didn't please me too well. As soon as she heard this, she said: 'It doesn't please you be-

cause you have plenty already. Give it to me, for I need it.'
By this she meant that I was fat enough already, while she was
skin and bones."

But he took also a keen interest in their up-bringing, paying
close attention even to details.

"All good qualities," he told their mother, "are the fruit of
those words which tell about them. They are nourished
through the ears which hear their names, and the glory of
those who are rich in them. Therefore see to it that if our
Adria does not learn as much virtue as we would like, she at
least acquires as much as she is able to. Then everyone will
give her praise and she will give pleasure to everyone."

"My dear Caterina, I beg you not to beg me, and I counsel
you not to counsel me, and I command you not to command
me to give Austria to the nurse you first suggested, nor Adria
to the governess you now mention. The first is scanty of milk
and the second deficient in character. Let my two daughters
stay in my own home."

"It is wise to take faults in hand before they grow too
strong. For that reason please break our daughter Adria of
her habit of obstinacy, which at present makes her so perverse.
Your sweet admonitions can do this. Then she, who is by
nature tractable and affectionate, will not keep on being scornful of those fatherly and motherly caresses with which we are
in the habit of bringing her up."

And he thought about their pleasure.

"I am sending Adria to spend the Carnival with you," he
wrote Sansovino, "and she can celebrate it for me. It will be
my Carnival to hear her tell about the bull fights, the crowds
and the masking. She knows how to tell about such things."

Yet when they were away from him, he was unhappy. "Indeed, I did let my daughter leave me to spend a week with
you," he wrote her old nurse, "but you saw the tears we both
shed when you came to take her away. It ought to convince
you that a child without her father, or a father without his

child cannot be happy. Bring her back today and we will rejoice."

In fact, there was only one thing that he would not do for Adria and for her sister. He would not legalize his relationship with Caterina Sandella, and thus make them his lawful offspring.

Often enough his friends urged him to take this step, but he was both firm and emphatic.

"There is no need for it," he said. "A decree signed by king or emperor would change nothing. They are legitimate in my own heart."

The sweetheart was Perina Riccia. If Aretino's love for the mother of Adria and of Austria had about it the calmness and the dependability which comes from the long years of hopes shared and hazards mutually faced that we may call marriage whether it has been legalized or not, that which he felt for this young person was different indeed. He was, as we have already noted, the all-sided man, and one side of him was the errant and playful, was the whimsical and fantastic one. Perina supplied the needs of this side — or what Aretino thought Perina was. For he was not exactly the realist about Perina. To the man who could strip all the veneer and lies from every court in Europe, who knew just what great ladies were courtezans and who among the dukes and marquises paid whom for what, there was always something startled and of the woodland about her. She was a hamadryad — to Aretino. She was a shy, dun fawn. She was a nestling, who had just cracked its fragile egg-shell, and was all fluff, and dark and frightened eyes, and amazement at the suddenly expanded world. If, to a less bewitched observer, she was also, at least at times, a scheming slut, a hard trollop — in plain English something of a gold digger who was equipped with everything from blond hair to the customary and ambitious mother — that is beside the question. Worldly-wise Messer Aretino did not see her so. Or he saw her so only on occasions and when he was angry.

And it is how Aretino regarded Perina Riccia that causes linotypers to have to deal with her name today.

He first thought of her as a father might think of his daughter. On a March day in 1537 — while Caterina still carried unborn Adria — Aretino wrote Barbara Rangone, wife of General Guido Rangone, thanking her for the fit of a dress of Lyons "dobblet." Its magnificence, as was to be expected, impressed him, for he was like a child in his great love for gaudiness and color. "It is woven through with gold thread," he exulted gratefully, "and its sleeves are of peacock-colored velvet. The coif that came with it is of gold and green silk." Then he added something significant. "I am going to give it to Perina Riccia, wife of one of my young men. She is no less virtuous than if she had been brought up by the angels in paradise. She calls me her father and mother, and in truth I am both to her. Indeed, I have adopted her. I am keeping her to take care of my old age, for whose ills there are no cure."

"God —" three years later he told Monsignor Zicotto, who was said to be her uncle, and who, even though a priest, may well have been nothing more — "did more for the friendship between you and me when he ordained that Perina should live in my house than even the Bishop of Verona did when he introduced us, for if you joined all the love that four fathers have for their children, you would not have even a small fraction of the affection that I have toward this animated and pretty girl."

"How many daughters have you?" Perina sometimes asked him after Adria was born. She was perhaps a little jealous.

"Two," he laughed.

And the truth was, he insisted, that he "put first her who, by coming into my household to comfort those infirmities to which I am subject, takes precedence over the one produced by my own blood."

He admired her just as a father might.

"There is no one like her," he said proudly. "No one in the world. Her innate goodness makes her always live a chaste

life, yet the pretty child does this with such tact and with such
gaiety that I weep for joy just to think of it. And I swear to you
that I have never seen anybody with so sweet a nature. Would
to God the gratitude she shows me for the little things I have
done for her were shared by some of those I really help. She
does not put on airs because she knows that she can have everything I own. And what is best of all, she and Caterina always
walk with their arms around each other."

She *could* actually have all he owned — materially and spirit-
ually. He gave her presents — not only Barbara Rangone's
giddy coif and dress, but silver scissors, golden thimbles, rings,
trinkets, silk stockings, glittering necklaces, embroidered
scarves. He spent days at a time "watching her when she sews,
reads, embroiders, or makes herself pretty — all in the gracious
way which she has learned from the cradle." He exulted —
and he also boasted — about her marriage.

"How is it possible," he exclaimed, "that although she is
scarcely fourteen years old, she knew how to choose a husband
who would prefer her to some wealthy marriage!"

"Messer Polo," he wrote Maddalena Bartolini, the mother-
in-law, "struts it like a lord whenever he is with Madame
Perina. You would hardly recognize her she has filled out so,
while she is more lovely looking and more good than ever.
She is a cup of gold which holds all those virtues which one
would wish a young girl to have. If you could see with what
tact, and with what reverence and respect, she lives with your
son, you would fall in love with her."

"Thanks for the olives," he added — Maddalena having sent
him a large jar. Then he went into a long dissertation on the
merits and demerits of the various kinds: Tuscan olives,
Spanish olives, Bolognese olives, olives from Apulia. He
tasted each one of them, and set down their sharp savor for
Monna Bartolini. Naturally the kind she sent him was the
best kind. It occurred to him that Perina would do better in
her married life if he became a fast friend of Polo's mother
and this seemed as good a way as any of accomplishing that

end. To say nothing of the fact that he would not object to having more olives sent him.

Even when he rebuked Perina he did it with a twinkle in his eye.

"My dear daughter," he wrote this staid matron, who was still hardly a grown woman, though she had been married now a year, "there is a proverb for little girls, and it says that every bargain is not a swindle. You and Messer Polo and Caterina with the groom and with the maid servant asked me if you could stay a week in the country. Now ten days have passed. Doesn't it seem to you almost time that you were coming home?"

For he wanted her back much more than he wanted to discipline her. She and her husband and her "stepmother." Without them, despite its retinue of male and female hangers-on, the Casa Aretino seemed lonely to him, and a little shabby also. 1537, 1538, 1539, almost 1540. That long, the happy interlude — the four-sided *ménage* of father, mother, adopted daughter and son-in-law — lasted. It was Arcadian — there, in that thieves' den, it was Theocritan. It was an idyll of the first water, all the more engaging because it sought the light and prospered in a place where, to say the least, idylls did not seem likely. Then suddenly it came to an end.

It was the "son-in-law," it was puffed-up young Bartolini who brought this about. He may well have thrust out his chest — as Aretino indicated — and cockadoodledooed like an aggressive bantam cock, when he was first married to Perina, for that is the way of shallow-pated young men when it goes to their head that they have made public demonstration that they have now reached manhood. But presently the innovation wears off and there comes a need for steadiness. Bartolini was not by nature steady, nor was, as a matter of fact, the pretentious palace on the Rio San Crisostamo exactly the place to acquire this quality. His eyes roved, then his fancy, then a good deal more.

Marietta d'Oro — her right name, or, golden Marietta, a

term of affection?—a tart of the first order and also one of Aretino's kitchen maids, was the particular one of his servant-concubines to receive this attention. Though married to one of Pietro's secretaries she looked up from her dish washing to reciprocate. Looks led to hands touching, to stolen embraces, to a whispered plot. One day Master Pietro woke up to find it carried out. He found two empty beds and a large painted *cassone* broken open. Silks and damasks had been blithely appropriated and a goodly haul of crowns and ducats absconded with. Some time during the night Messer Polo and his new lady love had flown the coop. Off the Molo, it was not hard to find a carrack or a round ship sailing for Spain, for Portugal, for Egypt or for Cyprus. They found one. Cyprus was its destination. That was far enough away to be safe from vengeance, yet it was still Christian and still Venetian. They clambered aboard. With Aretino involuntarily paying the fare, they could have a good cabin, live like *signori*. Oars took them from San Giorgio, with its brick-pink belltower, past that flat sand bar, which was known then, as it is today, as the Shore, or Lido. Then sails were unfurled and the breezes carried them. They were now probably past the last lateen-rigged fishing boat, and would soon see in the distance Istria and its white limestone.

Aretino's fury can be imagined.

"Please do not chastise the man who carried her away," he cried on a similar occasion to a military friend of his, who believed in direct action, "and *please* do not bring her back. I do not need the first—and I do not want the second. He has not only freed me from a trollop and a bad woman and from a thief, but from shame and expense and sin. If it were not wrong to be in debt to such an example of every kind of vice, I would confess myself indebted to him."

After that, he had bellowed like an angry behemoth.

"Sodomy and blasphemy and lying and embezzlement and adultery and sacrilege and incest! Those are the signs of the Zodiac for that kind of rogues!"

These words, or words much like them, probably now relieved his feelings. For there is a *catharsis*, worthy of the attention of Aristotle, in profanity. Then suddenly he realized that he had another problem — Perina.

The young wife was heartbroken, either because she really loved Bartolini (which by now she probably did not) or because (which was more likely) her vanity had been wounded and her pride hurt by being jilted. She wept passionately for days at a time.

Aretino tried to comfort her and it was his undoing. Just as if floodgates had been opened suddenly, he fell in love with her. But it was a new love which for the first time made him utterly unselfish. He asked nothing and made no passionate advances, seeming content merely to worship her and to adore her. For the moment, that is; because actually a deep, fiery longing for her almost consumed him. Then a second thing happened, checking Nature in her inevitable course and making "for the moment" last indefinitely. Perina became gravely ill. She had always been delicate, and grief sapped her powers of resistance. It turned out to be a hectic fever, tuberculosis. Aretino was in despair.

But — as always under any stress — he acted. He poured every energy he had into caring for her. He stopped writing and nursed her personally. He slept at her bedside, brought her broths and possets, did every menial duty for her. No woman could have been more tender. Huge men, great brawling masculine fellows are quite often thus. Finally, when the physicians in charge could make no progress, he sent for a specialist. This was Messer Elia Alfan, the able Jewish physician who had once cured Caterina Sandella of a serious illness and from whom, as Pietro put it, "one could learn to be a Christian."

Master Elia thumped, tapped, felt pulses, and then put his bearded visage to the young girl's chest. After that he made a modern pronouncement.

"Send her to the country."

This was doing something, and it appealed to Aretino, who at once put his villa at her disposal. To its mossy walls, fringed with oleanders, below which flowed the small and reedy Brenta — it was not, as we see it today, the ideal sanatorium for a consumptive, but it was better than blood-letting or the tidal damps of Venice, and the therapeutic value of clear mountain air was then unknown — he took her in person, then left her and returned to Casa Aretino. But all through the long winter he moved back and forth. It was a very stormy one. The roads were deep mud — sometimes frozen, always scored with ruts. The snow fell, or it rained and turned to sleet. The canals overflowed the piazzas and embankments, and the north winds howled down from the Dolomites. The shoal water of the open lagoon was lashed to whitecaps. Yet he wrapped close about him his great cloak with its vair lining, and he plunged into the fury. Often he had to curse his ferrymen; almost always bribe them with double fare, to make them leave house or tavern to go out into the tempest. But he never missed a trip. Frequently when he reached the mainland, the fresh water of his little river was frozen over, and his bark could go no further. He would disembark, call for a horse, and push on through the blizzard or the freezing downpour.

"I was no more troubled," he said later, "by the rains which descended on my head, the snow which drifted around me, and the winds that howled, than if the sheets of water, the flakes of snow, and the fury of the gales had been drops of dew, clusters of flowers and gentle zephyrs."

Gamberare at last! His villa! The sick girl!

The heavy door was flung open and a river of warm air flowed out. He strode into the obscure hall, shook the whiteness from his maroon cloak, stamped it from his wet boots, and then, a great fellow with moisture — melted snow or sleet — gleaming in a black beard already shot with silver, he mounted the stone stairway, bringing gusty healthiness and cheeks reddened and roughened by the frosty wind along with him. He softly entered the sickroom. There Perina lay. She smiled weakly—her hands parched from her long illness, but her face flushed from the slow fever—and in a faint voice tried to tell him that she now felt well. This touched him even more than her pain did and his eyes welled, filling suddenly.

"If she only knew it," he said, pitying himself, as a well man often does, because he had to pity her, "the suffering of my heart was as great as the sickness of her body."

Then he had to do something—he could not simply sit and give the comfort of his hand. He went out of the room and sought the doctor. "If there is a secret of medicine that my purse can bring to light, do not leave it untried."

That feeling that surges from the heart that somehow, the ducats—or pounds sterling, lire, francs, almighty dollars—that lie sterilely in bank or purse, which are bits of printed paper or of useless gleaming metal but which can acquire houses, silks, and jewels, rich foods and delicate wines and sometimes fame and power, can be used also as a sort of Danegeld to bribe the dark armies commanded by Azrael to go elsewhere!

After that he had the usual revulsion. What was the use? Not even the wisest physician, he insisted, really knew anything about medicine and what they cured one patient with killed another. But it was only a mood. He was harassed, was in desperation, was grief stricken; knew the helplessness, and the rage that goes with it, that a person of strong will always feels when he seems blocked by a stone wall. But the main thing he sought to accomplish he never let from sight.

At last he was rewarded. After thirteen bleak months of illness, Perina was pronounced cured. He brought her back to Venice. What he did with Caterina is not said; but he packed off Perina's mother to the villa with a long letter telling her to enjoy watching the corn raising its golden opulence from a tiny kernel, and the grape ripening on its pruned vine for the *vendemmia*. Then the man of eight-and-forty, and his nineteen-year-old dear one enjoyed a sort of honeymoon. This time he did ask — and was given. It was ecstasy. Then one morning he woke horrified to find an old scene played anew. There was an empty bed as before — only this time, that of Perina. There was a second, that of another of his so free-and-easy young men. There was also presumably, though he goes into no details, a rifled strong box with cash taken and some silks and dresses.

First of all he thundered.

Then he pretended that he had always seen through Perina. After that he was self-righteous about it.

"I will not go into details as to how she who came to my house in rags was decked with silks and brocades, with necklaces and pearls and was treated with honor and with reverence."

Finally he flung his scorn at her. The young man who ran away with her was punished enough for his misdeed just by having Perina with him. "In fact," Pietro said, "I pity him."

But the truth is that it was woefully sour grapes. Marietta d'Oro was just an escaped slut, but to Perina Riccia had he given his heart and the Lord knows how utterly. He was hurt, humiliated, in a fury at her shabby treatment of him, but he also wanted her back. At first he tried to keep this hid by roaring angrily even while admitting his love. "She who without any merit had me for her slave." "The error which for five years made me worship her." "I blush at my own stupidness just as she should blush at her iniquity." Then he almost inadvertently let it out. "I have no water to put out the fire of her love but perhaps it will go out of its own accord when she realizes how unworthy the object of it is." Then he still hoped?

Four years later he gave proof that this was literally the case. She came back to Venice, a bit down at the heels, but with head still high. Her young man — who "is known as a bad character and has the syphilis" — had had enough of her and God knows in what gutter or what brothel he had abandoned her. But not so Aretino. He asked her no questions, pried into no secrets of the sorry interlude, but simply took her in. He treated her with the same kindness and tenderness he always had. Very shortly the reason for her return came out. She was sick again. Her life as a trollop on the road had started up her old ailment and she was hardly in the Casa Aretino when she collapsed. Again Aretino took her to Gamberare, nursed her personally and got her every medical care. But this time it was too late. Even Elia Alfan was baffled. For three months she coughed up blood and serous matter. It was a marvel, said Aretino, that she lived even as many days.

Then one day she seemed better and he went to Venice for a while. It was the last time he saw her living. She died in the arms of her mother while he was away from her.

"I am glad," he cried, clutching at this consolation, "that in her last hours she was at least able to read the letter I sent to her. Then she could know what I really felt in my heart for her. But I wish death had come more swiftly. I have always loved her. I love her still. And I will love her always — until the Last Day passes judgment on the vanity of the senses."

He did not exaggerate. Death could not take her from his heart, he told a Captain Girolamo Romano who had lost his own mistress, two months later. He was a fool — he knew he had every reason to hate her — but he was more bound to her than ever. Two years later he still grieved for her, though he told her mother not to.

"O famous doctor of philosophy," he wrote Daniello Barbaro — and at that time Caterina was back with him; his second daughter, Austria, whom she perhaps bore to bring him consolation, walked and talked, "I know time is a physician who cures all the ills of the spirit, but I am sure also its years will never heal this wound. When Perina died, I died with her. I come to you only as a beggar asking peace. Why can't you teach me to forget?"

La Sirena was the soul-mate. She was the one lady, to put it with a little dignity, whom large Pietro loved platonically, according to Bembo's definition of Platonic; whom his heart went to without lust or passion; with whom his accord was of the intellect — Dante's *intelletto* and our word simultaneously; whom he was drawn to by nothing more than interests and tastes. Actually her name was Angela Serena — the serene one. But so poetic was the plane of their relationship that it did not seem other than appropriate to change a single vowel and make of her the Siren. A Siren is a fair creature with a bewitching voice who, since the days of Odysseus, has been a symbol for dangerously attractive feminine charm. But she is likewise mythological — which is a nice allegory even though Aretino probably did not intend it to be. It would only be for an imaginary being, or in this case, for his imagined concept of a real being, that Aretino could entertain feelings so ethereal. If it was not unfitting — poets being what they are, and he being, among other things, a poet of at least average distinction — that he should have at least one affair of this nature, it was necessary for him to have it in this way.

What the real Angela Serena was like we must piece out ourselves. She had this much in common with Caterina, that she came from (as it was accepted in Venice) noble stock. She had this much with Perina Riccia, that she was young, pretty, animated and gay. She wrote poetry — merely "of a sort," to be sure; but even poetry of a sort is highly appealing when its author is a gay, animated and pretty young woman. She came from Siena, and hence probably had a voice like a throaty nightingale for reading and for speaking. For despite the proverb *lingua toscana in bocca romana,* it is in the compact, walled, golden-brown city, with its exquisitely slender tower — the fairer daughter of a fair mother, the one that rises from the *Palazzo Vecchio* in Florence — and its peppermint candy cathedral, and the gold and clear blue and carmine of its almond-eyed madonnas by Duccio Buoninsegna, that the tongue of Dante is uttered most melodiously. She had dark hair, and complexion incandescent white. This might not suit Firenzuola, who wanted tresses like a yellow harvest moon and cheeks like tinted porcelain, but Aretino waxed ecstatic about her locks "falling about her shoulders and massed above her temples" that seemed "to gleam almost like hyacinths" and the "members of her inviolable chastity" than which "crystal is not more clear."

She was a friend of the Empress — and Aretino said that she, rather than his merits, had caused gracious Portuguese Isabel to give him one of the collars he so loved. She was vain, I think, and was susceptible to flattery; but she knew how to keep this in the background. She wanted Aretino's attention and she got it by letting him know she wanted it, the coquette thus serving the blue stocking. She too — like the others — was unfortunately married.

"Too much money is the reason for those scandalous ways which cause tongues to wag about you," Aretino wrote Giovanni Antonio Serena. "You are healthy, young and pleasant-mannered, and if you can only keep in check your bad habits you will live a long and happy life. Get rid of your false friends and cleave to your true ones. Associate with honorable people and not with scoundrelly ones, for the former give you a good reputation and the latter take away what reputation you have.

"But I am talking to the wind," he added.

For he knew well that you cannot change an inborn nature and that it was not possible for this self-willed, rioting loose-liver to leave following his catamites and gutter women while his purse was full.

"Not even Time who is a good hand at breaking headstrong colts will bridle him."

While his regard for Angela may have prompted all this moralistic oratory, something else bears in upon us. Like many of his nature, Messer Pietro Aretino was not very toler-ant of misconduct — except when indulged in by himself.

But if he was not tolerant, he took advantage. He would not have been fair to himself — and to his code of opportunism — if he had not. Polo Bartolo with his inveterate bedding with

the wrong woman had given him la Sandella, and the two
daughters he worshipped so; Polo Bartolini—the near simi-
larity of the names is curious—and Marietta darling (so,
really, I translate the *d'Oro*), Perina Riccia. Now Messer
Serena, whose vices were a bit more heterodox than either of
these two, threw his wife Angela under Pietro's influence and
he blossomed in his third kind of affair. It was unlike any that
he had ever engaged in before. It was as tenuous as peach blossoms on a sun-saturated hillside. It was not physical. There
were no intrigues leading inevitably and not even subtly to a
culmination in passion. *Platonicamento*—and with what
tender, novel, new and therefore strangely titillating platon-
ism!—he read intensely to this eager lady all the latest things
that he had written, and he listened to her reading to him;
her things and his as well—in that lovely, rich, vibrant, and
nostalgia-stirring Tuscan voice. He discussed Philosophy with
her; and Love; (purely in a theoretical and abstract way—he
who goes down in history because he had put love so blatantly
upon another basis!) and Virtue; and Religion; and the
Spirit. He even wrote a series of poems for her, and the words
in them were not vipers and scorpions, but lutes and
dulcimers.

> My heavenly Siren hath bright flashing eyes
> That make her hair shine golden in the sun.
> Yea, each blue orb the bright light hath of one
> That down to earth from God's sweet spirits flies.
> Her cheeks the color have of a blown rose
> That burgeons on a hill mid violets,
> And when she speaks angelically, she lets
> Her parted lips rubies and pearls disclose.
> Her gay bright laugh, the tenderness of her glance
> Do fill with such delight this earthly place
> As only when in Paradise you would expect.
> Her chaste breasts do forbid all dalliance,
> Yet she hath nature's miracle in her face,
> And all that's gracious in her intellect.

It is hard to imagine that the same person who wrote the sonnets against Adrian and against Clement was the author of this airy bit of verse.

Even when he gossiped with her—and he did undoubtedly while away some of their séances with salty anecdotes about the great persons he had known—he did so genially and without malice: I know these things, as it were, but do not take part in them. Plainly she appealed to the highest side of his nature, and men of his sort love to have their highest side appealed to. Especially when the one who does so is an exceedingly lovely-looking woman whose very charm and beauty is a constant and intriguing counter-appeal to their lowest side. It adds that variety which is said to be the spice of life.

How long Aretino would have maintained this idyllic attitude we need not tempt disillusion by inquiring. It was a novelty and his spirit, therefore, was willing enough. But the flesh is an obstinate campaigner and what it cannot gain by main force, it often essays by indirection. It was not given the opportunity. For Angela Serena's husband intervened.

He was urged on by various scandalized relatives who saw the family name at stake. Messer Serena himself could lecher and carouse, for that was expected of him as a spoiled and dissolute young man. But when tongues began to wag about his wife, it was another matter. La Sirena indeed—well, he has plenty of other sirens and we all know what he does with them! Not that I blame her—her husband you know! But with Pietro *Aretino*! So gossip in the churches and piazzas and in the dull bed of various licit bedchambers. One day the innocent if somewhat empty-headed siren was called into the great living room of the handsome palace, which was not far from the Ca' Bolani, now the Casa Aretino. She faced uncles, brothers, brothers-in-law, a husband. One of them began to talk, not the husband certainly, who must have been—if he had even the faintest trace of decency—just a little sheepish in his rôle of moralist. She was told certain things plainly and she had to listen to them. Not much later Messer Pietro went to call on her. A lackey informed him she was not at home. He went again. This time the cold reception was more definite. He wrote a letter to her. It was not answered — worse than that, a servant brought it back to him. One day quite casually he passed her on the narrow street. Velvet cap in hand, he greeted her. Most unkindest cut of all, she strode on, her head high as if she had not even seen him. That was plain enough. Deflation was, and ought to have been, complete.

To be sure he did not acknowledge this. That would have been treason to the one person he never was disloyal to — Pietro Aretino. Instead, first he was angry. Then he meditated revenge.

He found it in a way that entertained all Venice heartily. He sat down and wrote a second letter. This he sent his Siren's husband.

"Do you realize that there is no other great lady now living who can boast that the man princes fear, has so sung her that she will be remembered for ever? Are you aware that popes, kings, and emperors are happy when they are merely not vituperated by my pen? The Duke of Ferrara sent an ambassador laden with money just to induce me to visit him. A time will come when these very words I send you, and which I deign to sign with my own hand, will be a title of pride and of nobility to your descendants."

Thus he relieved his feelings.

And, of course, publicly.

For he took care that every inn and street corner should have a copy.

It was true, of course. The boasts were not exaggerated. Because their lives intersected his, Angela Serena and her sorry husband are remembered now when many greater ones are utterly forgotten. But they also had their ironic victory, whether or not they meant to. They had made him ridiculous in public, and that hurt him inordinately. It was his own fault, or was the price he had to pay for being what he was. He had left Bembo and even Firenzuola, with their Plato wa-

tered and twice watered, far behind him in his march toward
the realistic truth about why man seeks woman. That was all
right. He had a right to. But he should have stayed there. For
when suddenly a platonic mood came over him, there was no
one who would believe in him. Instead they laughed at him,
while also laughing at the two Serenas. He was hoist high
and soundingly by his own very efficient and effective petard.

CHAPTER XIV

The Secretaries of the Secretary of the World

BUT there were other complications too. It took a harem to take care of one side of Aretino's nature and consequently he assembled one, but his requirements did not end at that. If he needed love, he also needed adulation. The young men who gathered around him supplied this need. They flattered him, not because they feared him, but because they wished to emulate him.

In number they were almost as many as his women; Lorenzo Veniero, Polo Bartolini, Ambrogio degli Eusebii, Niccolo Franco, Leonardo Parpaglioni, Medoro Nucci, Lodovico Dolce, Agostino Ricchi, Anton Francesco Doni, Fortunio Spira.

Usually, they have been thought of as his secretaries — the secretaries of this self-styled secretary to the whole world — and two or three of them actually were. Most of them were simply hangers-on. Would-be poets in a rainbow array of one man's cast-off jerkin, another's cap, a third's hosen; down-at-the-heels pedants; hack writers, who gained some sort of a living by selling dedications to such deluded patrons as would cheat the jails by paying for them, or by serving up various made-to-order messes to the printers and booksellers, who were springing up in the city; they were — satellites or secretaries — as arrant a company of rakes and self-seeking but not utterly un-talented scoundrels as were ever sheltered beneath a single roof.

Such of them as were not born there came to Venice as the logical sanctuary for those rogues errant of the arts, who sprang up in Sixteenth Century Italy like the same plague of locusts that the scholars were a hundred years before them. They slept in filthy lodgings down the side *calli;* acted as porters, gondoliers, and even pimps; cadged for crusts of bread. Once there, however, they were drawn to Aretino by a kind of tropism. He did not discourage them. A scrawled letter of introduction from some petty prince who had once given him fifty ducats or an old doublet, or an incoherent laudatory sonnet scratched on foolscap, and his house and all he had in it was theirs. They could stay indefinitely, guzzling his wine, wearing out his shirts and shoon, and snuffling around him like a pack of mongrels looking for the scraps he flung them from the table of his food or of his glory. Some of them found in this a good living and from then on until the day he or they died, they continued as his unofficial but definitely not unpaid *entourage* of touters, overfeeding his already bulging self-esteem by singing fulsomely his praises both to himself and to all hearers, and also doing various dirty jobs for him, such as helping him when he wished attacks on enemies to be just a little too vindictive for his taste, for example, or even marrying women whom he wanted as mistresses. Others merely got upon their feet again, then became his rivals, or attempted to. A few fitted into both categories.

There was little difference. And reviewing the shabby story of their deeds, I do not think that we shall be able to escape the conclusion that, shrewd as Pietro was in detecting the faults and foibles of the great men of his age, he was an exceedingly bad judge of character. For to obtain his support and friendship, it was only necessary to bend the same knees of feigned toadyism and to offer the same buttered bread of extravagant praise — backed of course with bluster — as he himself did to the princes. But perhaps this was as it should be. Undoubtedly the most effective satirists have in them, to some degree, at least, those very weaknesses they take their flings at. That is why they understand them so well.

They were, of course, not all cut from the same cloth. Lorenzo Veniero was a nobleman. An ancestor of his had been doge, and that, further, in the days of greatness, before Turk militarism, which was to start mercantile, prosperous, and therefore intrinsically pacifist Venice toward its ultimate decadence, had more than just been heard of, and when the lion-pennanted galleasses of San Marco dominated the inland Mediterranean, or at least the eastern end of it. An uncle was to hold the same high office shortly, in the no less magnificent days of her splendor, when the rats had done a good deal of their gnawing, but were still unseen, and — by Venetians, at any rate — unsuspected. Lorenzo himself was to hold government position, was to be appointed governor of Dalmatia with its rugged island and deep inlets, its gleaming mountains of the white Carso limestone, and its little jeweled Italian cities; was to be sent to the mainland as *podestá* of Vicenza under verdant hills where the ogival and balconied buildings — Palladio had not yet left his cockleshell touch — looked like Venetian palaces set on dry land; was to sit in the proud councils of the proud, most serene republic; was to be given good jobs by his class and country and to do these good jobs very well.

Bartolini scaled a little lower. He was a Venetian and he came from a good family, but he was born a rogue and he died one. Like Aretino himself, Medoro Nucci was spawned by the gutters of the same fiery Tuscan hill-town that gave Pietro his name, but unlike him, he stayed upon the gutter level, a scoundrel of the first water. Lodovico Dolce was a poet — when he was not a hack writer, job translator, publisher's reader. "Thank you," Pietro wrote him, "for your poem about the little doves. It is so pleasing and musical that I can hear the roo-coo-cooing of a dovecote in its *terza rima* lines. Indeed, there is nothing you have written that does not have the quality of your name." Dolce means dulcet or sweet. Evidently an arrant manliness was not one of Lodovico's qualities though he did father a son and daughter.

Leonardo Parpaglioni was a little of both. Aretino found it necessary to praise verses he had written, though at the same time he cautioned him against vanity, warning him that "fame is the stepmother of death and ambition the excrement of glory." But his exit from the Aretino household was a tawdry one.

"Messer Ottaviano Scotto," Pietro wrote affably to one of the lesser noblemen who sent him gifts from time to time, "has just brought me the cambric shirts trimmed with embroidery that you sent me, and I like them very much. In fact I am going to take good care that they are not robbed from me like the crimson silk ones and the thirty *scudi* which you sent me from Mestre when you halted there on your way home from the wars in Hungary. One of my underlings not long ago decided to skip off to his native Lucca and at three o'clock of a dark night he called a gondola and placed in it a chest which contained the said shirts together with other goods of mine worth in all two hundred crowns. Then suddenly he remembered that he had left behind a pair of velvet hose. He went back to get them. When he returned, the gondolier had vanished with his gondola and with all the booty as everybody even in the last canal of Venice now knows!"

It was a familiar pattern, though most of Aretino's imbroglios with the ex-members of his household did not have this pleasant ending of the robber robbed which made it like a comedy by Molière. We have already seen how Bartolini found Messer Parpaglioni's larcenies far too small, and how he not only absconded with more money than that rhymester did and with more of Aretino's worldly goods but eloped also with one of worthy Pietro's women. Medoro Nucci wanted Aretino's protection, got it, did not find it enough, and gave vent to his dissatisfaction by publishing abroad certain illuminating facts about Aretino's origins that the great man did not wish known. That has likewise been recorded, and while we biographers must be grateful for the truth however it may reach us, it was a scurvy trick. Anton Francesco Doni's equally vindictive way of biting the hand that fed him — and delicacies, at that! — fits a later chapter. It was of a similar nature.

Indeed only two of Pietro's protégés never turned on him, Lorenzo Veniero, and Lodovico Dolce. A young rip with a flair for writing that was born out of his ebullient flair for life, the gay Lorenzo came into Aretino's household, not because he needed the patronage, but to sow his wild oats. He found ample fields there. He took part in the Aretine debauches and he became also a literary imitator. The former have not been recorded, and they would be dull to read about any way — vice having, through the ages, a certain sameness; but the literary imitations remain. They are two poems, *La Puttana Errante,* or the Wandering Harlot, and *Il Trentuno,* or the Thirty-one, which tells the sad story of a lewd trick certain rogues and rascals played on Angela Zaffetta. If possible — and in that case an all time low is reached — they are more indecent than anything that Pietro ever wrote. But they are also well written. And since Messer Aretino was supposed to have had a corner on well-written lewdness, they have often been attributed to him. He declined the honor — though not because he was ashamed of the work. By his own words, and as if proud of what his influence had brought about, he assigned (in a letter to the Marquis of Mantua, who was vastly amused by them) these two compositions to his noble "pupil." Young Veniero seems to have accepted the assignment, glad of even this sort of renown. Later on though, they must have been somewhat embarrassing, but unlike Shakespeare's Prince Hal (who became perhaps just a bit of a prig) he did not disown either them, or Aretino-Falstaff. Indeed, fifteen years later at the height of his grave state career, he asked his old friend to be his son's godfather. Aretino accepted. It was probably a credit to them both.

Dolce also stood by Pietro when he needed him, though he had less reason for not doing so than had Veniero. He was always a friend, and at one time he even became his copyist. It was something when you consider how busy he was. For besides all the jobs he did for publishers Giovanni and Gabriele Giolito, he wrote steadily and voluminously. He indeed was something of a record breaker. When he died at sixty, he was, counting translations and adaptions, the author of 112 books!

"I thank you," Pietro wrote this poet, "for your offer to prepare the second volume of my letters. I accept it gratefully.

For truly a well-copied and carefully punctuated manuscript is like a charming and beautifully dressed bride. Therefore, you must not be surprised that I wish mine to appear in the style your care will give it."

To be sure he followed this with the usual author's growl about careless printers and about typographical errors. But it was not at Dolce he growled. Indeed, Lodovico's devotion to him so touched him that it once moved him quite astonishingly to a burst of modesty.

"My good friend, the handmaidens of glory light my obscure name with a tallow candle not a torch. I carry ignorance in my hand. I had only an elementary education. I taught myself, and hence if I write in a scoundrelly fashion, there is more excuse for it than for those who have drunk deep from the Greeks and the Romans. If you read me, therefore, excuse me on the grounds that I am a prophet not a poet."

Like a large part of his self-analyses, it was a good deal more than half true.

But the relationships thus far reported had, when they came to their debâcles — excepting always the two that turned out well — the quality of irritations rather than catastrophes. If you should pepper a bull elephant with buckshot, he might think that whatever small insect pests even pachyderms are afflicted with were unusually active that day; but you would hardly bring him down. Perhaps they stung harder than that, for Aretino bellowed lustily at each so-called pin-pricking assault that was hurled at him. But there is evidence that he liked bellowing — particularly in print — and found it profitable. He understood publicity, and like P. T. Barnum, knew that it was good even when it was bad. "Even when I am railed at, I get my quota of renown," he told Marcolini. But he had two other secretaries, and in his dealings with them, mere annoyance festered suddenly into serious infection. His tripartite friendship with Ambrogio degli Eusebii and Niccolo Franco, followed by their three-cornered quarrel, for a moment threatened consequences that might have been devastating.

One aspect of it threw Aretino into a panic—he had several panics but this was the most serious one—that made him run for cover as a hare might. Another aspect cost him plenty of crowns.

They were a miserable enough pair. Eusebii was a fool rather than a villain, but it is not certain that in the long run folly does not do even more damage than villainy does. He came from Milan, and probably, despite his sounding name, from the gutters of that even then overgrown city. He was something-and-twenty, which is a good age to make a large idiot of yourself if you are gaited that way; for you have a self-confidence which does not, as a rule, come younger; and it is still just a little early to reflect. He esteemed himself greatly as a poet, though the few stiff sonnets of his which survive—and that only because Aretino printed them—have not led many others to agree with him. He had also no doubt that the beauties of Venice, when they saw him, would do battle royal for the honor of sharing his bed with him. He was agog, said Aretino, "to satisfy his desires with a woman so that he can make sport of Narcissus." Unfortunately, and that, as we have already seen, in spite of pointed advice from Aretino, he brought about this end by marrying one of Pietro's kitchen-maids. Next he decided to be a soldier. A train band with pennons streaming and with bagpipes playing went marching down the narrow street, while fair ladies leaned over balconies to call and wave to them, and it was all Aretino could do to hold him in check.

"It seems to me," Pietro told him, "that you are mad even to think of enlisting, and absolutely crazy if you carry out your purpose. It is as bad as if you became a courtier. Indeed, the court and the camp are much alike. In the first you find want, envy and old age, and you end up in the poor house. In the second, you gain wounds, a prison and hunger. It is all right to dream that you are a mercenary because that makes a man one of the heroes of Troy in his own thoughts, but I do disapprove of putting those dreams into effect. If what you want is to cut a couple of capers beneath the windows of your doxy with your head all bedecked with feathers, stay at home: you can do it as well right here. For a *'hip, hip hurrah, boys!'* in front of a hen roost, you pay by having no bread with your supper for a week. For a bundle of rags — and that's all your fine booty amounts to — or prison — where you will end up whenever God wills it — your reward is the right to limp home on crutches, and to sell everything you have so as to keep out of the hands of loan sharks. You would do well to change your mind, and since you can make a sonnet better than you could go through a drill, go on having a good time at my expense. The big prizes in the lottery are very few. Pin that on your chest, and then go and buckle on your tin armor!"

Niccolo Franco was less long on folly than Ambrogio was, but as far as trouble for Aretino was concerned, his arrant roguery about evened the score. "The wretch," Pietro said when at last his eyes had been opened, "is like a cur kicked from door to door and hated by everybody. When he sees a bone that he cannot sink his teeth in, he starts to growl sullenly. He is not ferocious. He is dying of starvation.

"I have seen madmen," he added, "insolent men, envious men, spiteful men, wicked men, destructive men, hard-headed men, arrogant men, villains and ungratful men, but I have never seen anybody whose madness, insolence, enviousness, spitefulness, wickedness, vanity, hard-headedness, arrogance, villainy and ingratitude were like his."

This *faciebat et iocabatur Francus,* as it says in the colophon of his "Temple of Love" was, further, "one of the leanest and most tattered pedagogues that ever gargled soup." When you went to war with Aretino, he moved up a heavy artillery of phrases that laid flat your strongest citadels. While the vehemence confirms their bias, investigation shows that they were largely true.

Niccolo was born in Benevento, and I do not suppose that the ruggedness and poverty of that place of origin, did anything to soften his disposition. Benevento — as of 1515, when

Niccolo saw the light of day there—had a great past and a starveling present. After the fall of Rome and the barbarian invasions, it became the capital of a potent Lombard duchy, and the bronze doors of its cathedral show that even in the early Middle Ages, it was rich and important. But latterly it had sunk into the obscurity of a southern hill-town, which had all the disadvantages of hill-towns generally, and none of the vitality that carried Tuscan hill-towns to great place. Niccolo shared its starved pride and want.

He was, according to conflicting stories, the son either of a poor country schoolmaster or of a rude ploughman. Scholars argue about this point, but there is no reason that the elder Franco could not have been both. His brother, Vicenzo, wrote poetry and was a schoolmaster too. Niccolo followed him in both occupations, but quite young he grew sick of teaching rag-and-tatters sons of provincial noblemen their Greek verbs and Latin declensions, and clambered down the crags to Naples. There he tried another way of making his living. He scratched out a series of Latin epigrams in honor of Isabella of Capua, wife of Don Ferrante Gonzaga, the viceroy. These appeared when Niccolo was twenty. There is no record that Isabella rewarded them, and it is indeed probable that the beneficiary of severe narrow Spanish rule would have been a little afraid to employ a fiery young man who by his own admission "would rather go without eating than not let fly my pen when the fancy takes me." But her husband, Don Ferrante, was a younger brother of Aretino's old patron, Federigo Gonzaga, and he may well have advised Franco to go to Mantua. The Marquis of Mantua would naturally have sent him on to Venice. It got him rid of a disturbing if talented stripling and it also did the youthful poet a service. He arrived there in the fall of 1536, and found shelter in the house of Quinto Gherardo. Quinto was a friend of Aretino's and Niccolo soon plied him for an introduction.

"I would serve Aretino as a slave if he would receive me as such," he insisted.

That was meat for Pietro, and he welcomed Franco with open arms. Rag, tags and patches, he led him into his great salon and sat him at a table.

"Take the hide of your hunger," he said, "and tell your lice begone. You can't live on half an ounce of *pasta* a day. Here are shoon of velvet for you and here too a bright beretta. Later there will be shirts to keep your back warm."

"This is too good for a wretch," replied Niccolo, but there is no record of his refusing them.

A maidservant set a bowl of broth in front of him and then had to run to the kitchen to keep from laughing in his face.

"My master," she announced to cook and scullions, "used to play host to princes and magnificos, but now he is the patron of a rogue's boarding house."

There is no snobbery in all the world like a servant's snobbery. But it is not often that the values it is based upon are false.

At first he, and Aretino, and Ambrogio degli Eusebii, got on famously. Why, as far as the young men are concerned, is obvious. Aretino fed them—and not crusts—and clothed them in their share of the finery which his pen earned him from the lords. It was pleasant to wear damask and to eat partridges. They looked up to him also in the rôle of master. With all due respect to his writing—and it was the most vivid and vital of an age packed with tremendous life—he was more than anything a literary racketeer. They who wished to be the same, paid him the admiring deference that all tyros do to the head of their profession.

Aretino, however, had equally good reason for wishing their good will, and they were not wholly altruistic ones. Printer Marcolini, his good friend, had promised him that as soon as he had published Serlio's book on architecture he would bring out a volume of Pietro's letters. They were the first ones in the Italian language ever assembled thus, and he was a good enough judge of public appetite and public taste to realize the sensation they would create. He anticipated the

reception they would get, and his corollary increase of income.
But in the meantime he faced a difficulty. When Achille della
Volta had attacked him fourteen years ago, he had not permanently injured him, but he had cut off certain useful fingers
from Aretino's right hand. This made actual writing something of a problem, the ideas flowing, but getting them on
paper being slow and troublesome. An amanuensis, therefore,
was a virtual necessity. But even for a man with ten digits, the
job would have been a prodigious one. Approximately 300
epistles were to be included, and each one had to be copied
on its sheet of foolscap in a clear, legible handwriting which
the printer could make out. They had further to be selected
from the many more that he had written. 2000 is his own esti-
mate. Nor did he even have copies of them all. Through
"faulty judgment" on his part which led him to think little
more of these his dashed-off improvisations than "a stepmother
does of her stepchildren"—and perhaps also from laziness—
he had very rarely retained duplicates. Now he had to seek
the originals. Princes, painters, prelates, magnates and great
ladies had to be importunated. Please send me the letter that
I sent you. It will be printed, of course, and you will get some
fame thereby. That also was part of the enormous task.

Messer Niccolo Franco and Messer Ambrogio Eusebii took
all this in hand. Aretino merely guided them. All through the
summer of 1537, therefore, the two assistants toiled away. It
was not more than normally hot, but a white sun made noon
unbearable, except when you remained in darkened rooms;
and the night damps shut down oppressively. There were
breezes upon the Lido, and sometimes even at the Piazzetta
and the Riva degli Schiavoni, but they rarely penetrated to
the S-curve of the Grand Canal where the Casa Aretino looked
upon the Rialto. Flagons of white Soave stood, however, on a
walnut table, and there were melons, figs, grapes, peaches, and
pears on silver salvers. And with these to refresh them they
copied, sorted, turned to Aretino for authority, and then
threw away, or retained and revised. They went to the cabi-

net where the letters were filed, took out, examined, either kept or returned. They relieved couriers of precious packets which when opened showed the large, familiar handwriting. Sometimes they even made suggestions.

"Here, Messer, is a grammatical error."

"Leave it. It is the speech used. It adds pith and vividness." Or, "Change it. I was hurried that morning."

"There, Messer, is a misspelling."

Or there was a garbled attempt — rarely, for he but rarely made a use of pedantisms — to introduce a Latin saw by the man who knew only such Latin as he had parrot-like picked up by ear. Former schoolmaster Niccolo Franco was particularly helpful in matters of the latter sort. But they both helped, and in every matter. The finished product was as much Aretino's as if he had had no assistants, but there is no doubt that the two young men were a lot more than stenographers. They were in a small sense at least collaborators in the work that perhaps as much as any work consolidated Pietro's fame.

Aretino did not forget this fact — indeed, rather, he acknowledged it gratefully. "These letters," he wrote to Marcolini, "were assembled by the love that my young men have for the things I write." He took the position, it seems to me, that they were worth more to him because his young men liked them. He proclaimed thus their judgment to the whole world.

But he went even further in these days of flushed exuberance. Franco had his own ambitions as a writer, and it occured to Aretino to give these a helping hand. He took four of Niccolo's sonnets and printed them with an effusive comment.

"This fellow, who after I am gone will be another I, and who nevertheless has been willing to spend his time copying out my writings, has written a hundred fine sonnets of which I select the following examples."

He did a similar service for Eusebii.

"As you know," he wrote, "Ambrogio has already done marvels. Indeed for a mere lad, there is almost too much judgment and style in the verses he writes."

He paid Niccolo the compliment of addressing to him his great letter against pedantry which sets forth his creed as a writer. Maybe this was two-edged, but I cannot feel that it was a dig at Franco's overload of book-learning, for the simple reason that he later transferred it to Dolce who was then on the closest terms of friendship with him.

"Follow the path which life and reality has marked out for you if you wish your words to stand out from the page on which they are written. Laugh at those who filch worn-out *clichés*. And realize that there is a wide difference between being influenced by, and blindly copying.

"Make use of the phrases that your own ears have taught you. People are tired to death of 'needs bes' and of 'else thou shouldsts,' and the sight of them in a book starts readers to snickering just as they would if they saw some bold fellow come prancing on to the piazza in a full armor with a steel helmet on his head all a-glitter and covered with dancing egret plumes. We would say that he was crazy or on his way to a fancy dress ball. Yet in another age this was the correct apparel for Duke Borso or for Bartolemeo Colleoni.

"The best way to follow Petrarch or Boccaccio is to express your own ideas with the same beauty and skill with which they expressed theirs, and not to plunder them of this or that phrase that today sounds stilted, or to lift bodily whole verses from their poems. It is only school teachers who think the way to write poetry is to imitate, and as they cackle into their notebooks, they transform beauty into rhetoric, a mere hodge-podge of meaningless words they have learned by heart. But, O wandering tribe, I tell you that poetry is a mere fantasy of nature in one of her ebullient moods. It requires nothing but its own frenzy, but if it lacks that, it is like a cymbal with no jangling bells to it, or a church tower without chimes.

"The alchemists, though they employ every device that

their patient, stingy avarice can suggest, have never yet made gold, but only a poor imitation of the same, yet Nature without the least effort has produced it pure and fine. The moral of this is: learn a lesson from the story about the wise painter I now tell you. He was asked whom he imitated, and he pointed toward a crowd of men. He meant that life was his model.

"Pay attention to the nerves and fibre and leave what is merely skin to the skin flayers who stand about begging for a penny-worth of fame with about as much genius as a pickpocket has.

"I tell you to be a sculptor of the things you feel and not one who paints miniatures with words."

He praised both of them in the fantastic dream-allegory which he made up in a letter to the ambassador of the Duke of Urbino.

He had climbed up the Mount of Parnassus, and he described that famed place with a grotesque irony and baroque sarcasm which was almost as if Dante had filched the pen of Rabelais. There he sat down in "an inn set by the wayside to ensnare the murderers of poetry." And he looked behind him.

"And even as I did so, I discerned my fine Franco coming up the very path which I had made over the mountainside, and it was not without pleasure and surprise that I saw him. I saw also that Ambrogio, my pupil, was clinging close to my heels and was hastening his footsteps."

They were the only two of his contemporaries that he saw fit to mention in this way and they were the two who would perhaps be the most appreciative. He thus fully paid his debts to them. And in the thieves' den of the written word that rose beside the limpid waters, good feeling reigned supreme.

But it did not reign for long. Nothing but the compelling needs of a definite situation could have held three such chemically active elements side by side inert, and once that had ended, there was inevitable explosion. It is not possible, for example, to imagine Franco "who is so puffed with vainglory that he spends the whole day writing odes to himself" being satisfied for long with the patronizing accolades Pietro gave him. Nor was he. Even when Aretino brought out his four sonnets with approving comments, he sputtered like a squib.

"Four or five of them have merit?" he fumed. "Everything I write is perfect, and not even Petrarch is qualified to cast slurs upon a line of it."

He had further, he wanted Aretino to know, though he took care not to invoke laughter by saying it in his presence, written dialogues and they were in the hands of a publisher.

"Any man of taste will tell you that they are far better than those of Lucan."

He was like the character in Thomas Kyd's famous tragedy. His speech showed him to be a Spaniard, being nothing but an inventory of his own commendations.

It is not any easier to conceive of Aretino continuing to give away free his eulogies, particularly when each generous bestowal of them was met only with a prayer or a demand for more.

Eusebii made the inevitable contributions of his hot-headed and impulsive temperament, for he had in his nature much of the Irishman in the story, who wanted to know whether this was a private fight or could anyone join in. It is to be noticed, however, that he never turned upon the man he called his patron. He was not overendowed with judgment, but he was basically loyal; and that will be evident, even if sometimes ludicrously so, through the whole course of his fantastic history. Unlike Niccolo, moreover, he was not hounded by a never-resting ambition. He wanted to write poetry, or to be a conquering hero, or to become rich and prosperous, but only if these ends could be attained by luck or miracle. Not certainly if he had to achieve them by hard work.

Three episodes, following each other in swift succession, brought the cataclysm about. It is not certain that Franco engineered the first of them, though it would obviously have been in character, and though Aretino assuredly believed he did. His responsibility for the second is challenged only by a very few and I feel it can be accepted. Of the third episode, there is, of course, no doubt.

On a Spring morning in 1538, one of those friends who always seem to be on hand to bring us evil tidings came hurriedly to the Casa Aretino, and hammering upon its gloomy portal, left a devastating bit of news. Charges of blasphemy were even now being sworn out against Pietro in the Venetian courts. They were to be followed, he said rumor had it, by charges of sodomy. The complainant was Giovanni Serena, himself adept in both of these matters, who thus took revenge on Aretino for the biting invectives he had let fly, when Serena took offense at his attentions to his wife. It was a very serious matter. By some process of human reasoning, verbal offense against the Lord Almighty — whom, if one were pious, one should believe capable of dealing with His own defilers — was punished drastically by human hands. The blaspheming tongue offended no longer, the head that held it being separated from body by sharp ax. The second offense, more logically if still somewhat severely, was likewise subject to man's law. A sodomite could be hanged in a cage from the campanile and left to die there. Aretino did not relish either of these ends. The florid countenance was content to rest on swollen neck, and he did not wish, either, to die slowly of hunger and thirst swinging in midair while the handsome robes he wore were dirtied hopelessly with what fellow citizens of imagination might produce from handy gutters. On the Brenta stood his villa, Gamberare. And though this time, at any rate, the charges were baseless, he took no chances. He escaped there hastily. Not until he was within its safe walls and looked down on the oleanders and the orange trees, did he breathe easily or feel secure.

The second episode took place a few months later. Aretino did not stay in exile more than a few weeks. Then his old adversary, the Duke of Urbino, intervened. Completely exonerated, he paraded back to the city, and his old splendor of living was resumed once more. But in August he was attacked again, and this time with his own weapons. An obscure printer in the city of Perugia brought out a little volume. Biancho dal Leon was his name, and the pamphlet's title was the "Life of Aretino." Its supposed author was Francesco Berni, now dead and not able, therefore, to deny the lie. In form, it was a dialogue. It began savagely with some would-be humor based upon a grotesque pun. The night before Aretino was born his mother dreamt that she had given birth to a skinful of wine (*Un otro di vino*). That was how Pietro got his name of the divine Aretino (*Aretino divino*). It next entered into that malevolent, distorted, but on the whole basically accurate relation of his early years which gives us the only outline which we have of his years of vagabondage. Then it took up present scandals. Assuming what gossip said of Aretino's flight from Venice to be gospel truth, it launched into a virulent, vivid, detailed but unquestionably highly-colored account of Aretino's doings with his friends, his friends' wives and his friends' sweethearts; it is literally unprintable. Last of all, it simply flung insults.

Hidden within the "Life" there was, further, an obscure remark Aretino must have noticed.

"I have heard," said an interlocutor, "that Niccolo Franco has brought out certain letters in competition with those of Aretino only a thousand times better."

This coupled with the final happening became instantly significant. In November of that same year, the French printer, Gardane, brought out Franco's *Pistole volgari*. Like Aretino's book, it was a collection of letters addressed to princes, prelates, writers, scholars and artists, and its handsome typography and pretentious title page were added insults. Aretino had called his plainly printed opus simply *Lettere*.

One, two, and three, they linked together. Franco had egged on Giovanni Serena to make his charges. Franco had written the life everybody knew dead Berni had not. Now Franco brought out his book of letters. The whole thing was a thought-out plot to steal Pietro's place.

Aretino could brook an enemy, but he could not tolerate a rival. He caught up with Franco on his marble stairway and he opened the attack by roaring at him.

"Do you know what your friend Bishop Leone said about you?"

It was to Monsignore Leone Orsini, Bishop of Fréjus, that Niccolo had dedicated his unfortunate book.

"He said that when he gave you a few lire for your gibberish, he was not rewarding worthless words, but keeping a poor beggar from ruin."

He then poured his accusations out in torrents. Franco was a liar, a plagiarist, a hypocrite, and most of all an unappreciative and disheveled rogue.

Franco tried to hold the maelstrom back.

"We are in the same trade," he blurted out.

"God forbid!" cried Aretino.

Then he took the quaking fellow by the shoulders and told him to get out. It is quite certain that Niccolo had not expected this outcome. Not, at any rate, immediately.

But he had no choice but to do as told to.

He did try to make his exit dignified.

"I would not stay if you implored me to. I have my own publisher and will steal your fame and Marcolini's living from him."

"But for my living and for Aretino's fame," laughed Marcolini when he heard about it later, "Niccolo would still be washing dishes."

Then he stumbled into outer darkness.

And the war between the two was on.

The first skirmish was fought out almost instantly. Quivering with chagrin and anger, Niccolo strode along the narrow *calle* toward a new hole in which to hide, only to look up suddenly and see the painter Titian coming down it in the opposite direction. It was too late to avoid him, but he did not want to anyway. Far better to display pique by showing how haughtily independent he now was. Ostentatiously he hid his cap in his jerkin so that he would not have to take it off, and then, bare-headed and with nose in air, he strode past this friend of Aretino's without speaking. The great artist with his tranquil, penetrating eyes was flabbergasted. Then, the astonishment over, his fine lips must have revealed interior amusement with the tremble of a not really completed smile. For, not long ago, at Aretino's suggestion, he had persuaded the Mantuan ambassador to give money to Franco, and it must have occurred to him that the moment would come when Niccolo would want similar assistance again, and would regret all the bridges he had burned.

Still in the same mood, Franco next encountered Sansovino, but this time he was able to be defiant again.

"What would you say," he asked cryptically, "if the man who just put your friend Pietro to shame should match the two hundred crowns Aretino got from the Emperor with four hundred from the King of France?"

He got no satisfaction whatsoever. Sansovino arched his Mongoloid forehead.

"I would be astonished," was his answer. "But where are they?"

They were, of course, nowhere, except possibly in Franco's wishful thinking, but he had not expected that the sculptor would deflate him so promptly.

Then, settled in his new lodgings he set seriously to work. First of all, he wanted the record clear.

"Aretino cannot say that I am ungrateful," he wrote the scholar Alunno whom he knew would report this to Pietro, "for even though I admit he sometimes fed me, he cannot deny that I repaid this courtesy sevenfold by the work I put in upon his things. Everybody knows that if it had not been for me, he would not have had the skill to translate all those legends of the Holy Fathers which he embroiders and passes off as his own."

This last reference was to three popularizations of religion, "The Seven Psalms of David," "The Humanity of Christ," and "The Story of Genesis," with which Aretino was at that time trying to bolster both his reputation and his pocketbook, and it so happens that of these the first two were published before Franco had reached Venice or even left the south of Italy, but he knew that several others were planned and realized that a blow struck in this way would be a blow struck at all of them.

Next he tried to counter one of Aretino's thrusts at him. Hearing of his boast to Sansovino, Aretino had laughed that far from getting any crowns Franco could not even sell a copy of his book and had hence ruined his publisher who was about to go bankrupt. Franco answered with a new edition. Bankrupt or not, the publisher was glad to bring it out, for a new letter to Envy (alias Aretino), which he promised to include, made it certain it would go like hot cakes.

Then he made direct attack. He wrote five neatly rhymed sonnets against Aretino, and in them he repeated every single charge of the nasty "Life." These he circulated. It was the first time since Berni that anyone had dared strike back at Pietro using his own name, and of course Berni had been safely far away in Rome. Obviously, there would be a counterattack. Waiting for it, Venice held its breath.

It was not long in coming, but when it did come, it was in an unexpected way. The attack was in words and Venice waited for a verbal answer; eagerly, for they knew Aretino's powers, and like Niccolo himself—in that same letter to Envy —they were willing to admit his arsenic could poison. But it was not even Aretino who struck the blow.

In his attempts to blacken Pietro and to cover him with scorn and obloquy, Niccolo had involved also Ambrogio degli Eusebii. He was one of Aretino's darlings, Niccolo rhymed, putting into that leering term every obscene interpretation that the Sixteenth Century could understand. He was a *marito* of his, a boy lady-love. Then he went one step further. He said Messer Ambrogio had played the pander to his own honor. That he had yielded his own wife to Messer Pietro; that he was not only a cuckold but a self-created one.

Whether or not this was true has little bearing on the case, the main issue being that Franco said it. The young fire-brand, who had married Marietta d'Oro for no other reason than to show what a fellow he was, could not brook such words. He thrust a slender knife into his sleeve, and marched across the city. He reached Franco's window, and there dared the traducer to come down. Franco did. He perhaps thought that words would be exchanged, and in that sort of contest knew himself the winner. Instead, Messer Ambrogio caught him by the collar, and set to work. The first cut was a slash across the face that Franco carried to his grave. Then he started slicing him to ribbons. He did a nice job — particularly on Franco's clothes — and then flung the howling poet into the gutter. Just before the peace officers who had heard the clamor reached the scene, he took nimbly to his heels.

He went straight to Aretino, and there panted out the story that his own blood-spattered garments but confirmed. Aretino made the gesture of rebuking him. Then, realizing the consequences that might follow, and not wishing Eusebii to get into serious trouble over something that at heart de-lighted him, he put on his cloak and hastened to the magis-trates. There he told a plain story of the provocations, and his influence and eminence were such that the charges Franco had already made were instantly dismissed. After that he went back to his study. He had his own debt to pay and now would do so. In his vitriolic attacks, Franco had had lots to say — largely because it helped strengthen his contention he was an important assistant — about Aretino's crippled hands. Now he, Niccolo, had been marked himself, and as light reading for his convalescence, Aretino made some sonnets of his own. A face carved until it was a gargoyle, was the subject, and to make sure they were appreciated, Aretino sent Ambrogio to recite them underneath his window. Agostino Ricchi was with

Franco at the time, and he listened without comment to Niccolo's plans as to how he, Ricchi, who was a mutual friend, could patch up peace between them. It was not necessary, Niccolo indicated, for Aretino to apologize publicly. He could make a private gesture.

Then the recitation began. And when the poems ended, Ambrogio degli Eusebii added features of his own. He paraded up and down the alley, letting all who dwelt there hear his challenges and taunts of cowardice. If Aretino did not incite Ambrogio's direct methods — and one does not think he did — he knew how to take advantage of them to the full.

But he knew also that enough was enough, and he did not want another brawl. And he was not sure that Ambrogio shared this feeling. Consequently, as the day neared when Franco would be able to go out, he decided he must keep the two apart. He had a chance to do this ready-made for him. For a long time the King of France had promised him 600 crowns, and now word arrived that if an agent were sent, the money would be paid to him. Who better could do this task than young Ambrogio? He sent, therefore, for his turbulent secretary, and asked him if he would like a trip to Marseilles. Expenses would be paid; he could pass through his native Milan *en route* and strut there in his acquired finery; he would see something of the wide, romantic world. All that he had to do was to collect a fat purse, and bring it to the Casa Aretino. By that time, Pietro felt certain, the affair which necessitated his departure would be old and forgotten. It would be a hard thing to imagine anyone of Ambrogio's temperament refusing such an opportunity. He did not.

He set out in the gayest spirits; reached Nice; crawled along the handsomely indented Riviera to his destination; there presented his credentials, and was given what he came for. But the crowns burned in his pocket. He must double them, and keep the profits — or keep part of them, his conscience added. A card game was in progress in the very house where he was given them, and those talking bits of pasteboard about which Aretino later made one of his most popular books, whispered their seductions to him. He laid what was not his own upon the table, and it was not there any more. Certain shrewd plays had been made, and Cardinal Rohan, smirking, swept the golden glitter up. It had not happened, it could not have happened, was his first thought, as it always is; and then suddenly his incredulity became bewildered belief and his bewildered belief gave place to fear.

What could he tell Aretino? He sat down and wrote a letter, saying, in a jumble of confused phrases, that the great men of the world were Aretino's servants, just as if that would somehow bring the money back. Then he realized that he was talking fol-de-rol. After which, he disappeared.

When next heard of, he was a long way off. How he got across the seasick English channel — and much more so in those days of fragile, foul-bilged cockles — is not certain, but the reasons that he sought the foggy isle seemed good to him. Even before he left Venice, he had heard that Henry VIII had also promised crowns to Aretino, 800 of them, it so happened. And he thought if he collected these, the 600 he had lost might be forgiven. Somehow or other, in London's crooked streets, he found someone who would introduce him to the right person, and in a large, draughty room, darkened with sombre, soot-black beams, he stood shivering, and also uneasy, before a square-jawed Englishman with straight black hair whom he set down as *Tomaso Cramuel, milorte di Privisel!* The phonetics are not difficult to decipher. It was Sir Thomas Cromwell, whose family later produced the great Oliver, and who, now that Cardinal Wolsey had overplayed his craftiness and in consequence lost his head, ruled Henry's kingdom for him as his forceful My Lord Privy Seal.

On this morning, he was affable.

"Yea," he said genially, "it is indeed true that His Majesty had thought of sending certain crowns to your master whose skillful pen we know of well."

Then he reflected a moment.

"But they were 200 crowns," he said, "not 800."

After that he dealt the crushing blow.

"Moreover, he has already sent them by a special messenger."

His smile indicated that he knew Ambrogio's weaknesses.

"He felt that they would get there far more expeditiously thus."

But he knew also the difficulties of underlings, and felt generous that day.

"However," he added, "here are eighty crowns which you can keep yourself. We know well the trouble you have taken."

Flanders next. There, in the Low Countries, a certain master of the Imperial Horse persuaded gullible Eusebii to lay out what Cromwell had given him in bills of foreign exchange which were guaranteed to pay 24 percent, and to sail to Portugal with him. Fortunately he was shipwrecked and could blame on an act of God what he would have lost anyway.

After that, he turned up in Portugal. The king of that country, it appears, was also making a donation to Aretino. But, Messer Ambrogio soon discovered, he likewise was sending it by special messenger.

"Whence all this royal suspiciousness?" he must have wondered.

"Your Lordship," he wrote Aretino, smitten by a sudden fear lest Messer Pietro share the same sentiments, "must realize that there are many who can do worse things than I have, but very few who would make the great amends I hope to, if I live."

"I now leave for the Indies," he went on, "and you will then see whether or not I am a worthless servant, for I will carry your renown to the Antipodes."

By telling—dare one suppose—the naked headhunters of the Amazonian jungles of the doughty fellow who did his headhunting for princes?

Aretino last heard from Ambrogio when he was in the heart

of South America. There, characteristically, he had attached himself to the service of the visionary and unfortunate Cabeza de Vaca. He wrote Aretino begging him to use his influence with the Emperor to help this leader out. For Cabeza, it so happened, was in dire straits owing to a revolt among followers who did not share his unconventional views about not robbing and torturing the Indians; and he was in fact later shipped home a prisoner.

"I will not write Your Lordship of the labors or the hardships we endure in this wretched land where we now are. I do not wish to afflict you with my woes. Let it suffice that we sowed and reaped, spading the soil as much as we could in the short time at our disposal; and that then, to discover this country, we marched through it naked and barefoot for thousands and thousands of miles, with a sack full of sorry meal on our shoulders, and a gourd filled with water at our belts. We cut down trees with our swords so as to make the very road we traveled on. The rain fell ceaselessly, and we had no shelter except the branches of some mighty trees. Often we came to a river which seemed wide as the ocean. This we would cross, rowing like galley slaves in certain little ships we built ourselves.

"The river on which we now are is called the Paraguay. The lower one which flows into the sea, and of which the Paraguay is a tributary, is called the Parana. The two rivers are two thousand miles long, and we have not come to the source of them yet. Where we now are is a thousand miles from the ocean. It took us six months to get here. We rowed the whole way.

"We are now going overland to a place where they say there is gold and silver. These treasures are owned by certain Indians called the Carcaras and the Mayas, and by others who are women and who allow no men near them except at certain times of the year. We think these are the Amazons.

"They dwell less than three hundred miles away from us, but the land in this part is uninhabited and very difficult of passage. However, at certain times of the year it is absolutely dry and our governor has already discovered a reasonably good road through it. Indeed, if it had not been that most of our party fell ill in this fever season when we were to set out, every one would now be worth twenty thousand ducats, but God did not will it so.

"However we will soon set out again, and may it please Him that this time we carry off the much or little that is destined to us; and I personally will bring back to Your Lordship from these Antipodes enough for you to flaunt in the beards of all the princes of Christendom how much your magnificent liberality can spend.

"I beg your Lordship not to be angry at the foolish things that I have done, because God intends everything to turn out well, and if you but pray to His divine mercy to grant me three more years of life, you will taste all the fruits of my having decided to journey here.

"In the meantime, let your Lordship not neglect to send me some rosaries made of azure glass beads about a finger long and thick as a reed pen; and some others made of small round beads either azure or green; and some large ones of various colors. For every two crowns you spend, I can make you two thousand by trading them to the Indian chiefs, who think that they are jewels. And send me four statues of yourself and some medallions and if possible your latest works. Address these to Scipione Grimaldi in Seville. He will send them to the Rio de la Plata.

"Into your charge as into a father's, I do put my dear beloved wife. Comfort her as best you can for my long absence from her. If I return to Venice—and I hope to, for I have not yet fallen sick in this land—she will find herself one of the best married women in Venice. First because I have had my fill of evil. And second because I am tired of seeing the world and of wandering here and there about it."

It was his swan song, and he made it in character.

Thereafter, there was utter silence, and we have no reasons

for not supposing that the great rivers of that continent, with their toothed caymans, and fierce cannibal fish, did not witness his last hours; and that the immense lianas of the tangled equatorial jungle, with its bright humming birds and orchids, its slow and crushing boa constrictors, and its stealthy, spotted jaguars, did not trail above his grave. It was just as well. It is not comforting to die far from one's country, but poor Eusebii's country now held nothing for him to which he could return. The dear wife he wrote about had taken her own consolation into her own hands. She had first become one of Aretino's mistresses. Then she had run off with one of Aretino's hangers-on. As for Aretino himself, there is no doubt that he was by now sick of Eusebii and the continual ridiculous scrapes he got into. If his fate had cast him back again on Europe, he would have been a beggar there. And he left it as a proud and bombastic young man.

Had Niccolo Franco flung off to the world's end in the same way, it would have spared Aretino many uncomfortable moments; but the second one of these two turbulent troublemakers remained. Stewing in his own juice to be sure—his confused noddle filled with the poisoned vapors of envy held in leash by impotence—but still on hand. For if he had gone off *à la* Ambrogio while any chance of getting back what he had lost remained, that would have been cutting off his own nose to spite Aretino's face, and Niccolo was, as his ex-provider of benefits neatly puts it into words for us, *piu tosto pessimo che pazzo*. The *pazzi* of the world—the light o'wits, the self-rhapsodizing, egotistical, impulsive Bedlamites (whether shut up or not) —find this sort of gesture satisfying. The *pessimi*— the unprincipled, not the crazy—realize that a nose left on face may still service a useful purpose, especially if a lean organ and adept at smelling out profitable evil. Franco's nose was both lean and adept.

He stayed largely in his own room. He had to. It was not safe to adventure abroad. After Messer Eusebii had set the fashion, wreaking physical vengeance upon this poor Franco for real or imagined grievances became almost a habit. And lord knows, considering the bitter tongue he had, the grievances were usually real.

"It was not," he wrote savagely, "because I wished to praise a certain gentleman, but because his high and mightiness paid me money to write filthy flattering lies about him, that I put him in my poems."

This was Lorenzo Veniero, and that high hearted young aristocrat was not quite the person to accept such words. He and a group of cronies filled themselves with wine one night, and then went to Franco's lodgings. They had a long wait, but at four in the morning he came sneaking in, and they caught him at his doorstep. They laid on him with leather belts, and took care to use the buckle ends. "Have you ever—" thus Aretino described the result—"seen a viper whose back has been broken? Though it cannot crawl away, it keeps lashing its tongue, lifting up its head and spitting poison."

Lord Giovangioacchino, a lesser nobleman, not otherwise made known to fame, did not even take the matter in hand himself. Stung by some of Franco's sarcasms, he sent one of his varlets who gave the fellow "as many drubbings as the unbridled rogue in his insolence pretended he had written letters to the King of France."

Dragoncino, author of the curious *Lippotoppo*, merely threatened.

"If I were not ashamed of quarreling with a lewd fellow, I would thrash him just as soundly as Madonna Giulia Riccia had him thrashed when the rat insulted her by making love to her."

But there was no guarantee that he would not master these scruples.

Finally, even the women made him a laughing stock. One day he went to the house of the Mantuan ambassador, and started holding forth against Pietro. Messer Agnello's mistress took him by the shirt collar and shook him. "If you say a word against the man who gave you this, I will snatch it from your back!"

It was a tribute either to his obstinacy or to his perseverance that he stuck to his position for a full six months.

But though persevering, he was not obtuse; and it dawned on him finally that his career in Venice was over. Aretino would never take him back again, and he could not suceed in Venice against Aretino's open enmity. There was not room for both of them in Venice, and Aretino was not dislodgeable. One day, therefore, there was an empty chamber and some tangled bedclothes and the few odds and ends always left behind when we pack hastily. Once more the poet-vagabond, who was much more the latter than the former, was on his way.

He went first to Padua.

There, brazenly, he knocked upon the door of Sperone Speroni, who looked up from a bit of preciosity that he was writing, and with near-sighted scholar's eyes, saw a shabby fellow with a haggard visage and a straw man's hair, who was swaying at its sill.

"I am," uttered the scarecrow, "Niccolo Franco—friend of Aretino," he added.

That was all Messer Sperone needed.

"Come in," he said, "and feed yourself."

Franco did.

Franco slept also, and borrowed pen and paper the next morning. This time he really sent the letter—did not merely print it and then say he had—and the gist was that Francis I of France could have the services of a man of genius at what came to bargain rates.

There was no answer, not even a refusal. It may be that His Christian Majesty was fed up with men of genius—particularly Italian ones—and that, after his experiences with some of them, would be understandable; but it is more likely he could not see how Franco fitted into that category.

Next, he tried Milan. Somewhat hastily, it happens, for it

would not do to stay in the gowned city long enough for his grammarian host to find out what his relations to Pietro Aretino really were. There "whipping schoolboys," or in other words acting as a crib, he tried desperately to gain a pittance. Enough, anyway, to pay for a fox's hole of a room and to fill his hollow belly with cheap wine and a plate of *pasta* at least once daily.

Chance intervened at the next stage. Leaving Milan, and *en route* to nowhere in particular, he stopped, merely because he had to stop somewhere, at Casale, in the Mantuan-dependent state of Monferrato. The lord paramount of that little capital in the Ligurian Alps was Sigismondo Fanzino, and if, intrinsically, he was nothing but a small-town despot, he had swelling ideas. He wanted to be a Casale Medici, and to set up in his minuscule seigniory a famous literary court. All he lacked were men of genius—and of course money to tempt them there.

Niccolo was made to order for him. Famous Aretino's equal—nay, his master even! (So, at any rate, he called himself.) Driven out of Venice by his jealousy! He sent instantly for the poet and with a soft smile to offset professionally scowling brows, he spoke to him.

"I am about to found a literary academy to be called the Argonauts."

"Yes."

"And I want you to be head of it."

Franco nodded.

"Thus many crowns will be your salary."

Not as many as he had hoped for, but a few crowns were better than no crowns, especially now that, as Pietro succinctly put it, "his lice had come back again."

Nor could even Niccolo warm himself to an illusion that the distinguished fellow members would take any large place in future histories of Italian literature.

"Of course," Sigismondo went on, "you will have to help Messer Ubaldini with state papers."

Niccolo was fidgeting up and down in his anxiety to accept quickly without showing an undue eagerness. He was on Lord Fanzino's payroll before he left the chamber. He at last had a patron of his own.

What happened thereafter, happened swiftly and was definite.

"Messer Titian," is how Mantua's ambassador reported it from Venice, "told me that he went yesterday to the house of Aretino where he found him in a state of fury. He was dashing off a pamphlet against your Lordships"—i.e. the three regents who now governed the city—"and for that matter against everyone in the realm. The artist reproved him for this and asked him why he was doing it. Aretino answered that his enemy, Niccolo Franco, was being sheltered in the house of Sigismondo, and that Franco had composed a book dedicated to this Fanzino in which very many slanders were said against him. Aretino was convinced, further, that the book was not written without your Lordships' knowledge. Consequently, he was going to take vengeance on you by writing and saying publicly all the evil that he can. Messer Titian is your friend and he feels, speaking as your friend, that I should tell you this, and he feels also that it would be well for you to placate Aretino with a few reassuring words and also by forbidding Niccolo Franco to write against him."

Copies of the offending opusculum soon reached Venice and the reasons for his irritation were at once no mystery. Sitting in his Casale room, scrawny Niccolo had at last struck back. He had worked steadily and with a widening cat-and-the-canary smirk upon his face, until the piled foolscap in front of him enshrined the most amazing product of a monomania that the world had ever seen. One, two, three, four—ultimately 298 biting sonnets were upon the bits of paper. After the dedicatory ones, they had but a single subject—Pietro Aretino. And they were a rogue's symphony of abuse and of foul speaking.

These he published, using the false date line of Turin to

avoid possible later difficulties arising from the fact Casale was imperial territory. Then he added insult to injury. He started writing his *Philena* which was an autobiographical imitation of Boccaccio's *Fiammetta*.

"Here lies Sannio," he said smugly as the tale moved toward its climax, "born of humble parents, but made noble by his genius. He was cherished by the good because he was known to be virtuous himself. He was hated by rogues because he hated roguery in others. He conquered Envy itself, for when, scarcely five and twenty, he was set upon by one who envied him and brought him down with mighty blows. All Italy hailed his victory."

Sannio was Franco himself.

Philena was tedious and prolix—as also, to a certain extent, was the book it imitated—but the sonnets were succinct and quotable. Quotable, that is, by those who felt no qualms about using all the five-, seven-, and nine-letter Italian gutter words (whose Anglo-Saxon equivalents as a rule have four letters), out of which they were largely made. The princes at Mantua, Ferrara and Florence, the Roman courtiers and the elevated and erudite gentlemen of Venice did not feel any. They quoted them, and I am afraid laughed neither considerately nor decently. The one sonnet by Berni excepted—and it can be, for it was an isolated instance—it was the first time that he who had so blithely transfixed all who had incurred his wrath or even irritated him with his scathing, apt, and not forgettable phrases, was himself transfixed in the same manner. He could now know what his victims felt like. For Master Pasquino had at last met a worthy foeman, and Aretino was on the defensive for the first time.

He did not—you can be very certain—stay in that position long. He was not made for defending citadels but for storming them, and the gray threads that at nine-and-forty silvered his black beard and temples were the proud banners of mature strength, not of enfeebling decrepitude. But the very carefulness of the steps he took showed how seriously he took the onslaught. He left nothing unprovided for. Niccolo's barbed taunts in rhyme had dwelt iteratively upon the thesis that he was a huge fellow "as wise as Cicero" in being a rogue, diddling the princes, guzzling wine, swilling rich food, and self indulging it in bestial love, but hardly able to piece together two sentences without ghost-writing Franco at his side. He met this by setting down upon paper two comedies, and they were good enough to answer any charges of incompetence. Niccolo had further hinted that he was friend only of sycophants or riff-raff. He met this with his own second edition. This new printing of his letters carried as an appendix forty-four letters not written by Pietro but to him. Bembo was among the writers of these, also Sperone Speroni, Michelangelo, Veronica Gambara, and Vittoria Colonna. This done, and then only, he launched his counter-attack.

"I spoke," said the Mantuan ambassador, "to Pietro Aretino about what Messer Titian had said to me and found him in an apologetic mood. He admitted that he had lost his temper but he now promised that he would not make a public issue of it. He did grieve, however, that Franco had held forth against the Emperor—" while attacking Pietro, Niccolo had heaped scorn on Charles V because he now paid Pietro a salary—"and he was afraid that if your Lordships did not take some action the whole world would believe it was done with your knowledge and consent since the book was both written and published in your dominions."

A week later,

"I again saw Aretino and found him in an ebullient mood. He told me that so great was his regard for the late Duke of Mantua that he would always be loyal to the regents and indeed to all the house of Mantua, but he threatened to excoriate Fanzino, and I think he will.

"Furthermore," added the busy little Agnello, "I heard gossip that he still grumbled threats against Your Lordships and against Mantua.

"To me, however, he talked most politely."

Another fortnight,

"Aretino is still angry. However, he is a Christian, he says, and if Fanzino would write him a letter saying that the book was not dedicated to him with his knowledge, I am sure everything could be made smooth."

That long, the iron fist was gloved in velvet. Then he struck with it.

Ludovico Tripidale was another Mantuan, and he was walking in Venice one day when he heard his name called. There was Aretino in a gondola.

"Come with me," he said, "I wish to talk to you."

Tripidale did. He clambered into the small craft only to have it almost capsized by a savage gale of angry words.

"He launched into the greatest complaints you could imagine against the regents," Tripidale reported, "and particularly bewailed the fact that since he had been so good a friend to the house of Gonzaga, Franco was allowed not only to write against himself but against the Emperor who paid his pension to him."

Tripidale tried to calm him.

"The regents," he said soothingly, "can do nothing. They are powerless. The book was not printed in their territory."

It was a zephyr trying to outblow the whirlwind.

"I dare you," Aretino shouted, "to secure copies of the book, and then compare the type with the type used by Caretto in Casale. I have already done this. I have, further, letters of Franco that prove it published there. And besides that a gentleman of the household of the Duke of Urbino has just visited me. He passed through Casale. He saw Franco at Fanzino's table and the rogue not only blatantly admitted the attacks but threatened further ones."

What answer can be made when facts are roared at you? Tripidale sat silent.

Then Aretino shot his final bolt at him.

"I am sending," he said, icily cold, "copies of the book to

Rome and Madrid. The Pope and the Emperor will be quite competent to judge where it was printed."

And whether it behoved them to take action or not.

Tripidale, a courtier, quaked in his shoes and then having reported it to Mantua waited the answer. It was not sent to him and it was not, either, what he had expected.

Ercole, the Cardinal, who was Federigo's churchman brother, headed the regents, and he wrote briefly to his ambassador, and he did not even notice Tripidale's words.

"Thank Messer Titian," he wrote, "for his good offices in the *affaire* Aretino but tell him that I can see no reasons whatever for placating the fellow. Nothing he could do alarms me."

"I would like to see Cardinal Gonzaga in person," answered Aretino.

And tell him, one supposes, what were the risks that he incurred.

Then he very promptly changed the subject. For he knew well that Ercole had called his number, and he did not want other princes to find out that it could be called.

Thereafter, he fought out his battle without outside help and with his usual fusillade of epithets.

"*Più tosto Turco che Franco,*" he said. It was a savage pun, Franco meaning French and Turco's meaning being obvious.

"I will now give you some bad news, you scoundrel, and that is that I now find myself able to do more than ever and my health is so flourishing that you would die of fury if you merely saw me."

"Your writing things against me comes more from the fact that you are jealous of me than from your having reached a point where you can look down on me, yet because I once kept you from starving, I can't take the trouble to hate you. If you want to be as famous as I am, write against vice instead of virtue; tell the truth instead of lying; and stop bringing your talents to shame by using them against one who is as good as you are evil !

"*Poveretto, poverello, poveraccio, poverino !*"

You poor, silly little rogue, is the only possible translation of this eloquent crescendo of belittlings.

Once he did relent a while. In 1545, Niccolo fell ill.

"It would be right for me to rejoice at your bad fortune just as you grieve at my good. But the limitless generosity of my nature is such that I feel very sorry about it. So take care of yourself and have good hope. The true doctor is God. Fortify your conscience and have faith in Him. If you do this you will get well and cure your fever."

But a letter to Domenichini gave his reasons.

"I am sick even to the soul that you-know-what fellow may be dying. I want him to live and I want the envy that he feels to gnaw at him. If he should die, how can I get the revenge of his finally realizing what a sorry villain he is?"

Even when he begged Captain Bovetti not to murder Niccolo, this ultimate coming out on top was in his mind. The good, he pointed out, are fortunate when rogues abuse them, and he went piously into the Christian virtues of returning good for evil.

But he had already told Franco what he hoped would happen and in fact had prophesied it.

"Your ill deeds make it certain that you will end upon the gallows."

And he did not wish the knife to cheat the rope.

In the long run, he had his wish. Aretino was fourteen years in another world when a white-haired, long-bearded man "who was more venerable than otherwise" was marched through the streets of Rome to the Sant' Angelo bridge. "This is too hard a punishment," he said, as a rope was placed around his neck for his libelous attacks upon Pope Pius IV's two nephews. And the crowd, hearing them, and looking at him, was sorry for him. Then he danced on Roman air.

But he did see his debâcle as Fanzino's protégé. Niccolo had but one song, and it now grew monotonous. In 1545, he was still working at a new edition of his sonnets, and the only other book that he had written was both blasphemous and filthy. In 1546 Aretino learned he was a wanderer again. "The naked, bare-legged, starving Franco," he exulted. "I feel the sort of pity for him that the fortunate have to feel for wretches. He knew nothing—that was pardonable. What he thought he knew brought ruin to him." The long contest appeared to have been won.

But it was not certain that it was not a Franco victory.

"The vendettas of the pen," said Aretino, "last longer than vengeances of blood feuds."

His vendettas—for he was boasting.

But Messer Niccolo's did also. For in the four centuries since the two men died, it is what Franco wrote about Aretino that has set the tone of most opinions of Pietro. He was not a villain because Franco said he was a villain, but a large part of all the evil we attribute to him was reported by this Niccolo's pen.

CHAPTER XV

The Egregious Messer Titian

ARETINO and his women; Aretino and his disreputable young men. Between them we get a gusty picture of this fine-looking, well-fleshed fellow, with his all-embracing appetites, convenient lack of principles, and measureless energy and vigor.

But it is not quite the complete one.

For a full life, even to a man so exuberant, does not mean merely an animal or even a worldly one. And Aretino — although admittedly he sought the fleshpots — had more to him than large and largely carnal ideas, brought to their fruition by his firm purpose and his unsurpassed self-confidence. He was a type person of the refulgent Renaissance, and the love of beauty, even in the abstract and often sublimated form of art, was another attribute of that amazing age that matched every Sigismondo Malatesta, Caesar Borgia or Pierluigi Farnese with a Fra Angelico, a Pietro Perugino or a Raphael of Urbino.

We have a plethora of pertinent examples. Cosimo de' Medici the Elder, moved by his *"voluptas pulchri"* to pause for a moment in the shrewd, cool, clear-headed scheming by which he raised up his businessman family to its mighty estate, so that he could bestow the accolade of paying for the pictures or the statues they created, upon Paolo Uccelli, Benozzo Gozzoli and Donatello, or to countenance some prank of Fra Filippo Lippi. Criticized for the latter, he was the age's mouthpiece when he said: "The vagaries of great geniuses should be forgiven for they are celestial beings and not beasts of burden." Francis I, not only leaving for an hour or so his famous stag-hunts but daring even to laugh at his latest mistress, Madame d'Etâmpes, so as to put Benvenuto Cellini in the mood to finish for him his incomparable saltcellar. Il Moro, the usurper of Milan, finding work for the great Bramante and for even greater Leonardo, while he plotted, as he thought, his own pinnacle of high aggrandizement and cared not, though he ruined all of Italy.

Nor are these exceptional instances. The feelings manifested in them were shared by all the era. To create beauty by the brush or chisel or the burin; or to enable others to create it; or to enjoy it by absorbing it, was as much a necessity as a desire, and it was possessed fully in its latter aspects not only by the above named mighty men but by popes as different as Pius II Piccolomini and Alexander VI Borgia; by noble lords like Federigo Gonzaga, Alfonso d'Este and the Duke of Urbino; and by plain, bourgeois Milanese and Florentine citizens.

The very *cassoni* of the latter, those exquisitely painted chests in which they stored their decent and rosemary-scented linen, were Sistine Chapels and Halls of the Great Council in miniature. It flourished in the ambient air which all men breathed.

Aretino possessed these tastes also, and indeed intensified them as he did virtually every quality of the time in which he lived his life. There were various reasons for this. Though he scorned *satraps*—the word is today, I believe, *tycoon*—he was a satrap of a sort himself and he tried studiously to emulate satrapic ostentations. But it was also sincere to him. He loved art and he was drawn to its practitioners. They also were drawn to him. When he was a student at Perugia, Pietro of that city was putting his last, exquisite, finishing touches on the tiny but precious jewel box of the Sala di Cambio, and no sooner did he get to Rome than Aretino found himself in possession of the confidence of Perugino's most illustrious pupil.

"If Chigi were alive," Lodovico Dolce quotes him as saying years afterwards, "he would bear witness that Raphael Sanzio used to show me all his pictures before he exhibited them to the public."

He was at that time little better than a lackey, but Dolce makes the story credible by himself not only using Aretino as his mouthpiece when he wrote his "Dialogue on Painting," but appropriating from Pietro very nearly every idea which he incorporated into that interesting little essay on aesthetic values (All, as a matter of fact, that he had not first appropriated from Baldassare Castiglione's "The Perfect Courtier").

Vasari chose him as the recipient of that long letter in which he described all the festivities with which the city of Florence welcomed the daughter of the Emperor who had come there to marry her negroid Duke. Among the decorations on this gay occasion were paintings by the hand of Messer Giorgio and he wanted to make sure they were appreciated.

Fra Sebastiano del Piombo was, as we have already seen, his daughter's godfather.

Giovanni da Udine called one day at the famous Ca' Bolani, and not finding Aretino at home, he left upon an inside panel of the door one of his priceless sketches as a calling card.

He was looked up to by Il Tribolo and by Danese Cattaneo and of course obviously by a horde of lesser men. The pictures which we have already seen hanging in the sumptuous chambers of his residence were left there by artists who regarded him as one who understood them and who was their friend.

But it was not merely as the friend of artists and as their admirer and appreciator that Aretino made manifest his love for all the beauty they created. He bestowed on them his accumulated practical wisdom and he lent also the influence of his power and position. There is no better example of this than in the long and tumultuous story of his relations with Leone Leoni. Messer Leone was a fellow Aretine who should be far better known than he is; for he was very nearly as good a sculptor as Benvenuto Cellini, almost his equal as a goldsmith, and quite on a par with him in violence of character. He was also Benvenuto's vindictive personal enemy.

Aretino advised this fine fellow in his salad days. He had stopped off at Padua and done a fine medal of Pietro Bembo and was paid a sum of money. Then suddenly he discovered

TITIAN

"The egregious Messer Titian . . . who is another myself."—*Aretino.*

that Cellini was there also and had done merely a model in wax and had been paid for it a larger sum than he had for the completed task. Forgetting that Cellini was an established artist and he merely a young man in search of reputation, he flew into a fury. He wrote Aretino.

"Keep your anger until it is needed," Aretino answered him. "If it is indeed true that Bembo has given much more for what you rightly call a mere sketch of a portrait, you must remember that Benvenuto is an old friend and that old friendship often influences us in these matters. In the meanwhile you have been rewarded liberally."

He counselled him when he rode the crest of the wave.

"Fra Tommaso, who has kindly presented me with your letter, brings me the good tidings that you study no less to serve God than you do to delight your fellow men. You do well to do so, for from Him cometh all our knowledge and our power to work. It is He who moveth your graver when you make coins and inspireth your genius when you think, and the honor which you acquire with your chisel is the gift of His clemency. Think of your recent gifts from Jesu's mercies to you. The Pope himself listens freely to all stories of your talents. You have a treasure of a wife and you have children. The man who persecuted you is in prison. You are in Rome, glory of the arts, mother of reputations, and fountain source of wealth and fortune. Most important of all you are young, well, and appreciated. But as I have already told you, the above mentioned blessings must be attributed to the goodness of God. For if you take credit for them yourself you risk making an enemy of Fate who has already prospered you and who will continue to prosper you as long as you forgive injuries done you no matter how grave they may be. For the Son of the Most High is pleased more than anything else by a manifestation of that same spirit who not only led Him to forgive those who crucified Him but to pray also to His Father to forgive them.

"For that reason I beg you to pray the Pope to set free your adversary. The poor unfortunate is a craftsman of ability. He is a hard worker. He was once the darling of the papal court. Besides that, you owe more to him than to the Pope himself; for His Holiness would not ever have known the sum total of your abilities, if it had not been for the fellow's spirited rivalry. What if he did boast that he would kill you! It was that which brought your fame to you!"

This was not either pseudo-piety or smugness, but exceedingly sound advice. For the poor unfortunate to whom Aretino referred was none other than again Cellini.

"I have no other enemies," Benvenuto testified before the papal court that sentenced him, "but a certain Girolamo and the sculptor Leoni. Both of them wish me ill. Leoni shouted at me that I lied in my throat, and that not only in the papal chambers, but in the presence of many witnesses."

He now lay in the deepest and the dampest dungeon of the Castel Sant' Angelo, and there is much evidence (including his own testimony) that rage at his confinement made him for a while nearly as mad as the castellan who was his jailor and who had the illusion that he was a bat. The focal point of his fury was "Messer Leone, the goldsmith of Arezzo," and the incoherence of his rage at him led him to state, first, that Leoni had joined a conspiracy to murder him by crushing up a diamond and putting it in his food, and second, that he had been so mean that he had stolen it and substituted a green beryl which was not hard enough to do the business. Aretino knew that when papal rage had blown over, Benvenuto would be released, and remembering his quick blade, he thought it better all around if Messer Leone had appeared to urge the setting free himself.

He also helped the tempestuous artist when Leone was himself in serious difficulty.

On a May morning in 1540, Aretino, basking in the limpid air that blew in through his study window, received a bulging letter by a messenger from Rome. When he started reading it, he frowned. It was from one Jacopo Giustiniano, a friend of Leoni's, and its contents were alarming. Master "Lion's" temper had betrayed him and he was himself a prisoner. When Benvenuto had gone to the Castello, Leoni had been given his position at the mint, and this quick rise had brought about some jealousy. Sullen in his resentment was one Pelligrino di Leuti, a German, who not only loved Cellini but perhaps hoped for the job himself. Messer Pelligrino was patient. He bided his time until he saw certain things, and then he made the most of them. Leoni was accused of counterfeiting. He did not wait to answer the charges, but tracked down the German, and then drew his dagger.

"You are a rogue," he shouted, "and you have not only falsely accused me, but you attempted to attack my wife."

Then he set to work on him. But he had no more than slashed his face when he was arrested. Leoni was haled before a papal judge, told what he had been charged with, and urged to make a full confession, and then when he refused to do so, ordered to a gloomy torture chamber and stretched out upon a rack. Three times the cords were tightened until his bones and muscles cracked, but the artist, his face clay white, said nothing. Then his mother and his wife were led before him.

"They will be tortured also and you can witness their agony and hear their screaming if you refuse to speak to us."

This made him admit what they said that he had done, and confess many things more beside. The vindictiveness of his punishment might seem almost incredible. He, who had wrought so much of beauty with it, if he did also much violence and harm, was sentenced to have his right hand severed at the wrist. It was not a death sentence, but it meant abject beggary. The executioners actually stood before him and his hand lay on the block, before reprieve came. It was almost as grim as the original punishment. A life sentence as a papal galley slave! He was now somewhere on the Tyrrhene sea, his artist fingers growing clumsy and calloused as he tugged a heavy sweep. His captain was one Meo da Talamone, a Corsican, and the seafarers of that craggy island were noted for their savage ruthlessness. His best hope for release was that some corsair out of Algiers or from Tunis would sink his craft. Under the waters there would at least be peace.

Giustiniani, telling the story of this, and painting a picture of the woes of Messer Leone's wife and children, who had lost their breadwinner, begged Aretino to use his influence to help the fellow out of his dire plight. Aretino did. He was on good terms with Andrea Doria, the papal admiral, and he wrote him an eloquent letter begging for the sculptor's release. It accomplished what it set out to do.

Less than a year after the day that he was sentenced, Messer Leone proudly strode the streets of Genoa, a free man.

But his character was not in any way tempered by this episode and from then on until the day he died, Aretino had to help him out of troubles and to put up with annoyances from him. To begin with, he refused to stay in Genoa. Aretino had hoped that he would repay Doria by remaining in his service a while, but he did hastily not more than two or three medals and he then decamped to fields of greater promise. Nor did he give up acts of violence. Fortunately — for him — it was not until after Aretino's death that he nearly, and for no reason but a simmering jealousy, murdered Titian's son Orazio; but it was not three years after his days upon the galley that he hired bravos to attempt to kill a former assistant who refused to return to his service. At that time Aretino broke off relations with him for a period of at least two years. He tried counterfeiting again, and but for Aretino's intervention, would have danced from the gallows at the orders of the Duke of Ferrara. All Aretino ever got from him personally (besides letters of complaint and praise) was a single medallion showing on its face his bearded countenance — yet but for Aretino, Messer Leone would have not walked upon this earth long enough to make medals at all.

Writing to the Duke of Ferrara, Aretino gave his reason for this patience. He said that even if Leoni were guilty, he should be forgiven because he was so distinguished an artist. And by putting up with all that Leoni made him, he gave proof that

in this matter he practiced what he preached. He satisfied also
his own urgency, and the urgency of the age he lived in, to do
well by anyone who did excellently by art.

It was this aspect of Aretino's multiplex nature that led inevitably to the most engaging passage in his whole interesting
and intriguing career. I refer to his great friendship with the
painter Titian. We have seen its beginning in a chance encounter with Jacopo Sansovino in the narrow artery of the
Merceria. Sansovino presented him to Titian. His old comradeship with the skilled stoneworker, whose almost faun-like
St. John's, fey Madonnas and wonderfully rapt young Bacchus
glowed with well-nigh living warmth even though carven out
of chilly marble, was reborn to an enduring steadiness, as they
both worked, and both prospered in the canal city. It is evi-
denced by the fact that when Sansovino wrought the bronze
doors to the sacristy of St. Mark's cathedral (and they are sec-
and only — if that — to the bronze doors by Ghiberti on the
Baptistry in Florence) he put Aretino's bearded countenance
upon them in the guise of one of the evangelists. But the
strong ties that bound him to the splendid painter need another name. Brotherhood is a trite and sentimental word, but
it is an apt one. They were *compari* by mutual agreement, but
though the dictionary gives "gossip" or "godparent" as the
exact translation, not even in its Elizabethan sense is it quite
warm enough to carry over the meaning.

They were bound together by an incredible congeniality.
They shared every interest they had, and they talked over
every conceivable topic, the details of their households, and
the annoyances; the problems of their respective progeny;
how Aretino missed Venice on a short trip to Verona. "Oh
brother, veritably insupportable is my home-sickness for the
Grand Canal, and I can assure you that I never put my feet in
stirrups that I do not long for the ease and comfort of a gondola: truly it is a break-your-back and a pound-your-breeches
to ride a-horseyback! If I get back alive, I will never hurry off
again!" The unreliability of the lords, and the "quicksilver-

like vagaries of their fantasies"; the difficulties of dealing with such men, and conversely the advantages that could be derived from making use of these difficulties; Aretino's troubles with his sycophants; Titian's troubles with the men and women who sat for him; whether Titian liked ancient art better than modern art. What he thought—and love Venice though Aretino did, he pined for them—of all the splendid sights and treasures of Rome.

Nor were they afraid to talk to each other plainly. There was no reserve between them. Many people flattered Aretino, but Titian was quite willing to rebuke him sharply for his immoral way of living, and to tell him that the disordered life of his servants, who robbed and cheated him at will, and who treated him as an equal, was making him the laughing stock of the city.

"Instead of being angry that my servants take advantage of me," answered Pietro, "it makes me happy. For just as Philip of Macedon, father of Alexander the Great, in the midst of his triumphs prayed to the gods that they would humiliate him a little, so I, who am feared rather than loved by the great ones of the earth, am pleased that my grooms and kitchenmaids do not respect me. It keeps my head from being turned."

Aretino was equally outspoken. When Titian turned out a hasty picture as a result of having accepted too many orders, he did not hesitate to rebuke the painter's "greediness." When Titian allowed his success to make him haughty, Pietro was bluntly candid about it.

"Although I have only received one letter from you since you reached the Imperial Court," he wrote Titian on the occasion of the latter's visit to Augsburg, "I will not yet believe that the favors of His Majesty have so filled you with conceit that you are scornful of old friends. Yet if that which I cannot believe is true, instead of congratulating you on your success, I deplore it. For that fortune is a misfortune which makes a man over pleased with himself. But even if ambition has made you a snob, you had better act toward me with your

old-time modesty. I would talk back to the Emperor himself
if he treated me too diffidently. So clear yourself of all suspicion by writing two or three lines to me. In the meantime,
Sansovino and I send regards to you."

It becomes evident that save for Giovanni delle Bande Nere
there was no person who had come into his life whom he favored with esteem so slightly qualified. "Titian is I," he said,
"and I am Titian."

"When I write you, it is the same as if the letter were from
Titian."

But the final summing up was even more sweeping.

"The egregious Messer Titian . . . who is another myself."

It was, of course, not—anyway in any literal sense of the
phrase—other than remotely true. The two men were bound
together by ties golden and immortal, but it is not easy to
imagine human beings who could be more different. They
were different in their temperament; different in their character; different in their dispositions; different in their approach
to life. And if there were not a thousand other ways of knowing this, one need do nothing more than compare any one of
Titian's splendid, but revealing portraits of Pietro, with such
a painting of himself as the grave one that hung in the
Prado, or the thoughtful one in Berlin. The contrast is ar-
resting. There is no arrogant boldness in the face of Titian.
There is no sure effrontery. There is no animal coarseness—
but there is no animal exuberance either. The forehead is as
high and the eyes seeing and penetrant, but they are sad with
too much knowing and with feeling too much. Look at Aretino as he faces you from the walls of the Frick gallery and
you can see instantly his essential ruthlessness. When he flays
rogues, mountebanks and villains—and also princes, prelates,
poets, captains and great ladies—they are but subjects for his
fierce lampooning, and not palpitant fellow humans who
might flinch even at the thought of the whiplash. Titian, on
the other hand, has gone so deeply, as he paints, into the sensi-

tive interior of the men and women whom his brush immortalized that he shares something of their secret and disturbed
psychology. His "Man with the Glove" was certainly a product
of one of the same courts that gave Aretino his *Cortegiana* and
his *Marescalco* with their ludicrous buffoons and fawning sycophants; but his frayed finery and baffled countenance reveal
tragic frustration that the artist shared while painting it. So
does his "Man in the Red Cap" which hangs next to Aretino
in New York. Nor did he penetrate less deeply when he did
his lovely Venus', and his gross and worldly-looking rulers,
like the Elector John Frederick of Saxony. If Titian's mouth
was strong, it was also fine as a thoroughbred's. The sum total
is the reflective and perceptive face of an artist. Aretino's
visage is that of a mercenary captain — of an ex-footsoldier who
had made himself a Duke.

If this had not been the case, then we would have to say
that there is nothing either to heredity or to environment.
For the two men were both shaped differently by each of these
important forces. Titian's origins were other than the origins
of Aretino. Titian's background was not the same. He had
another sort of parents; another boyhood; another youth;
another early manhood. He was molded differently from another sort of clay.

He was born high among the Dolomites in Pieve di Cadore,
which is a small town set upon the hilly saddle that connects
two lofty peaks. The house in which he spent his boyhood —
if he was not born there — still exists. It is modest in size, but
not small; white with a slant red-tiled roof; and it has two
ample chimneys — for there is need of roaring fire in Pieve —
one of which rose generously from a sort of kitchen lean-to.
But it is tidy and neat, and its plain lines have an Italian
aspect, thus showing the connections with the south, though
it is but a little further to the northward that you encounter
the wooden upper storeys on the Swiss or Tyrolese style of
architecture, and churches with the bulbous south Germanic
steeples.

Cadore itself—Cadore the province—was an Italian fron-
tier. On its south border lay the Coniglio, then a great forest
of beech, pines and larches which supplied Venice with the
timber for her masts, oars and ships, and even for the rotless
piles she stood upon. During the season of spring freshets, they
were floated down the otherwise almost dry Piave, in those
huge rafts or *zattere,* which have given their name to a whole
stretch of Venetian waterfront. Bears and wolves roamed
through the thick-grown trees, while on the sharp snow-clad
limestone peaks above—Antelao, to name one of them, towering 11,000 feet—you could see roebuck and chamois. Underneath precipices, there were caves Gothic with stalactites and
stalagmites.

At Forno, which you could reach only by a difficult mule
path, there were ancient but still productive mines of silver,
lead and iron. They had been worked almost continuously
since that day in the late Stone Age when some swart savage
had discovered that the gleaming stuff which had been melted
down by accident in some fire of his was brighter and more
valuable than shells and beads, or stronger and more work-
able than flint. Red apples and even juicy pears grew in such
of the valleys as were protected from the icy blasts; but the
main industry was the grazing of large herds of sheep and
cattle, which fed on the tender Alpine verdure, and produced
wool and hides for export, and milk, butter and cheese to feed
the Cadorini. Being on the *Strada Allemagna*—the road to
Germany and Central Europe—it had more things to fear
than the sudden storms, destructive cloudbursts, and the noisy
avalanches for which it was noted. For from the days when
the Huns and Avars burst upon the disrupt Roman Empire
until Titian's own time and later, there was no lengthy period
when the Cadorini might not have to retire suddenly to the
hills and look down upon the smoke of their own farms and
orchards, as marauding Slavs, Hungarians, Germans and even
Ottomans showed their bright weapons in the rugged glens.

Titian's father, Gregorio Vecelli, was a public servant in

this little nation. As painted by his own son and now visible in the Ambrosiana at Milan, he has the withdrawn wild-bird look of a dreamer, though it may be that it is merely that of one who lives in empty spaces. But actually he was a practical man and solid citizen. He was captain of the local defense forces, "centurion of Pieve" is the exact title; overseer of the grain stores; superintendent of castle repairs — something of a job, for the castle of Pieve was sacked at least three times during his lifetime; and finally inspector of mines. He was the descendant of a line of lawyers. Guecello the first — and the law which makes Teutonic *w* become Italian *gu* as in *Guelph-Welf, Ghibelline-Waiblinger, Gualtiero-Walther* leads us to suspect a northern origin — had been appointed *podestá* by the then feudal lords, the counts of Camino, in 1320. The name Vecelli may well not long ago have been something like Wetzel. But Guecello second, and Conte one, two, three and four — the last being Titian's grandfather — had pled causes in provincial courts, and such office as they may have held was incidental. Of his mother much less is known. Her name was Lucia. She bore Gregory four children, Francesco, Titian, Caterina and Orsa. We can see her as the old woman with the basket of eggs in "The Presentation of the Virgin Mary" that is now in the Accademia at Venice. Despite her fine face with its courageous chin and with Titian's own prominent nose, it is not likely that she could either read or write.

A tough race of hardy mountaineers, who could band together almost communistically to acquire and to store a common food supply — Cadore itself could produce each year only three months' sustenance; who were daring enough to cut off a puissant German Emperor both from his breadbasket and from his line of retreat; yet who at the same time did not lose a manly and occasionally even a quarrelsome individuality, was a sounder source to rise from than a city proletariat, which had learned by sad experience that he who has the least scruples goes the furthest, only provided that he is not hanged while getting there.

Gregory, the administrator, even if a small one, was preferable as a father to poor shoemaker Luca.

And Lucia, whether she was literate or not, possessed probably, and could hence pass on, more of those qualities that go into making what we call character, than Tita did, devoted though she was to son Pietro.

Cadore had one other gift to give to Titian, and though it does not bear on the immediate subject, it should be mentioned here.

"Among these Venetian Alps," said an observant English visitor of a hundred years ago, "when clouds and mountains mingle, they retain their separate embodiments. The clouds roll down in force, the mountains resist with might, the landscape becomes bright and dark in powerful contrast."

That dramatic luminosity which shone always in the background of his glorious pictures—that contrast between light and darkness which lent such power to them—must have come to him from his Cadorine air.

It would not be profitable—nor would it be pertinent in what is, after all, the life of another man—to try here to puzzle out just what were the interior physiological changes that produced suddenly in a line of matter-of-fact men of practical affairs not merely an artist but one of the half-dozen greatest painters of all time. But the transformation was definite. For not only did Titian become a painter, but so did his brother Francesco—though he was a soldier and a public servant also—and thereafter there were a son, a nephew and perhaps other relatives who gave up fitting into their appointed places in the little hierarchy of this Alpine province to carve marble or to smear pigments. Titian even had a namesake who was so good at this that if the job had not been already done by his illustrious uncle, he might himself have made the name Vecelli last forever. Moreover it demonstrated itself early. There is a pretty story of Gregorio's second boy astonishing the Pieve townsfolk by rendering a fresco of the Madonna on an outside wall of the small house he dwelt in.

It was still visible, though faded, as recently as the middle of the last century, and local tradition had it that the grave lad who knelt therein was Titian himself. Supposedly it was painted with the juice of Alpine flowers. Titian's father, says the tradition, denied him what he regarded — with the logic of a *pater familias* who knew that it was difficult enough merely to feed and clothe four children in Cadore — as the extravagance of paints. Thereupon Titian and his sister Orsa went out upon the sloping hillsides and picked wildflowers there. From their juices he prepared the needed colors.

Whether this is true or not, the future artist displayed his special talents at a sufficiently young age to be sent — say both Dolce and Vasari, and they knew him — at about the age of ten to Venice. He was to study painting there. His first teacher was Sebastiano Zuccato, the mosaicist, and the regard that he had for him is indicated by the fact that a half century later he and Sebastiano's two talented sons were the best of friends. But though the color of mosaic-making must have appealed to Titian, its stiffness definitely did not. He transferred himself to Gentile Bellini.

Contrasting his pupil's fluent and spontaneous way of working with his own relatively methodical procedure, Gentile made a surprising comment:

"He has no future as a painter."

Titian moved his paints and brushes to the studio of Giovanni Bellini. He fared better there, and there are enough of his paintings — notable among them the "Madonna of the Cherries" — with distinct traces of the Bellini influence to show that the time spent with Gentile's brother was not wasted. But not even Giovanni Bellini was the right man to bring out Titian's powers. Intrinsically he was too austere. "Even his doges are priests," a critic said of him.

A miracle in the world of art made it possible for him to become what he was destined to, in short order without either years of difficult experiment or being led by inappropriate influences up sterile byways. Messer Giorgio of Castelfranco arrived in Venice, and his essential realization of the pleasant and the lovely possibilities of this world we live in — dryly, his "inherently secular point of view" — coupled with his restrained and refined gaiety and feeling, and his love of color, and his subtlety of mood, made him the one person who could show Titian the way he wished to go.

Titian became Giorgione's pupil and he took over the Giorgionesque manner for a long period of his life. Indeed a great number of his early pictures — though a shrewd eye could detect a difference, and could realize that it would grow — seem but surer Giorgiones. His first demonstration of an independent reputation came by accident. Giorgione was commissioned to do frescos on the outside walls of the Fondaco dei Tedeschi, and he assigned certain of them (those less conspicuously placed) to Titian.

One day, Messer Giorgio walked to look at them with a friend.

The friend commented:

"These, Messer Giorgio, are by a long way the finest you have ever done."

Giorgione admitted they were Titian's but was so chagrined that he would not leave his studio for several days.

Thereafter, Titian advanced in his own name, and when Giorgione died prematurely, he had no competitor. When he and Aretino met, he was an established painter. He had done his fine romantic paintings of St. Anthony for the Scuola del Santo. He had finished Giovanni Bellini's "Bacchanals" for the Duke of Ferrara; and perhaps also his own "Reclining Venus" and his "Bacchus and Ariadne." He had painted "The Three Ages," the "Pesaro Madonna," the "Sacred and Profane Love," and the "Death of St. Peter Martyr," and a large number of his earlier and more poetic portraits. He was working on — or supposedly working on — his battle painting of the Doge's palace; and he had received public ovations at the unveiling of his "Assumption of the Virgin Mary" at the Frari. Domestically, he was enjoying a happy and contented, if a modest and an almost bourgeois, wife. Two years before, he had married his half-Polish mistress, Monna Cecilia, in the presence of a jeweler and a marble dealer who were at that time among his closest friends. He lived now in his recently purchased house in the distant and the tranquil San Casciano quarter. All around it, there were gardens. It fronted the lagoon. And it looked northward toward a line of far blue mountains. They were snow-crested, and they looked almost like surf breaking on some distant shore. High above them towered Antelao, and on rare days of absolutely crystal clarity it was plainly visible. With his feet in Venice, Titian faced his boyhood home.

The fine friendship that began without prelude at this midway period of the two men's lives had perhaps the most color and most gaiety in their frequent and convivial gatherings for recreation. It is thus we often think of them. When Cecilia died — in 1530 — Titian retired to Pieve for a while, but when he returned he took up a most animated life. He and Aretino — often with Sansovino and with others — gathered in some garden near the water. There they put aside the ardors of painting, sculpturing and setting words on paper. Lutes were strummed, and the conversation had great wit and gusto. The grammar teacher, Priscianese, was present upon one of these occasions.

"I was invited," he wrote, "on the day of the Calends of August to celebrate that festival which they call the *ferr'agosto* — why I don't know, though it was discussed a great deal during the course of the evening — in the delightful garden of Messer Tiziano Vecellio, an excellent painter as everybody knows. There were present there — birds of a feather flock together — some of the most original wits of the city. Messer Pietro Aretino, for example, that new miracle of nature. Likewise Messer Jacopo Tatti, known as Sansovino, who copies nature as skillfully with his chisel as our host does with his paint-brush. Finally, Messer Jacopo Nardi, and myself. So that I was the fourth member of so distinguished a group.

"Though you could still feel the sun's heat, the place was well shaded. Consequently, we passed the time before we sat down to the table admiring the life-like figures in the excellent paintings with which the house was filled, and in regaling ourselves with the beauty and charm of the garden. It seemed wonderful to us all.

"This garden was situated in one of the outlying parts of the city. It was beside the lagoon, and overlooked the pretty island of Murano, as well as other pleasant places, and as soon as the sun had set, the surface of the nearby water was filled with thousands of little gondolas, aboard which were lovely ladies, who sang and played various instruments. Until midnight, this served as an accompaniment to our gay repast.

"At last the dinner was brought on, and it was not less well-planned than plentiful. For it was supplied — in addition to the most delicate viands and the most delicious wines — with all those pleasant and agreeable things which were due to the time, the company, and the festive occasion. Finally, when the dessert had been placed on the table, your letters arrived. They were like fruit of some new and delicious kind which had been lacking to the perfection of the splendid party.

"One of my pupils brought them to me, and as I could not contain myself, I opened them and read them before all. I knew that because of their charm, everybody would be entertained by them.

"And so they were. Especially when they heard the account of the delightful banquet you had in the gardens of your very reverend patron Monsignor Ridolfi, and of the conversation which took place there. However, they were a little annoyed at the incivility, not to say spitefulness of that thorny old pedant, as you call him, who thrust the bitterness of grammatical argument into the pleasures of dining and the gay conviviality.

"More than any of the others, Aretino grew angry as a handsome devil when he realized that he was attacking the Tuscan tongue. If we had not restrained him, I think that he would have set his hand immediately to the most cruel invective in the world. For he cried furiously: 'Paper! A pen!' without, however, ceasing to take part in the verbal maledictions.

"But at last he was quieted and the meal finished in gaiety."

Nor was this the only time when good food and the magic which is hidden in the grape made the two men—as they foregathered—large and expansive.

Count Manfredo di Collalto made Aretino a present of some thrushes.

"As I tasted them," he wrote in acknowledgment, "I found myself humming that old ditty 'Of all fine birds the finest . . .' Indeed, they were so good that our friend Titian, seeing them on the spit, and getting a whiff of them in his nostrils, gave one look at the snow which was swirling down outside, and decided to disappoint some gentlemen who were giving him a dinner party."

The Cavaliere da Porto sent Pietro two brace of grouse.

"I certainly enjoyed them, as did also Sansovino, the reputation of marble, and Titian, the glory of paint. Although my servants could only tell me that they came from Vicenza, and although all the knights in that city are generous, I knew them to be your regal present to me."

The ladies, too, were not always left drifting about in gondolas. These three were men of the world; they liked completeness; they had a wide range of tastes; and Venice was renowned for her women. Titian had painted them. They were his Danaës and Europas, his St. Catherines and his Virgin Marys. In some cases, Sansovino had used them in his sculpture. Aretino knew them intimately. Also *la vie bohème*—whether it be lived in Renaissance Italy, Murger's Paris of the late Nineteenth Century, or Greenwich Village of the 1920's—has a certain convention to live up to.

"We expect you to dinner tonight," thus Pietro wrote a certain Franceschina. "Titian and Sansovino and I do. But on one condition. That is that you bring Messer Ippolito with

Venice

ARETINO AS AN EVANGELIST

When Sansovino wrought the doors to the sacristy of St. Mark's cathedral, he put Aretino's bearded countenance upon them in the guise of one of the evangelists.

you. Then if my food lacks flavor, your singing and his ac-companiment may bring savor to it."

"A pair of pheasants and I don't know what else are ready to regale you tonight," he wrote Titian. "Angela Zaffetta will be here. So please come. For if we are continually gay, old age, who is the spy of death, will not report that we are gray-ing."

Incidentally, how these three men made a contrast with each other! As in public, Aretino, in private, is all impulse and energy. He wants pens and paper. He wants to pour out what is seething in his mind while it is still molten, before it grows cool and will not flow. The same way in his dealings with the ladies. He holds nothing back. He gives out all his abundant personality to them. He flatters them, makes them laugh, fills them with his own exuberance. He makes very little distinc-tion between the most open courtezan and the finest great lady. Quite often, therefore, the most open courtezan became like a great lady as far as her dealings with Pietro were con-cerned. The reverse was also true. Sansovino, with his bulbous head and his short red beard, is nervous and changeable. Some-times he has Aretino's mood, sometimes Titian's. Neither be-longs to him. He is a great artist, but you cannot help feeling that he fits badly as a man. At all times, he is self-conscious, at most times introspective. Titian is aloof and self-contained. You see him as the observer, hardly ever as the participant. Even in the wildest of their evenings, he maintains a kind of dignity.

Congratulating Sansovino on some amorous exploit, Are-tino made the observation that Titian did not go in for that sort of thing.

"Indeed, I marvel at him. No matter with whom he is, or where he finds himself, he always maintains his restraint. He will kiss a young lady, hold her in his lap, or fondle her, but he never goes further.

"We ought to be corrected by his example," he added.

No one, however, who has looked at Titian's magnificent

paintings, which are hymns to the human body and *gloria in excelsis*' to the senses, will make the quaint error of imagining that he lived the chaste life of a monk or an eremite. He did not, and Aretino knew that he did not. But there were some things that he felt it was decorous to be reserved about, and fitting to keep to himself.

If we knew only this aspect of the relationship between the two men, we might imagine that theirs was nothing else than one of those tavern companionships which, since the days of the Mermaid, have been dear to all romantics. But this friendship had more depth to it. Aretino had a very real concern in everything that touched Titian's life and this is nowhere shown more charmingly than in a letter that he wrote to one Angelo degli Organi. In it, he asked Angelo, "the light of your art," to make a harpsichord for Titian, "the splendor of his." In return, Titian would paint Angelo's portrait.

"No more high-principled deal could be imagined," he said. "You are to construct one of those contrivances whose sweet harmonies make the soul prisoner to rapture. He is to set down your face in one of those paintings which astonish all people. The world awaits the outcome."

The same very real concern is shown in the interest he took in Titian's children. Nothing could be more patient or more fine.

As we have seen, Aretino was genuinely fond of young people. His love for his own daughters was one of the most appealing sides of his character, and to a degree that was only perceptibly less he was drawn to all others of the same generation. When they were young, he wrote to them. When they were older, he used his influence to advance them. If they were successful, he congratulated them. If they were in difficulties, he tried to help them out. All the while he paid them the most effective compliment that a grown person can pay a growing one: he took them seriously. Yet he was never solemn with them. And he never forgot that their extravagances were the extravagances of his own younger days, were the extravagances once indulged in by the very persons who were most horrified by them.

"If there is such a thing as right," he wrote a parent, "certainly the wrongs done you by your son would justify you in cutting him off without a *soldo*. Yet if you stopped to think what you yourself did at his age, wouldn't you forgive him and laugh heartily too? What you should do is to return him a hundred for one, spending some of the money that you have saved for him, on gay clothes and love affairs."

This was a line of attack that youth could comprehend better than moral lectures. Consequently he won his way into their hearts.

Titian's eldest son, Pomponio, was one of those young people in whom Aretino felt the keenest interest. It was not the less, we can suppose, because of the boy's distinguished father. But also there was a certain spirit about Pomponio, a certain independence about him that could not help appealing to the man himself whom no one had been able to tame or bridle. We are quite aware that Aretino paid some attention to Titian's other children, that he wrote to them, and was glad to hear of them. Orazio, however,—like his father, he was a painter—and Lavinia, the lovely daughter, were content to let their lives flow smoothly in the safe channels which had been dug for them. For that reason, they could not really attract Pietro. Their ways were very normal and very even. To him it was the dramatic that made appeal.

His contact with Pomponio began early, and it appears even that he had some influence with him. At any rate, when, at twelve years old, the boy showed his first signs of rebellion by refusing to return to school, Aretino was called on to reason with him. He did so in the following communication:

"Your father has just brought me the greetings you sent me, and they pleased me almost as much as the two partridges that came with them. Incidentally, I gave the latter to myself. He told me to present them to some deserving gentleman!

"And now that you have seen how big-hearted I am, let me

repay you 'A thousand, thousand, times, That all the night long sings and chimes,' requesting that you give the leanest ones to your little brother, Orazio, since he has forgotten to tell me what his latest fancy is about spending this world and the next as soon as possible. Your thrift is a better way of getting rich, and since you are to be a priest, I am sure that you will not depart from that old priestly custom.

"And so good health to you and my best wishes. But now I have some very bad news.

"It is time to get back to work, for as I recall it, there are no schools in the country, while in the winter, the city is a very pleasant place.

"So come back to Venice, where with your twelve years and your Hebrew, Greek and Latin, you will drive all the learned doctors in the world to despair, just as the fine things your good father paints puts to rout all the painters of Italy.

"That is all.

"Now keep warm and enjoy your supper!"

It continued all through the long course of Pomponio's varied career.

Young Pomponio, as that letter shows, was destined for the church, and while Titian's influence could do much for him, Aretino could do even more; just, therefore, as if the lad had been his own son, he kept up a constant pressure for him, with the secretaries of princes, with the pope's priest confidants, with the princes themselves, with their chancellors and ambassadors. Let him be given a benefice. Let him be given a better benefice. In general, this campaign was successful. The Duke of Mantua made Pomponio a canon. Pope Paul III, an abbot. Later he was given a rich curacy near Treviso.

Furthermore, Aretino's patience outlasted even that of Titian. Pomponio repaid all his father's efforts and all those of Pietro with conduct so disordered that even Aretino could not disregard it. Yet his attempt to correct the young man was a good-tempered one.

"I realize that it is true that old age is something youth cannot believe is really possible, just as youth is an extravagant fairy tale to old age. That is why youth laughs at old age when it really should weep, and why old age laments at youth when it really should laugh. I am telling you this so that one like yourself won't take lightly a moral lecture just because it comes from one like me. Here is the situation. The other day your father came to my house and he was in so great grief that it made me suffer to see him. He wanted you to change your way of life. And I have to admit that your goings on are like a low farce which, although it pleases the actors, is distasteful to the audience. Go back to your studies, and let your fine mind show that it is the equal of that of any learned man there is. For it is not right that the wealth amassed by the paint-brushes, the labors, the wisdom and the long voyages of so great a man as your father, should be thrown away in riotous living. It would be more to your credit to double it."

The point was a well-taken one. The son of a poor shoe-maker was a free agent, and could do as he wanted to. The son of a great man had a standard to live up to.

Pomponio did not see it that way, however. He may have read the letter, but he did not allow it to influence him. He went on with his dissolute ways. He whored, ruffled, and ran into debt. Finally his conduct was such that Titian, his heart wrung with anguish, was obliged to write to the Duke of Man-tua and ask him to transfer the benefices to a nephew.

Small wonder that Aretino looked on his own offspring with redoubled pleasure.

"Happy are they whose children are daughters," he said. "I thank God that He has given me Adria and Austria. With His aid, I can at least count on their goodness."

Poor Titian, he must have agreed!

But it was not even in these intimate aspects that the friend-ship of the two men took on its greatest significance. It was in the effect Aretino had on Titian's painting. Directly, of course, he did nothing or said nothing that made the artist draw a truer line or fill in a finer picture. That would have been beyond his powers. But he helped Titian to a renown that must have heartened him to superlative effort. Those, therefore, who consider the man of Cadore to be one of the supreme manifestations of human genius as it deals with form and color, must, even if reluctantly, acknowledge themselves in Aretino's debt.

He was admirably qualified to do this job. It has been said that no person can truly understand all those many factors which are involved in putting certain pigments, mixed with white of egg or oil, upon canvas in such a way as to produce what is great and beautiful, unless he has himself been a painter. But Aretino had studied painting in Perugia. It is said that to appreciate those sorts of things one must have lived in contact with them. But at no period in his life was he far from either art or artists. Finally he was an excellent critic. "I will listen to you gladly," Gian Francesco Fabrini told him, "for I know you to be a man of great understanding and judgment, and most of all in things which appertain to painting."

His own dicta on art show why Fabrini felt this way about him.

"Those who prefer Michelangelo are for the most part sculptors who think only of his draughtsmanship and power. They consider that the light and graceful manner of Raphael is too facile and hence not really art. They do not realize that ease is the best argument in favor of art and is the hardest to attain."

"I say to you that Leonardo was equal to the greatest. His limitation was that he had so elevated a genius that he was never satisfied with what was done."

"Granted that foreshortenings are difficult, it does not follow that the more often one uses them the more credit he deserves. A painter should not demonstrate one quality but all of them."

"Painting is largely to afford pleasure. Hence the painter who does not delight will stay unknown to fame. But by delight, I do not mean that which pleases the eyes of the vulgar

or even of a person who regards it for the first time. I mean
that great delight that more increases the more times you look
at a picture."

"Above all things, avoid too much refining of your work. If
I am not mistaken, Apelles used to say that although Pro-
tagones was his equal and perhaps his superior in most things
that had to do with painting, he was the superior in one matter: he knew when to stop working on a picture."

"Conception, design, color — these are the three important
parts of painting."

Though some of these words of wisdom ring now with almost trite familiarity, it must be remembered that they had
not been said quite so often four packed centuries ago, and
never by an artistic popularizer.

Indeed only one tenet of his has since been adjudicated to
have been wrong or at least vulnerable.

"Tizianus emulus naturae imme magister — Titian, an imitator of nature, hence a great master."

Photographic reproduction of what the eye sees is not now
regarded as art's highest achievement. But there are three
things to be observed about Aretino's defence of it. First, that
despite stories of Zeuxis and the bees, art first became successfully representative in a literal sense during the age of Titian
and that it had to be able to be representative before it could
proceed to other conquests. Second that taste — even where it
concerns great art — has something of the latest fashion about
it and that it is quite possible that our present anti-literal
trends may go out of vogue again. And thirdly that the most
you can ask of any critic is that he can distinguish between
the good and merely adequate, according to the canons of his
age. And this Aretino could do, and did.

Having these qualities, which put him in a position to see
Titian's true value and therefore lent sincerity to his eulogies,
Aretino knew the thing to do with them. No one had to tell
him that the secret of promotion is repeating constantly. That
he knew instinctively.

Did he have an occasion, therefore, to praise a statue by Tribolo? It was a chance, then, to admire a painting by Titian. Did he write a lord? He threw in a hint that it would be well to have Titian immortalize him. Did he make a present? He tried to include something Titian had recently completed.

Suppose it were not paid for, or only paid for moderately? Well, at least it would give him a chance for further heralding.

"The medallion," he wrote Count Maximilian Stampa, "on which Luigi Anichini has engraved the head of Mars would not be much of a gift, my lord, were it not for the crystal bucklers and the mirror of the same material, as well as the painting by Titian which I am sending you by Rosello Roselli. Incidentally, you must not value this last because I gave it, but for the skill which makes it valuable. Look at the softness of the curly hair and the pretty youthfulness of St. John. Look at the flesh tints so skilfully rendered that they are like snow tinted with vermilion, and seem animated by living pulses and warmed by the spirit of life. Of the crimson of the cloak, and of the lynx fur, with which it is lined, I will say nothing. Painted, they match real crimson and the skin of an actual lynx. They are life itself. As for the lamb, it would make a ewe bleat, it is so real. But since neither the skill nor the gift is of any real moment, let your lordship accept my heart with it. It is invisibly part of what I send."

This, incidentally, is merely one example, chosen half at random out of many.

Titian.

The immortal Titian. The Apelles of our day and age.

Aretino's audacity was unbounded. He buttonholed the Doge in full piazza and reminded him that his portrait had not yet been painted by the greatest artist in the city over which he ruled.

He saw to it that his friend was given the opportunity of painting Pope Paul Farnese, and then took good care that the renown of the portrait of the aged yet still crafty fox was trumpeted through all of Italy. It might well be. Portraiture has not a greater masterpiece. As it hung in a window in Bologna, the people hurrying by paused to bow in reverence. For a half moment they thought it was Farnese himself.

He persuaded Titian to attempt the Emperor.

Also he cautioned him against worrying too much about the price he would receive.

"Not Apelles nor Praxiteles nor any of those others who have painted or carved out portraits or statues of whatsoever prince or king can boast of having received gold or gems that even approach the reward your genius has received from His Majesty. The fact that he deems you worthy of being called to him in such a time of great disorders is the greatest tribute an artist could receive. By this, he shows that he holds you more important than any of the leagues or alliances which he has to organize against the world. Furthermore he once swore that he wanted no portraits or statues to put him on the plane of the gods, and that he was much more contented to be carved and painted merely in the hearts of the good and the wise, yet he has consented — merely to pay tribute to your unique ability — that you should record his appearance. Therefore, go to him, and when you are at his feet, worship him with all your being. And do this in my name also."

He realized that the fame Titian got from portraying the great Charles would make it worth his while, if he did not receive even his living expenses. It was not this particular picture that he was promoting. He was promoting Titian's whole career.

The importance of all this can hardly be exaggerated. Admirers of Titian who dislike having to admit the part played in his career by a man of Aretino's reputation, point out that the artist was in his late forties when Pietro met him. They point out that he was already well-known. They say that Aretino had nothing to do with his development. They assert that Aretino merely took advantage of Titian's glory to give a certain standing to himself.

This is at best partially true. Titian may well have been forty-seven or even nearly fifty when he and Aretino met — and even according to the modern but less probable chronology, which sets his birth in 1490, he was not less than thirty-seven — and he was known then through all of Italy, but simply as a great painter. Aretino made him known as the greatest painter. He made him a fashion. He convinced princes that it was necessary for Titian to paint them if they wished to be immortal — quite as necessary as it was for him to write about them. It was due to Aretino's pen and tongue that when Titian departed for Augsburg, a crowd stormed his studio. They wanted to buy every picture there. They were afraid that he would never leave the emperor's service. They were panic-stricken lest a god be gone for good.

Yet at that the great friendship was not a one-sided one. It was not that Titian served Aretino in a similar fashion, though in a way he tried to, jogging the memory of this prince and that marquis or duke about pensions overdue, and writing from Madrid and Rome how this grandee or that grandee asked for him, and how it was: "Aretino said this," "Pietro said that," "Did you hear the witticism of the Scourge of Princes?" It was more that he brought out all — and there was much — that was the best in Aretino.

As they associated together, some of Titian's poise and finesse began to show itself in Aretino. Without even trying to, he began to be less of a ruffian. Also Titian awakened in him that fine sense of every sort of beauty which was one of the most unexpected phases of his character.

One letter will bear witness to this. It was addressed to Titian. It was written when Aretino was fifty-two years old. He was ill. He was bored. He was disconsolate. So he went to the window and saw something that made him marvel. This is how he set it down:

"Having eaten alone, my good friend, which is contrary to my custom; or to put it better, having eaten in the company of an annoying quartan fever which did not even permit me to taste my food, I arose from the table fed up with the same despair with which I had sat down. And then, leaning my arm against the window sill, and on my arm my chest, and indeed almost my whole body, I looked at the marvelous scene outside.

"Infinite boats, some laden with foreigners, others with people of our own city, entertained not only the onlookers but the Grand Canal itself, entertainer of all who plough its waves. In front of my eyes, two gondolas, each manned by famous boatmen, were having a race. This gave great sport to the people. And they crowded the Rialto Bridge, the fish markets, the *traghetto* of Santa Sofia, and the Casa da Mosto, to see the gay sport.

"Then, while this group of people and that one went their way applauding joyously, I, who was almost a man who has become so revolting to himself that he does not know what to do with his thoughts, turned my eyes upon the sky. Since God had created it, it had never been more beautified with a subtle pattern of lights and shades. Indeed the quality of the air was such that anyone who wished to make a record of it, would have been consumed with envy at not being you. You will see this when I tell you about it.

"To begin with, the houses, although they were of real stone, seemed to be some unreal fabric. Next you must visualize the atmospheric effect. In some places, the air was transparent and living, in other places turgid and dead. Think, too, of the wonder in my heart at clouds which after all were nothing but condensed humidity. In the center of the scene, some of them seemed to touch the roofs of the houses, while others receded into distance. On the right hand, they were like a poised mass of gray-black smoke.

"Certainly I was astonished at the various colors they showed. Those near at hand burned with the flames of the sun's fire, while those in the distance had the dull glow of half-molten lead. Oh, with what clever strokes the paint brushes of the world around us gave perspective to the very atmosphere, setting it back from the palaces, just as you, Titian, give it distance in your landscapes. In certain places there appeared a blue-green and in others a green-blue which was truly composed by the errant fancies of nature with the skill of a great master. With lights and shadows she brought forth or subdued in manner that which she thought ought to be brought forth or subdued.

"So that I, who know that your brushes are the very soul of her soul, cried out three or four times: 'O Titian, where are you now?'

"By my faith, if you had painted what I have described to you, you would have turned men stock-still with the same astonishment that confounded me as I looked at the scene I am telling about and realized that its wonder would not last."

If you concede — and I do — that Titian awoke in Aretino those feelings which made it possible for him to write suddenly like a painting by Turner, that alone evened up the whole score.

CHAPTER XVI

The Sweat of My Ink

IT WAS during these crowded years — the non-literary activities of which would alone have filled up a very strenuous life — that Aretino turned loose upon the world the full flood of his voluminous writings. Though his pen had been his sword, though he had begun winning the material as well as verbal tributes that made it possible for him to live overlooking the canal like a great, swaggering robber baron long before he set up his Venetian residence, that which he had written had been relatively little; that which he had published even less:

The thin, juvenile book of poems, which had slipped swiftly into the usual and deserved obscurity of youthful imitating (it was forgotten even in his own lifetime and only rediscovered little more than fifty years ago) ; the "Testament of the Elephant" with its maturing if still awkward sarcasms; the sheaf of irreverent pasquinades about the papal election of 1522; the indecent sonnets; a few laudatory poems such as the *Laude di Clemente VII, the Esortazione de la Pace tra l'Imperatore e Il Re di Francia* ("A Prayer to the Emperor and the King of France that They Sign a Peace Treaty") , and the *Canzone in Laude del Datario;* his first comedy, *La Cortegiana* ("Life at Court," not "The Courtesan" is the English for it) , which he circulated at this time though he did not have it printed; the first ones of his devastating series of *giudizii;* a handful of his more mordant epistles.

Even when you make due allowance for the fact that the Renaissance writer had no typewriter and few other mechanical aids to help him rush any undigested idea he might have into more or less enduring permanency, it was not an incredible amount.

Now at thirty-five, he stepped ashore upon the Molo at the exact age when Dante set out on his imaginative voyage to the lowest depths and highest peaks of human psychological experience; at the exact age when Boccaccio started the *Decameron,* he settled seriously to business. The results were on the same scale as every other thing he did. Indeed, the mere list of simply those compositions of his which he found time to publish during the first two decades of his Venetian sojourn — and he wrote always more than he gave the printers — is a little breath-taking.

Mazzuchelli's inventory will do to begin with. According to that periwigged Brescian nobleman scholar of the Eighteenth Century, whose careful study of Aretino was the by-product of his prodigious book-collecting, he brought out in 1532 the first two cantos of the never really finished *Marfisa.* In 1533, he brought out his second comedy, *Il Marescalco.* In 1534, the first volume of his notorious dialogues, the *Ragionamenti;* "The Seven Psalms of David" (his first religious work) ; and a revised version of the *Cortegiana.* In 1535, "The Three Books of the Humanity of Christ." In 1536, the second volume of the *Ragionamenti.* In 1537, the first volume of his "Letters" and the "Stanzas in Praise of Madonna Angela Sirena." In 1538, his "Conversations about Courts" (*Ragionamenti de le Corti*) ; his "Story of Genesis" and the short narrative poem, "The Tears of Angelica." In 1539, he brought out *Fra Zoppino.* In 1540, the "Life of St. Catherine of Siena" and his third comedy, *Lo Ipocrito.* In 1541, "The Life of the Virgin Mary." In 1542, his fourth comedy, *La Talenta;* a revised edition of the first volume of his letters; and the first edition of his second volume of letters. In 1543, the "Life of St. Thomas Aquinas." In 1544, his *Strambotti alla Villanesca,* poems. In 1545, his *Carte Parlanti* or "The Talking Cards." In 1546, his last comedy *Il Filosofo;* his tragedy, *l'Orazia,* and the third volume of his letters.

This does not include works only doubtfully ascribed to him (and that largely on account of their indecency) , such as the *Commento di Ser Agresto* ("Master Sour Grapes") ; the *Diceria de Nasi* ("Observations about Noses") ; or the dialogue, *La Puttana Errante* — not to be confused, as it often has been even by scholars, with the poem of the same name by Lorenzo Veniero. It does not include the *Astolfeide* and the *Orlandino,* two lively burlesque poems obviously written at this time but only published much later. It does not include the five cantos in honor of the Marquis of Vasto. Nor the various laudatory or sarcastic sonnets scattered through his correspondence. Nor his fulsome *capitoli,* long eulogistic poems in *terza rima,* which he compared to "colossal statues of gold or silver where I have carved the forms of a Pope Julius, Emperor Charles, Queen Catherine, or Duke Francesco Maria, with such art that the outlines of their inner nature are brought into relief, the muscles of their will and purpose are shown in play, the profiles of their emotions are thrown into salience." Nor does it include the "Poetic Combat between the Divine Aretino and the Bestial Albicante."

At one time, according to Francesco Coccio who was with him daily, he was thinking out and putting down on paper as many words in a single day as the printers, not having linotype machines, could set down in two of them.

"I live by the sweat of my ink, the lustre of which has never been extinguished by the blasts of malignity or the mists of envy!" he said exultantly.

At that time, it was a highly typical mood.

True, he was not always undespondent.

"Old age," he complained to a friend, "is beginning to paralyze my wit, and the love which ought to wake me up now puts me to sleep. I used to turn out forty stanzas in a morning. Now I can barely write one. It took me only seven days to compose the 'Psalms,' ten for the *Cortegiana* and the *Marescalco,* forty-eight for the two dialogues, and thirty for the 'Life of Christ,' yet I suffered six months writing the poems about La Sirena. I swear to you by that truth which is my guide that beyond a few letters I have written nothing."

But that was in 1537 when all his working hours were taken up with the vast labor of editing his correspondence, and when he published nothing. A writer is a kind of a drug addict who is soothed only by what flows from his pen. When he writes nothing or when — even more important — he has nothing published, he is apt either to be gloomy or cantankerous.

A short time later his old *élan vital* returned to him.

"The *Filosofo*," he announced to the Duke of Urbino, "was composed in ten mornings, and the *Talanta* and the *Ipocrito* in the sleep robbed from twenty nights."

"It seems to my thus made nature," he said also, "that to spew forth all I knew in two hours of each day is to do enough. If I spent in composition even one-third of the time I throw away, the printing presses would have time for nothing else but to bring forth my works."

And these compositions which he tossed off in such a fury of mad haste were read all over literate Europe. They were translated into French. (As a matter of fact, the first volume of the *Ragionamenti* was first published in Paris — even before it was published in its own country; Brantôme, an authority on such matters, and talking of a not much later period, tells us of a Venetian printer in the Rue St. Jacques who "did once tell me, and swear to it, that in less than a year, he had sold more than fifty of the two volumes of Aretino to very many folks, married and unmarried, as well as to women, of whom he did name three very great ladies of society." And "all at their weight in gold.") They were popular in Hungary, Poland and the Netherlands. Johann Herold said that Aretino and Machiavelli were the only Italians read in Germany, and he implied that they were civilizing the country. His works reached the Tudor court in London, where they started the vogue of Italianizing that was to bring forth such good and evil under a later sovereign. The *Inglese Italianato* who, according to the proverb, was *un diavolo incarnato;* the young son of a gentleman or an earl who followed Oxford or Cambridge with a grand tour of the brothels of Florence, Venice, Genoa, Ferrara and Milan, and came back a rotten and a discontented fruit of pleasant corruption and unprincipled intrigue, was one product of this influence—but so also was Elizabethan drama: Greene, Webster, Johnson, Ford, and even gentle Shakespeare, were to some degree his work.

Curiously enough, however—for a prophet, whether before the fact or after, is said never to be without honor save in his own country—it was in Italy itself that Aretino attracted the most attention. There he became at once a sort of fashion and the sensation of the hour. Indeed, there is no parallel for the way what he brought out was received until we come to Lord Byron. Just as "Childe Harold" was swept up from the book-stalls faster than it could be printed and bound, so everything that Aretino wrote was snatched up by a seething mob that literally fought around the tables.

Bernardino Theodolo was in Rome on one of these occasions.

"Even at the opening of the papal law courts, I never saw such a press of litigants striving to be the first to enter as there were men striving to be the first to purchase your new book. A sign, 'Letters of the Divine Pietro Aretino,' was hung up. Suddenly there was a great crowd of people, followed by as much noise and jostling as there is in certain cities when, on Holy Thursday, they give alms to the poor.

"And so great was the sale that I can assure you that there were plenty who went off with empty hands.

"I had not taken care to be among the first, and consequently I would have been one of these, if it had not been for a certain courtier. This is what a fool he was! He and his companion each bought a copy of your book, and in spite of all the push he began to read it then and there. Then, wishing to see whether the book bought by his friend was exactly like his own, he picked this one up and laid down the other on the counter. No sooner did he do this than I snatched it up, and withdrew. When he discovered how silly he had been, you should have heard his uproar. He made more noise than the whole crowd put together. Indeed, what with his swearing and cursing, you would have said that Renzo, Jacobacci, Malatesta and all such windy braggarts were nothing.

"After that, seeing that oaths did not avail him, he began to beg and plead. He uttered more prayers than Fra Stopino has in all the years he has been trying to be made Bishop of Gaeta. Or even Rimini who wants to be a cardinal.

"However, it was I who went off with the letters, and since then I have read them not once but ten times over."

But it was not only the mob of Roman fashion that stampeded to buy his work. From all over the peninsula and from men of every sort, tributes came to him. One correspondent said that he would rather have received Aretino's letter with the enclosed sonnet than if it had come from the world's greatest ruler. Another — Bernardo Accolti — confessed that the "Tears of Angelica" brought tears to his own eyes. A third, Giovanni Pollio, himself a reasonably good minor poet, announced that he had praised the *Marfisa* so long and so loudly that the base crowd must have come to the conclusion that he was a mere adulator. Not so the learned, he added. Veronica Gambara, blue-stocking as any literary lady of Eighteenth Century France or England, and as a poetess third only — in her own age — to Gaspara Stampa and Vittoria Colonna, found every single one of his works "exceedingly dear to me." The "divine" Molza called the *Ragionamenti* "very pleasing." Duke Cosimo de Medici took the trouble to thank Aretino personally for his comedies. Gian Antonio da Foligno said that in his time he had "committed many sins and done many wrongs" but that Pietro's religious writings had set him on the road from error.

Add to this testimony, other testimony that is not limited to words of praise. Fausto Longiano, writing a treatise on the Italian language, did not see how to make it complete without including Aretino's work. He wrote respectfully asking for the necessary permission. Alessandro Piccolomini, attempting to translate Ptolemy's "Astronomy" and his other scientific works, did not know what to do about technical words. He took counsel from Pietro. Beside that, Aretino was sought after by all the staid academies. That of Siena was the first one to elect him a member, but the Infiammati of Padua chose him in 1541, and the Florentine Academy in 1545.

The literary log-rollers had joined popular taste and the considered and judicious in acclaiming him. He was a great writer for his own age and for all time also. We begin now to understand Joseph Addison's comment and to wonder what has happened in the meantime. But perhaps we should not wonder, contemplating with malicious pleasure, rather, the moral there contained. Only two centuries ago, he doubted if there were a single man then living who did not know who Aretino was.

The reason for the popular part of his vogue is not hard to find. The Italians were a great nation of readers. Where, in that effulgent century, not only the barbarity but even the illiteracy of the French court was conspicuous enough to evoke written comment; where the English lord, (whose grandson was to patronize the bright Apollos of the Mermaid Tavern, to say nothing of writing competent sonnets himself), was a blond and raw-boned fellow, thoughtful of his staghounds and his brawling retinue, but who had much difficulty in scratching out slowly his own name, even the ordinary Italian was not only literate but devoured everything that he could lay his hands on. It was part of his tradition. When there were no books — or none anyway except those hand-copied onto parchment or vellum which no one but the really wealthy could afford — the hard-headed burghers and artizans, from whom even his princes were descended, had been a nation of listeners. They had crowded, during the Dark Ages, into the square piazzas of the mediæval cities, as the *cantastorie* — the gaily colored wandering street singers of that day — told their merry, generally racy *fabliaux,* or sang their long romantic cantos about Charlemagne and Arthur. *Il Reali de Francia* — the high stories of the legendary Kings of France — were preserved, even if they were not created, in Italy, rather than in the country whose sovereigns they celebrated. They are cherished by the people there even today.

The art of printing, therefore — the ability to produce books that men only modestly well off could buy — did not so much create a need, as it supplied one, for until then the ordinary person's library had been his memory. At the same time the Italians had then, as they have today, a great love for the personal. The abstract made a thing much less appealing to them. If a robustious tale were told, it had to be about a real person. If a pithy saying were uttered, someone actual had to utter it. The short stories of Sacchetti give an excellent example of this. Just as all our economy stories used to be attached to Calvin Coolidge, so in Sacchetti, if a poet overhears a rude clown misquoting something he had written, and confutes him wittily, it is Dante Alighieri. If there is a cruel lord, it must be Bernabo Visconti. If there is a shrewd painter, it is Giotto. But the same thing is also true of even so conscious and so cultivated an artist as Boccaccio, and indeed the two writers often deal with the same otherwise obscure men.

Coming into maturity at a time when the printing press, now a half century old, was beginning for the first time to function efficiently, Aretino was equipped, by every quality he had, to be the man of its need. His great energy equipped him to supply the publishers at a time when they needed things to print and to sell as fast as possible. And the sharp acid of his sarcastic nature and the acuteness of his observations made it certain he would write what buyers wanted. *"Parla male ma dice il vero,"* says one character to another, in his comedy, *La Talanta*. "You speak maliciously but you tell the truth." It is Aretino in exactly six words. Maliciously he did speak, but with due allowances, and at that with modest ones, he spoke truthfully. It was what made him the loadstone that drew all eyes.

But it is not merely that he was the supplier of urgent needs that makes Aretino deserve our consideration and thought. That made him a social phenomenon, but he was

also a literary one. He made a definite contribution to Italian
literature and it was an important one. Indeed, it is not much
of an exaggeration to say that but for Aretino, Italian literature might have flowed almost indefinitely through impossible
channels. And that, since a large part of the great literature of
northern Europe stems from the Italian, but for the Pietro
we are now examining it would surely have had a different
and a less happy course.

To understand just exactly what is meant by this and why
and in what way it was true, it is necessary to digress a little
—to leave Aretino for a moment and to go into Italian writing
as a whole. Italian literature, as a separate and important
entity, had its birth during the extraordinary Thirteenth Century. There is some difference of opinion as to what began it;
but whether we take Francis of Assisi's vibrant and crystalline
clear *Laudes Creatorum* as the first notes of its unequalled
music, or whether we incline more to the love poetry of the
Provençal tradition which was naturalized at Palermo during
the intellectually stimulating reign of German-Sicilian Fred-
eric II, they were all sounded within its hundred years. Yet
it was not more than fifty years after the close of that century
that it had reached heights not surpassed in any language.
Dante Alighieri had gone down to hell and up to heaven.
Boccaccio had dredged legend and history and the streets and
courts of Florence, Naples and the world, for his so animated
men and women. Petrarch had made love music that was
approached by no man; and among the other sex, only by
Greek Sappho.

Then suddenly the whole thing ended. To be sure, there
was Lorenzo de' Medici—the great diplomat never quite sufficiently appreciated even in his own country as a poet—who
amused his leisure hours by writing pieces in the vernacular
that were as fresh and jocund as the Florentine countryside;
and there was his friend Angelo Poliziano, almost equal to
him. But Angelo and Lorenzo were almost sports, and the
bulk of Italian talent—and it was large and had ability—

turned to the dead language of Cicero and Virgil. It was not fitting—and it was hardly even respectable—for anyone who thought he had an intellect to write except in Latin. The result was that when Italian came into vogue again it had no tradition except these three. But Dante was regarded as inimitable. Petrarch and Boccaccio, therefore, became models and saints, and since there had been no healthy growth, men, otherwise sensible, turned to them in abject worship. They knew all, and anyone who knew anything they did not know, knew nothing. To write poetry that was anything but thinned-out Petrarch was a sin against the spirit. To write prose that was anything but watered Boccaccio was to fail utterly. The categories of good taste became the limits set by imitation. It was poor form to be original. It was crude and uncultivated to do anything they had not done before.

An example of just how far this could be carried is given forcibly in a colloquy by Sperone Speroni. And he expressed but a very common view.

"Having in all truth," he wrote, "from my earliest years, been desirous beyond all measure to speak and to write my thoughts in our mother tongue, and that not so much with a view to being understood, which lies within the power of every unlettered person, as with the object of placing my name upon the roll of famous men, I neglected every other interest, and gave my whole attention to the reading of Petrarch and of the 'Hundred Novels.' I exercised myself for many months in these studies without a guide and with very little profit. Then, inspired by God, I betook myself to our revered Master Trifone Gabrielli. With his kindly assistance, I arrived at perfect comprehension of those authors, whom, through ignorance of what I ought to have noted, I had frequently, up till then, misunderstood.

"This excellent man and true father of ours, first bade me observe the names of things; then gave me rules for knowing the declension and conjugation of nouns and verbs in Tuscan; and lastly explained to me articles, pronouns, participles, adverbs and other parts of speech, so that collecting all that I had learned, I composed a grammar for myself, and by following this when I wrote, I so controlled my style that in a short space of time the world held me for a man of erudition, and still does.

"Then, when it seemed to me that I had taken rank as a grammarian, I set myself to making verses, to the utmost expectation of all who knew me. My head full of Petrarch and Boccaccio, for a few years I produced things that seemed wonderful to my judgment.

"But after a while, coming to the conclusion that my vein was beginning to dry up—inasmuch as my words frequently failed me, and not finding anything new to say, I often rewrote my old sonnets—I had recourse to what the whole world now does. I composed a rhyming dictionary or vocabulary of Italian phrases. In this way I classed by alphabet every word these two authors had used. Moreover I collected in another book their various ways of describing things such as day, night, anger, peace, hate, love, fear, hope and beauty. In this way, not a single word or thought came to me that did not have its precedent in their sonnets or tales."

It would have been most surprising if in all Italy with its immense mental vigor, there had been no one with enough common sense or enough human vitality to cry out at such futile and such sterile subservience. It so happened that there were at least two.

In his "Book of the Courtier," Baldassare Castiglione stood out very valiantly and with cogent reasoning for a new order.

"I cannot—" and with wise choice he makes Giuliano de' Medici the interlocutor to say this—"and in reason ought not to contradict any man who says that the Tuscan tongue is more beautiful than the others. Nevertheless, it is true that in Petrarch and Boccaccio are found many words that are now discarded by the custom of today; and these I, for my part, would never use either in speaking or in writing; and I believe that they themselves if they survived until now, would no longer use those words."

He went further, and, though fully and fairly stating the case for the conservative opposition, he elaborated a clear, logical defense of the Italian language, that language to be based on the tongue actually spoken. Language was fluid, he realized, and to take the mother tongue as an example, "if those earliest writings in ancient Latin had survived, we should see that Evander and Turnus spoke differently from the last Roman kings and the first consul." And of course, Virgil, Circero and Horace differently from these.

"Therefore I for my part should avoid using antique words save in certain places and but seldom there, and it seems to me that he who uses them otherwise makes no less a mistake than he who, in order to imitate the ancients, should wish to feed on acorns after wheat had been discovered."

It was a telling and convincing phrase.

But there was one limitation to Castiglione, and it put definite bounds to his effectiveness. He was a scholar and a gentleman, and such cannot lead even literary revolutions. Words still had to him a certain sacredness. They should be "beautiful, ingenious, acute, elegant and grave — according to the need." A more vigorous leader of attack was needed. It was found in Aretino. He was unable — because of his background — to become one of the Petrarchizers, and even if he had been able to, his temperament would have prevented it. Partly, therefore, because he "made a virtue of necessity" — this exact phrase, incidentally, occurs in his writings, and he thus used it more than half a century before it was made a proverb by Shakespeare — and partly from very real conviction, the son of the shoemaker, who became the terrorist of the pen, was called on to lead the conquering assault.

He did this with his habitual thoroughness and gusto.

His first attack was against the institution itself.

Sending a few stanzas of the *Marfisa* to the Marquis of Mantua. he made the following illuminating comment:

"I do not deny that there is invention and style in them, but I confess to a faulty language. This not wishing to make use of my native idiom is a strange fantasy of mine. The reason is that every pedant has made a dry skeleton of the Tuscan way of speaking. If the souls of Petrarch and Boccaccio are so tormented in the next world as their writings are in this, they ought to forswear their baptism."

The reason that he took this attitude, he explained elsewhere with a back glance at the pack of schoolmasters who like jackals were ready to snarl at a safe distance, was not that he did not know the works of these two masters. That he knew them and admired them his own writings give plainest evidence. It was because he did not wish to lose time, patience and reputation in the mad attempt to convert himself into something not himself.

"It is better," he cried out, "to drink out of one's own wooden platter than another's golden goblet. A man makes a braver show in his own rags than he does in velvet robbed from someone.

"What have we to do with stolen goods?"

His next attack was on Petrarchism's most obvious fault. Proceeding with the argument we have already listened to, Sperone Speroni launched into his theory of poetic diction.

"While numbering and weighing Petrarch's words one by one, I realized that I found none base and none common; few harsh; all clear; all elegant; and all, moreover, so adopted to common use that one might have supposed that he had selected and accumulated them with assistance of all Italy. Among these — like stars amid the limpid space of midnight — a few shone with special lustre. Some were ancient words, but not unpleasing in their age, such as 'needs must,' 'whenas' and 'ofttimes.' Others were beautiful and graceful words, like jewels that delight the eyes of all men. All were such as are used only by high and gentle intellects. Time would fail to tell in detail of the verbs, adverbs and other parts of speech which make his verses noble. One thing I will not pass in silence. When speaking of his lady, he generally avoids the proper names of things, and by some wonderful art adorns each with words appropriate to something else, calling her head fine gold; her eyes suns, stars, and sapphires; her cheeks now snow, now roses, now milk, now fire; rubies her lips, her throat and breast now ivory, now alabaster."

In other words, the language of a writer was to be a rich ornamented brocade rather than the strong, serviceable home-spun of actual usage. His phrases were to be exquisite, but artificial.

This struck Aretino as utter nonsense, and he set out to say so. Root out of your compositions all the terms of Petrarch, for they are the clogged-up superstitions of the language, he admonished. Get away especially from just those particular archaically affected words that are held out by Sperone Speroni. Avoid Master Ofttimes like the death, Sir Ne'er as if he had the pox, Don Hence and my Lord Hereby like hostile armies.

Again it was common sense rather than ignorance that guided him.

"If you do not see them in my poem, it is not because I do not know them. I know them just as well as any of these half and half poets. But the love which that comely wench Laura gave to Master Petrarch was not as crude as the love Rome, *coda mundi,* gave to the Spaniards and the Germans. My words have to be foot-soldiers and arquebuses."

Elsewhere he made his point with irony.

"The conclusion of the dream was," he wrote Giancopo Leopardi in fantastic allegory, "that I found myself in a market place where starlings, magpies, crows and parrots were all making as much noise as a flock of geese. With these birds were certain togaed, bearded and wild-eyed pedants whose only occupation was to teach them to chatter by the points of the moon. Oh, what sport you would have had from one blue jay who kept repeating, 'ne'er,' 'needs must,' 'lissome,' 'oft-times,' 'hereby,' and 'hence.' You would have split your jaws to see Apollo, mad with fury, making a blockhead leap because he could not teach a nightingale to say 'I' troth !' He broke the bottom of his cithara over the fellow's backside while Fame split the handles of her trumpet."

Logic had not ousted all this time-worn nonsense from the house of custom. Perhaps repetition would. Repetition, and an occasional irreverent loud laugh.

But it was not simply to destroy old critical values that Aretino put up a hard fight. He was positive as well as negative. He could build up as well as destroy.

And the principal thing that he aimed to build up was the idea of looking at the scene in front of you. Do not be bound by the old conventions. "If my actors come on the stage more than five times in a scene, do not be surprised. The chains that hold the mills on the river do not bind the madmen of today." Do not follow classic models. "Men live in a different fashion in modern Rome than they did in ancient Athens." Use the language of your contemporaries; the customs of your day and age; the flavor of the world you live in. Above all, have something to say; something based on the fantastic mixture of farce and tragedy that swirls around you; something based on that strange drama with its shams and its sincerities, with its lusts and its loves, its hatreds and its generosities, its crude humor and swift heartless disasters. Something made of your own bone, your own feelings, your own vision. This is the most important of all. If you do not, "you will be like an industrious workman from Bergamo who has in his hands the instruments of his trade but nowhere he can use them." You will be like a "tailor who having no cloth or any other thing he can cut, still brings his scissors to the shop."

It is hardly necessary to point out the essential soundness of this approach. Art is a matter of instinct rather than logic —"an innate way," to use his own phrase, "of considering the excellencies of nature that comes to us when we are in our swaddling clothes." The consequence is that there are many exceptions. Yet, by and large, it is just that art which has been conditioned on actual existence which is most apt to be real and valid. What may need pointing out, however, is that Aretino was as qualified to carry out these dicta as he was to formulate them. Unlike many in whom the critical sense is highly developed, the creative sense was highly developed also.

The result is that everything he wrote had a singular vitality. His florid *canzoni,* for example — those rococo, verbal lapidary inscriptions praising the dead and living mighty ones — were not poetry in any possible sense of the word, but they did have a kind of gusto and a way of seeming sincere (perhaps they actually were sincere, for Aretino could apparently convert himself genuinely into a given mood, if it was profitable, almost at a moment's notice) that made them stand out among most occasional laudatory stanzas of the day, and made it easy to see why they were sought after with such avidity by the men they celebrated. If they were not Michelangelos and Sansovinos, they were at least statues by Bernini. Simplicity was lacking in them, but they had a kind of ornate magnificence. The crude satire of the *Orlandino* and the *Astolfeide,* brief mock epics about the heroes of Charlemagne, not only made every clear-headed reader laugh loudly, but in a small way anticipated *Don Quixote*'s job. They made chivalry — which despite high beginnings by now fully deserved it — and they made poems of chivalry, a laughing stock. Tasso to the contrary notwithstanding, after the *Orlandino* it was always going to be a little hard to take any new *Orlando Furioso* quite seriously.

The religious works — those "Psalms of David" retold, "Stories of Genesis" at the mental level of the illiterate, wordy lives, even more romantically chaotic than the wildest painting by a Tintoretto, of St. Catherines, Virgin Marys and St. Thomas' of Aquinas — were not only accepted at their face value by the most pious and in some cases most intelligent men and women of the day. They were so vital, for all their over-writing and exaggerations, that even when after his death they were placed under papal ban, they were brought out

under another name. Partenio Etiro—this was the one used
—is not an author of the Seventeenth Century but an anagram
for Pietro Aretino. In their lurid and dramatic style, in the
way Aretino spun fact out with his fecund fancy, they might
almost be called the forerunner of the most popular if not the
soundest modern biography.

Certain Italian critics, and at least one French one, have not
hesitated to place his tragedy, *Orazia,* on the level with Shakespeare. It is of course fantastic; but in its historic truthfulness,
its willingness to portray action rather than to report actions
which had happened offstage, and in the naturalness of the
language used in its blank verse, it did start tragedy down a
new road, so that the Elizabethans owe a debt of at least
moderate gratitude to him.

The "Conversations about Courts" and the "Talking
Cards" with their comments on sycophancy and gambling
paint a true picture of certain aspects of contemporary life,
and if their allusions to obscure episodes and to the obscure
dramatis personae of the day make them a little difficult for
the general reader, they are at least as much worthy of study
as Greene's "Groate's Worth of Wit" and his "Disputation between a Hee and a Shee Conny-catcher," and for the same
reasons.

Even his more ambitious poems, bad enough in any general
sense, were as good as or better than many serious poems of
the day. To uncritical ears, at any rate, their brilliancy of
improvisation dazzled out their defects. Their fluency drew
eyes away from their lack of inspiration. Referring to the
Marfisa, one contemporary said that it not only carried on
Ariosto's story (the *Orlando Furioso*) but surpassed it. It took
more than a little time—plus the withdrawal from the scene
of Aretino's personality—to find out that this was not even remotely true.

So far we have dealt only with Pietro's minor works, with
such writings of his as were admittedly of the second order.
As we have seen, even these—though it is quite obvious that

they have few, if any, claims to make upon a modern reader
— do not lack their share of merits. But in three categories at
least, Aretino went even further. It has been said that his
comedies were the only vital contributions to the Italian theatre before Goldoni; and this is incontestable if you leave out
Machiavelli's *Mandragola* — which is, incidentally, though
entertaining, more a dramatized off-color story than the
pointed commentary upon actual life that a true comedy
should be.

The six volumes of the letters — three of them were published during the period which we are now considering — contain approximately four thousand pages of begging, fawning
and flattery which are now, as befits the work of one intrinsically a journalist, and as befits also anything basically unfelt
and artificial, just about as dead as last month's newspapers.
But the four or five hundred pages remaining are not only
among the best writings of the Renaissance: they are as read-
able as if they had been written today.

Last of all we have the *Ragionamenti*. They can be compared only, among modern writings, with the work of Rabelais. They perhaps lack his large laughter and his huge
robustiousness, but they make up for it with their vivid, if
disturbing, sense of realism. Indeed, they are the first realistic
fiction since the *Satiricon,* and they are far more normal than
that novel by the Roman writer. Whether or not we deplore
the fact — and there is much in them to test broad-mindedness
— they must be set down among the great books of all time.

It is not practicable to go into these writings at great length,
nor is it in any way necessary. We are telling Aretino's life
story, not writing a critique of Renaissance literature. But
some mention of them, is, of course, called for — to help us
see exactly what he was.

The letters, naturally, come first. For if there is more useless
lumber amid their many pages than is usually the case in
works of talent, they contain also Aretino's finest handiwork.
And they can be read today without apologies. They are versa-

tile and many-sided. They contain vividness—the letter to my lady Fontanella; boldness—the defense of the lewd sonnets; calmness and warmth—the letters to Caterina Sandella; playfulness and affection—those to and about Perina Riccia; manly hero worship—the one about the death of Giovanni delle Bande Nere; wit and humor—which are quite different, and love of taste, touch and color, as in the descriptions of the delicacies sent to him, and of his house in Venice, and of a Venetian sunset, and of the various paintings by Messers Titian, Vasari, Sebastiano del Piombo, etc. An anthology of the best fifty or sixty of them has never—insofar as I know—been made in any language. If one should be, it would not only paint a portrait of the man that wrote them, which would be as good as any self-portrait ever done, but would be also a source book for the Renaissance that could not be equalled. It would show how a man having every Renaissance taste and quality lived and thought. It would automatically become a classic. It would be reprinted in every compact library and as much read as any volume there.

The comedies have a double appeal. In themselves—if you make due allowance for change of taste as it regards what is seemly—they are really very good theatre. They are diffuse, padded with non-essentials (but so was even Shakespeare at times), badly bound together, and they have only one plot: that of a fool made an ape of by a charlatan though that might be said of half the comedies ever written. But they are also animated, vivid and diverting. They could be acted today—if the audience and the censor would permit them and if you could take out or explain purely local allusions of the moment and the place.

But besides that, they were a step in the development of comedy. Before Aretino turned to the stage and wrote plays for the merry and the erudite Company of the Calza to enact before scenes painted by Vasari, the Italian theatre was the Roman one with names changed. The two Menaechmi (Plautus' creations), Davus the parasite, and Miles Glorious were merely given Italian-sounding appellatives and cuirasses or jerkins, as the case might be, and long and twirling mustachios instead of Roman toga and cropped poll. But the thoughts, lines and situations were the same.

Aretino made them people of his day and age. The hypocrite of *Lo Ipocrito* has been called shrewdly a "Tartuffe anticipated," but he is not only an Italian Tartuffe but a Cinquecento one. Il Marescalco in the comedy of that name — the man who hates women and thinks the Duke of Mantua is going to make him marry one — is not only of the peninsula but of the very province. The plot of *Il Filosofo* is not from Terence, but from Boccaccio, and it is Boccaccio modernized. *La Cortegiana* with its Roman street scenes, strident fish vendors, insolent servants, poor bedevilled Jews, lewd procuresses and wayward wives, and with its portraits of court life and the cruel villainies and cruel disappointments thereof, is so much Rome between 1516 and 1524 as to be a document. Captain Tinca with his Spanish oaths and braggadocio seems alone anachronistic. He is still the Miles Glorious. But that is not because Aretino's observation failed him. It is because no change has taken place. It is because Captain Tinca and his Roman equivalent remain the same.

But the most striking of Aretino's works (if not the finest), the most argued about, the most read both in its own language and in numerous translations, are the two volumes of the famous *Ragionamenti*. They are the one writing that almost everybody has heard about. Unfortunately that is more due to their lewd reputation than to the real merit they have. Because of their crude subject matter and their absolute fidelity to even the most blatant details, they have never been appraised judiciously. They have been taken over whole-heartedly by the filthy-minded and the collectors of pornography, and for that reason the fact that they have worth and stature has been lost sight of. Consequently a case for the defense is needed. And there is no better way of giving it than by telling what they are in full.

Their framework is a simple one. They are cast into the form of dialogues, and Nanna and Antonia, who do the talking in them, are two courtezans. Nanna has a daughter, Pippa. She does not know what to do with her. Shall she make her a nun? Shall she marry her? Shall she establish her in her own lucrative and ancient career? Antonia proposes that they sit under the shade of a certain fig tree and consider the three occupations. This they do. The first day they tell anecdotes about the life of nuns. They are incredibly ribald — they also, despite Renaissance standards, most probably libel seriously what was not certainly a wholly corrupt institution — but they are but little worse, and of course infinitely more convincingly set down, than the fierce charges made in the diatribes of Martin Luther. Nanna had been a nun, and knew, she said, what she was talking about. The second day they tell tales of married life, which read like transcripts of the testimony in the most lurid divorce cases. Nanna had been married also. The third day they relate the doings of the courtezans. Nanna comes to her conclusion, and it is the obvious one. She will set up her daughter, Pippa, in the latter occupation. Why? it is the most respectable one. "The nun betrays the sacrament and the married woman destroys the sanctity of matrimony. But the courtezan attacks neither the monastic life nor her husband. She is like the soldier who is paid for doing wrong, and for that reason should not be held accountable. That is what her shop has to sell."

The second part of the *Ragionamenti* is merely a continuing of the first — but unlike most instances where the author of a best seller tries to imitate himself, there is little falling off, if any. During its first day, Nanna instructs Pippa in the ways of making men's lusts fill a pocketbook, all complete in easy lessons. It tells the manner of beginning such a career; how to lure on the timid; how to keep a lover when you have him; how to play one lover against another; how to use vanity, jealousy, curiosity and every other weakness to which poor mortals, especially when male, are subject, as a means of get-

ting and furnishing fine chambers, and of living, eating and
drinking therein in plenty if not in magnificence. It is a guide
book of cosmetics, and a short volume on elementary psychology. It tells when to feign innocence; when modesty; and
when, though perhaps inexperienced, to act like a veteran of
a life of brothels. In the second day, Nanna tells some of the
frauds men are willing to perpetrate on women of this sort.
If the other was a guide to success, this is a warning of dangers.
The third day seems at the outset less relevant, and because
it deals with those who might be called the middlemen —
mezzana is good Italian — of a very sordid occupation, it is by
all odds the nastiest. Nanna and Pippa, seated in their garden,
listen to a nurse and an old gossip discoursing on the art of
being a procuress. But it is not, as it first seemed, the weakest
part of the dialogues, but their logical conclusion. No matter
how profitable there would now never be a sequel — Aretino
had said all there was to say about this shabby trade.

But it is not simply as a lewd treatise or "Bawd's Hand-
book," as it would have been called in the age of Queen
Elizabeth, that these "fantastic and pleasant" bits of reporting
are to be regarded. Had this been so, they would have been
swallowed long ago by that limbo of oblivion that gapes just
as eagerly for bad smuttiness as it does for the most sloppy-
sentimental. Aretino's object may have been to titillate the
corrupt lords; but the great artist that lay within him forced
his hand. Willed he, nilled he, he breathed breath of life into
what under less inspired hands would have been a catalogue
of dull obscenities. Though born in a fertile brain and exist-
ing only as printed on paper, Pippa and Nanna are very real
people. Though this is merely a technical matter, their speech
is real speech. It has the cadence, the vocabulary, the sound
and the taste of the language of tough people of his day. You
do not even have to know Italian very well to be aware of this.
There is a common denominator between it and the modern
American equivalent that makes recognition inevitable. Going into matters that are more essential, their comedy is the

comedy of things that might and in some cases probably did, actually happen. Their shabbiness is real shabbiness; their hopes, schemes, bewilderments, betrayings and betrayals, *bona fide* ones. The swift pace of their various adventures carries the conviction of episodes that have truly taken place.

It would not be desirable to quote at any length from the pages of this writing, and I have a fairly good suspicion that it would not even be legal. An idea of the vividness can be gained from the description of the sack of Rome already cited. The language was completely outspoken. Aretino, as he set them down, made absolutely no compromise, and every word that Pippa or that Nanna might have used is there in its stark, and uncompromising nakedness. Though the episodes are Boccaccian, there is none of Giovanni's graceful paraphrasing. Yet even at that, as the *Ragionamenti* appeared, they shocked nobody. There was some protest but it was against their rawness and their ugliness, rather than their nastiness. Aretino was regarded as the Zola or the Dreiser of his age, not as its pornographer. More generally they were received with enthusiasm. The reaction of the great Spanish general, Antonio de Leyva, was typical. "This Pietro is more necessary to the human race than preachers," he said. "Preachers set simple folk on the road to righteousness, but his writings reached to the mighty and to the great ones."

Characteristically enough, Aretino made no such claim to moral motives.

This is what he wrote Vittoria Colonna, one of the few really virtuous people of the time.

"I am extremely happy, most modest lady, that the religious works I have written are not displeasing to your taste and your good judgment. And I am aware that your doubt as to whether you should praise or blame me for having used my talents on anything but sacred themes is prompted by your worthy soul that wishes every word and thought to turn to God, who is the giver of all goodness, and all wit. I confess, too, that I am less useful to the world and less acceptable to Christ when I spend my time on lying trifles and not on the eternal truths.

"But the cause of all this evil is the lewdness of others and my own necessity, for if the princes of the world were as truly pious as I am indigent, I would use my pen to write nothing but *Misereres*.

"Excellent lady, all men have not the grace of divine inspiration. Most are ever aflame with fleshly concupiscence. You are lighted up every hour with angelic fire. For you, offices and sermons are what masks and revels are to them. You would not turn your eyes to look at Hercules on his funeral pyre. They would not have a St. Lawrence on his gridiron or a flayed St. Bartholomew in their chambers.

"Look at my friend, Brucciolo. Five years ago he dedicated his translation of the Bible to that King who calls himself Most Christian, yet so far he has not had an answer. Perhaps it was not well translated or well bound. At any rate my *Cortegiana* which was rewarded with the chain of gold will not laugh at his 'Old Testament,' for that would not be decent.

"So you see my trifles have at least this excuse. They were composed to make a living, and not from maliciousness.

"For that reason, may Jesus inspire you with the thought of having Master Sebastiano of Pesaro—from whom I have already received thirty crowns—pay me the rest.

"I owe them—since you have to know the truth!"

John Addington Symonds, an unqualified admirer of Vittoria, is irritated into saying that this letter which is "one long tissue of sneers, taunts and hypocritical sarcasms" gives "the complete measure of Aretino's arrogance."

In a way, this describes it accurately.

Yet the letter gives also a complete measure of Aretino's candidness, and his lack of insincerity.

He does not even deceive himself.

He knows just exactly what he is doing.

And he does it very well.

Chapter XVII

The Scourge — and the Friend — of Princes

WE ARE now ready for the grand climax of Aretino's extraordinary career. Step by step, we have set down faithfully the episodes of his life; and if at times — indeed, almost always — the incidents of our narrative have read more like a picaresque novel than a documented and authentic biography, it is not our fault. We have told nothing about our subject except that which happened to be true.

Yet, Lord, what a romance of adventure it has turned out to be! The street urchin of a crowded Arezzo tenement, the shoemaker's brat, the alert ragamuffin of a crowded Central-Italian slum. He ties up his few belongings in a scarf or handkerchief, and sets off down the white and dusty road to seek his fortune. He becomes an art student (which is what he wants to be), a renegade and vagabond (because of his temperament), and he becomes also, when his hunger compels him to, a household menial, cleaning out privies and doing any sort of dirty job his master tells him to, for the lean privilege of eating sorry food in a damp and fetid servants' hall — not getting money for this, of course, for the reasonably frequent usage for a Renaissance employer was to take on a groom or valet for a month's trial without salary, and then discharge him when the month was over, thus getting a month's work without paying for it.

Then his wits serve him — and his luck does also. As the result of a piece of clever insolence which might have earned him a sound beating or a dripping prison cell with rats for company, he is led into the presence of the very man his pen insulted and is given employment by him. And for money, this time. Paid clown, and paid rhymester and buffoon to fat Pope Leo! Thereafter, his rise is swift and steady. When Leo dies, he has already impressed Cardinal Giulio de' Medici that his scathing tongue is a useful political asset, and for the brief duration of the unfortunate conclave at which Adrian was finally elected, he is in Giulio's employ. Even when Giulio has lost out, and when, as an unsuccessful candidate trying to regain influence with a new and very strait-laced Pope, he finds Aretino's efforts on his behalf have become embarrassing, he does not wish or dare merely to turn him out. So he sends him to the Marquis of Mantua, and to Giovanni delle Bande Nere. In that way — and aided by his sparkling talk and geniality — he becomes the intimate, the entertainer, the adviser, the drinking companion and the comrade in debauchery of a great nobleman (there were few still in the seats of power of an older lineage than the Gonzaga), and of the first general of modern Italy.

But now at Venice, as we have seen, even this has been improved upon. True, the ex-rogue is still living a somewhat ruffianly life. The coins that come to him are mulcted from the bestowers of them by a ruthless process that was not much, if any, different from blackmail. He is the sultan — to omit less engaging private disorderliness — of an almost oriental harem. He is the patron of a figurative, if not literal, gang of thieves. But he has become also the close and trusted associate of that fine artist and sterling gentleman, the painter Titian. He has made himself the center of half the literary adulation and of all the literary controversy of the period. He has convinced people that he is the wielder of the most influential pen in Europe; and he is, in fact. He is rich — at any rate until he has spent his latest levy; lavish; even though this seems incredible, respectable.

But he still has a little further on his road to go. The epithet bestowed upon this man of opportunity by Ludovico Ariosto has already been referred to:

> Behold the Scourge
> Of Princes, mighty Pietro Aretino!

It was during these days of glorious Venetian summer — it

was, to be specific, in 1532—that he was so labeled by the
fluent poet of Orlando in his madness. We will now see how,
though it was flattery when it was written, it became shortly
both accurate and exact description. It will now be related
how the man from Arezzo did actually become the stinging
scourge of the second greatest prince in Europe—and became
also the friend of the first.

To do this, it is necessary to retrace our steps. As we have
more than once stated, the first problem of a Renaissance
writer was to find a patron. The painter had already become a
merchant; indeed had always been one. He started in a *bottega*
or workshop, and quite often the master himself was but the
head workman who produced panels and altarpieces with the
assistance of his employees, much as someone else might produce steel armor or boxes of tooled leather, and with no
thought whatsoever that connoisseurs and critics would one
day try to establish with every deductive device at their disposal that a given artist had done a given bit of work, and
thereafter make boast of this as bestowing greater value. The
patron, therefore, as far as the artist was concerned, was but a
glorified customer—someone who commissioned you to do
work, and often in sufficient quantity to take all your time
and skill, rather than dropping in at the place where you
painted, and buying what you had on hand.

The writer found a different situation. There were no copy-
rights, and even after the invention of printing, it was not easy
to sell enough copies of a book he had brought out to do
much more than pay his printers. He had two choices, as a
result. Not having a private income—and he usually did not—
he could either find somehow or other a church sinecure, or
he could secure someone to endow his career. Machiavelli and
a few others did get state employment, but such opportunities
were most infrequent. For the satisfaction of seeing his name
upon a title page followed by a eulogistic dedication, there
was always some lord or magnate, who would count out at
grudging intervals a pitiful stipend, and perhaps give you his

cast-off clothes. You were not more than a half step upward from a lackey, however. For you not only had to disfigure your volume with the nauseating words of praise, but you had also to act as private secretary, making use of your skill with words to weave out his tissue of state lies, and acting also as a literary pander by writing all his persuading love letters for him. It is small wonder that, among writers of the Renaissance, cynicism flourished like a corrupting weed. The wonder is that any ever were sincere.

Aretino fared no differently from the rest, and the long story of his complicated relationships with Pope Leo, Cardinal Giulio de' Medici, Giovanni delle Bande Nere, and Federigo Gonzaga, was, as we have seen, with one exception, the long story of a search for someone who would not only supply Aretino with butter but with bread to put it on. Then came the cumulative cataclysm. Leo had been long dead, and Cardinal Giulio, now became Pope Clement VII, went publicly puritanical on him. After that Giovanni delle Bande Nere met his end in battle, and it thereupon turned out that Federigo Gonzaga was more interested in having the good will of one close to that peerless leader than he was in Messer Aretino himself. Aretino fled to the canals.

Then suddenly, after not entirely fruitless efforts to regain at least technical support from Federigo and the Medici, he saw a broader target. He made a *volte face* toward the King of France. That *roi galant* of the romantic-minded; that hero of at least one of Balzac's droll improprieties; that lover of the fair and the capricious Madame d'Etâmpes, who was the predecessor of all those Diane de Poitiers', Madame du Barrys, Pompadours, Ninon de l'Enclos', and Madame de Maintenons, who have had such potent influence upon Gallic polity, was the next one selected by Pietro to be his chief contributor. If he had accepted that post, the French monarch would have gained a staunch ally who would have supported every cause of his with the first mechanism for effective propaganda that man's ingenuity had devised. And since the word has a way of conquering that surprises even its most confident users, modern history might have taken a new direction. But instead Francis sent the famous chain of gold only after Aretino had begged for it so long that it was tarnished when it got to him. Thereafter, he received nothing but "French promises" which "dissolving into French smoke" made him "despair of French courtesy." The old national closeness—or what Italians call the old national closeness—and the French conviction that when a man is once bought, he will stay bought, had come into play. Aretino grew angry. He could not understand all this yea-and-nay-ism, as clear financially in the French ruler as it had been politically in Pope Chameleon. He fumed angrily, and threatened this and that. To be sure, he had no real intention of carrying out his own threats, but that did not make them sound less terrible.

All at once he stopped. For the long column of letters, messengers and indeed ambassadors, each with gift enclosed or borne in hand, and asking in return no more than a word or paragraph in thanks—but of course published, and of course circulated abroad—made him realize that he had no need for Francis or for anyone else. He was his own patron, and required no other.

But all that has been already told.

Yet in spite of this new independence, Aretino still hankered for the moral support that came from the favor of one prince. It was not purely old habit, and it was not certainly the cash involved. The cash was, in comparison with his other income, far too insignificant. It was rather the prestige of the thing. Phrasemaker by appointment to His Majesty! Francis having failed him, Charles V, Holy Roman Emperor, Lord of Austria, Lord of Burgundy, Lord of the Netherlands (which in those days not only included present-day Holland, but a good part of Belgium also), King of Castile and of Aragon, King of Naples and of Sicily, master of the Americas, and at least theoretical overlord of north Italy, was the next one for whom Aretino set his cap. He did so successfully. Cold and calculating where the writer was impetuous, he seemed Aretino's exact opposite, and the last one with whom Pietro could come to terms. "The Pope told me," wrote a Venetian ambassador, "that when His Majesty was negotiating with him, he carried in his hand a written memorandum of every matter which he planned to discuss." But he matched Aretino in one thing, his steady purpose, and in another, his willingness to use any method necessary to realize it. He was determined to hand over his hereditary and elected realms to his successor unimpaired; and beset on all sides — with Germany divided by religion, Spain often in revolt, the Low Countries restive under his high taxes, France trying to acquire Burgundy and Milan, and the pirates of North Africa harrying his coasts — he needed every ally he could get. Moreover his specialty was taking enemies into his own camp.

Aretino had been an enemy.

"The Spanish ambassador," this was his own boastful way of referring to the matter, "is always hastening to accuse me before the Venetian signory, crying out *usque ad sidera —*" even unto the heavens — "that I am guilty of *lèse majesté* because I have taken in vain His Catholic Majesty's jaws."

Charles' Hapsburg cant-hooked and protruding chin, which passed on to his descendants, was not something it was hard to be sarcastic about, but there is printed evidence that Aretino's comments on the Emperor were not limited to such purely physiological matters.

When, therefore, the word got abroad that Aretino was receptive, the realistic ruler who, although a good and for that matter a passionate Catholic, had not hesitated to win over to his side German Lutherans by means of compromise, did in this case also what was necessary.

Grave Spaniards in suits of black mounted the dark stairway of the Ca' Bolani, and swallowed all the insults that its occupant had heaped upon their race in many letters and comedies.

"Pietro Aretino?"

"At your services, *señores.*"

"His Catholic Majesty has long been aware of your preëminence among those who write."

"He is generous, Your Excellencies."

"Nothing but the affairs of state have kept him from taking earlier cognizance of this fact."

"I am grateful, Your Excellencies."

"He now bids us offer you two hundred crowns a year as a measure of his appreciation."

"*Mil gracias, señores.*"

"But observe the conditions."

Aretino stiffened.

"He has noted how many kings promise, and then in the stress of affairs, forget what they have said. These crowns, therefore, only come to you, if you will accept them from the grain revenues of Milan. They will then not be subject to any whim or any memory. They will come to you with regularity."

Aretino smiled broadly. No contract. Then he could accept it.

"I kiss the feet of His Most Lavish Majesty," he said, Spanishly grandiloquent, "and I will say shortly those things about his god-like generosity it most richly deserves."

"The Emperor," snorted Benedetto Agnello when the news got abroad, "has just given our friend Pietro Aretino a pension of two hundred crowns. This has set tongues to wagging. Many say that His Majesty was very much annoyed at being obliged to make this gift, and that he only did so because he feared what Aretino might say about him. Particularly in the matter of his sister-in-law."

Benedetto, it should be remembered when trying to decide what value to put upon this statement, was the Mantuan ambassador, and Duke Gonzaga, now nearing forty, had never made peace with Aretino. Yet this much is known about the matter. It was at least common gossip that the great defender of the Catholic commonweal—and of his family interests in the rule thereof—was carrying on an amorous intrigue with the handsome and the intelligent Beatrice of Savoy, who was thus related to him. And that upon one occasion, if not oftener, Aretino had put this scandal into writing. It may be, therefore, that the shafts winged by ill-tempered annoyance hit the target of truth. It may be that this new contribution to Pietro's revenues was not only the gift made to an artist and the wages paid a journalist, but the bribe exacted by a blackmailer as well.

But whatever you call it, Aretino not only accepted the money, but lived up to the conditions implied. To do this was a matter of business integrity which was also business sense, and that was something he respected. Charles wanted praise? Then he would give him a good measure of it.

"Having always regarded Your Majesty as nearer God than any man that ever was."

"I, O Caesar, must compare you to a torrent. Swollen with rain, snow and sun-melted ice, it is swallowed by the fields that think they are drinking it, whereas really its proud course is making a bed of them."

"O greatest ruler of all peoples and of all kingdoms!"

Charles wanted present virtues to ring as loud as past faults?

"I salute," said Aretino, "the faith, the religion, the pious conduct, the mercy, the kindness, and the prudence of Caesar."

Charles wanted an ally in his campaigns?

"I tell you that this new onslaught shall come to nothing, just as every one ever made against you comes to nothing, and just as every race, every banner, and every name who contends with you comes to nothing. For who fights against Caesar fights against God, and who fights against God meets destruction."

"It cannot be denied," Aretino wrote at about this same time, "that Your Majesty deserves shrines and altars, and that you have your place in the skies with the other gods. Nevertheless, it would seem to writers that your rare deeds will not endure unless record is made of them. They contend that pens and tongues armed with steel that always cuts and fire that always burns will enlarge the realm conquered by your name just as much as your captains do the bounds of your empire."

His pen took up the Empress also. Realizing that despite wayward fancies—*"car il aymoit l'amour, et trop pour ses gouttes,"* said Brantôme—and despite even steadier intrigues such as the alleged one with Beatrice of Savoy, Charles was the devoted husband of the wise and lovely-looking Isabella of Portugal, whom he had married for reasons of policy but whom he now adored because he utterly respected her, Aretino put all his most decorated language into a prose passage that hymned her praise.

"Adorned then with grace and beauty, with the simplicity that shines from your forehead you bring serenity to minds that are clouded with affliction. That tranquillity which calms the tempest in our hearts shines forth from beneath your eyelashes where we see honesty and a grave seriousness together. Your eyes, so modest in their glance, console the spirit of anyone who looks into their sweet affectionateness, and their graciousness refreshes him just as if he had gazed upon a vista of green and emerald meads. Your cheeks are the flowers of our hope. With a glance, you bring reward unto the virtuous, and a mere nod is sufficient punishment for the wicked. Your slightest actions teach us how to do virtuously, and your countenance shows us how a saint should look. Charity opens your hands and mercy moves your feet. Constancy, humility and concord are your ministers and your companions. In your walk and in your presence, you reveal the presence of heaven. Faith and religion bear witness to your good sense and to your innate worthiness. And with the glory of those virtues which adorn you you make no fewer conquests with your courtesy than the Emperor does with his arms. Hence the world is half yours and half his."

It was as if he had wished to demonstrate that his pen and his tongue were the ones best fitted for any service whatsoever that the mighty ruler might require. It was as if he wanted to show Charles that a poisoned dagger was not the only weapon in his armory; that he could bear aloft also the mace of courtierlike obeisance and that he could wield a gleaming sword.

But he was soon given an opportunity to serve his new benefactor with something more than merely pleasing phrases — with words still, to be sure, but with important words; with all the talents at his disposal, with all the skill and genius he could command.

The French King went politically mad. His long conflict with Charles had been the one unbroken incident of their two reigns, for while Henry of England and Francis, and Henry of England and Charles might exchange blows or stage Fields of the Cloth of Gold as the mood struck them, it was not possible for Charles and Francis to do other than do battle with each other. Every interest the one had imposed upon an interest of the other. The Low Countries blocked France upon the north; Germany blocked her in the east; Spain faced her from across the Pyrenees; and there was Italy beyond the Alpine passes. Charles, therefore, as far as Francis was concerned, was never to be allowed to prosper. Francis never did allow him to prosper and the fact that after nearly twenty years of contest, he still held virtually everything that he had started with except the north of Italy, and that he had once driven Charles from Provence and was ready to and able to again, was in itself something of a victory. But the French ruler did not have the temperament to be content with this dry fact. A knight errant born too late into the world, he thought himself a new Orlando, and the black day of Pavia still was unavenged. Not till Charles sued at his feet, would he be satisfied.

And now suddenly the man to help him to this end revealed himself. A strong ally — or rather, strong potential ally — loomed in the Near East. Suleiman the Magnificent, the latest and the greatest of Turk conquerors. The armies of that pale, sallow Commander of the Faithful with his aquiline nose, long, thin neck, and his moody and haughty disposition, stood upon the plains of Hungary, and his swift fleet, led by the pirate Keyr-ed-Din Barbarossa, swept out from the hill-encircled harbors of North Africa to challenge Western domination of the Mediterranean. Incidentally Keyr-ed-Din was himself interested in a French understanding.

In 1534 ambassadors of the corsair king and admiral landed in France and were taken to Paris where their swarthy visages and the wrapped folds of their turbans—they looked, said an observer, "like the three kings of the gospel"—aroused seething popular curiosity. They came merely to investigate. But in 1535 the recapture of Tunis by Charles and his Spanish army, and the establishment therein of the deposed Muley Hassan as a puppet king, made the pirates really anxious for French support. Jean de la Forêt, a veteran of the French foreign office, was already in Algiers with detailed instructions as to how far Francis was prepared to go to get an alliance with the pirate fleet, and Barbarossa now helped him toward the Golden Horn. When he got there, Suleiman was away fighting the Persian Sophy, but the undiscouraged Frenchman pushed his way to Azerbajan where he met the Grand Turk. A summary of the European situation impressed the latter, and they came back to Constantinople together for more detailed talks. The talks were successful, and in 1536 a treaty between France and Turkey was made public. It was "strictly commercial in its nature,"—as all such agreements always are—but since the agent of every wide-awake government knew exactly what de la Forêt had set out to accomplish, and since Barbarossa now assembled a huge fleet at Negroponte, and since Suleiman himself marched an army toward Avlona in Albania, it was not hard to imagine a secret military treaty behind it.

Then corsair galleons anchored at Toulon, and were provisioned there. No denial now was worth the paper it was printed on. France stood beside the infidel! A fierce wave of anger swept the continent. It was followed by a wave of panic. For a Turk invasion and horrible atrocities seemed synonymous. In the tense state of their nerves, men almost heard the axes that were cutting down and sharpening the stakes that would impale them. Women dreamed of slavery in some harem. Even the children had a sense of something dire impending. There was not a red-roofed town from the Strait of Messina to the Gulf of Genoa, from the Catalonian border to the gates of Hercules, there was not one from Otranto, where the Turks had once butchered before, to the strong border of the Venetian Republic, that could see a distant sail — it might be merely a lateen-rigged fishing boat — without expecting fire, death and captivity. It was a sword put into Charles' shrewd hands. For all that he had to do to make this folly of the French king turn into armies fighting on his side was to find someone to make these sentiments reverberate. And the one to do it was now ready for him.

Not only because he served the Emperor, but because he conceived the interests of his beloved Venice to be menaced, Aretino wrote forthwith two letters. They were nominally to the King of France but actually to public opinion.

The first one was relatively mild. He began first by tactfully pointing out the altruism and the sacrifices of the Venetians. Though they had received generous Turkish offers and though to keep on bad terms with Suleiman meant not only pouring forth their gold but risking all their eastern possessions, they had still aided the forces of the Pope and Emperor. This was good politics, for France counted on Venice as an ally. Next he asked Francis what his strongest feeling was — hatred of Charles or love of those who worshipped Christ? If hatred of Charles, he said, let Francis look well that his expression of it did not jeopardize his title of Most Christian, for this could not fittingly be worn by one who was the ally of the unbelievers. Then he reminded him of the French attitude in other days. When 350 Ottoman vessels had attacked Castro, 2,000,000 gold francs went to the rescue. After that he played upon the French ruler's love of glory. Not so had Pépin done, or mighty Charlemagne. Those Frenchmen had restored popes, not assailed the defenders of the pope's religion. Last of all, he touched upon the heart of the matter.

"Ah, worst of all passions, the desire to rule! Ah, cruel desire to achieve revenge! And to think you should lodge in the mind of the most noble king there ever was!"

The most noble king was given thus a graceful way out. He could demonstrate his great nobility.

He did not take it.

The second letter, therefore, was a thunderclap. No punches were pulled, and it was merciless.

"I am aware that, as the world sees it, it is not fitting to speak or write to a person of royal birth on a matter of such importance without being asked to. Yet since the word of God forbids deceiving, and since in Christ's republic there are no distinctions of rank, I have decided to continue in the same tone as in my former letter. In that one I doubted whether as a Christian, I could call you 'Most Christian.' In this one, I regret bitterly, as your servant, that I can call you neither King of France nor Francis, for how can one truthfully be called either King or Free—which last is what France and Francis mean—when he goes begging the aid of barbarians, who are both enemies of his race, and rebels against his creed?

"My lord, for so I still address you, you have thrust the Ottoman sword into the heart of Christendom, and so doing you have wounded fatally the magnificence of your hitherto unconquered glory. Moreover, while doing the Emperor little or no damage, you have strengthened all his reasons for calling you his foe.

"Besides that, is there any Christian prince who will not turn at least his sympathies against you now that you have chosen such an ally? Look at the wise King of England. A while ago he was estranged from both Pope and Emperor, but no sooner did he hear that Turkish fury was directed against the west than he turned his pious arms against you. And if for one reason or another, other princes have not yet done the same, either they will do so shortly, or else—which is very important—they will direct both their prayers and their influence against you. They will implore God that the same ruin will come to you that would come to them if the Heavenly Father—which He will not do—should let the arms of Caesar meet defeat."

But suppose that the French cause were victorious, would you expect the Turks to keep faith with you? Look at history with its long series of moral lessons on this subject. The Turks never would have entered Europe at all if they had not first been called as allies by the men of Trebizond. The Roman Republic never would have conquered Capua if the Capuans had not summoned her. It was the Greeks who needed assistance in taming Philip of Macedon, who first brought their Latin conquerors into the country. In more recent times, how did Milan become slave to Charles except through the arms which they themselves put into his hands?

"These things mainly happened between infidel and infidel or between Christian and Christian, yet you think that you can be safe with the head of the enemies of your faith. Do you imagine, then, that he does not realize how much treasure and what lavish blood your predecessors poured out against the Mohammedans? That he is not aware that if the Christian armies were united under your royal hands, he would see the unconquered standard of Christ in front of him and that you would be the chief and the director of Turkish ruin? Do you imagine either that he does not clearly realize that it is neither lack of religion nor love for him, but solely your hatred of Caesar that bands you to his cause?

"Abandon, then, this unholy alliance. It is the only way that you can justify your Christian faith and the only way you can carry out the glorious French tradition. In the days of Camillus, this indomitable people climbed the wall of Rome and reached the very Capitol. In the days of Laelius Emilius and of Caius Stetilius they terrified the Italian peninsula and forced the Republic to arm eighty thousand horsemen and

seventy thousand foot soldiers. They once crossed Asia itself
where they left behind them the name of Gallogrecia. Under
Charlemagne, they tamed Spain, and Germany and the Sara-
cens. Yet now France feels constrained to bow down and ask
the aid of the enemies of her race and of her God, and to sue
for the banner of a greedy corsair, of a vile, infamous pirate!

"I would like to write you with that deference which is
due both to your rank and to your past merits, but I cannot
help being more conscious of an evil present than of a laud-
able past, and for that reason I lament more at your fault of
today than I honor your good deeds of yesterday. Jealousy of
Caesar is what moves you. Either, then, so govern your heart
that his greatness does not trouble you, or so act that you are
his equal or superior. Take up, as he has done, an honorable
sword in Christ's behalf. Cast out this venomous serpent from
your breast. Do not permit Turkish scorn to parade through
your cities and your palaces and the temples of your God.
Break with this proud monster who is not a friend but a foe.
The Christian princes who fear the Turkish despot urge you
to do this. So do private persons who fear being made slaves
of the barbarians. So do all women who fear to see their own
honor and that of their daughters soiled by Turkish lust. So
does that Christ who gave you all the honors that ennoble you.

"When you have done that, you will pardon the insolence
of your rash yet faithful servant just as readily as I hope you
will ask God to pardon you. And if what people are saying
reaches royal ears as it reaches private ones, you will not blame
me for writing. You will blame me for waiting so long."

It is not here the moment to go into at great length the
obvious inconsistencies amid this whirlwind of words. Popes
had themselves, and that in recent times, found it quite possible to do business with Islam, and even—so, at any rate,
their enemies reported—to urge Ottoman fleets against Italian
shores. By supporting Muley Hassan, even Charles was, in a
sense, merely picking for his ally a weak follower of the
prophet, instead of a strong one. And the very writer of these

epistles would within a few years address "the greedy corsair
. . . the vile, infamous pirate" as "illustrious king, worthy
pasha, unconquerable warrior" and speak praisingly of his
"generosity" and refer to "the graciousness and benign majesty" of his master Suleiman when he wished to get something
from Barbarossa.

The important thing was rather, that here was a private
citizen who, clothed with no authority but his own robust self-
confidence and the conviction (proven to be right) that ten
million voices would thunder "Aye" to him, dared stride up
to an anointed king and confront him with unpleasant truth.
Not since the days of the Hebrew prophets had such boldness
been known, for even Dante's fierce Isaian strictures seemed
pale and bloodless by comparison. The words, therefore,
spread through Europe, and the whole continent held its
breath. And though they accomplished his purpose, even
Charles, if he had been able to read into the future, must have
been alarmed. For during the next four centuries, more than
one man and woman in whose veins flowed his blood were to
pay with shame and exile and with life itself to the new power
revealed thereby.

As for Francis himself, he did what was obvious. He realized
what a costly matter his economies had been, and he set out to
retrace his steps.

Very shortly Aretino received a letter. It was from a certain
Hieronimo Comitolo of Perugia, who had been an old comrade of his, and who was now in the French army.

"My honored lord. I can never forget the obligations under
which I am to Your Lordship, and therefore wherever I am,
I always want to act in such a way that you will at least realize
that I have an interest both in your honor and your welfare.
For that reason I want to tell you what happened yesterday.
When I was riding with the Grand Master who was personally
inspecting the fortifications, we happened to meet the Duke
of Atri who knew you in Venice. We fell to talking of various
matters, among them yourself. The Duke told me that the

KING FRANCIS I

"I regret bitterly that I can call you neither King of France nor
Francis. For how can one be truthfully called either King or Free —
which last is what France and Francis mean — when he goes begging
the aid of barbarians who are both enemies of his race and rebels
against his creed?" — *Aretino.*

other day he and the Grand Master and Luigi Anichini were together when it happened to be related that the Emperor had given you a pension of two hundred crowns on condition that you would make his deeds immortal and that you would cease praising France as quickly as you honorably could. To this the Grand Master replied that if you would write about the Emperor and the King of France just as their deeds and the strict truth merited, he would persuade the King to give you four hundred crowns. He also said that he would like to see some of your works.

"I mention this merely because if you could do such a thing, it would be to your glory and also to your advantage. As far as my weak powers are able to, I guarantee this offer. If it is defaulted you can call me ungrateful."

There were two excellent reasons—quite aside from his innate prejudice against burning bridges behind him—why Aretino did not simply turn this offer brusquely down. Owing to the Imperial wars, which, with at least five fronts, and as many potential adversaries, were waged continuously, and the Emperor's consequent always urgent need to keep every bit of money he could lay his hands on, an installment of the interruption-proof pension was now overdue, and Aretino had no way of knowing when or whether it would be paid to him. More seriously, he was at the same time threatened by the machinations of a clever forger.

There was now in Milan a certain Giovanni Alberto Albicante, as notable a literary brigand and in some respects as able a one as Aretino, though, of course, far less versatile. He and Aretino had alternately worked together—as, for example, when they attacked, and, according to legend, literally caused to die of heartbreak a young poet, Broccardo; or when Albicante helped Pietro wreak revenge on Francesco Berni by bringing out after his death a ludicrously garbled version of his rewriting of Boiardo's *Orlando Innamorato*—quarreled, and made up again. "Brother," Aretino said upon the latter occasion, "the fury of poets is but a frenzied stupidness."

But that was after Albicante's documented references to Aretino's difficulties with the law and more particularly to the fact that he had once lent him ten ducats — the very smallness of it was an added sting — when he was in trouble, made him realize that the Milanese poet could give him "bread for biscuit" as the saying goes, tit for tat.

This man was approached by the French, and persuaded, with the customary inducements, to circulate a series of scurrilous attacks upon the Emperor, and upon his household. He signed them with the name of Aretino.

Aretino could not be sure that the angry and the categorical denials which he sent promptly to Gian Battista Castaldo and to Cardinal Carraciolo as men close to the Emperor, would be believed.

But he soon had the answer to both his questions.

The overdue pension was counted into his hands with apologies that were more than perfunctory. Castaldo answered diplomatically that it was as easy to tell black from white as it was to tell imitations of Aretino from his own writing. Cardinal Carrociolo said more emphatically that he had never for a moment supposed that Aretino had written the attacks, and that he was passing on Aretino's communication to his superiors with this comment. The sense of both was that there was no danger that he would lose the Emperor's favor.

This decided the matter.

He wrote two letters — one to the Duke of Atri, and the other to the Grand Master. The meaning of each one was the same and the tone of each one was suave irony. He appreciated the good wishes of both men, though it did not surprise him for he had always counted on their kindness. As for the King of France, he was and would forever be loyal to him. But he had had bitter experience of French nature, and the way all French promises turned to nothing. When the four hundred crowns were actually counted into his hand, he would speak praise of the King with all the truth that he was noted for. In the meanwhile, he was their humble servant. It was a diplomatic way of refusing, for the moment, the overtures, but at the same time it did not leave the door closed.

Then, lest his nuances be too fine for certain blunt natures by whom he did not wish to be misunderstood, he wrote his friend Agostino Ricchi.

And this time, he exploded.

"Do you know what the Grand Master of France sent to tell me? 'If Aretino will speak and write of his Emperor and my King truthfully and as each one deserves, I will give him a life pension of four hundred crowns.' So you see how I could sell my talents if I were as money-grubbing as I am lavish, and also if I did not know Charles' merits."

After that, his course was a steady one. He might dicker with France; he might even send Ambrogio Eusebii to rake in a few handfuls of coin; but the star to which he hitched his wagon was the Imperial one. He followed it loyally and to the best of his ability. He flung out his best phrases in its behalf. He trumpeted it as effectively and almost as loudly as his own achievements. And presently he had a crowning reward.

This happened in 1543. Charles, moving restlessly about a stage that was hardly big enough for his abilities even though it was the largest any man had played on since the day of Constantine, made his second visit to Italy. He was urged onward by pressing necessity. He had suffered a grave setback in Algiers. An autumn storm had scattered, where it had not wiped out his fleet; and starving on a ration of dates and unsalted horsemeat, his army had forced him to withdraw. The French monarch had launched a war on every front without even taking trouble to declare it. But though his case seemed desperate and though he had to pay heavily even papal neutrality, he was, as he rode toward the Brenner Pass to strike France through her German back door, still the first ruler of Europe. For he could still re-form his lines once more. Consequently the princes, who were the politicians of the day, swarmed around him. Each one had something to get from

him. Among them was Guidobaldo delle Rovere, Duke of
Urbino, son of Francesco Maria who had been so admired by
Giovanni delle Bande Nere yet whose ineptness or whose
treachery had caused Italy such sorrow. Guidobaldo, like his
father, served the Venetian Republic, and he went to lay her
needs before the Emperor. He asked Aretino to go with them.
Aretino agreed.

Their own trip was a kind of a triumph itself. Save for his
flight and hiding five years previously, it was Aretino's first
visit to the mainland since he came to Venice and now he was
a world figure. Their first halt was at Padua. There Aretino
was almost mobbed by his admirers. Padua is the city of St.
Anthony and of the great church built there in his honor. It is
the city of the grave and holy Giotto frescoes of the life of
Christ, wherein man's faith, as it was held in days more simple,
is forever recorded for us in the clear blues and crimsons, and
in the serene faces done by the peasant who watched sheep
before he became the modern world's first painter. It is the
city of the Gattamalata, the first epic statue of a man on horseback since pagan hands wrought that green-bronze Roman
emperor who stands now on the Roman *campidoglio*. But it
is also the city of the university, and from *Il Bò* — the old ox,
as Paduans call it in memory of the days when it was a tavern
of that name — with its handsome columned courtyard, and
with its coats of arms of all the great who studied there, poured
forth some several thousand students.

Aretino! Evviva Aretino! He was the man of letters triumphant, he was what they all (except the medical students,
and students of divinity) hoped to be one day — was what they
would be. They clutched at his handsome cloak; they tried to
touch him, have a word from him. Indeed, after a whole day
and night devoted to receiving them, he had to make his
escape just as if he were a fugitive. Next Vicenza. The town
surged, but obviously the scenes of welcome and of curiosity
were more subdued. Then Verona. There he and the Duke of
Urbino met the four other Venetian ambassadors, Gabriel

Veniero, Carlo Morosini, Lodovico Faliero, and Vettor Grimani. All bearers of the noblest names in Venice. They rode on together to the little village of Peschiera standing at the blue-green outlet of Lake Garda, where the Emperor was expected. They were still in the middle of a crowd.

From Peschiera, Aretino and the Duke continued down the road to greet their overlord. It was Guidobaldo's expectation that they would be well received, and there is no question that one reason he took Aretino with him was that he hoped Charles' eagerness to see this sensational person would help his own interests. Even at that, he was hardly prepared for what ensued.

In the distance, they saw a white cloud of dust which took form as it drew nearer. First it was like smoke rising from beyond the horizon. Then it was a thick, opaque mass. Then they could discern the cavalcade.

Lances flashed in the bright sunlight, banners with the black Hapsburg double-headed eagles flapped their folds of crimson. Dust, however, clung to bright caparisons just as it made white the vine leaves at the roadside. Two hundred men at arms, completely equipped; four hundred archers with ashen pikestaffs and with arquebuses; behind them a mule train, laden with baggage and with treasure, and further off still the foot soldiers. How many, they could not tell.

As it grew close, they could see, too, one man, who though not prepossessing, seemed to dominate it. He wore simple clothes and a beretta of plain black velvet. He had a long outthrust under-jaw and a half starved blond beard that was like corn stubble. He had quick, nervous eyes, but they were penetrating. It was the Emperor. It was Charles V, whose rule ran from Poland to Peru and Mexico.

Duke and writer were off their horses in an instant. Caps were in their hands, they were on the ground, they were kneeling, they were obeisant. Hardly had they found this position, though, when this man spurred up to them.

"Which one of you is Aretino?" he asked.

"I, Your Majesty."

"Rise and ride beside me."

It was done as commanded. Side by side, and Pietro on the right hand, the two men rode through the applauding lanes. One of them ruled half the known world and was nominal lord of an unknown one. The other was the son of a shoemaker. One listened. The other talked. And it was the great Lord who did the listening. Charles' conversation was limited to showing deference.

"When I met with disaster at Algiers, your letter was the one that heartened me."

Aretino had felt — with most of Christendom — that even to be repulsed by the infidel was better than not to face him at all.

"When my beloved wife died, your message was the one that consoled me."

Aretino had touched that string also.

"Every gentleman in Spain knows all your writings — they read everything of yours as fast as it is printed."

Charles knew how to consolidate this friend.

Peschiera again. Bustle and confusion. Generally this little Italian village with its plastered houses and its weathered Lombard church is noisy only on market days. Then you hear cattle bellowing and pigs squealing. Now on this hot July day it was filled with seething humanity. Prelates who glared at other prelates. Ambassadors who were so polite it cut to other ambassadors. Soldiers who frowned at other soldiers. Marquises, and counts, and dukes. Each one of them had some favor to ask, yet the man whose *yes* or *no* crowned or ended their hopes only attended to Pietro. Charles talked of his campaigns and hardships. Pietro who had lived in a camp himself listened attentively. Pietro offered his services and his praise.

They came to Vicenza. There Charles had business to take up, and for a while Pietro receded into the background. He had letters to write; his friend, Brenzone, who had a cool villa with groves of oranges and lemons, with cedar hedges, and with olive, fig, cherry and pear trees, to visit. And he rejoiced in them as city dweller does if he does not stay in the country too long. But he soon stood before the Emperor again and this time he held some sheets of paper.

Finally Charles saw him.

"What have you?"

"A poem, Your Majesty."

"Read it."

It was an ode of triumph and of welcome, and line followed adjectival line in a bewildering succession of compliments. Charles listened, and was tactful enough to seem pleased by it.

That night there was a state banquet, and again Aretino was given the place of honor. Great lords and mighty churchmen were pushed into lower places. Pietro sat at the Emperor's right hand. The Emperor asked him if he would accompany him to Germany.

"I am sorry, Your Majesty, but I have sworn never to leave Venice."

The next morning he was not on hand. His own statement is that he was afraid that the Emperor would compel him to go with him to the north, but the truth probably is that he had decided he would be more noticed if he were absent. Charles did notice him and turned to the Venetian ambassadors.

"Take care of him, and recommend him to your government. Remember that he is dear to our person."

It was all over. The Emperor rode Tyrol-ward and then to Germany. Princes and prelates had been obliged to cool their heels while the first monarch of Europe showered his favors on a mere upstart.

As for Aretino, he returned to Venice where the whole city was ringing with his exploit.

Giovanni Betussi, the editor and biographer of Boccaccio, was writing in his study, when a friend entered the room. He seemed all worn out.

"Where have you been," Betussi asked, "that you should look so tired?"

"I have come from the house of Aretino where everybody is gathering to congratulate him on the measureless marks of affection bestowed on him by the Emperor."

Betussi weighted this statement, then said something himself:

"I hear that His Majesty, besides making him many gifts, had him ride at his right hand for many miles and also recommended him to the Venetian government as very dear to him."

"So it is."

"What do the pedagogues say?"

The pedagogues! Those feeders on the dust of the dead, those arch enemies of all things vital!

"They confess that there will never be another one like him."

Even his old adversaries, then, could speak no ill of him!

Let us take the most matter-of-fact view possible. Let us say that the whole treatment accorded him by Charles was planned out, calculated, came from the head not the heart. Let us say that he found Aretino a great rogue with a flourishing black beard; utterly distasteful to him; utterly crude, raw and corrupt; merely some one whom he wanted on his side. Let us say that he realized that there were many prelates in the world, many noblemen, many ambassadors, but that he knew that their needs were so pressing that they would not turn from him even if they were slighted. Let us say that he realized that there was only one Pietro Aretino, a man of temperament, and that he could be lost as well as won.

Then the very fact that Pietro seemed worth all this effort only made the tribute a greater one. Remember Aretino was given no handicaps; whatever he attained, he attained through his own qualities.

Aretino himself was aware of this, and he crowed triumphantly.

"With a goose quill, and a few sheets of paper, I can laugh

THE EMPEROR CHARLES V

"The Spanish ambassador is always hastening to accuse me before the Venetian Signory, crying out *usque ad sidera* that I am guilty of *lèse majesté* because I have taken in vain His Catholic Majesty's jaws."

—Aretino.

at the universe. They say that I am the son of a prostitute. It may be so. But I have the heart of a king. I live free. I enjoy myself. I can call myself happy."

Even the old slanders had no longer any power to trouble him. He was sitting on top of the world.

CHAPTER XVIII

The Handsomest Old Man in Venice

THE next stage is the decline. The human body is like any other piece of machinery. Parts wear out, become creaky, cease to function perfectly. For a while they can be repaired, patched up, made to work at least after a fashion. But it is a race against the inevitable. It is Canute giving orders to the tide. Aretino was no exception. Though he pulled the noses of the popes and princes and accepted deference from the great and from the mighty ones, he was still subject to the relentless graybeard with the sickle and the hourglass. His declining years had one further difficulty. He had reached his apogee. After his meeting with Charles, he still had a fifth of his days ahead of him, but they were at worst an anticlimax and at best merely level continuance. That is the one "out" about achieving all you ever hoped for. His boundaries had been delimited and staked out. There was very little further he could go.

Yet we must not make the mistake of imagining that he moved into a decrepit old age. Though his years grew weightier, he did not ever pass beyond the fifth of Shakespeare's seven stages, and he probably would not have, even if he had lived to ninety. His generous, rather than fair, "round belly with fat capon lined"—or with white-fleshed partridge or with gamey francolin—was much more in evidence than any "shrunk shank" for which, as the poet puts it, "his youthful hose were a world too wide," and since he was not—as Boccaccio was at the same age—wasted with the beginnings of an unpleasant disease, he did not have to retire to the somberness and gloom of lonely contemplation. Instead he lived among men—and among women—as he always had. And he lived vividly. Wit, liveliness, and his amazing energy never deserted him. His mental faculties were unimpaired. His tongue was just as sharp and possibly as active as it ever had been. His physique—though he often grumbled, for he was the type of large man who always complains of feeling badly, and though we know of many spells of fever and have a little unreliable gossip of syphilis—served him adequately. Scipione Ammirato reports for us the impression that he made walking by the Rialto in these days of sunset. "You would have had a hard time to see a handsomer old man, or one who was garbed more splendidly." Old man? He was only fifty-two when Ammirato saw him thus, but in those days men either felt their years earlier or were more honest.

Titian's famous portrait bears this out. It hangs now in the Pitti Palace in Florence, and Aretino, who, as the sitter, was perhaps the hardest person to satisfy, testified that it was a good likeness.

"Certainly it breathes, its pulses beat, and it is animated by the same spirit with which I am in real life," he told Duke Cosimo who was paying for it.

Let us look at it. The gold chain with its little enamelled red tongues—the one given him by the King of France—hangs over a vest or jerkin of a stylish coffee brown. The long robe is of rose silk, ample, generously cut, sumptuous. It was not the fur-trimmed robe famous in another Titian portrait. That was hung up in his wardrobe for some chillier season. But he still looked like an alderman. The eyes are dark and penetrating (intelligent eyes, eyes that see clearly), the nose finely shaped, the forehead broad and intellectual. If the complexion is a little sallow, it is not unhealthily so. He was graver perhaps in that year 1545, when this restrained masterpiece was sent by its subject to the chilly (and for that reason, in a worldly way successful) son of the hot-blooded Giovanni delle Bande Nere; slower in his walk; less like some captain of fortune and more like some pompous old Venetian senator; but he was still virile, still forceful, still swelled up like a turkey cock. There was a gray frosting in his black beard, but even that could be remedied.

He was thinking of dyeing it, he said gaily, and he hoped

that he would have better fortune than a certain friend. That fellow's came out blue, and the poor devil had to go into retirement for a while.

"Titian," he informed Gianbattista Fossa, "spoke the truth when he said that I am living as joyous a life as I ever did."

Why not? It seemed to his exuberant nature that he could make mock of time with its burden of years just as easily as he could tame fortune with its gifts of greatness. "As long as I keep up a youthful point of view," he maintained, "the weight of my age seems a thousand pounds lighter." Except for a certain stoutness, he boasted, he was in no way different from when he was an art student in Perugia. He cried out — and he wished to believe so — that the flavor of life was as keen as ever, as keen as when he was a wild stripling or only a boy.

These statements appear to have involved only the slightest and most pardonable of exaggerations.

He still entertained his Angelas, Paolinas, Pocofilas, and other ladies of a far from doubtful reputation, since there was no doubt whatsoever as to what their reputation was; and he still poked a lot of fun on this subject at Sansovino and Titian who (thank God) were even further from the year in which they were born than he was.

"Messer Jacopo," he dashed off in a note to the first of them, "the respect which I have for you and Titian is the reason I did not let you know that I had Virginia to supper the other night. I did not say a word about it, but kept it entirely to myself, so that you and your good friend would not hear. And to this I was counselled by the love that I have for the (alas!) somewhat advanced age of both of you. For it is good, wise, and seemly that I should keep you away from all lustful temptations. And even if the attitudes of love do not any longer allure you, the beauty of Virginia is such that she would move Continence itself to a wish to enjoy her. So much so that she can be compared to those dishes which not only tempt hungry people to eat them, but even those who have just risen from the table."

Titian

Venice

ARETINO IN 1543

"Certainly it breathes, the pulses beat, and it is animated by the same spirit which I am in real life." — *Aretino*.

In 1547, his second daughter was born. He named her Austria in honor of the hereditary dominions of his mighty emperor just as he had named his first daughter Adria after the sea ruled over by Venice. His progeny, apparently, just like his books, were always dedicated and, of course, to some person or power whose good will would be useful to him. It was an occasion for exultancy. "I have all my youthful powers," he wrote a friend, "and not more than four or five months ago, love and nature made me father of a lovely daughter." He was then fifty-five years old and was bursting almost childishly with his proved virility. Given his philosophy, it was all important to him.

As for the activities of his pen, they were maintained with the same overflowing vitality. Though he wrote less than in the full height of his greatest productivity, six books of his were still to be brought out. Three of them have been already discussed: *Il Filosofo,* his final comedy; *L'Orazia,* the tragedy in blank verse; and the third volume of his letters. All three appeared in 1546. The last three were volumes four, five and six of his epistles. They were as portly as the first three volumes and the average of their quality about as high. There were fewer masterpieces among their pages — none of the great letters we have already quoted coming from them — but a deeper wisdom which was sometimes even mellowed by tolerance.

Last of all, in 1551, he carried out his greatest feat of editing and publication.

Under the three winged angels bearing a scroll written with *"Veritas Filia Temporis"* — Truth, Daughter of Time — of printer Francesco Marcolini, who was once again his friend, he brought out two well-packed tomes. These were the "Letters Written Unto Signor Pietro Aretino by Many Lords, Republics, Worthy Ladies, Poets and Other Excellent People." I have them bound in parchment on the table in front of me as I write, and while I look upon their handsome pages printed in italic, I measure them as the first conscious effort in per-

sonal promotion in all literature. They were to show Pietro
Aretino as a person of immense importance. And they did so.
875 closely set up pages, they were made up of a careful
selection from the massive correspondence which had been
indited to him by nearly every distinguished person of the
period, and by many undistinguished ones as well. The ones
from the undistinguished persons were couched in terms of
fulsome praise while those from the mighty or learned were
addressed as to an equal or a superior. Though his enemies
tried to pretend so, there is no evidence that they were forged,
and little that they were really rewritten. And they set Aretino
on a pedestal of public fame which no writer had attained before, and few have since. If the meeting with the Emperor
was the crown of his life's work, this was its robe of ermine.
The tribute which he gathered so industriously was not entirely paid in gold.

In the meantime, the days, weeks, and months went by.
They brought with them their characteristic gifts. Things to
grieve about. The death of his sister Francesca, which called
forth a long letter to his soldier brother-in-law. It was full of
deep feeling, mellowed by revery. Aretino was fond of his sister, possibly because she idolized him, possibly because he
helped her all her life and we love those who owe us gratitude, possibly because she was the one member of his family —
and hence tie to his youth — that, his mother having gone, he
could be fond of. The death of his father, which hardly
touched him, and was mentioned almost in passing; he never
liked Luca; he resented Luca's being just what Luca was. The
death of King Francis I. This perhaps affected him the most of
any death, since the French monarch — though he had never
met Pietro's demands — was the last link with the great days
with Giovanni delle Bande Nere, which were growing, as he
grew older himself, more and more legendary. Controversy;
his strange quarrel with the stormy Michelangelo; physical im-
broglio; his set-to with the English ambassador. Family cares.
Adria's marriage with the joys and with the sorrows that en-

sued therefrom. At any rate, it can be said with safety that his last years were not dull through any lack of events.

The quarrel with the knotty stone carver, who, for the second time in his career, was engaged upon a titanic job of painting which would gain him more public fame, if less artistic reputation, than all of his sculpturing, was the first one of these episodes in point of time. And in biographical significance it was not second. For it showed Aretino in a somewhat unfamiliar rôle.

Ordinarily he was the friend of artists; getting them — as we have seen over and over again — jobs; praising their paintings; giving them advice; firing them with his own mighty enthusiasm. There is, of course, that merry story of the small difference of opinion with Jacopo Tintoretto. Aretino had criticized the young artist publicly and the latter guilefully invited him to his studio to paint his portrait. Pietro accompanied him there and when he was seated, Tintoretto suddenly produced a mighty pistol and flourished it. "What are you doing?" cried the journalist. "Taking your measure," the painter answered coolly, meaning it both literally and figuratively, and proceeded to lay off the huge quaking fellow in pistol lengths. It was a good way to make sure of favorable press notices. But another attitude was far more usual, and indeed during those very years it which he was contending with the Florentine, he showed that it was the normal one by the time spent and the trouble taken to aid Sansovino. The sculptor-architect had been pitched headlong into a damp Venetian dungeon when the façade of the library he was building, opposite the Doge's palace, collapsed, either owing to faulty design or because he skimped — so as to make greater profits — on the materials. Aretino button-holed Doge and member of the council; he addressed prince and foreign ambassador; he even wrote Titian who was at the time in Rome, until he had the sentence commuted to a fine, and until later he had even the fine removed. But the reason that he quarreled with Michelangelo was the same reason that he was the friend of other artists. It was his whole-hearted, if acquisitive, love of art.

As far back as 1537, friends of Aretino told him of the Florentine's engagement in as ambitious a project as had yet been attempted by a painter. This was no less than to cover the whole altar wall of the Sistine Chapel with a prodigious "Last Judgment." The figures were to be many times life-size. The drama of the composition was to be on the same scale as the terror and wonder of the subject. The graphic arts, which had won supreme laurels with the pastoral lyric and with the calm of narrative, were now to essay a Greek tragedy. And for once Michelangelo, who had dreamed of carving a whole marble promontory into a single mighty statue, was not bound by any unpleasant necessity to hold himself in reserve.

It is almost a waste of breath to say who was the only other man in Italy who was capable of responding to such size and boldness. It was he whom we write about. This was something like his own doings — like his making bids for kings and emperors. But he saw also an opportunity of a more practical sort, for we must remember that he always made his enthusiasms, though genuine, pay dividends. Here was one artist whom he certainly had neglected. No Michelangelo painting, or even drawing, darted glance of fury from beside the priceless masterpieces by Titian, Sebastiano del Piombo, Giulio Romano, Giorgio Vasari and all those countless others in his famous salon. Might not he now have a chance to get one if he spoke his heart out? "Pens!" he called for. "Paper! My ink bottles!"

"Just as, venerable man," began his letter, "it is a sinful and a shameful thing for the soul not to be mindful of God, so it is a reflection on the worth or judgment of anyone who has either worth or judgment, not to pay reverence to you."

Then he started stringing phrases together.

"For that reason, I, who with my praise and blame have spread abroad faults and virtues in vast quantity, hasten — so that the little which I am does not become nothing — to salute you, and I would not dare to do this, if it were not that my name which has reached the ears of every living prince, had not thus lost a great part of its worthlessness.

"But it is fitting that the world should treat you with respect, for the world has many kings and but one Michelangelo.

"Indeed, what a mircle it is that nature can produce nothing anywhere that is so majestic that you do not find it out and impress it on your works with the immense power of your pencil and your chisel. Thus, he who sees you, does not have to regret not having seen Phidias, or Apelles, or Vetruvius, for their spirits are but as shadows compared to your own."

And now, so Pietro was informed, he said, Michelangelo was engaged in a "Last Judgment" which he hoped would surpass his "Birth of Adam." Well, he would help out by telling him how to handle it.

"I see, in the middle of a crowd, Antichrist himself, with features such as you alone could imagine. I see fear written on the faces of the living. I see extinction on the sun, moon, and stars. I see the spirit leaping up, as it were, from fire, earth, air, and water. I see all nature, horror-struck, barren, shriveled up in its decrepitude. I see Time, emaciated and trembling, who, having come to the end of his term, is seated on the withered trunk of a tree. And while the trumpets of the angels shake the hearts of all, I see Life and Death thrown into utter confusion, the one weary of raising up the dead, the other making ready to strike down the living. I see Hope and Despair guiding the cohorts of the good and the rabble of the damned. I see the theater of the clouds lighted up with the rays which come from the pure fires of heaven. On these, amid His hosts, Christ is seated, cinctured with splendor and with terror. I see the refulgence of his countenance and the flashings of those flames of light, which fill the righteous with gladness and the evil-doers with fear. I see the ministers of the abyss who, to the glory of saints and martyrs, deride Caesars and Alexanders, since to have conquered oneself is something different from having conquered the world. I see Fame with

her crowns and her palms trod under foot, flung down beneath the wheels of her own chariot. Finally, I hear the Son of
God pronouncing sentence. I see his words come down in the
form of two arrows, one bringing salvation, the other damna-
tion. And as I watch them come down, I hear fury cracking
through the mechanism of the elements, with great cracks of
thunder undoing and dissolving all. I see the lights of Paradise and the furnaces of Hell which cut the shadows of the air
of Chaos.

"And I am so moved by the thought which this image of
the final day inspires, that I find myself saying: 'If you so fear
and tremble seeing the work of Buanarotti, how much more
will you fear and tremble when you stand before the Judge
himself?'"

After that he asked Michelangelo if he did not think he
would have to break the vow he had once made never to set
foot in Rome again, if only so as to see the great painting.

"I would rather make myself a liar than to do your picture
the injustice of not seeing it."

In its own way, it is quite a masterpiece. It was, of course,
impertinent, but its impertinence has been greatly exaggerated by those who do not like to realize that in his own time
Aretino was regarded as a great writer, and that in those days
many a famous artist — though none quite so irascible and so
independent as the Florentine with his lined brows — was
quite glad to have his theme suggested by a man of letters. But
its love of art stands out all over it, and its eloquence, if showing the beginnings of baroque, is really notable. But what is
most to look at is the cold purpose that is always concealed behind its fire. It was an opening move of more than reasonable
skill.

Curiously enough, Michelangelo, who was generally un-
communicative, paid it the compliment of answer.

"Magnificent Messer Pietro, my lord and brother, the receipt of your letter brought me joy and sorrow together. I
rejoiced exceedingly because it came from you, who are with-

out peer in the world of genius. Yet at the same time I grieved, for having already finished a large part of my picture, I cannot avail myself of your conception. Yet it is so vivid that if the Day of Judgment had come and you had seen it with your own eyes, you could not have described it better.

"Now in answer to what you wrote me: not only did your letter please me, but I beg you to continue in the same vein, seeing that kings and emperors deem it the highest favor to be mentioned by your pen. And if I have anything you would like, I offer it to you with all my heart.

"Last of all do not break your resolve of never revisiting Rome merely on account of the picture I am painting. That would be too much."

The irony was entirely apparent, but even if it had not been, something Michelangelo did at about this time would have made it so. At the right hand of his angry Christ, he was sketching in St. Bartholomew and it suddenly occurred to Messer Buonarotti to give him the face of Pietro. Following the convention he placed in the flayed saint's hand a knife, but the skin which he held in his other hand — instead of being his own skin which it should have been — had the face of Michelangelo. It was if he were pretending fear of what would happen to him if he did not comply with the writer — just as a large schoolboy does when threatened by a little one. "Do not flay me alive!" it seemed to say. But Aretino, although not obtuse, did not choose to take it this way. For he thought he saw his way clear.

Not having, he replied, one of those vases of emerald in which Alexander the Great kept the works of Homer, he had sighed when Messer Jacopo Nardi brought him the letter. It was so lavish a gift and he could pay so little honor to it. However, now that he had read it reverently, he would do the best he could. He would place it with ceremony with the privilege which he had received from Charles V in a golden jar given him by Antonio da Leyva. And since it was a shame for Michelangelo to have wasted valuable time answering his scribblings, he wanted to add modestly that he had not written him with the idea of telling him how to paint his picture, but merely to show him how any other conception of the subject must fall flat beside that of the great artist.

Then he came to the point of the whole business. Michelangelo had said that if there was anything of his he wanted, simply to mention it. Well, there was. Did not his devotion to Michelangelo deserve from the prince of sculptors one of those fragments of cartoons which he was accustomed to consign to the fire? He would treasure it, he said, during his life, and when he died, take it to the tomb with him. Thus he opened his campaign.

And he fought it out, as was his custom, with every strategy that he was capable of, making use of every weapon he possessed. Flattery. Might not even thorny Michelangelo be susceptible to his fine eloquence besmeared with honey? Innuendo, hinting, obstinacy. Constant repetitions of his importance with the implied corollary that it could benefit the artist. Constant reminders of the gifts of their works which other artists had been willing to give him. They had been many, God knows; and so too did anyone who had been rowed in gondola down the slapping serpentine of the Grand Canal and had entered the Casa Aretino. Outright begging, subtlety, persuasion, every kind of scheme.

After Peschiera and the triumph of his reception by the Emperor, he wrote Michelangelo telling him about it, and then added that he considered it an even greater honor merely to have been born in the great sculptor's century. "Why not," he went on, "reward my admiration with but a scrap torn from one of those sketches that seem so worthless to you? I would value two of your pencil marks on a bit of paper more than all the cups and collars I have received from all the princes in the world?" It was true — so help us.

He enlisted his friends. "Last of all," he besought Carlo Gualterazzi, "in view of your close relations with Michelangelo, I beg you to ask him how long he thinks I can wait for the drawings he promised me. I look forward to them as eagerly as I am anxious to serve him."

He took every vague phrase as a definite hint.

"Your letter," he wrote Jacopo Cellini — and not Benvenuto, as many writers on the controversy have it, perhaps being unable to imagine that there could be more than one of the name Cellini in a single century — "is particularly pleasing because of the greetings from the divine Buonarroti it brings me. Now I hope to be made proud by the gift that I await so expectantly. But in case he holds out any longer I must lose faith in the integrity of this very great man."

But not reverence for his art, he added. The man who had considered a whole winter not too much to spend in wheedling eight shirts from the procrastinating Marquis of Mantua, had definite ideas as to how to carry on a siege.

But at last after eight years, it became apparent that he would never win out. In the spring of 1545, certain sketches arrived but they were merely copies, the work of an inferior artist. Then Aretino took out his last arrow and fitted it. It was the poisoned one. He wrote Michelangelo telling him emphatically that these would never do, requesting something genuine. He then added a hint that there were many things a scathing tongue might say about the great artist, and that so far he had not uttered them. Several days elapsed, and no answer. Several weeks, finally several months. And then all at once it dawned upon Pietro that the stubborn Buonarotti was not planning ever to send him any of his work, and indeed never had thought of doing so. So he let the bowstring loose.

"Sir," he began very deliberately, "now that I have seen copies of your finished 'Last Judgment,' I acknowledge that I recognize the distinguished charm of Raphael in its agreeable beauty of invention. However, as a baptized Christian, I blush before the license, so forbidden to a man of genius, of which you have made use in expressing ideas connected with the highest aims and final ambitions to which our faith aspires.

"So, then, that Michelangelo, so great in his fame; that

Michelangelo whom all admire; that Michelangelo renowned in prudence, has chosen to display to the whole world an impiety of irreligion which is only equalled by the perfection of his painting! How can it be that an artist who, since he is divine, does not consort with human beings, has done this in the greatest temple built to God, upon the highest altar raised to Christ, in the most sacred chapel upon earth, where the mighty hinges of the church, the venerable priests of our faith, the Vicar of Christ himself, with solemn ceremonies and holy prayers, confess, contemplate, and adore His body, His blood, and His flesh?

"If it were not infamous to introduce the comparison, I would plume myself on my virtue when I wrote the *Ragionamenti*. I would demonstrate the superiority of my reserve to your indiscretion. I, while handling themes lascivious and immodest, used language comely and decorous, spoke in terms beyond reproach which were inoffensive to chaste ears. You, on the contrary, presenting so awful a subject, exhibit saints and angels, the former without earthly decency, the latter without heavenly honors."

After that he elaborated his charges. The pagans, when they modeled a Diana, gave her clothes; when they made a naked Venus, hid with the hand of modesty those parts which are not shown. Yet here came a Christian who because he rated art higher than the faith, deemed it a royal spectacle to portray martyrs and virgins in improper attitudes, to show men dragged down by their shame. His art might be at home in a brothel but certainly not in this sacred chapel, and it would have been better if he had denied Christ altogether than, believing in Him, to turn into derision the faith of others. Why shouldn't he at least restore the picture to repute by turning the indecent parts of the damned to flames, and of the blessed to sunbeams? Why wouldn't he imitate the modesty of Florence which hid his David's shame beneath some gilded leaves?

"As I wish God may pardon you, I do not write this out of

resentment for the things I begged of you. Yet the truth is that if you had sent me what you promised, you would only have done what was clearly in your own interest, for this act of courtesy would have silenced the envious tongues of those who say that only certain Gerardos and Tommasos can obtain them."

But if the treasure bequeathed to Michelangelo by Pope Julius so that he would finish his tomb was not enough to make him keep his promised word, he went on, what could Aretino expect from him? Incidentally, neither the great artist's avarice nor his ingratitude could keep that mighty Pope from enjoying immortality, since God had willed that Julius should live renowned forever, earned by his own virtues which were more than any towering monument. In the meantime, Michelangelo's failure to discharge his obligations was nothing but a theft.

"Our souls need the tranquil emotions of piety more than the lively impressions of plastic art, so may God, then, inspire His Holiness with the same thoughts that He instilled into Gregory of blessed memory. That Pope chose rather to despoil Rome of the proud statues of pagan dieties than to let their magnificence turn the people from the humbler images of the saints.

"Finally," he concluded, "if, when you set about composing your picture of the universe and hell and heaven, you had steeped your heart in those suggestions of glory, honor and terror proper to the theme, which I sketched out in the letter which I offered to you, and which the whole world reads, I venture to assert that not only would Nature and all kind influences never regret the illustrious talents they endowed you with, but Providence itself which sees all things would continue to watch over such a masterpiece as long as order lasts in the hemispheres."

Last of all, he added an insidious postscript.

"Now that I have blown off some of the rage which I feel against you for the cruelty which you showed my devotion,

and have taught you that while you may be divine (*di vino*),
I am not of water, I bid you tear up this letter, for I am ready
to do the same. And do not forget that I am one to whose
epistles kings and emperors reply."

It was a malicious letter, one of the ugliest and most insolent
ever penned. Yet even after we have made pause to say that
about it, we have to pay a tribute — as so often — to its diabolical skill. For though it appeared to hurl every insult that Aretino hastily could dig up, in reality it used only those that had
particular power to hurt the artist. The comparison with
Raphael. Michelangelo's testy strength hated the delicacy and
softness of works done by the handsome man from Urbino,
and indeed many agree that Raphael only became great when
he borrowed some of Buonarotti's iron. Then — for instance,
in the chamber in the Vatican — he equalled the Florentine.
The reference to the tomb of Julius. Michelangelo's own conscience always troubled him because he had not ever fulfilled
his plain contract by completing it, but he had been powerless
to do differently. The ribald leers about his young men. The
great sculptor was perhaps foolishly sentimental in his affection
for Tommaso Cavalieri and that other Gerardo, as rugged men
sometimes are when they let the barriers down, but he was not
a sodomite. The charges of his indecency and irreligion — for
he was at heart a Puritan. The devout hope that the Pope
would have the picture destroyed. It might add impetus to a
movement which was already started, and which resulted later
in the picture's being bowdlerized by Daniele of Volterra who
thus earned the proud title of breeches-maker. Even the smug
hypocritical reference to his own epic of the stews and leaping
houses showed his ingenuity. He sensed the coming age — when
it was not wrong to sin if you were pious publicly. As for the
postscript, it was plain as plain could be. I have not yet given
this letter to the world, it said. I need never give it. And I will
not — if you pay the price.

Yet for all that, it never did its job. For even after this verbal
assault with intent to commit verbal mayhem, no picture, not

even a fragmentary sketch, forthcame. It is as one might expect. For if Michelangelo thought on the same dramatic scale that Pietro did, he was likewise equally tough-minded. He was used to enemies. He was used to bitter attacks. And the man who dared defy Julius II, who was the most fiery, if one of the greatest Popes ever to occupy the Vatican, was not likely to be cowed by any son of any shoemaker even though princes and prelates often were.

Next in order was Aretino's set-to with the English ambassador. It was less stirring than his quarrel with Michelangelo, but it was more typical. Aretino and these emissaries of princes! To the last pages of his life we shall be reading about them! But this time he could not rant, and then save his apparently sensitive hide by suddenly becoming obsequious. This is the thing to wonder at: that he so often could.

As far back as 1538, Henry VIII had followed the example of the other lords and rulers by sending Messer Pietro Aretino —after the mission of the unfortunate Eusebii—a certain princely gift. Two hundred crowns it amounted to, and though, as has been recorded, they were slow in coming, Aretino acknowledged them. First merely by phrases. Then in 1542 he dedicated the second portly volume of his letters to the bluff, many-wived King Hal. "To the great and the magnanimous Henry VIII," he inscribed them. This he followed with three pages of eulogy. Henry brought "glory to the possession of dignities," made "lordship worthy of reverence" and "exalted the high state of being a king." Aretino worshiped "the sacred shadows of the throne" he sat on. He contrasted Henry's "humanity" with "the pride of other rulers." He noted his accomplishments. "Peoples who were lawless, faithless and without virtue, you have reduced to right-doing, piety and obedience." Of "the common folk" whom Henry "ruled with fatherly compassion," he would not speak, since "the peace, well-being, and prosperity" with which he "kept them quiet, contented, rich and esteemed," begged him to be silent. "But I will say that the whole world, seeing resplendent in your character both the torch of worthiness and the taper of wisdom, bows to you and you only."

We know Henry, and we do not seem to recognize the portrait. But Henry must have been a little puzzled himself. Especially in these latter days, when his Katherine of Aragon trouble, Charles V trouble, Cardinal Wolsey trouble, had broadened into general wife trouble, Thomas More trouble, Thomas Cromwell trouble; when his wrangling with the Church caused the Defender of the Faith to join the heretics; and when the fistula on his leg informed him that the sins of the fathers do not always wait to visit the children. Well-fleshed English Harry whose so simple actions led him into such complexities, did not often receive such glowing commendations. He was particularly touched because they came from the Italian peninsula, and even more so because they emanated from a man, who, although Henry had rewarded him, had handled very little of his money.

To be touched was to be generous royally.

"We will send him another gift — this time three hundred *scudi,*" he directed.

Word of this came swiftly to Venice, where it was received by the person it most concerned with due rejoicing. One thing that must be said of Aretino is that he was always appreciative. All he now wanted was the actual cash that would make the promise come true. A new letter would then be in order. And certainly it would surpass the first.

But to promise all this money was one matter, and to pay it was another, especially when your treasury was chronically overburdened. Aretino waited. A year passed. No crowns. Two years, three years, four years, five years. Royal Harry died. Then another friend in London — Denny by name — wrote Pietro saying very specifically that the crowns had been sent. They had been sent to Sigmund Harwell, English ambassador. Aretino waited. Still no money. Rightly or wrongly he concluded that he knew what had happened to it. To conclude was to act. To act was to put into words.

He now realized where his crowns had gone, he wrote to
the Mantuan ambassador. Master Harwell had appropriated
them. He absolved Henry of all complicity, though the act,
said he, was characteristic of "that insolent race of shopkeepers." (He thus beat Napoleon to his famous phrase.)
Then he published the letter, and all of Venice read it avidly.
So, apparently, did Harwell.

A few days later Aretino was walking down a narrow side-
street. All at once he saw that his way was blocked by six men,
all armed. At their head was the ambassador. Aretino looked
for a way of escape, saw none, so turned and faced them. The
first thing he knew, he was seized, thrown to the ground, and
cudgelled from head to foot. Some hours later his servants
found him. When they lifted him from the gutter, his right
arm was hurt, though not seriously, and he was black and
blue from head to foot. His adversaries had vanished into thin
air.

As can be imagined, the affair made a tremendous noise.
Many considered that the English ambassador had done right
thus to silence an insolent tongue, but the majority felt that
his act was an outrageous bit of bullying. Here was a not
youthful man set on by six ruffians and beaten without mercy,
while the victim of his words stood by perfectly safe, with his
hand on his dagger. If Harwell had taken on Aretino personally, it would have been another matter. Even then the odds
might have been unequal, but the provocation would have
been held to justify it. If he had stabbed Aretino in broad
daylight, the Italians would have understood it. But this
playing-certain business of making sure you had an over-
whelming physical majority on the side of righteous indignation was beyond their comprehension. There was an under-
tone of real rage.

In the meantime, the victim himself did nothing. The
bravos who surrounded him urged him to let them murder
the foreigner. He asked them not to. Cooler heads begged
him to lay his case before the magistrates. He refused to.

"They did me no harm and they did not frighten me," he said calmly. "I wish no revenge upon anyone." These temperate words, though they may have been studied, made a big impression.

Presently all of public opinion was on his side. And not merely Venetian public opinion, either.

"I am very much upset about the unexpected affair of Pietro Aretino," wrote Duke Cosimo de' Medici, "and certainly you must be too. It seems to me that the freedom of speech which all Christian princes have agreed to grant the man has been violated. Nor could the English ambassador have offered more convincing proof that Aretino spoke the truth. Otherwise he would have kept his temper."

Don Diego de Mendoza, sallow personal agent, in Venice, of the Emperor Charles V, expressed his indignation in terms no less certain.

One after another, other princely emissaries followed suit.

Harwell soon saw that he had made a false step and he hastened to undo it. He went to Aretino and apologized without reserve. "I acted hastily," he said. "I was misled by reports of what you said about me. If it would do good, I would wipe out the fault with my own blood." After which, he offered tangible proof of his sincerity. He disgorged, or at any rate paid over, the three hundred crowns which caused the controversy.

Aretino was exultant. "Christ must have forgiven my sins," he cried, "since he has thus allowed me to show I have no rancor!" The coins jingled in his purse — which they might not have if he had resorted to violence. He had warmed old friends and possibly, in Harwell, made a new one. And the few bruises he had were already healing. "I am glad I had the opportunity to forgive an affront."

But it was not either one of these affairs that left the deepest mark upon his peace and his tranquillity. His quarrel with Michelangelo showed how vindictive he could be when he was crossed, but we have seen him crossed before and seen

Rome

ARETINO AS ST. BARTHOLOMEW: DETAIL OF
MICHELANGELO'S 'LAST JUDGMENT'

"Do not forget that I am one to whom kings and emperors reply."

—Aretino.

the way he acted. The set-to with the irascible Briton showed his pliability. He could put on Christian forbearance when he needed to, and when he knew that it would gain his end with far less risk to hide than anger would. But Adria's marriage left a deep scar on his heart. It showed that he was human, and knew pity, and love, and tenderness, even though his exterior was crude and brutal, even though he was blatant and arrogant, even though he seemed simply ruthlessness and selfishness incarnate advancing to the sound of a loud noise.

We have long ago noted what he said were his feelings for this exquisite little girl. "Adria is not my daughter," he cried feelingly, "but my life itself." We have seen also how he told Sebastiano del Piombo that his one prayer was to live until he saw her safely married. Now, in 1548, she was eleven years old and as such matters went in Italy, it was time to take steps to have this prayer of his granted. He must find her a husband. He must gather together a dowry. Since all the money that was paid into his hands found its way out again very shortly, this last meant a new appeal to the great.

The question of the husband was settled very promptly. No sooner was it known that Adria was to be married than a claimant for her hand appeared. He was a young man whose parents came from Bergamo, but who had been born and who lived in Urbino. His name was Diotalevi Rota. He was twenty-nine years old. He had inherited lands and houses worth five thousand crowns, and he must have had a good head for business for he demanded a portion of one thousand ducats and insisted it be paid in gold. Aretino, once more judging character badly, passed over the probable implications of this, and thanked Christ very joyously—in a letter to the Duke of Urbino's ambassador—that His mercy had provided Adria with the sort of a husband he desired. "For I am more anxious to have someone worthy than someone great or noble. My genius will supply all the honor and prestige that is needed." Even in the moment of providing for that daughter who was very nearly the only person he loved now or had ever loved disinterestedly, he could not forget to posture or be vain.

The dowry was another matter, however, and to assemble it took all his efforts. The Cardinal of Ravenna, who had once helped him similarly with his sister, had promised him five hundred *scudi*. Aretino wrote reminding him of this, and the churchman sent two hundred to him. There was no hope for any more so he thanked His Eminence effusively. He was a good judge of when the limit had been reached. Don Diego de Mendoza contributed one hundred, and one can presume it was with Charles V's approval. Last of all, he applied to Cosimo de' Medici. The Duke of Florence promised three hundred, but the money did not appear. Aretino wrote a second time, and this is how Cosimo answered him:

"It is not because we do not believe that your daughter is to be married that we put off giving you the money we promised, but because we wish to be sure that it will go where it is meant to. Send the future husband with an order and the crowns will be paid to him immediately. It will be better for you to have the money go into his hands directly than into yours, for from your natural liberality, which is no vice, you will put it to some other use. Keep up your good works, and we will never fail you." It appears the son of his old comrade understood his man.

Pietro even went so far as to swear roundly that if he could not raise the money otherwise, he would pawn the golden collar given him by Philip II. And as greatly did he adore and cherish Adria, that he might have, at that.

But one way or another the money was assembled without this necessity, and in June 1550, Aretino wrote a friend, Antonio Gallo, that Rota was on his way to Urbino and Adria, now his bride, with him. "Not one *soldo* of all the thousand ducats is still due him." At the same time he bid Diotalevi farewell by telling him that he did not regard him so much as his son-in-law as his own offspring. Then he sent a letter to the Duke of Urbino, begging him to receive his daughter kindly. She was so dear to him that he dared to make this request, he said, even from a lord so great as Guidobaldo.

Guidobaldo granted it. Bells jingling, a cavalcade of prancing horses rode down from the little city to meet Adria and her husband, finding them eight miles from its gates. It was headed by the handsome Duke himself. He got off his cream-white charger and kissed the little bride as if she were a princess. Then they started upward again. All the road was lined with Guidobaldo's subjects, and as they moved along cheers greeted them, and they were showered with rose petals. That night torches wavered beneath their windows, and there was a serenade until nearly daybreak. The next morning Adria was received by the Duchess, who welcomed her as she might have her own daughter. When she and her husband wrote Pietro Aretino to tell him of their joy at seeing her, the cup of his happiness was full.

But it was empty again only too soon. As might have been expected, Diotalevi, who had insisted on her dowry being paid in cash, had no other interest in Adria than the money he could get from her; and that paid to him, he treated her with planned brutality. So did his brother, and his sister. Perhaps thinking that her inevitable complaints would draw bribes from her father, they often shut her up in her room; took the keys of the provision closet and wine cellar; berated her because she wore bracelets and chains. Rota, eager to have everything that she possessed, even abused her like some foulmouthed carter because she would not sell the diamond her father had given her as a farewell present, and turn over the price to his rapaciousness. She was struck, thrown about, and taunted with reminders that she was a bastard. For clothing she was given nothing but rags.

At last she could stand it no longer, but fled to Venice where she told her story to her father. His friends listened to it, and Titian among others was moved to tears. One and all they urged her to stay with Aretino. At first she said she would, but after a while she changed her mind. After all, a wife's duty was with her husband. She had promised to obey him always. She must go back.

Three days after her arrival, her ill treatment recommenced. This time she did not flee but wrote her father. He appealed to the Duchess of Urbino.

"In the name of God and nature and charity, I beg you to give her your protection, for she is worthy of it."

The Duchess was glad to intervene, and presently Adria found shelter in the Ducal palace.

But it was too late.

She had been brought up in the most ill-reputed house in all of Europe and had seen nothing but kindness. Now her own husband showed her inhumanity. The disillusion was too much for her. Her heart was broken. Very soon she died.

And in her death Aretino received one of the two hardest blows that Fate had given him. Just what he said when he received the tidings we do not know, but we can realize the dagger stroke. So we remember other words spoken on another occasion.

"When Perina died, I died with her."

Only this time, it was his own flesh and blood, his own daughter, his own little winsome Adria. And this time he was too old for the healing processes of time, which in the case of the other loss, though he had doubted their efficacy, had finally brought him relief.

CHAPTER XIX

A Second Jubilee

IN 1549, Pope Paul III died. Close to seventy when, fifteen years before, the triple crown had been placed on his head, Alessandro Farnese, the first Roman citizen to become head of the Roman church in something more than a century, reigned, nevertheless, with a fierce and youthful vigor that belies the hectic old-man complexion and the bloodless if dynamic hands in that famous family group painted by Titian. The bending, hunched-up body in its pontifical robes of white and old rose may be fragile and it may be withered as an autumn oak leaf, but the will power behind the crafty old eyes did not yet burn low. And this will power shaped out a great papacy. Or at least a notable one.

Alessandro Farnese had formed his ideas in the great days of Alexander VI, Julius II, and Pope Leo X de' Medici, and as nearly as possible he brought back all the brilliance and the vividness of their vanished era.

Art returned to the Eternal City for its brief turgidly-colored *tramontana*, for it was during Paul's papacy that Michelangelo was haled back to Rome to do the virile storminess of "The Last Judgment," which brought forth such a disturbing controversy with our Aretino.

Nepotism became respectable again, and for the first time since greedy Spaniards and lustful Teutons had laid sacrilegious hands upon the Bride of Christ, the Pope's son and grandsons — to say nothing of his sisters and his cousins and his aunts — received due acknowledgment, and fitting secular or ecclesiastic honors. Benvenuto Cellini's gadfly, Pierluigi Farnese, the sodomite, with his greasy beard, bulging eyes and his penchant for sleek furs and white satin neither desired nor was suitable for a church appointment. Consequently fox Farnese made him Duke of Parma and of Piacenza. (Incidentally the

Parmegiani, who though not fastidious, drew the line at some things, found it ultimately necessary to murder him, which they did with a ruthless brutality which was, considering the victim, almost admirable.) Grandson Alessandro, however, was made a cardinal. He was not worse than many cardinals, though it can hardly be said that the red hue of his robes went very becomingly with his sallow, dissolute complexion. Grandson Ottavio, a young man on the make, if there ever was one, (and a slimy and cold-blooded young animal if you can judge from his portraits) was married to the daughter of the Emperor. Granddaughter Vittoria was married to the illustrious Guidobaldo II of Urbino. She was a homely little girl, but she had a gentle if insipid face. Maybe one member of that family was not calculating, did not scheme!

Pope Paul also renewed the old battle for the Pope's temporal power, and since he employed craft rather than power, made a reasonably good job of it. At least he prevented the Council of Trent from accomplishing anything significant, and since the object of that gathering was to reform Catholicism by modifying the absolutism of the Pope, that was considerable.

Indeed, those who like metes and bounds, will find 1549 quite as good a date for the end of the Renaissance as 1453 was for its beginning. For as long as Pope Farnese sat, like some ancient spider, in the Vatican, no new age could really begin.

Paul III was succeeded by the third Julius. To outward appearances, the former Cardinal Del Monte was another temporal ruler of the same lavish Renaissance tradition. He had his extravagances. He had his favorites, male and female. He had his soaring ambitions and hopes. Actually, however, his short rule — for he was Pope hardly more than four years — was an interlude. He lacked the ability to carry on Paul's restorations of Papal power and splendidness, and he did not have the temperament to bring into being those considerable reforms which seemed necessary and wise to the more realistic pontiffs who succeeded him. Even his one petulant attempt at the vicious favoritism of the High Renaissance was more ludicrous than it was either venal or indecent. For a prince of the church to see a young fellow skipping over the house-tops of Bologna; to be struck by his physical comeliness; to adopt him; ultimately to elevate him to a kind of *papier maché* eminence (the mincing young fellow finally became Cardinal del Monte, but no one—not himself even, one thinks—took it very seriously) was a tame sequel to alleged intrigues with the ox-eyed and flaxen Lucrezia; to the devil deeds of Caesar Borgia; to making delle Roveres and Pier Luigis dukes of bona-fide dukedoms. To most clear-eyed observers, Julius was, therefore, an easy going and perhaps even not too immoral old man in whose slack hands the papacy lost, almost without knowing it, most of what energetic Paul had regained for it. Aretino, however, saw him in a different light. To the scourge of princes, Giulio Terzo was a fellow citizen of Arezzo, with whom, and particularly with whose family, he had always taken wise pains to curry favor. He was, consequently, the first pope since the early days of Clement, to whom Aretino could appeal with some chance of being listened to. Now at last, then, he had found someone who would aid him in that final step upward which he had long contemplated. And which, if he was able to take it, would be the crown and climax of his whole career.

To find out what this was, we must go back into the past. Twenty years earlier, it will be recalled, Aretino was engaged day in and day out in his endeavor to win back the favor of Clement VII which he had lost when he had quarreled with Giberti. Very nearly the whole story of this has been told, and with utmost detail, but the one thing that is now significant was omitted. When Clement finally made peace with Aretino and sent him, as a pledge, five hundred crowns, he entrusted them to Girolamo Schio, Bishop of Vaison. Schio forwarded them with a letter.

Here are the five hundred crowns, this said, and they are

merely a beginning. For if, it went on, Aretino should continue in papal good favor, other rewards would come to him.

"A rank fitting to your merits," was one of them.

What was this rank?

With true diplomatic caution, it was never mentioned, but it is not hard to guess it. It had something to do with the church. It had something to do with a red hat and with a ring of amethyst. No wonder Messer Aretino was tempted to behave.

It, of course, came to nothing—and in fact it is not easy to imagine that Clement with his disposition could have given more than the most fleeting of a passing thought to making Aretino a cardinal—but under the next papacy it was seriously considered again. Indeed, grandson Ottavio Farnese himself advanced the claims of Messer Pietro to his Pontiff grandfather.

"Holy Father," he said formally, "every day in your life, you make men who are poor and of low degree, cardinals. And for no other reason than that they have been faithful agents of our house in its every need. That, certainly, has been a wise and a praiseworthy thing to do. But if those persons seemed fitting to so exalted rank, consider what you would gain by bestowing it on Aretino. Though he is poor and base-born, he is in the good graces of every prince in the world, and if he should receive this dignity from you, he would make you live forever."

Then he went into the details of his argument. Had not the great Titian just finished an immortal series of portraits of the Farnese family? And who had urged him to do this? Was not the Farnese Pope trying to build up a family and hereditary state just as the Borgia and the Medici had tried before him? And who could state the case for this the most effectively? Even Charles V, the austere Emperor, had not hesitated to put Aretino on his payroll.

"These are modern times, my grandfather."

Paul reflected. The temptation was indeed great, but were

Others were addressed to the various princely patrons of Pietro:

"To the Majesty of the Most Unconquerable Charles V, Emperor worthy of a thousand empires."

"To the illustrious and most worthy lord, Guidobaldo, very worthy Duke of Urbino."

"To the illustrious and very excellent Lord Duke Cosimo."

"To the Serene Doge of the very worthy republic of Venice, that unconquerable stronghold."

Point by point, they assembled every insult imaginable that could goad Messer Aretino into incoherent fury.

"Your father was a lay Franciscan, and your mother a lay sister. You are, then, virtually the son of a nun and of a priest."

"You say that Kings and Emperors brought you tribute just as the three Magi brought tribute to the Savior. Yes, but what a difference! He spoke righteousness, lived even better, and taught virtuously the word of God. You, who write evil and live even worse with your Nannas and Pippas and other filthy courtezans, have published only villainies. His divine Majesty is the salvation of princes and you are their scourge. Christ founded the church, and you, with your pasquinades and satires, have tried to ruin it, lashing out at cardinals and stinging bishops and prelates."

"Pietro means head, and reading Aretino backward—for you are the reverse of all Aretines—you have Onitera (*Ogni terra*). Almost, you might say, the head rascal of all the world."

"You allege that Duke Alexander wanted to give you the Strozzi palace. Do not believe, O great beast who are swelled up like the bladder of a hog, that His Excellency really meant this, for he was a prince of great judgment, and if he gave you a few crowns, it was simply as a chattering buffoon. What right would a person like you have to such a noble residence? But if he did say so to shame an enemy of his, was not this his meaning? 'I am going to put the most wicked man in the world in the most honored house in Florence so that it will

be disgraced for ever.' Yet I swear in the name of your villainy that if this had happened, not only the Strozzi faction,
but the Medicis themselves would have burned it down with
you inside of it."

He resurrected the old bit of gossip about Francesco Marcolini.

"No man in the world ever treated you better than he did,
yet you boasted — and in public — you had cuckolded him."

It was the libel which Doni had already spread by word of
mouth, and he now made doubly poisonous by printing it. He
meant business when he turned his words on Aretino. The
earthquake was really out to topple the colossus. Who was
hurt beneath the falling débris, Doni did not care.

But perhaps his most effective onslaught lay in the long list
of the disasters which — he said — had shortly afterwards befallen all who had befriended Aretino.

"Didn't you say so many things of the keen mind of that
generous lord, Pierluigi Farnese, that he wanted to send for
you and to keep you in Piacenza like some precious jewel?
That and no other thing, that alone I tell you, was the cause of
his being assassinated."

"Didn't the Marquis of Vasto, who with such solicitude collected taxes on the Milanese wheat and then gave you the
money like a king, suffer many reverses for having shown you
this courtesy?"

"They say that Antonio da Leyva was carried off by the
devil. I don't believe it. Yet that is what they say, and I will
tell you why. It is because he gave you so many and such lavish
gifts."

"The Emperor has been, and is, beset by sickness and by
long wars simply because he persists in letting you enjoy the
sweat and blood of those poor gentlemen who have to contribute to your pension of two hundred *scudi*. And I know
certainly that as soon as he stops giving you this, peace will be
concluded."

"The Marquis of Marignano is dead for no other reason

per, Tongue, Pen, Ink, Sacred Rites, GOD and GIULIO TERZO himself—the last two printed entirely in capital letters—were marshalled up and down like troops in review before a pleased conclave of pompous generals (and just as helter skelter as the metaphors I have used to describe it). Comparisons wove in and out with the intricacy of ballet dancers. "Streams of Generousness" and "Rivers of Love" flowed from "the Mountain—" a play on the Pope's name of Del Monte— "of Valor, Grace, and Sense, which equalled Sinai and out-towered Olympus." I would like to print it in its entirety as a kind of ironic memorial to the great boast that Pietro made that his only weapon was truth, for rhymed sycophancy certainly never reached to greater heights. Space forbids, unfortunately. But it was rhymed sycophancy that aimed toward a definite end. And it got its reward.

The first thing that happened was that the city of Arezzo appointed its most notable living son as its honorary chief magistrate. Julius' hand was discernible, or at least brother Baldwin's, but it pleased Aretino no less mightily. For beneath a tough hide the great pen-wielder was, like many public figures, sensitive, and had always felt hurt that his native city had rarely shown how proud of him she was.

Then, he received a thousand golden crowns. They were counted out to him in cash, glittered brilliantly if briefly, and were presumably gulped down by his triple-mouthed extravagance.

Next, he was brought tidings that he had been made a Knight of St. Peter. This appointment carried with it a small salary. Eighty *scudi* a year. Not princely, but, at least a lot better than nothing. This time, at any rate, he would not be a knight without revenues. He accepted with glee.

But what delighted Aretino most was not the receipt of these honors. It was new tidings of the prestige he had.

One day he was handed a letter from an old crony, Captain Faloppia.

"I am overcome with joy at a letter which I have received

from Messer Geronimo Romano. In it he says that you are so
highly regarded by the Pope, that there is no one he esteems
more. Indeed, His Holiness said the other evening that if you
came to Rome, it would be like another jubilee, for everyone
would come to see you. According to what Messer Geronimo
writes, they expect you, and he asks me to tell you that if you
come, you will make a thousand crowns for every one you
spend. You had better make the best of this."

Shortly after this, he received another communication. It
was from one Vicenzio di Poggio who had paused in the
Eternal City on his way to the Holy Land. He wrote Aretino
that he heard as much talk of him in Rome as he did by the
Grand Canal.

"Everyone not only speaks well of you, but does it with all
the love and sincerity possible. It seems to me that poets of all
times ought to envy you, for not only the great give you deserved praise and wish you every happiness, but in the streets
and in the houses people are laying wagers as to what future
honors you will receive. It is said publicly that His Holiness
and his friends love you and esteem you immeasurably. They
say that your virtue is like the hydra. When one head is cut
off, seven new ones spring up in its place. I have heard and I
have seen things about you that I cannot possibly tell. Your
old enemies are now your fathers, your sons and your brothers,
according to their age. What more can I say? When the
Knights of St. Peter met, they all surrounded me and asked
for 'news of Signor Aretino.' 'How is he?' they cried; 'when is
he coming here?' I was delighted to answer such a tumult, and
I said: 'He's well; he's coming soon; his affairs are prospering.'
The long and short of the matter is that all people want you
back at Rome again."

Only Giovan Angelo Baccamazzo dissented. He had just
visited Venice, but he had missed seeing Aretino, and he now
wrote to express courteous regrets.

"I am delighted," he went on, "to hear of the gifts given you
by the Pope. Everybody now says that you are coming to

Rome. I can't believe that at your present age you are willing
to become a courtier, especially in so sorry a court. I think that
the mere fact that the Vicar of Christ and his Roman followers
desire your presence, is enough to proclaim your goodness and
merit to the worthy, and to rout all the mob of hypocrites."

Even he added a postscript, however.

"Nevertheless, I am looking forward to seeing you."

Then came the opportunity.

A letter from Guidobaldo delle Rovere, Duke of Urbino,
who had just been appointed Captain General of the Church.
He was going to Rome to accept the insignia of office. Would
Aretino go with him?

It was a sign from heaven. It was Guidobaldo who had taken
him to the Emperor, and "it might," reasoned Aretino, "even
please God to let his illustrious Lordship see me received at
Rome by Julius III with some part of the favor with which he
saw me received by the mighty Charles V at Peschiera." It
might also please God *not* to let lightning strike twice in the
same place; but your opportunists, who are, of necessity, opti-
mists, never argue that way. He had made an old rule that he
would never leave Venice and above all never go to Rome, but
he decided to break it. He always broke any rule that stood in
his way.

But he would not make the voyage in an unbecoming manner.

"The worthy Master Jacomo Terzo," he wrote Guidobaldo,
"has just paid me one hundred golden crowns in the name of
your humane, kindly and courteous Excellency. For this new
act of generosity and help, the knee of my thus relieved poverty bows lower than the ground. I thank you affectionately,
I will repay you with praises, I remain very whole-heartedly
under obligations to you.

"But since all this goodly sum has been—as they say in
Rome—like a platter of soup before twenty friars, I beg your
magnificent greatness to send me an additional fifty ducats.
You see I want to appear at the court not in my own worthless

capacity—for which any old rags are good enough—but as befits a follower of Duke Guidobaldo whose merits equal those of any prince or king. So if you don't give me what I ask for, I will have to spend, in your honor, the dowry of my youngest daughter, which is already in the bank.

"For half of what I have already received has gone for a robe of velvet and wool, which is no less seemly than handsome, and besides this I need four others to wear at our receptions and on the road. Nor have I yet even mentioned such things as hosen, greatcoats, caps, shoes, slippers, riding boots, hats, valises and strong boxes. Nor the livery for my serving men. Nor lodgings for the attendants that I will bring with me to Urbino. To say nothing of what I will have to leave behind me for the staff which is taking care of my house."

That much for a starter. For if you could wheedle, there was no need to demand.

"Remember, too," he continued, "that the treasury of St. Mark and the strength of Hercules would not be enough to get me to leave Venice for a single day, and that by persuading me to come to Rome, you alone have been able to accomplish what the Emperor, the Pope, and the Duke of Florence were not able to do."

Then suddenly, for greater persuasiveness, he sent back his memory on a reconnoitering expedition.

The last time he was in Rome?

A narrow street in the crooked Parione quarter and the dagger of Achille della Volta.

Might this not happen again? he wondered.

It was a considered opinion, he discovered, that it would be foolish for him to leave the city of the canals. Priestly poison (this was a good menace to stumble on suddenly and then to brandish) would undoubtedly, in that place where priests were regnant, "send him to Hallelujah." Or the Pope—poor old bumbling Del Monte Giulio Terzo who had already showered him with favors—was planning to have him murdered secretly. These were convenient bogey-men. Then, too, there was the summer climate of Rome. He shivered. It would be the death of him.

All nonsense, and all, probably, hastily improvised nonsense, but he wanted Guidobaldo to think that he was leaving Venice reluctantly.

But suppose Guidobaldo should take him seriously, and not press the invitation? That would never do!

"Nevertheless," he said swiftly, "O my patron and benefactor, I am coming on this trip simply because you command me to come. That is enough augury for me. I would like to set as a condition that you not only send a boat to meet me but someone to go with me. But if that is too much to ask from you, I am coming anyway."

For in his attempts to coax Guidobaldo into larger donations, he did not wish to risk losing the whole trip.

And this large-sized eagerness to revisit the scenes of his early manhood was not caused, certainly, by any desire to revive a long-abandoned way of life.

"Courts, ah!" he had once thundered. "Courts, eh! Well, I personally would prefer to be a gondolier here than a chamberlain there. Let's have a look at your poor courtier. He spends his life on his feet. He is martyrized by the cold and eaten alive by the heat. Where is the fire to warm himself with? Where is the water to refresh himself? If he falls ill, what room, what stable even, or what charity ward is there to receive him? Look at the rain, the snow, and the mud which do him to death when he rides out with his patron, or upon his patron's business. Where does he get fresh clothes to put on? What do they do to him in return for all this? Isn't it a cruel thing to see children who have been made court servants grow into bearded men before their time, and young men turning white-headed after a life spent at the tables, at the entrance hall, at the privies? 'You can have my share of them!' cried a certain good and learned man who in his old age had been hunted to the gallows because he would not commit some piece of pimpery. Courts, eh! Courts, ah! It is better to live on bread and capers than on the smell of fine viands served on silver platter. And just as there is no suffering like that of a courtier who is tired and has no place to sit down, who is hungry and has nothing to eat, who is sleepy and must keep awake, so there is no pleasure like my own. I sit down whenever I am fatigued, eat as often as I am hungry, go to bed when I choose. All my hours are my own. What shall we say of the abject souls of those who think that being able to stumble into a bed of straw is ample compensation for any servitude and and fidelity? For my part, my very wants make me happy, since I am not obliged to take my hat off to any papal favorite."

Elsewhere he had been more specific.

"Please put a stop," he told a friend, "to any movement that has been started to bring me back to Rome, for I would not live there with St. Peter, let alone with his successor. And I would sooner spend ten years in a prison than the same number of years in a palace."

Nor had he any ambition to turn out an inveterate old wind-hover like the Messer Pietro Piccardo he caricatured so pleasantly.

"I could spend whole days listening to him recount how Cardinal San Giorgio (Pope Julius II) won sixty thousand ducats from my lord Franceschetto, the brother of Innocent, and how with these winnings he built his palace in the Campo di Fiori. He will tell next about the flasks with which Caesar Borgia poisoned himself and his father, thinking he was brewing it for their Reverences. He remembers the blow which Julius gave Alessandro *in minoribus* on the bridge. He has been present at all the schisms, all the jubilees, and all the councils. He has witnessed all the whorishness. He saw Jacobazzo go mad. He knows where the pox comes from and every other courtly ribaldry. Certainly they ought to put him up in marble or bronze over the door of every servant's hall with a Bible at his feet which contained the names of all the popes and cardinals he has known."

But there was one bait which could inveigle him, and that bait was set before him. Now or never he would be made Cardinal. Consistency went flying. Once he had said that to call a man a cardinal was to "murder his honor," and had absolved Medici and Lorraine from "the disease—" avariciousness—"that attacks red hats" because they hardly ever wore their robes. But that was before he visualized the brightly colored folds over his own shoulders, saw the wide brim sheltering his own forehead. With Cardinal Pietro Aretino—or perhaps he would have had the last insolence to call himself Cardinal Pietro Bacci—it would be different. He prepared to set out.

He left Venice on an April morning in the year 1554. He embarked from the Piazzetta, walking to his gondola between the two statues of St. George and St. Theodore where, almost exactly twenty-seven years ago, he had stepped ashore a fugitive, and a homeless even if not exactly an unknown adventurer. Now the city, which had come to be his city, came to see him off. Is it presuming too much to imagine that it was a bright day, and that the great clock on the Orologio was blue and gold and all aglitter? At any rate, on his right hand was the newly finished library of Sansovino. His work in part, he could think quite truthfully.

His boat lay off the Dogana, and soon he was aboard it. Presently the anchor chain clanked, the sails began to belly, and they were under way. They went past the island of San Giorgio Maggiore, which even then had a church, though not in those days the Palladian one with its handsome façade, with which we are now familiar. They headed toward the Lido. Presently the channel turned northeast and they were clear of the city. On their port side, they could see Sant'Elena, Vignole with its farms and vineyards, the forts on Sant' Erasmo, and the empty Lido of Treporti. They could see also low sandbanks, intersected by marshy canals, and scarcely rising from the lagoon—Venice, as it was before the first terrorized citizens of Altinum fled from the barbarians. It was desolate but it was amazingly appealing. Then they came to the entrance, and sailed outward between the spits of sand. After that they turned south, following the seacoast. The sky was pellucid, the sea hazy azure. They passed bright-sailed fishing vessels, two-masted with lateen rig.

The first place that they left on their right hand was Chioggia, its towers showing above the dull dunes. It must have been pointed out to him for it was well-known in song and story. Now it is only a fishing center, where shawled women make lace beside the straight, miniature canals, and where nets dry on the pavement, but once Genoa and Venice fought out their duel there. They passed the Po with its many mouths, giving it a wide berth to avoid bars and shoals such as always are found at river mouths. They passed Ravenna of the famous pine forest and of the tomb of Theodoric. Dante had left his bones there, and later Byron would leave his memories. They passed Rimini, which is the first city south of the Rubicon, and saw it stretch along the level shore. Finally they reached Pesaro.

At Pesaro, Aretino quit his vessel and from that place he rode inward and upward to Urbino, half cabochon topaz, half eagle's nest. It was the handsomest city in all Italy and was set amid rugged Apennines, which were still, even in the magic Italian springtime, snow-covered. There he met the Duke. But we do not know how he was received. Did a cavalcade ride out eight miles to meet him as it had for Adria? Was he almost mobbed, as he had been in Padua, by his admirers? We do not even know whether he saw his unhappy daughter who had not yet fled to the Duchess, but it is safe to imagine he did. We have no recollection of any conversation with that sad specimen, Diotalevi Rota. If so, his mood must have made him feel like limiting his conversation to the fellow's name, Diotalevi, God carry you off (for it could be misspelled to mean that as much as 'God bring you up' as intended). Might God do so indeed!

From Urbino, he set out to cross the peninsula. Now he had the Duke with him, and he traveled with more state and with more congeniality. The way is one of the most thrilling imaginable. You pass Gubbio, where' (so legend says) St. Francis of Assisi with his gentle words tamed the ravening wolf so that he went from door to door like a friendly dog, and was mourned, when he died, by the sturdy citizens. From Gubbio, the road crosses the peaks of central Italy looking like the white wake of a ship in the midst of a tumultuous sea. The rocks are gray, and except where you see some distant village, it is as desolate as a view in Montenegro, which is like a slag heap left by the giants. But the yellow *ginestra* — English broom, the *plant à genêt* which gives its name to a romantic dynasty — was in every crevice of them. It may have been beginning to bloom as Aretino rode by. On May 2, he was in Perugia. His old friend Comitolo — the same one who had tried to win him to King Francis — was still there, and in the beetling city with its sombre arches and its thick Etruscan walls, they talked back through the four decades that had elapsed since Aretino had been a student there. Aretino felt both elated and sad. This is apt to be the case at such reunions.

Then he turned south again. On his left was Assisi, nitid on its east slope of Mount Subasio, and filled with the whiteness of a character who, it may be assumed, interested Pietro but little. Then Foligno; Spoleto (with its Roman aqueduct) ; Narni; and Orte. At Orte, he encountered the Tiber, still, to some extent, a swift mountain stream. But gradually it lost its pace. Gradually the space between its mountain embankments widened. Presently the Campagna; meadows filled with lush grass, and with flaming poppies. Cattle grazed, and they were sleek-sided. All at once, he could see domes and towers clustered in the distance. It was like an oasis to a traveler in deserts. He pressed forward. A Duke at his side, he rode in triumph when he was two and sixty, through the same city gates, out of which he had hurried like an escaped criminal in his three-and-thirtieth year. Before June had come with its heat that thrust like lances, he had reached his goal.

And his reception there was no less enthusiastic than he had expected it to be. The old crowd was gone, his enemies Berni and Giberti having been cut down by the same relentless scythe which had harvested his friend, Vaison, and his patron, Cardinal de' Medici, later Pope Clement. Raphael was dead, and Guilio Romano, and Fra Mariano, and Messer Andrea, and Chigi, and fat Pope Leo. Even the aspect of the city was changed. Rome shone as before the Sack, but to rebuild is not to restore exactly, and he saw little that was still familiar. Nevertheless, there were plenty to welcome him. Agostino Ricchi, the Pope's physician, was a friend of long standing. Baldovino de Monte wanted to acknowledge his gratitude. The Pope wished to see him. He "kissed the foot of Julius" but after that "was greeted with fraternal tenderness." As for the scholars, the writers, the pedants, the artists, the courtiers, the curiosity-seekers, they swarmed around him. They made him presents both in cash and in flattery, and they bothered him for favors. Not for nothing was he the most talked-of man in Europe, the most notable as well as the most notorious. As had been predicted, to have him there was a Roman holiday for Rome.

But the thing that he came there to seek was not even mentioned. Though Titian could write from Augsburg, with the authority of court gossip, and with the implication of imperial sanction, that "in Venice, Rome, and in all Italy everybody believes that His Holiness is about to make you—something or other" and that "Caesar shows in his countenance that he is entirely pleased," from the Vatican hill, which was what really mattered, there was no hint, no move, no suggestion of steps to be taken. Was what he dreamed of merely some *fata morgana* that would dissolve into nothing? Was he not destined for his new triumph? Were the great of the world to betray him again? Would this trip be as large a failure as his last trip to the mainland had been a success? Would he have to creep back to Venice in chagrin?

It was now June. The foliage of the trees was dark and

lifeless. At noonday, the sun was so brilliant that the eyes could hardly bear it. There was a fragrance of flowers, but the odor was heavy rather than pleasing. On the mottled walls, lizards basked rather than darted.

It was then July. Out in the country, the wind, when there was a wind, rippled through wheat that was beginning to turn golden. Grape clusters, though still green, were swelling and promising. The heat was like a heavy blanket. It choked you and it took your life away.

Finally, it was August. Miasma. The close stench that comes from narrow streets and from badly disposed-of sewage. The stench of dead dogs and of human offal. Overhead you could hear the piping swallows, and in the distance, if you climbed the Pincian, you could see the Castelli Romani, the Alban hills and the Sabine hills, the white daub that was Tivoli. There, there would be groves, cool and shady, and you longed to get to them. Still no word.

When Aretino came to the end of his patience, he came to it suddenly. It must have been toward the middle of August when he realized that the Pope did not have the slightest intention of elevating him to the Sacred College. He packed up immediately. We have no record either of angry recriminations or of pleading farewells. He simply retraced his own steps. Back across Umbria that was now the burnt golden of the color it gives its name to. Over to Urbino. There he took his first steps toward repaying the vain help given him by the Duke by writing and by publishing two sonnets in praise of the Duchess. These, at least, he could do with good grace and without silly fawning since they were for past favors rather than for favors anticipated. Then down to Pesaro and up the coast once more. He was in Venice again, or very close to it, by September first.

There, after some reflection, he decided that the best way out of the whole matter was to proclaim that he had never wanted the high rank. He did this in a roundabout manner.

"Regarding the haughtiness which your master shows to

me," he wrote an acquaintance, "I will explain it as follows. We have different natures. He is a cardinal and I have never wanted to be one."

Elsewhere he hinted that he had been offered a creation, and had declined it.

He did not, however, launch into any attack against Julius as he had against Paul. Possibly he had grateful memory of the thousand golden crowns, but it is more likely he was still thinking of that lesser amount, the eighty which were still coming to him. He would not be so impractical as to bite the hand that was feeding him, whatever resentment he might feel. Not, at any rate, so long as it continued to feed.

CHAPTER XX

Return to Paradise

BUT the return to Venice, though it undoubtedly should have been, was not quite a return to Paradise. The pigeons greeted him, strutting no less swollen-chested than he did; and the first freshness of sparkling September reminded him that autumn would soon be at hand — that incomparable Venetian autumn, merely to think about which causes any true Venetian to burst into poetry, talking of its opalescent magic, of its bright noontimes, of its mother-of-pearl morning and evening mists that cling to the warm walls of Gothic palaces, bringing out their many colors until the whole city gleams like a rich yet subtle watercolor. The streets were familiar to him; the soft water-lapping of the canals; the *pali* heavy with seaweed; the airy balconies and the surprising, hidden, brick-walled gardens. The citizens spoke to him — so, too, did the obsequious shopkeepers. And Austria — "that adorable little girl of mine" — who was now seven years old, tripped down to the Molo and threw her arms about his neck and kissed him delightedly.

Certainly, it compared favorably with the hopes deferred and with the renewed intrigues of his last foiled attempt to storm the Roman citadel. But there were other matters that were not so pleasing. Aretino's life sometimes seems almost as if lived step by step just to demonstrate that there are few heights to which boundless energy and self-confidence cannot carry you. It was equally a demonstration that in such a career, there is little, if any, peace.

To begin with he could not go back to the famous Casa Aretino. Landlord Domenico Bolani had evicted him.

Aretino, of course, tried to make it seem as if he had left voluntarily.

"Distinguished and honorable sir," he wrote, putting on a

tone of haughtiness, "I herewith restore to you the keys of that house which I have dwelt in for twenty-two years, and to which I have given the same care that I would have if it had been my own. And I will not give any other reason for this than that it is falling to pieces in every part, so that I can no more repair its decrepitude than I can shore up my own old age.

"I will not mention the little respect that you have shown to me — me, on whose behalf, the Emperor himself interceded, asking the four Venetian ambassadors to secure for me the good will of the Venetian signory. Yet if you had treated me as someone dear to His Majesty, he would have acknowledged himself eternally in your debt. I will not mention this. Indeed, I will say only that if you look in the room where I had hoped to live my days out happily, the figures on the ceiling, the graciousness of the terrace, the decorations over my bed and over the mantelpiece, all will combine to show you that I avenge even discourtesies with my courtesy.

"The daughters which have been born to me, the treasure everyone in the world knows about, the works which all see, I have begotten, I have amassed, I have composed here. Thus I have potent reasons for loving and for reverencing forever, not only the place, but Your Excellency as well.

"Therefore, when I go tomorrow — may it please God, with good fortune — to pay twice the rent in the lordly and commodious apartments which I have taken on the Riva del Carbon, it is with a wish to be still the same humble servant and friend to you that I have always been. For no perverse injury can make me change my nature."

It was a piece of gaudy braggadocio, a lie told to keep his courage up.

For the "lordly and commodious apartments" still stand, and we can go to look at them. They are not utterly despicable. They are set back from the canal, it is true, behind a noisy street crowded with business, and they are sombre where his other quarters were sunny. But the house is handsome with a warm, Fourteenth Century façade and with white tri-lobed windows, and, though narrow, it is deep and roomy.

But if Aretino paid twice the rent, or even half the rent, he was beginning to dodder.

The truth is that he was not only habitually tardy with the installments due Bolani in return for occupying the old establishment, but that there is much reason for believing that he generally neglected them altogether. Bolani's patience outlasted any on record in the long history of landlords. Then, after two decades of forbearance, he came to the conclusion that doubtful glory plus a single published eulogy was a lean income from what the tenant himself described as the best site in the fairest of possible cities. And Aretino had to find another home.

The next episode to disturb his evening calm was another of his quarrels with an ambassador. This time Pero, the Florentine, was the victim of Pietro's anger; and it turned out that even though age had come upon him, his tongue still had its youthful sting.

The *casus belli* was, as usual, money Aretino did not receive. Cosimo de' Medici, now Duke of Tuscany, and founder, therefore, of a new dynasty rather than the last member of a dying one, felt that he had been sufficiently lavish in his gifts to the writer. Three hundred crowns upon one occasion; more on others; and he was now paying his rent for him. But he was the son of Giovanni delle Bande Nere who had loved Aretino and whom Aretino had loved and also praised, and old habit made Pietro feel that no price would be enough to pay for this. When, therefore, it developed that generous presents were not prelude to a regular pension, he moved here and there through Venice, uttering insults. And he was thoroughly impartial about this. If he said a world of nasty things about Cosimo, he lashed out at Messer Pero too.

Being a diplomat and knowing that, for odd reasons of his own which it was not fitting for an ambassador to inquire about, Cosimo still wished to maintain his friendship with Pie-

tro, Pero took the one way he knew about to avoid a show-
down. He did his utmost not to meet Pietro. This worked for
several months. Then one day happened the inevitable. He
walked into the house of the Spanish ambassador—from
which he had heard Aretino on account of "certain doings of
his" was now excluded—and the huge fellow stood in front of
him. He was talking to the Spanish diplomat and the word
"Florence" uttered scathingly came floating out across the
room. Laughter followed it. Even at that, Pero attempted to
withdraw.

But Aretino saw him and he turned across the room to him.

"Ha there, my lord Ambassador of Lenten Fasting!" he
cried tauntingly.

Pero bit his lip, and did not answer.

Then Aretino starting talking for his benefit.

"The son of the great Giovanni delle Bande Nere—is that
what they call your Duke Cosimo? And on what grounds, I
ask you? Because he stormed Siena. Because with trained
Spanish soldiery to do his fighting for him he beat down the
resistance of that little city and put her to the fire and the
sword. But I tell you the storming of Siena was a trick worthy
for a widow's spoiled darling who has not yet cut his apron
strings, and not that of a son of Lord Giovanni!"

After that, he made, one after another, further remarks
which are recorded by the Florentine's incoherent anger only
as "a thousand other poltrooneries."

Pero felt his gorge rising, and at last he could contain himself no longer.

"Pietro, you clown!" he shouted. "Pietro, you clown! You
go about looking for what you have deserved very richly since
the day you were born!"

His hand gripped his sword, and he said a few things of his
own, which, according to his description, were worthy enough
of Pietro, but perhaps not so much so of a Florentine emissary.

Thereupon Aretino, if we can believe this particular
witness, turned tail and fled "like the vile creature he is."

According to the ambassadors, he was always fleeing from ambassadors. But he paused at the threshold, and he flung back a warning.

"Beware," he said. "Beware, Master Emissary, for I am writing such a letter that in a month you will be recalled from here."

Then he darted through the arras.

"I want you to know all this," Pero concluded his account to Cristiano Pagni, the Florentine chancellor, "and I put into your hands the office of doing whatever it seems fitting for you to do. Certainly it seems to me that this ruffian deserves as many beatings a day as the Duke gives him ducats a year. He never ceases his continual noise-making. I know very well that the Emperor's ambassador has been informed of his wicked life, and he has taken it upon himself to awaken His Majesty's conscience in regard to the pension he has given him these many years." News had been given out in Venice, he added for the enlightenment of Pagni, that the Sienese had won back their city, and it was this news that had heartened Aretino into speaking so outrageously. "But I do not think this could be possible," said Pero. Poor old insulted Florentine—he was loyal to the last!

What Pagni evidently thought was fitting, was to smooth over the whole affair. Pero was continued as ambassador, and Aretino was not cut off from his supplies. It may even be the pot was sweetened a little, for very shortly Aretino had a change of heart. He now hymned Cosimo and his rape of Sienese freedom, just as loudly as he had previously scoffed at it.

The ambassador was more rigid, however. Word was brought to him that Pietro, presumably as part of an agreement, had praised him in a letter to the Duke, and he grew chilly. "I have no pleasure in being praised by Aretino," he said. "To be praised by that sort of man seems to me more evil than good." Make one of these self-controlled fellows really vindictive and you have done something. He will carry his vindictiveness to the grave.

But aside from all this — or perhaps even including it — the ordinary activities of Pietro's life continued with very little change. At this time of his life, just as ten years earlier, he refused to be relegated into discard. He insisted on living actively and vigorously. He refused to be considered, or to consider himself old.

As ever, he was profusely grateful to his princely and unprincely benefactors.

"My not having written to you in the nine days which have elapsed since I arrived from Pesaro," he wrote the Duke of Urbino, "is due to my having been sick in bed. Indeed, if illness had not interfered with my desire and my duty, I would have told you long ago that the ship you sent me in was suited for a prince, as was the entourage with which I was honored, entertained, and served."

He added generous words regarding Simone Bonami, the ducal majordomo who had been his escort. Because of Simone's courtesies, said Aretino, he was "worthy of the everlasting favor of the gracious Guidobaldo." He sent with the epistle twelve pieces of gilded Spanish leather. These were for the Duke himself.

He still pleaded their cause with the old fervor.

Word came to him that the Duke had at last formally received that honor which had taken him to Rome, and he broke into a hymn of triumph.

"O everlasting mansion of the eternal and omnipotent God," he addressed the Roman Church, "it is your just and powerful arms that make the religion increase and wax glorious, and cause it to be feared and obeyed. Wherefore the soldiery of God's armies call you the Church Militant. And now Julius, father of Christianity, inspired by Jesus, has elected as Captain General that Guidobaldo, who, in valiance and in wisdom, equals, in the camp and on the battlefield, any other leader that has ever been. He will exalt with his strength and industry not only your powers, your cities, your peoples, but those sacrifices, those altars, and those rites, which glorify your heart and soul. Therefore, since it is the duty of every member of the faith to honor this illustrious choice, loyally and with such skill as nature gives my pen, I celebrate in the following lines, the pomps and ceremonies used by your blessed ruler and son in bestowing the terrible and triumphant baton. The recipient deserves it because his life is praiseworthy in every respect. He deserves it too because he is of the mighty line of Sixtus, Julius, Innocent, and Paul, those immortal Vicars who magnified you, won you crowns and mantles, and made your rule eternal, giving it both holy and religious fame."

The accompanying poem was even longer than the *capitolo* in praise of Julius, and it sounded with the same blare of trumpets.

He continued his famous charities.

"I have read the note," this was to a certain unnamed woman, "which you sent me. It was written more by the pen of misery than by your own. Therefore, I send back a ducat by the servant who brought it. I would like to do more, but my always wanting to help my neighbor has put me where I cannot. In two months, I have given away more than three hundred golden crowns. Yesterday I helped bury a man. He was so poor that even a Turk would have had pity on him. Besides that, one gondolier after another comes to me, and asks my purse to stand godfather to his children. It is now near Christmas, and I would like to come through that season still solvent. I will — if street musicians, beggars, friends, and my too large household staff do not make me pawn my very flesh and blood. What more can I say? Even now as I am asking your pardon because I can give you little or nothing, here is a note from a poor scholar who wants a cloak so he won't freeze to death. I myself live but from hand to mouth. So you will have to forgive me, dear lady, if I don't do any more for you just now."

He went on with his own begging.

Vargas, who carried in his pouches a semi-annual installment of his imperial pension, was tardy in transferring it to
him, and he wrote urgently Charles' Venetian ambassador asking him to see that it was paid over. Mary Tudor — Bloody
Mary of the Protestant legend — now reigned in England and
he addressed letters to various English lords, praising that
severe, inhibited lady and her ludicrously younger husband,
Spanish Philip. To the latter he appealed directly. "Imitate
the generosity of your imperial father and instead of praising
me send me a subsidy." He eulogized Catherine de' Medici
and hinted to the plain, unhappy, strong-willed Queen of
France that it would not be unsuitable for her husband,
Henry, to emulate Francis I by giving him another golden
chain. But Henry was too prudent or too parsimonious to
do so.

He kept up his sprightly relations with his friends. He asked
Titian to forgive his erring Pompeo who was returning like
the prodigal son from Rome. He refused to settle an argument
as to whether sculpture was a greater art than painting. Sansovino was involved in this. "My judgment," he told him, "is
that to do this, would be to canonize nonsense with further
nonsense." He wrote frequent and lengthy letters to Agostino
Ricchi.

Even the ladies still played an important part in his scheme
of things.

There is an entertaining correspondence with the Cavalier
Gualtiero of Arezzo on the subject of "four or five rosaries of
gold and ebony," which the Cardinal of Montepulciano had
promised him "in exchange for some gloves of Portuguese
leather." Like many other churchly gifts, they were slow in
coming, and Aretino felt called upon to ask Gualtiero to press
his case. He wanted them "not for the muses of Parnassus, but
for the nymphs of Venice," he said.

There was also a letter to a certain "gallant" lady, Roberta
by name, who was changing her way of living. "I kiss your
hand, while regretting this greatly," he commented.

Irony? Or was he still a practicing amorist?

He still had the power to be gay. Indeed, there were only two outward changes that showed that inwardly he was not quite the same. He was not writing very much.

"In your very kind note you ask me," he wrote the historian Parabosco, "to tell you what I am working on at present. I can only answer: 'Nothing!' Though I admit that my pen ought to be laboring night and day, spreading the fame of the Most Holy Emperor abroad to the whole world."

Fatigue, shown by a sort of lassitude, was at last leaving her traces on him.

The other change was a loss of his mental self-confidence.

A friend sent him a book of philosophy he had written.

"I accept it," he replied, "and then send it back to you. Therefore, take it in the same spirit that you offered it to me. For since doubt is the only certainty to one who tries to find out the nature of things, I, who am trying to live resolutely, have no use for it."

A bad omen. For in the days when he had been sure of his powers, he did not even allow himself to think about the questionings of others.

A young lady asked him about certain matters of faith.

"O my daughter—for you are my daughter in spirit, just as you are Madonna Maria's in flesh—you must learn to hold all those miracles of death followed by resurrection as nonsense, foolishness, jests, dreams, chimeras, and sheer madness. Only the rabble takes them seriously. They are like magic art, voices from the dead, mind reading, prophecy, and augury. They are comedies to people of our times, just as they were serious matters to men of old. So laugh at them, and do not be awed by them."

Hitherto, like so many of his temperament, he had accepted the tenets of the church without question. Even though he did not often go to mass, he had been a good Catholic and as firm a believer as the next man. To be sure, he had attacked individuals connected with the church and had lived pretty well as he chose to. But the first matter had nothing to do with faith and the second would be attended to by God's mercy. Now, however, he turned his cold rationalizing toward the awful gulf, and it won a sombre victory.

1554 ran its course, and was followed by 1555. 1555 was critical. For, according to a mediæval superstition which was still credited by the timorous, he who lived through his 63rd year would live on indefinitely. 1555 came to an end. Aretino was still alive.

Chapter XXI

The Earthquake of Doni, the Florentine. The End

THE year 1556; and, one after another, every person and episode that connected the great Scourge of Princes with his days of glory and power, dropping away. Henry VIII had joined his ancestors — Martin Luther's "Squire Harry", Shakespeare's "Bluff King Hal", that large man with the fine brain and the porcine, squinting eyes; matrimony's unquenchable optimist, who married nearly every mistress he had, cut her head off, and then looked forward hopefully to his next wife. But he left a daughter, and her name was Elizabeth. So too was Francis I, French, gallant, well-spoken, and likeable; a fine duellist, but a poor general, since he was at the mercy of every shift of his feelings; a good swordsman, in the Rabelaisian, as well as the military sense of the word; a true son of the Renaissance.

Now Charles V, the last of the great trio with whom Aretino had had dealings, joined the procession. He was not dead, to be sure, but had buried himself alive. In his beloved city of Brussels, the capital not of his empire but of his heart, he had ridden, clad in simple black and wearing only the small insignia of the Order of the Golden Fleece, to the great hall of the Dukes of Brabant. There he read his abdication, his voice choking with tears. "Not because I do no more desire dominion, but for the good of my states." Shortly afterwards he made his way toward the castle of Souberg on the Flemish coast. He went on shipboard there. And presently, a sick, trembling old man — in whom nothing burned hotly but the spirit, that being unquenchable — was moving across Spain toward the monastery of Yusté in the lonely, rain-drenched Estremadura Mountains, where he was to live the austere life of one who had taken monkish vows, hoping morbidly to make his peace with God thereby.

Philip II, shy, haughty, morose, and almost psychopathically religious, was his successor. He took up the reins dropped by Charles with such eagerness and with such lack of even feigned reluctance, that one cannot help wondering about his filial affection, about which so much has been said. And in due order, the Duke of Alva was turned loose in the Netherlands, and Christ, like some bloody Moloch, was given 30,000 human beings.

Cardinal Caraffa — Aretino's hypocritical Chieti — sat in the chair of St. Peter. He was the old kind of pope, but he lived to the new tune of keeping up appearances. He had "nieces" and "nephews," but the avuncular fiction was strictly maintained, and they were obliged to make public demonstration of piety, even if favored with high offices. For the rest, the renewed fires of the Inquisition sent a black cloud of smoke toward Heaven; and the Jesuits, sincere but ruthless, gathered fuel for them.

Indeed, only in the graphic arts were there survivors. Michelangelo still lived and still worked, and so did Titian, but these two, one of whom died at ninety, the other at ninety-nine, dwelt on this earth so long that they seemed literally, as well as figuratively, immortal. As far as the south of Europe was concerned, the great flowering was dead and buried. It was ready for the inscription on its tomb.

Yet the keen voice from the Riva del Carbon still spoke on. On April 20, 1556, Pietro Aretino was sixty-four years old. It was an anniversary, and this time an important one since he was no longer that fatal sixty-three; and knowing his love for anniversaries, we can imagine that he celebrated it with gusto. However, if we can believe one of his enemies, he had little to rejoice about. He existed rather than lived, this man pleasantly tells us. Disease racked him. He was afflicted with erysipelas, epilepsy, syphilis, and palsy. His old wounds bothered him. He was defaced with scabs. He was afflicted with a serious rupture. His face was a *mappamondo* — a literal cosmographer's chart of the world he lived in—because of the tracings of old scars.

Even allowing for the violence of a foe's vindictiveness, it is plain that, at last, years were doing their work on him. It was time, for he had lived hard and never conserved his resources. Yet at that, if he were only given a little tranquillity, just a little ease of mind, there was no doubt that he would be able to live out the three score and ten that supposedly are allotted to us. And then another decade, or even two or three, like his mighty adversary and his mighty friend.

But such ease of mind was the last thing he was to have. He had risen by controversy, and controversy was to go with him to his latest moment. His power had come to him from written and from spoken outrageousness. A bit of written outrageousness—this time with him as the victim—was to round out his tumultuous career.

And the man by whom this hard blow was struck was none other than that old friend of his, Doni. The same one who had talked garrulously of the House of Aretino and the Street of Aretino. The same one—incidentally—who had given him the book of philosophy. A man who had eaten his bread and accepted his favors for a decade. Once again Aretino's ironic destiny overtook him. This was that, although he could almost always deal successfully with his enemies, he was usually undone by his friends.

Anton Francesco Doni was a fit person to be added to this sorry group. He was a rogue, if the Lord ever made one, but that went with the business he followed. He was half mad—as witness his last days when he lived, solitary, in a tower on the mainland, and came out only at night and then naked. He had wild hair, and a long and tangled beard, and starting eyes that also were penetrating. Besides that—and of course important —he had a sort of genius. "He, truly, even more than Aretino, was the father of modern journalism." It is overstatement, but he had, certainly, a journalist's aptitude for catching ideas on the fly, and he wrote best under pressure, as a journalist does.

"What I set down," he once boasted, "is read before it is
written and printed before it is composed." There are men
using their pens and having a following, of whom this can be
said even today.

He was born in Florence, in the year 1513. His father was
a scissors-maker. Cutting, therefore, came to him by heredity,
but his cutting was to be with ink stamped on paper, rather
than with tempered blades of metal. Two times he did try to
settle down into a steady calling. He became a Servite monk
until he was chased out of his monastery for an act of moral
turpitude. He studied law at Piacenza. But the large part of
his early days were spent in wandering. He was driven from
Rome for his scurrilities; from Florence for a vile printing
press which he ran; and from Piacenza — during a second visit
— for literary indecencies he was associated with. In many
ways, as was the case of most seeking Aretino's protection, this
part of his life was much the same as Pietro's had been. In his
later days, he was actuated by the same motives. Only the lines
he drew were lower. He said that he was willing to do anything
from being a court poet to becoming some lord's pander if
only he could find some one who would hire him. All that he
needed was a fuller measure — he had more than most — of
Aretino's ability to become a second Aretino. There were
many, and there still are, in the same situation. But that, although they do not realize it, is a large lack.

In 1547, when he was thirty-four years old, Doni came to
Venice. There he established himself permanently. It was the
only place in Europe where, in those days of growing Catholic
self-consciousness, an unfrocked monk could live with anything like safety. By flattery and persistence, he soon worked
his way into Aretino's confidence, and presently the latter was
helping him. He told Doni whom to see. He got work for
Doni as a free-lance. Doni's books now began to crowd from
the printing presses, and if he had been willing to be content
with this, he and Aretino might have lived upon good terms
indefinitely. This would have been to the advantage of both.

But he was not content, and hardly could have been as long as he lived in a garret on one of the most shut-in and most foul-smelling of all the small canals in Venice, and Aretino in a sumptuous, if debt-ridden palace. Consequently he started to poach.

To one after another of Aretino's patrons, he made cautious advances, and finally he had success. Through one of his secretaries—and probably because he thought that he was helping one of Aretino's friends—the Duke of Urbino sent a purse with money in it. After which came the crow of cockerel. "I now have a patron on my own account, and need fawn no more to Messer Aretino." But cock-a-doodle-doo rang out too soon. Word came to Aretino, and he was dumbfounded. Then he went into a fury. He snatched up a piece of paper, and put words upon it.

"To *Gian* Francesco Doni," he began ominously almost as if he did not know the man.

Then he launched his accusation—Doni had not only tried to steal the favor of Duke Guidobaldo, but had slandered Aretino to Aretino's own publisher.

"Therefore if I had known you were at Pesaro as I thought you were in Apulia or Rome, I would not have waited so long to let the Duke know about your bad qualities. I will now do so. I will set them down shortly, and when I have done so you will have a few things to think about to your public damage and shame, since I write nothing that is not the truth. I will portray you as the high protector of all evil, and I will seek out every damaging fact about you and I will write about it to Duke Guidobaldo."

Doni would have a hard time to defend himself, he added. For the Duke looked upon him as a son.

It was a good opening fusillade—bewildering because sudden, and effective because it was a lot more than merely partly true. Furthermore, Doni knew that it would be followed by others—he knew well that a battle was on.

He had, consequently, only two choices. He must act swiftly

or retreat with equal promptitude. But if he drew back he was lost for good, and doomed definitely to a lasting subserviency. This was something he could never possibly tolerate. He sat down, therefore, and prepared the counter attack. It was a written one also.

"Earthquake of Doni, the Florentine," he scratched across a piece of foolscap, "with the Ruin of a Great Bestial Colossus, the Anti-Christ of Our Age."

Then a pause to think a moment.

"A Work Written," he continued, "for the Honor of God, and for the Defense and the Well Being not only of Prelates but of all Good Christians.

"Divided into Seven Books."

What would the seven books be?

"The Earthquake."

Next?

"The Ruin."

Next?

"The Lightning; the Thunder; the Thunderbolt; the Life and Death; the Burial and Obsequies."

The text followed as fast as pen could set it down — a series of letters it was, each one of them as venomous as possible, twenty-three of them in all. And he promised more. Two hundred and sixteen, to be specific. One for every word in Aretino's own letter.

"To that disgraceful scoundrel, source and spring of every rascally deed, Pietro Aretino, stinking member of diabolical lying, and true Anti-Christ of our century."

"To that long-faced coward, Pietro Aretino, the clumsy fool of our age, and a disgrace to mankind."

"To his divine hogsheadedness, one time Master Pier of Arezzo, a divine wine-jug."

"To Aretino, the tilting dummy of all worthless fellows, gilded if you like, but wooden inside."

"To the hoggishness of that wild hog, Aretino, venerable gulper-down of roast hog meat."

Others were addressed to the various princely patrons of Pietro:

"To the Majesty of the Most Unconquerable Charles V, Emperor worthy of a thousand empires."

"To the illustrious and most worthy lord, Guidobaldo, very worthy Duke of Urbino."

"To the illustrious and very excellent Lord Duke Cosimo."

"To the Serene Doge of the very worthy republic of Venice, that unconquerable stronghold."

Point by point, they assembled every insult imaginable that could goad Messer Aretino into incoherent fury.

"Your father was a lay Franciscan, and your mother a lay sister. You are, then, virtually the son of a nun and of a priest."

"You say that Kings and Emperors brought you tribute just as the three Magi brought tribute to the Savior. Yes, but what a difference! He spoke righteousness, lived even better, and taught virtuously the word of God. You, who write evil and live even worse with your Nannas and Pippas and other filthy courtezans, have published only villainies. His divine Majesty is the salvation of princes and you are their scourge. Christ founded the church, and you, with your pasquinades and satires, have tried to ruin it, lashing out at cardinals and stinging bishops and prelates."

"Pietro means head, and reading Aretino backward—for you are the reverse of all Aretines—you have Onitera (*Ogni terra*). Almost, you might say, the head rascal of all the world."

"You allege that Duke Alexander wanted to give you the Strozzi palace. Do not believe, O great beast who are swelled up like the bladder of a hog, that His Excellency really meant this, for he was a prince of great judgment, and if he gave you a few crowns, it was simply as a chattering buffoon. What right would a person like you have to such a noble residence? But if he did say so to shame an enemy of his, was not this his meaning? 'I am going to put the most wicked man in the world in the most honored house in Florence so that it will be disgraced for ever.' Yet I swear in the name of your villainy that if this had happened, not only the Strozzi faction, but the Medicis themselves would have burned it down with you inside of it."

He resurrected the old bit of gossip about Francesco Marcolini.

"No man in the world ever treated you better than he did, yet you boasted — and in public — you had cuckolded him."

It was the libel which Doni had already spread by word of mouth, and he now made doubly poisonous by printing it. He meant business when he turned his words on Aretino. The earthquake was really out to topple the colossus. Who was hurt beneath the falling débris, Doni did not care.

But perhaps his most effective onslaught lay in the long list of the disasters which — he said — had shortly afterwards befallen all who had befriended Aretino.

"Didn't you say so many things of the keen mind of that generous lord, Pierluigi Farnese, that he wanted to send for you and to keep you in Piacenza like some precious jewel? That and no other thing, that alone I tell you, was the cause of his being assassinated."

"Didn't the Marquis of Vasto, who with such solicitude collected taxes on the Milanese wheat and then gave you the money like a king, suffer many reverses for having shown you this courtesy?"

"They say that Antonio da Leyva was carried off by the devil. I don't believe it. Yet that is what they say, and I will tell you why. It is because he gave you so many and such lavish gifts."

"The Emperor has been, and is, beset by sickness and by long wars simply because he persists in letting you enjoy the sweat and blood of those poor gentlemen who have to contribute to your pension of two hundred *scudi*. And I know certainly that as soon as he stops giving you this, peace will be concluded."

"The Marquis of Marignano is dead for no other reason

than that he sent you a hundred crowns, and promised to send you the same every Christmas. But he died before even the first payment was made, so that you should not have the money, and so that it should be demonstrated how unseemly this was."

"The chain with its pendant tongues, which King Francis gave you, was the reason he was made a prisoner, and King Philip owes his misfortunes to another chain with which he encircled your neck."

"Don't you allege that Lord Giovanni delle Bande Nere gave you bread? Don't you assert that you were his favorite, and that one day he would have made you Lord of Arezzo. By God, yes, you say. Well, I swear to you that the musket that carried him off, to the great ruin of Italy, did so because of the curse that has been put upon you, the curse that makes you infamous and ruins your friends."

"The reason that Pope Clement was shut up in the Castello was because at one time he fed your hunger, and Rome was sacked because she did not murder you after all those pasquinades in her dispraise."

On the other hand, "Pope Paul reigned sixteen happy years because he never gave you anything."

"I tell you, Master Pietro," Doni explained, digging his pen into the paper, "that you are like some deadly sickness."

Did it not occur to Messer Doni what this attack might do to Aretino's income if there was but one lord among his many paymasters who was superstitious? Was he not very probably making a deliberate assault upon the one place where Pietro was vulnerable? Upon the fellow's purse?

But there was one further thing that Doni had to say, and that thing was perhaps the most interesting of all. So far he had merely ranted. So far he had merely embroidered an old theme with new violence—and also, it must honestly be said, with new eloquence. So far he had done merely what Berni had tried to do, and what Niccolo Franco would have liked to have done.

Now, however, he ventured into specific prophecy, his rage causing him to disregard all the cautious noncommitalness by which oracles from Delphi onwards have gained their reputations. Now brashly he gave orders to the three sisters whose spinning and whose snipping set the course of human destiny.

I have not said my whole say, he thundered. I have not done my last injury. A new part is to follow—nay, for that matter is now ready for the printing presses.

"In it you will see how I have prophesied correctly that you will die during this year of '56."

And with that said, he ended his assault.

He then rushed his manuscript to a printer and by March 7 all Rome was reading it. By April, it had reached Venice. The month passed, though, and he was still a liar. May followed. Then June, July, August and September. Half a year had gone by and the Scourge of Princes still flourished. He still strolled along the Riva every day, being looked upon by strangers and greeting all his many friends. His hair now was snow white, and his walk certainly more slow and marked by longer pauses, but his eyes still regarded eagerly, and his voice and talk were still as keen.

It was now October, and on the twenty-first day of that month he was still very much of this world. There was on that evening a merry foregathering in a tavern of the neighborhood, and Aretino attended it. Wine was on the table and he ate, drank and laughed with the best of them. He had never been more gay in all his days.

The blow came, therefore, with all the more dramatic suddenness. It was the third hour of the night. He was tilted back in a chair laughing heartily. Suddenly the chair swayed, did not catch itself, and hurtled over backwards. Aretino crashed to the floor. His friends rushed up to him, found that he was still living, but that his face was flushed, his breathing heavy. He had had a stroke of apoplexy. They carried him back to his own house, swaying and groaning, for he was large as Falstaff; laid him on his bed. Then they summoned a doctor and a priest. The first of these could do nothing, and what the latter could do is questionable though there is an affidavit that he died confessed. Incoherently he talked to himself for several hours; then grew quiet. By whatsoever miracle it had happened, the prognostication of Doni had come true. In the morning, Aretino had blasted his last adversary. The mighty Scourge of Princes was now dead.

It was a great stillness that followed. Ordinarily the house of death is hushed; for standing before the one thing we can never understand, even the most irreverent find somehow that their hearts (or maybe, it is but self-pity) lay a hand across their mouths; even the most light-headed sense a kind of speechless awe. But this silence seemed to reach through all of Europe. It was deeper than the customary silence, just as the voice that had preceded it was louder. It was the loudest voice of a whole continent. It was the loudest voice of a whole age.

But unfortunately it did not last for long. No sooner was it plainly realized that he could never answer back, than the flood gates of malice held in check by fear of reprisal burst asunder. Almost instantly, the cautious became fierce and furious. Almost immediately, all those sorry ones who like to play safe, became brave and swaggering.

Pero, the Florentine, was the first one to show his venom.

"The mortal Aretino—no longer the divine—was carried off into the next world last Wednesday. No decent man was sorry to lose him."

Ludovico Nelli followed suit.

"Poor Aretino is dead and he died in as mean a way as possible."

Soon a third scandal-monger made gossip really ugly.

"Do you know how Aretino died?"

"How?"

"He was recounting the escapades of his sisters, and he laughed so immoderately that he fell over backwards and cracked his skull."

"Sisters? Then the great beast had sisters?"

"He did. They kept a bawdy house at Arezzo, and it was their filthy deeds he was laughing at."

Last words were invented for him.

While he was unconscious, he had been anointed with oil, preparatory to receiving extreme unction. Recovering consciousness, he had pushed the priest away. This is what he said:

> Guardatemi da i topi, or che son unto.
> (Keep rats away, now that I'm all greased up)

Even an imaginary epitaph was contrived:

> Qui giace l'Aretino, poeta tosco,
> Chi disse mal d'ognan fuorche Dio,
> Scusandosi col dir, Non lo conosco.

Let us look at it in English:

> Here lies Aretino, the Tuscan poet.
> He slandered everyone but God.
> This was his reason. "I never heard of him."

The old lion being dead, the jackals now could snarl at him and not risk answer. And that—evidently enjoying themselves —they proceeded to do.

But it so happened—and one is glad that it so happened— that these were not the only opinions of the dead man uttered. His friends said something also. They engaged stone cutters, and gave them words to carve. These they fastened to the walls of San Luca, and there, during the Seventeenth Century, a traveler from Germany saw and copied them.

> Da infime stirpe a tanto altezza venne,
> Pietro Aretino, biasmando il vitio immonde,
> Che de color che tributava il mondo,
> Per temenza di lui tributo ottene.

This is a translation:

> Although base-born, Pietro Aretino rose to towering
>   height
> By blaming the foul vices of the world.
> Therefore those to whom the world pays ransom
> Paid ransom to him
> Lest he should tell the truth about them.

Think it over carefully, and then ask yourself if it was not as true as what the others said. At least — and maybe more!

But that is the strange thing about Pietro. He had so wide a character that it is hard to libel him. Omit details, and every poisoned word his adversaries spoke about him describes him eloquently. But so too do all the eulogies of his admirers. Truth does not lie between the two extremes, but it embraces both of them. Not thus with most men that we read about. That probably is why he is the type personage of the Renaissance, for that period was made of contradictions. That certainly is why he is one of the most amazing ones who ever lived.

EXPLICIT VITA PETRI ARETINI

A Note on Research

To LIST all the fonts of information direct and indirect which have gone into making this biography would be to make a small volume itself, for it is laid in a source period of our western culture, and I — like most of us — have absorbed my background knowledge of that period, here and there, and often almost unconsciously, as long as I have been exposed to reading and books.

I have, therefore, in the appended bibliography, set down only those books which I consulted for the specific purpose of writing about Pietro Aretino. In each case, incidentally, the edition listed · is the one I happened to find it most convenient or most practical to use. I used, for instance, the Lanciano edition of the *Ragionamenti,* rather than the handsome Elzevir one of 1660, or those French and Italian ones of the Sixteenth Century, for the double reason that it was easier and more economical to acquire (though I finally did indulge, as an extravagance, in the Elzevir edition) and that it was not in any way a defacing of valuable property to underline relevant passages and to pencil notes in the margins.

Of course, all the items are not of equal importance. Aretino's own writings remain the No. 1 source for information about the man and it is by an analysis of them, or rather of the autobiographical passages which almost every one of them contains, that we best establish the outline and the details of his life. Next in order come the letters written to him, and the scurrilous but not always inaccurate anti-Aretino literature of his contemporaries. The so-called Berni "Life" is an example. Last but not least, come the modern and amazing studies by Prof. Alessandro Luzio, particularly those dealing with his early days in Venice and his relations with the Marquis of Mantua. If every other phase of Aretino had been dealt with as fully and as competently, a pen would have been only slightly more important to his biographer than scissors and a pot of paste.

Besides reading these books, I have also taken pains to visit every place — with the single exception of Fano — in which there is any evidence that Aretino ever stayed even for the shortest time, and I have likewise hunted out and examined every real or supposed portrait of the fellow. I consider this a very important part of research. For the putting together of a biography is, among other things a bit of literary detective work. And as I understand it the really Grade A sleuth always arms himself with photographs from the rogues' gallery and also visits the scene of the crime.

Bibliography

Albèri, Eugenio: *Relazioni degli ambasciatori veneti al senato.* Florence. 1839-1869.

Aretino, Pietro: *Le Carte Parlanti.* Lanciano. 1914.

———: *Lettere.* Paris. 1609.

———: *Opera Nuoa . . . zoè Strambotti, Sonetti, Capitoli, Barzellete e una Desperata.* Venice. 1512.

———: *Poesie.* Lanciano. 1929.

———: *Prose Sacre.* Lanciano. 1914.

———: *I Ragionamenti.* Lanciano. 1914.

———: *Ragionamento de le Corti.* Lanciano. 1914.

———: *Teatro.* Lanciano. 1914.

Armstrong, Edward: *The Emperor Charles V.* London. 1929.

Bandello, Matteo: *Novelle.* Bari. 1910-1912.

Baschet, Armand: *La Diplomatie Venetienne.* Paris. 1862.

———: *Documents inédits tirés des archives de Mantoue concernant la personne de Messer Pietro Aretino.* In "Archivio Storico Italiano." 1866.

Batiffol, Louis: *The Century of the Renaissance.* New York. 1935.

Batelli, Giuseppe: *Esame critico sulla vita di Pietro Aretino attributa al Berni.* Turin. 1888.

Berenson, Bernard: *The Venetian Painters of the Renaissance.* New York. 1894.

Berni, Francesco: *Vita di Pietro Aretino.* London. 1821.

———: *Opere.* Milan. 1864.

Berni, Francesco et al: *Opere burlesche.* London. 1734.

Bertani, Carlo: *Pietro Aretino e le sue opere.* Sondrio. 1901.

Betussi, Giuseppe: *Il Raverta.* Milan. 1864.

Bonnet, Theodore F.: *Pietro Aretino.* In "The Lantern." 1917.

Bourrilly, L.: *L'ambassade de la Forêt et de Maurillac a Constantinople.* In "Revue Historique." Paris. 1901

Brantôme, Pierre de Bourdelle de: *Oeuvres completes.* Paris. 1848.

Buraglii, Federigo: *Venezia e la fortuna di Aretino.* In "Le Tre Venezie." 1931.

Brinton, Selwyn: *The Gonzaga—Lords of Mantua.* London. 1927.

Burckhardt, Jacob: *The Civilization of the Renaissance.* London. 1929.

Campori, Giuseppe: *Pietro Aretino e il Duca di Ferrara.* Modena. 1869.

455

Cappelli, Antonio: *Pietro Aretino e una sua lettera inedita a Francesco I.* Modena. 1865.

Cartwright, Julia: *Isabella d'Este.* New York. 1905.

Castiglione, Baldassare: *The Book of the Courtier.* New York. 1929.

Cellini, Benvenuto: *The Life of, written by himself.* New York. 1906.

Chasles, Philarète: *Études sur W. Shakespeare, Marie Stuart et l'Arétin.* Paris. 1851.

Chubb, Thomas Caldecot: *La casa dell' Aretino a Venezia.* In "Gazzetta di Venezia." 1935.

Cian, V.: *Gioviana.* In "Giornale storico della letteratura italiana." 1891.

Cima, Antonio: *L'Orazia dell' Aretino.* In "Propugnatore." 1877.

Crowe, J. A., and Cavalcaselle, G. B.: *Titian, His Life and Times.* London. 1877.

Currey, E. Hamilton: *Sea Wolves of the Mediterranean.* London. 1910.

Diehl, Charles. *Venise.* Paris. 1921.

Dolce, Ludovico: *Dialogo della pittura.* Lanciano. 1913.

Doni, Anton Francesco: *Il Terremoto di M. Anton Francesco Doni contro M. Pietro Aretino.* Lucca. 1861.

——: *La vita dello infame Aretino.* Citta di Castello. 1901.

——: *La zucca.* Venice. 1551.

Dumesnil, M. J.: *Histoires des plus celebres amateurs italiens.* Paris. 1853.

Encyclopedia Italiana. Milan. 1929-1938. Articles on Aretino, Doni, Niccolò Franco, etc.

Firenzuola, Angelo: *Opere.* Milan. 1802.

Flamini, Francesco: *Il Cinquecento.* Milan. 1898-1902.

Franco, Nicolò: *Le pistole.* Venice. 1542.

——: *Rime contro Pietro Aretino.* Lanciano. 1916.

Gauthiez, Pierre: *L'Arétin.* Paris. 1895.

——: *Jean des Bandes Noires.* Paris. 1901.

Gaye, Johann: *Carteggio inedito d'artisti.* Florence. 1840.

Gilbert, J.: *Cadore or Titian's Country.* London. 1869.

Giovio, Paolo: *Elogia.* Basle. 1571.

Gnoli, D.: *Storia di Pasquino.* In "Nuova Antologia." 1890.

Graf, Arturo: *Attraverso il cinquecento.* Turin. 1888.

Grassi, Paride de: *Il diario di Leone X.* Rome. 1884.

Gronau, Georg: *Titian.* London. 1904.

Guasti, Antonio: *Alcuni breve di Clemente VII sulle ferite e la morte di Giovanni de' Medici.* In "Archivio Storico Italiano." 1888.

Guasti, G.: *una figlia di Pietro Aretino.* In "Archivio Veneto." Venice. 1885.

Guicciardini, Francesco: *Istoria d'Italia.* Pisa. 1819-1820.

Hourticq, Louis: *La jeunesse de Titien.* Paris. 1919.

Hutton, Edward: *Pietro Aretino, the Scourge of Princes.* London. 1922.

——: *Aretino, the First Journalist.* In "The Nineteenth Century and Afterwards." 1922.

Kennard, Joseph Spencer: *The Italian Theatre.* New York. 1932.

Lanciani, Ridolfo: *The Golden Days of the Italian Renaissance in Rome.* London. 1907.

Lettere Scritte al Signor Pietro Aretino. Venice. 1551-1552.

Lorenzetti, Giulio: *Venezia e il suo estuario.* Venice. 1927.

Lucchesi, G. B.: *Documenti tratti dal R. Archivio di stato in Firenze.* Venice. 1874.

Lumbroso, Giacomo: *Memorie italiane del buon tempo antico.* Turin. 1889.

Luzio, Alessandro: *L'Aretino e il Franco.* In "Giornale Storico della Letteratura Italiana." 1897.

——: *La famiglia di Pietro Aretino.* In "Giornale Storico della Letteratura Italiana." 1884.

——: *L'Orlandino di Pietro Aretino.* In "Giornale di Filologia Romanza." 1880.

——: *Pietro Aretino e Pasquino.* In "Nuova Antologia." 1890.

——: *Pietro Aretino nei primi suoi anni a Venezia e a la Corte dei Gonzaga.* Turin. 1888.

——: *Un prognostico satirico di Pietro Aretino.* Bergamo. 1906.

——: Review of Giorgio Sinigaglia's *Studio di un un saggio su Pietro Aretino.* In "Giornale Storico della Letteratura Italiana." 1883.

——: Review of Vittorio Rossi's *Pasquinate di Pietro Aretino.* In "Giornale Storico della Letteratura Italiana." 1892.

Machiavelli, Niccolo: *Tutte le opere.* Florence. 1929.

Marchetti-Ferrante, G.: *Rievocazioni del Rinascimento.* Bari. 1924.

Mari, Giovanni: *Storia e leggenda di Pietro Aretino.* Rome. 1903.

Mazzuchelli, Conte Giammaria: *La vita di Pietro Aretino.* Brescia. 1763.

McElwee, W. L.: *The Reign of Charles V.* London. 1936.

Michelet, Jules: *François Ier et Charles Quint.* Paris. 1880.

Mignet, M.: *La rivalité de François Ier et de Charles Quint.* Paris. 1886.

Molmenti, Pompeo: *La storia di Venezia nella vita privata.* Turin. 1885.

Muratori, Ludovico Antonio: *Rerum italicorum scriptores.* Milan. 1723-1751.

Nerli, Ferdinando: *La tragedia italiana.* Florence. 1904.

Panzacchi, Enrico: *Pietro Aretino innamorato.* In "Nuova Antologia." 1885.

Pastor, Ludwig: *The History of the Popes.* London. 1906-1938.

Peignot, Gabriel: *De Pierre Arétin.* Paris. 1836.

Percopo, E.: *Di Anton Lelio Romano e di alcune pasquinate contro Leone X.* In "Giornale Storico della Letteratura Italiana." 1896.

———: Review of Pierre Gauthiez' *L'Arétin.* In "Rassegna Critica della Letteratura Italiana." 1896.

Petrucelli della Gattinara, F.: *Histoires diplomatiques des conclaves.* Paris. 1864.

Pittoni, Laura: *Jacopo Sansovino Scultore.* Venice. 1919.

Plon, E.: *Les maîtres italienne au service de la maison d' Autriche.* Paris. 1887.

Putnam, Samuel: *The Works of Aretino.* Chicago. 1926.

Robertson, William: *The History of the Reign of the Emperor Charles V with an Account of the Emperor's Life after his Abdication by William H. Prescott.* Philadelphia. 1904.

Roeder, Ralph: *The Man of the Renaissance.* New York. 1933.

Roscoe, William: *The Life and Pontificate of Leo X.* London. 1846.

Rossi, Vittorio: *Pasquinate di Pietro Aretino ed anonime per il conclave e l'elezione di Adriano VI.* Palermo-Turin. 1891.

———: *Un elefante famoso.* In "Intermezzo." 1890.

Sanesi, Giuseppe: *Un libella e una pasquinata di Pietro Aretino.* In "Giornale Storico della Letteratura Italiana." 1895.

Sansovino, Francesco: *Venetia, città nobilissima.* Venice. 1663.

Sapori, Francesco: *Jacopo Tatti, detto il Sansovino.* Rome. 1928.

Sicardi, E.: *L'anno della Nascita di Nicolò Franco.* In "Giornale Storico della Letteratura Italiana." 1894.

———: *L'autore dell'antica "Vita di Pietro Aretino."* In "Miscellanea Nuziale Rossi-Teiss." Trent. 1897.

———: Review of Pierre Gauthiez' *L'Arétin.* In "Giornale Storico della Letteratura Italiana." 1897.

———: Review of Carlo Simiani's *La vita e opere di Nicolò Franco*. In "Giornale Storico della Letteratura Italiana." 1895.

Sinigaglia, Giorgio: *Saggio di un Studio su Pietro Aretino*. Rome. 1882.

Sorrentino, Andrea: *Francesco Berni, poeta della scapigliatura del Rinascimento*. Florence. 1933.

Suida, W.: *Le Titien*. Paris. 1935.

Symonds, John Addington: *The Life of Michelangelo*. New York. 1928.

———: *The Renaissance in Italy*. London. 1920-1927.

Tassini, Giuseppe: *Curiosità Veneziane*. Venice. 1933.

———: *Di Angelica Sirena amata di Pietro Aretino*. In "Archivio Veneto." 1886.

———: *Della abitazioni in Venezia di Pietro Aretino*. In "Archivio Veneto." 1886.

Van Dyke, Paul: *Renaissance Portraits*. New York. 1905.

Vasari, Giorgio: *Le Vite dei piu celebri pittori, scultori e architetti*. Florence. 1925.

Virgili, Antonio: *Francesco Berni*. Florence. 1881.

Young, Col. G. F.: *The Medici*. New York. 1910.

Zeller, J.: *La diplomatie francais vers le milieu di XVIme siecle*. Paris. 1880.

Index

461

3/4

Ap 4

129